KU-456-823

*This book is dedicated to my husband and wonderful children
who are the joy of my life.*
—Joyce J. Evans

About the Author

Joyce J. Evans is a dynamic communications professional with a lifetime of experience in instructional design and human interaction. Her talents are continually growing to meet the needs of students, clients, and colleagues. With over 10 years of experience in educational training, speaking, tutorial development, Web design, and usability, she faces every challenge with a genuine concern for the user.

Joyce founded, designed, and maintains the Idea Design Web site (**www.je-ideadesign.com**), a Web design studio. In conjunction with the ID Bookstore and other various clients, she keeps herself very busy in the online development world.

Authoring the *Fireworks 4 f/x & Design* and the *Integrating Flash, Fireworks and FreeHand f/x & Design* books has given Joyce the opportunity to use all of her skills, from basic writing and tutorial development, to advance interface design and information architecture. She also has contributed to *Dreamweaver 4: The Complete Reference* and is currently working on other book projects. For speaking engagements and updated book information, visit **www.JoyceJEvans.com**.

Acknowledgments

First and foremost I want to acknowledge my God who provides the calm and peacefulness to complete what I set out to achieve in life.

I couldn't have brought this book in on time without the help and support of my loving family. I especially want to thank my husband who did most of the shopping, cooking, and serving Sunday morning breakfast. Also my appreciation goes to my children who help with the cooking and supply the coffee and water when the deadlines are looming.

This book had a lot of help and contributions by many people. They are all listed in detail in Appendix B, right in the front of the Appendix. There are so many people who contributed that I didn't want to leave anyone out no matter how large or small the contribution because even the contributions of an image helped in the final compositions.

I am very grateful that Hillman Curtis, author of *Flash Web Design*, took time out of his busy schedule to write the introduction to Flash in Chapter 13 and for the contribution of the interface that Scott Hamlin, author of *Flash 5 Magic*, provided for your use. I also want to thank the folks at Fig Leaf for the banner ad projects they provided and thanks go to Tracy Kelly (formerly of Fig Leaf Software) for writing much of the ActionScript in the Flash section.

The FreeHand section had the assistance of Ian Kelleigh of the FreeHand Source and Ron Rockwell, the author of *FreeHand 10 f/x & Design*. At the last hour Brad Halstead of the Pretty Lady Web site volunteered to write the layout instructions for the Horse Adventure Web page in Dreamweaver—many thanks Brad.

I'd also like to thank the fine folks from Macromedia who offered assistance, Mark Haynes, Doug Benson, Elizabeth Siedow, David Morris, and Delores Highsmith.

It's been a pleasure working with the crew at Coriolis who worked so hard to get this book to press in a timely manner. Thanks go to my project editor Sean Tape who was always patient with my many questions and my wonderful tech editor Mary Rich who carefully tested every project. I also appreciate that Bill Sanders lent his expertise for the Flash section. The other important person in the making of a book is the copy editor, and mine was great, thanks Tiffany Taylor.

And thanks to everyone else at Coriolis who made this book possible, Alisha Blomker and Beth Kohler—Acquisition Editors; Michelle McConnell and Chris Nusbaum for their work on the CD-ROM; April Nielsen and Laura Wellander for their work on the Color Studio; Meg Turecek, the Production Coordinator; and Patti Davenport, Product Marketing Manager.

—*Joyce J. Evans*

Contents at a Glance

Table of Contents

Introduction

I'm thrilled that you are taking the time to read this introduction. Whether you've just purchased this book or you are thinking about buying it, I want to tell you why I've written *Integrating Flash, Fireworks and FreeHand f/x & Design* and what you can expect from it.

About Flash 5, Fireworks 4, and FreeHand

Flash is the premier tool of choice for serious developers and producers of Web movies and motion graphics. The addition of ActionScript in Flash 5 has expanded its capabilities greatly. It's almost overwhelming how much you can do in and with Flash. You'll be exploring and using ActionScript firsthand in the Flash section of this book.

Fireworks was originally developed by Macromedia to do superior image editing in preparation for Internet presentations. Today, Fireworks 4 is the premier image-editing program for serious Web designers who want a tool designed specifically for their Web-centric needs. Making navigation systems complete with HTML code and JavaScript is all part of the power of Fireworks.

FreeHand is the trendsetting leader of illustration programs, with innovative new features such as the contour gradient tool and the ability to use multiple master pages. You can even open multipage PDF documents in FreeHand. The compatibility between your FreeHand files and Flash may truly amaze you.

I didn't neglect Dreamweaver in this mix. Appendix A is devoted to editing your Fireworks images from within the Dreamweaver environment, as well as producing a complete and complicated layout in Dreamweaver using features such as layers, cascading style sheets, and rollover behaviors.

Who Needs This Book

Some of the individuals who will benefit the most from this book include professional designers, freelance designers/Web developers, teachers, and project managers. Because this book is written for users at the intermediate to advanced level, a working knowledge of Flash, Fireworks, and FreeHand is vital.

You will not be taught how to use every program. You will, however, be taught how to use the functions in each project and the major functions of each application. Because the interpretation of exactly what constitutes being an intermediate user is so nebulous, it's impossible to guess your learning level; so, great care has been taken in writing precise project instructions.

f/x & Design Philosophy

This *f/x & Design* book will help you gain a better understanding of how to best use the best workflow features of Macromedia's top applications. You will learn what each program does best, resulting in increased productivity for you and/ or your Web team.

Because the best way of learning is doing, the techniques taught are quickly reinforced with real-world projects. Each step in each project is taught prior to the project. If a technique is explained in more detail in another chapter, then a reference is given so you can read more details about that technique if necessary.

As I noted earlier, it's impossible to know exactly the level of experience an intermediate user has gained, so all steps necessary to produce a project are listed, no matter how basic. The end result is an intermediated to advanced technique presented in a manner that a broad range of users can understand.

How This Book Is Structured

This *f/x & Design* book focuses on the strong points of Flash, Fireworks, and FreeHand and how to best use the strengths of each application in a production workflow. This book is divided into three major sections: FreeHand, Fireworks, and then Flash. This structure by no means indicates an order of application use. Each application will have its benefits to you and the way you work. Each section is independent of the others, but they also all work together.

When features of applications overlap, we will look at the differences between them and how they vary. There are also times when a topic is discussed at more length in another section or chapter; in these cases, I give you chapter references (and usually a section name, as well) for further study or practice. As an example, users of Fireworks may not be as knowledgeable about how to use the vector drawing tools; so, the instructions are a bit more basic in the Fireworks section, and the FreeHand section references the instructions in the Fireworks section. Using the same example of the vector drawing tools, in Flash we discuss the tools that function differently in FreeHand and Fireworks.

The instruction for the FreeHand section is not version 10–specific. The screenshots were captured in version 10 because it is the version I use, but all files are exported into FreeHand 9 format so you can still use them with FreeHand 9, Fireworks 4, and Flash 5 (because FreeHand 10 was released after

Fireworks 4 and Flash 5, they can't read FH10 files). If Flash 6 and Fireworks 5 are released when you get this book, then compatibility will be a non-issue. I also didn't want to assume you would upgrade all your programs right away. The project using contour gradients is a FreeHand 10–only project, because this is a new tool in version 10.

The Fireworks section deals primarily with working with bitmaps, using the color tools, masking, and compositing, as well as slicing and optimizing your images. Features such as optimizing images are found in all three applications, so you'll have to decide which works best for you. Personally, I prefer the wide range of options and ease for optimizing and naming the images and slices in Fireworks. Although the focus is on bitmap images, the vector capabilities and animation capabilities of Fireworks aren't neglected.

The Flash section starts off with a bang with an introduction from Hillman Curtis, renowned Flash designer and author. This section will not teach you how to use Flash—so many excellent books are available for learning to use Flash that I didn't use valuable book space trying to teach you the basics. Instead, we concentrate on intermediate and advanced aspects of Flash, such as writing your own ActionScript. You will be provided with starter files when needed and completed files for comparison if you get stumped. If a project doesn't work, please check your spelling carefully; it's an easy mistake to make. (I'm speaking from experience.)

The projects were chosen for their potential usefulness in the real world. For example, at first glance you may think a puzzle will be useful only for a game site. But if you begin to look beyond the obvious, you'll realize that the same techniques work for dragging clothes to a model and similar applications. Plus, this project and all its variations will teach you valuable lessons about loading movies to different levels and many more techniques. In addition, you'll find obvious projects such as using the print functions, and the lure project for use in displaying merchandise of any type.

I have endeavored to focus each section on the strongest features of each application while still providing information about most of the major functions of each application. When you add a drawing from FreeHand into Flash, I will tell you which chapter it was made in as well as provide the file in case you didn't do the projects in that chapter. Or, when you use a Fireworks image in FreeHand, I'll tell you which chapter it was produced in, and so on.

Because I wanted to illustrate Flash, Fireworks, and FreeHand techniques with real-world projects, I have included complete interfaces and Web pages for the projects in this book. Parts of several projects are made in different sections throughout the book to illustrate specific techniques. When the project is assembled, references are made to the chapter where each portion was made. If you'd rather not make certain parts of a design from scratch, no problem—the image file is included in each chapter's resource folder, ready for your use. Some of the projects are actual working Web sites; you can't get more real world than that. The only things not included are copyrighted fonts. The fonts used in the projects are for display purposes only; you can substitute any font you'd like. The fonts used are always mentioned, in case you want to use or purchase them.

About the CD-ROM

I had demos for you for Dreamweaver, Fireworks, FreeHand, and Flash. In fact, the book makes reference to the demos on the CD-ROM. I have included so many project files that in order to include all these demos, I'd have to leave out the bonus tutorial movies. Because I've gotten such a wonderful response to the movies, it was decided that the better value to you would be the movies. You can still get the Macromedia demos free of charge to use for a full 30 days by going to this link: **www.macromedia.com/downloads/**. I apologize for any inconvenience this may cause you.

To fit as many movie tutorials as possible, they were compressed. You will need a program such as WinZip, which you can get "free" from **www.winzip.com** or StuffIt, which is also "free" from **www.stuffit.com**.

Great care and effort has been taken to give you the best book possible. I've enjoyed writing this book tremendously and hope you enjoy it, as well.

Feel free to keep in touch. I have a companion Web site to this book at **www.JoyceJEvans.com**, where any updates will be posted, along with new tutorials.

Joyce Evans

July, 2001

Part I

FreeHand

Chapter 1

Using FreeHand Drawing Tools

In this chapter, you will become familiar with FreeHand's powerful drawing tools. You will learn the tool's strengths and uses, and will practice editing your paths.

FreeHand Resources

One book on FreeHand you may want to check for more detailed and design-related information is *FreeHand 10 f/x & Design* by Ron Rockwell. He has offered his advice and assistance for parts of this section. Ian Kelleigh, who runs The FreeHand Source at **www.freehandsource.com** contributed and helped out as well. You can learn a lot of great tips and techniques from The FreeHand Source.

Note: I would be remiss if I neglected to mention that FreeHand has powerful print functions, making it a valuable tool for both the Web and for print. Because the focus of this book is the Web, the multiple print capabilities will not be covered.

Introduction to Part 1, FreeHand

The FreeHand section of this book covers Chapters 1 through 6 and is not meant to teach you all there is to know about Freehand—doing so would require a very large book.

You will learn about the major Web functions of FreeHand and how to integrate FreeHand into your Web design workflow together with Flash and Fireworks. This section focuses on tasks that FreeHand simply does better than Flash or Fireworks. At the end of the FreeHand section, you will find a summary of what you accomplished and an outline of what you need to do in Flash and Fireworks to complete the projects.

Drawing Tool Basics

In this section, we will discuss some basics of using the FreeHand drawing tools. These essentials affect most of the tools.

All objects you draw in FreeHand contain points. The position and number of points determine the shape of your object. FreeHand uses three kinds of points: corner points, curve points, and connector points. You will see them in detail in the section "The Pen Tool."

When you place two points, a segment automatically connects them; when you place another point, another segment is added. In FreeHand, segments are known as *paths*. You can generate straight or curved paths. Paths can also be open (the points don't meet) or closed (the points meet).

You use the Pointer tool to select, move, and alter objects. You can see the objects' path and point information in the Object inspector (Window|Inspectors|Object). The Object inspector tells you whether a point is selected and what kind of point it is, and will allow you to collapse the point's handles, adjust the handles, and provide the point's X, Y coordinates. You can change a point's type by selecting the point and then clicking the appropriate icon in the Point Type area. If a path is selected, the Object inspector tells you how many points are in the path, the type of fill, and whether the path is open or closed.

Handles

When you use the Pen or Bezigon tool, FreeHand adds handles to curve points. Handles are hidden until a path is selected. If you can't see a handle after the path has been selected, then the handles are *retracted*. To get control of the handles, choose the Pointer tool, press the Alt/Option key, and drag the point. Repeat this step if you want two handles. To hide the control handles, select the point and click the Retract button in the Object inspector. Manipulating handles is discussed in the section "Editing Shapes" later in this chapter.

Automatic Control Handles

If you select the Automatic checkbox in the Object inspector, FreeHand estimates the placement of the control handles and the adjacent path to conform to the existing path. This method may be fine for a particular project, and if you need to move a point, you can still do so manually. The Automatic option is deselected by default.

Icons and Cursors

You will see various icons and cursors throughout this chapter. To see the visual clues that your cursor provides as you draw, be sure your preferences are set for Smart Cursors (Edit|Preferences in the General tab). Your cursor will then offer you more information about the operation you are performing. Figure 1.1 shows the icons in the Object inspector for the types of points.

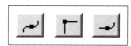

Figure 1.1
Icons for curve, corner, and connector points, respectively.

Figure 1.2 shows the Smart Cursor tips you'll see most frequently in this chapter. The plus sign (+) is the standard crosshair cursor. The plus sign with the little minus (-) sign appears when your cursor passes over a corner point that you can delete. The plus sign appears when your cursor passes over an area in a path that you can add a point to.

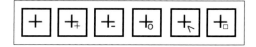

Figure 1.2
The Smart Cursor tips for paths.

The Pen Tool

The Pen tool can make both straight and curved segments. When you click and drag a point, you make a curved segment. If you hold down the Shift key while clicking to the next point, the movement is constrained to 45-degree increments. (If you need more basic instruction on how to use the Pen tool, see Chapter 8 in the Fireworks section of this book.) You can make three types of points using the Pen tool: corner points, curve points, and connector points.

Corner Points

Corner points offer the most flexibility. (To change a point's type, select the point and make the change in the Object inspector.) Corner points are solid squares until you select them; then they become hollow. Each corner point can have two control handles, one on each side of the point. You can add these handles by selecting the corner point and then clicking and dragging in the direction you want to add the handle. These handles move independently of each other. While dragging a corner point, hold down the mouse button and press Alt/Option; the trailing control handle will be locked, allowing you to position the leading control handle independently.

Curve Points

When you insert a curve point, FreeHand adds a Bézier curve. Curve points turn into hollow circles when selected. Curve points also have two handles but each control handle is restricted to one axis. As one handle rotates, the other rotates in the opposite direction. Curve points make it easier to produce smooth curves in your paths.

Connector Points

Connector points maintain a smooth transition between a straight-line segment and a curved segment. Connector points turn into hollow triangles when selected. The movement of the control handles is restricted to the same direction as the straight-line segment. You can move the handle only in and out—not side to side. To make a connector point in Windows, press and hold the Alt key and right-click with the Pen or Bezigon tool. On a Mac, press and hold the Control key and click with the Pen or Bezigon tool.

The Bezigon Tool

The Bezigon tool performs much like the Pen tool. The main difference is it can produce only straight segments. By using modifier keys, you can determine which type of point is laid. Handles are automatically added to all Bezigon points.

Using the Pen and Bezigon Tools

The Pen tool and the Bezigon tool have many functions in common. You will see in the following exercises how they are similar and how they vary.

Drawing an Umbrella Shape Using the Pen Tool

In this exercise, you will draw an umbrella shape so you can get a feel for how the Pen tool responds. Follow these steps:

1. Choose File|New.

2. If your rulers aren't visible, choose View|Page Rulers and select Show. Pull guides onto your document. You can refer to Figure 1.3 for an idea of how I set up the page for this example. The size isn't important; the lines are just guides to help you produce a better shape.

3. Select the Pen tool from the Toolbox. Click the left side of the document on the bottom guide to place the first anchor point. Figure 1.4 shows the completed shape, so you can see where to place each point as you continue this exercise.

4. After you place the second point, click and drag the handles of the center point on the top of the line to form the curve. As you drag to

Note: The first anchor in this example is a corner point. When using the Pen tool, you can press the Alt/Option key and drag a control handle while you are placing the corner point. The control handle you drag will affect the next path segment.

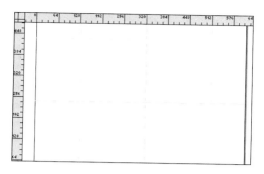

Figure 1.3
Guides in place to draw an umbrella shape.

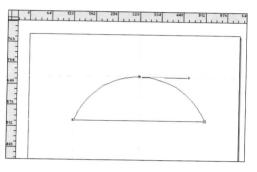

Figure 1.4
The completed umbrella shape.

the right, the handles will be horizontal to your guide when the shape is at the correct curve.

5. Click the third point on the bottom guide.

6. Hover your cursor over the first anchor point until you see a little O next to the cursor; it indicates that when you click to add a point, the path will be closed.

7. Open the Object inspector (Window|Inspectors|Object) and select the first anchor point you placed. In the Object inspector, you can see that it is a corner point. Figure 1.5 shows the Object inspector and the active corner point icon.

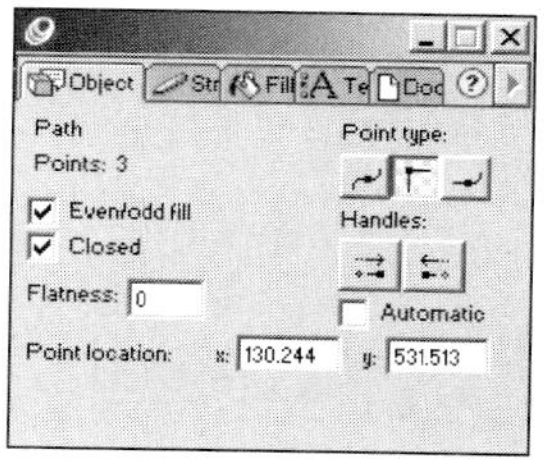

8. Click the center point; you will see that it is a curve point. The third one is another corner point. Of course, the spot where you connected the path is also a connector point, but it doesn't show up in the Object inspector.

Figure 1.5
The Object inspector shows that the anchor point is a corner point.

Drawing an Umbrella Shape Using the Bezigon Tool

You will see in this exercise how the Bezigon tool differs from the Pen tool. Follow these steps:

1. Set up your page the same way you did for the Pen tool example in the previous section.

Note: In this exercise, the guides will help constrain your bottom line. If you are drawing a shape such as a zigzag and want to constrain the line to a 45-degree angle, hold the Shift key while you set the anchor point.

Note: You can move the point as you set the curve point. You do not have control over the handle, as you did with the Pen tool—but this is not a bad thing, as you will soon see.

2. Select the Bezigon tool from the Toolbox.

3. Click to set the first anchor point on the bottom guide on the left side of the document.

4. To place the curve point using the Bezigon tool, hold the Alt/Option key and click. Notice how the handles extend automatically. These handles control the segment preceding and following the curve point. Figure 1.6 shows your shape so far; it doesn't look like much yet.

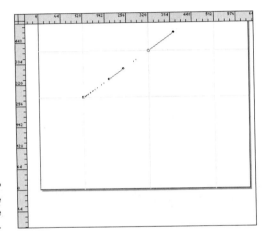

Figure 1.6

The first two points set for the umbrella shape using the Bezigon tool.

5. Now you will really begin to see how the Bezigon tool differs from the Pen tool. Click the third point on the lower guide on the right side. The curve point you added affects both path segments and guesses the curve you want to produce. (Isn't that neat?) As you can see in Figure 1.7, the curve is just what you want; but if it isn't, you can adjust the handles normally to tweak the shape.

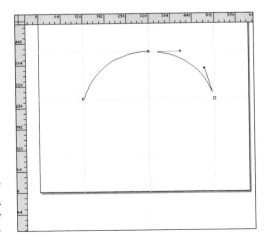

Figure 1.7

When the third anchor point is set, the two curves automatically adjust to the umbrella shape.

6. Close the umbrella shape by hovering your cursor over the first anchor point and clicking when you see the small O.

Adding and Deleting Points

It's quite easy to add and delete points using the Pen tool or the Bezigon tool. The cursor icons will help you with visual clues. To add points to an existing path, follow these steps:

1. Select the path you'd like to add a point to.

2. Pass the cursor over the area where you want to add a point; a little plus sign (+) appears in the right corner of the cursor. Click to add a new point.

To delete points, follow these steps:

1. Select the path you'd like to delete a point from.

2. Pass your cursor over the corner point you want to delete; a minus sign (-) appears to the right of your cursor. Click to delete.

3. If you are trying to delete a curve point, you will see the upside-down V next to your cursor. Click once on the point, and the minus sign will appear; click to delete.

> **Note:** If you want to delete multiple points, Shift+select then press the delete key.

Moving Segments

To move a segment, select its beginning point, Shift+select its ending point, and then drag. Rectangles made with the Rectangle tool are grouped by default; so, when you select the path, you won't be able to move a segment. Select Modify|Ungroup (Ctrl+G/Cmd+G) and then proceed as you would for other segments.

Connecting Points

Sometimes, you will draw a path that you think is closed until you try to fill it and nothing happens. To close a path, the points must be connected. Using the Pointer tool, Shift+select or marquee-select the two points you want to join and choose Modify|Join (Ctrl+J/Cmd+J).

Closing a single path is a bit different. For instance, if you did the umbrella-drawing exercise, do it again and don't close the path. Or, simply draw a jagged line using the Pen or Bezigon tool. To close this sort of path (select it), open the Object inspector and select Closed. FreeHand adds a segment connecting the last point with the first point.

This following exercise demonstrates closing two separate paths and presents another problem. Follow these steps:

1. Open a new document (File|New) and select the Pen tool.

2. Choose Edit|Preferences, click the General tab, and be sure Smart Cursors is selected. Click the Object tab and select Alt-Drag Copies Path (Option-Drag Copies Path for the Mac).

3. With the Pen tool, click to set the first anchor point. Hold the Shift key and click another point about two inches below the first one.

4. Select the Pointer tool and duplicate this line by holding Alt/Option and dragging a copy away from the original. Put the duplicate about an inch from the original line.

5. To connect these two lines, use the Pointer tool to marquee-select the top two points.

6. Choose Modify|Join. You didn't get the result you expected, did you? The bottom two points, which you didn't even select, were connected. FreeHand joined the paths according to the path direction; the bottom two points are the ending points, so that's where the join took place. Choose Edit|Undo.

7. To alter the path's direction, marquee-select the two paths and choose Modify|Alter Path|Reverse Direction. Marquee-select the top two points and choose Modify|Join; the top two points will be joined.

8. You can't perform the same joining action to close this path, because it is no longer two paths but one open path. You can close the path several different ways; choose which method works best for you:

   - Open the Object inspector and select the Closed option.

   - Select the Pen tool, click one of the bottom anchor points, pass the cursor over the other end point until you see the little O, and click.

   - Drag one point on top of another. Of course this technique also alters the shape.

> **Note:** If you had drawn from the bottom up, Step 7 would be unnecessary. But who the heck draws that way?

Editing Shapes

After you've drawn a shape with curves, you may want to make adjustments to it. You work with the control handles by using the Subselection tool and clicking a point on the path. Control handles are visible when you select a path with curve points on it. To practice manipulating curves using control handles, follow these steps:

1. Select the Pen tool and click three points in a row. Double-click the ending point of the path; see Figure 1.8.

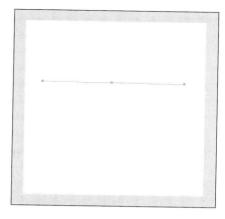

Figure 1.8
A line on which to practice
Bézier curves.

2. Select the Subselection tool and click any point. If no handles appear
(they won't, on this straight line), press the Alt/Option key and drag the
middle point down. When you release the mouse button, a control
handle will be visible. Figure 1.9 shows how your curve should look.

Note: To change a straight
line into a Bézier curve, hold
the Alt/Option key and drag a
point. You will actually be
dragging a control handle. To
change a Bézier curve back
into a straight line, select the
Pen tool and click the point of
the curve you'd like to be a
straight segment; the curve
segment of that point will
become straight.

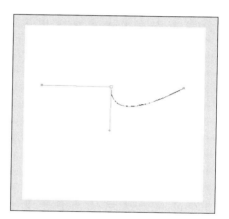

Figure 1.9
A Bézier curve added to the
middle point of the practice line.

3. Hold the Alt/Option key, click the same point, and drag straight up.
Figure 1.10 shows the result.

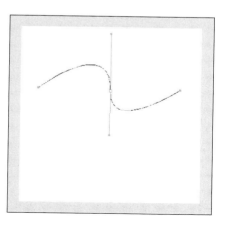

Figure 1.10
Two handles on the Bézier curve.

4. Working with Bézier curves takes practice, so you can get a feel for what direction to pull and turn the handles to get the desired shape. Click and drag the top control handle to the right and down. You can move it up, down, and all around.

PROJECT Drawing Puzzle Shapes

In this project, you'll add a puzzle made in Flash to the Horse Adventures children's Web site (you'll build this site in Fireworks in the next section of this book). The shapes for the puzzle are best drawn in FreeHand, particularly because of the Bezigon tool, which Fireworks does not have. To draw the puzzle shapes, follow these steps:

1. Open puzzle.gif from Chapter 1 resources folder on the companion CD-ROM, which contains the tracing image shown in Figure 1.11.

Figure 1.11
The puzzle shape that will be traced.

2. Open the Layers inspector (Window|Panels|Layers F2), select the puzzle image, and click the lock on the Background to lock the layer.

3. Open the Stroke inspector (Window|Inspectors|Stroke or Ctrl+Alt+L/ Cmd+Option+L) and set the Stroke size to two. In the Color Mixer (Window|Panels|Color Mixer or Shift+F9), click the System Color picker (bottom color icon on the left) and choose a bright green color. Drag this color on top of the color in the Stroke inspector.

4. Select the Bezigon tool. It works well for this project because of all the curves.

5. Begin tracing the first vertical line on the left. Click to set the first anchor point at the top of the line. Click another anchor point just before the curve starts, and then press Alt/Option to set a point in the center of the curve. Figure 1.12 shows the tracing at this point.

6. Click the next point at the end of the curve. Figure 1.13 shows the completed curve—it isn't bad at all. Because this is a puzzle, the shapes don't need to be exact. If you want them to be exact, you can edit the handles later.

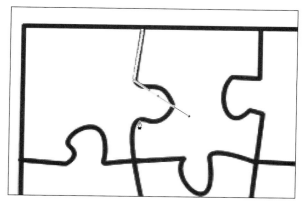

Figure 1.12
The tracing with a curved point added to the first curve and the Bezigon tool ready to click the next point.

Figure 1.13
The tracing with the first curve completed.

7. Continue down the rest of the first vertical line using the same techniques. Don't forget to press Alt/Option as you set the point in the curve. Figure 1.14 shows the completed first line. As you can see, it needs a little editing.

8. Select the Pointer tool and select the second curve you traced. Figure 1.15 shows the control handles on the curve.

9. With the Pointer tool, click the top handle on the center of the curve and drag it up to form to the shape of the curve. Edit any of the other curves as necessary.

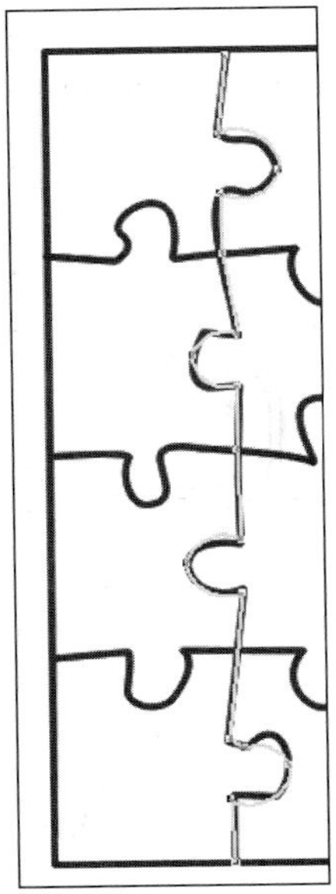

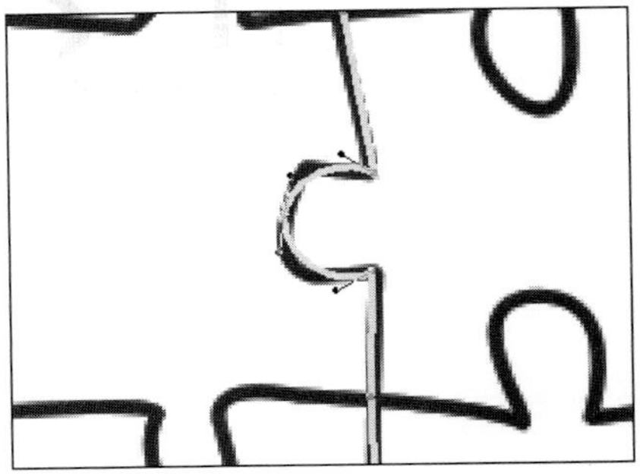

Figure 1.14
(Left) The first vertical line traced and ready for editing.

Figure 1.15
(Right) The control handles on the selected curve.

> **Note:** If your line isn't selected and you need to edit the control handles, select the path using the Subselection tool and edit the control handles with it.

10. This pattern includes some curves that you won't be able to trace perfectly, such as the last one in this vertical line. You need to add a point if you want the tracing to conform better to the curve. Figure 1.16 shows the Pen tool in position, ready to add a point (notice the plus sign). Click to add a point. With the Pointer tool or Subselection tool, adjust the control handles to fit the shape.

Figure 1.16
The Pen tool in position and ready to add a point.

11. Figure 1.17 shows an area that doesn't conform to an extra curve in the first curve you made. The Subselection tool is pointing to it. Let's change the type of point from a corner point to a curved point. Open the Object inspector.

12. Select the point that you want to convert; you will see in the Object inspector that it is a corner point. Click the curved point icon. Control handles are added to the point you selected, and the point below it is

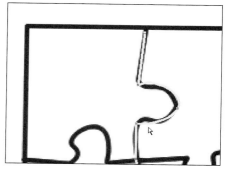

Figure 1.17
A point that needs to be changed from a corner point to a curved point.

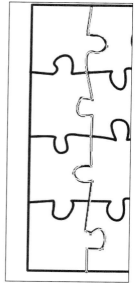

Figure 1.18
The first vertical line with its control handles adjusted and points added or converted as needed.

also affected. Adjust the control handles and move the point to fit the shape. Figure 1.18 shows the first vertical line with its control handles adjusted and points added or converted as needed.

13. Repeat the same techniques you used for the first vertical line for each vertical and horizontal line.

14. Select the Rectangle tool and draw the rectangle bounding box for the puzzle.

15. To use this puzzle shape in Flash, it's very important to be sure that all the lines touch. The horizontal and vertical lines will touch, because they are one-piece lines that cross over each other. However, you may have a problem around all the edges (see Figure 1.19). Using the Subselection tool, select and pull the point until it touches the outside bounding box. Do this for all lines that need to touch the edge. Use the Zoom tool to check that all line edges are touching.

Figure 1.19
A line that doesn't touch the outside edge.

Note: Even if you are using FreeHand 10, do not save using the FreeHand 10 format—unless, of course, Flash 6 is released by the time you read this. If it is, then you don't need to export; simply save as a FreeHand 10 file.

Note: The Pen tool produces more points only if you click to follow the trace closely. If you are very good with the Pen tool, you probably can complete the trace with no more points than with the Bezigon tool. I personally found the Bezigon tool to be easier to use for the curves, but it all depends on your skills and preferences.

16. You are now ready to export this file as a FreeHand 9 file (more on exporting in Chapter 6). Choose File|Export and select FreeHand 9 Document from the Save As Type drop-down menu. Name your file and click Save. A copy of this puzzle called puzzle.FH9 is in the Chapter 1 resources folder, ready for Flash.

Variation: Using the Pen Tool

If you are more comfortable using the Pen tool, doing so is an option. However, in this case it produces far too many points if you are inexperienced with adjusting handles as you draw. Figure 1.20 shows the same vertical line traced using the Pen tool. If you use the Pen tool, be sure to select Modify|Alter Paths|Simplify and enter a number to simplify the path as much as you can without altering the shape.

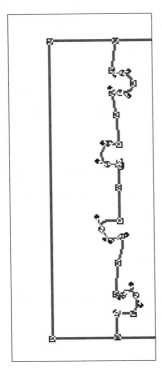

Figure 1.20
The same vertical line traced using the Pen tool before simplifying.

PROJECT Tracing a Car for the Point of Purchase Web Page

The car you'll trace in this project was drawn by Jeffrey Roberts in FreeHand. It is used on the Point of Purchase Web page. (You'll draw and color the car in FreeHand in Chapter 4.) Figure 1.21 shows the interface in which the drawing will be used. The pedestal will contain a car that rotates in Flash.

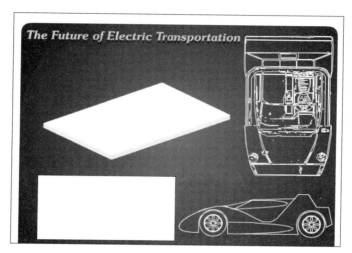

Figure 1.21
The interface in which you'll use the car.

To begin tracing, follow these steps:

1. Open the electric car.FH9 file from the Chapter 1 resources folder.

2. Open the Layers inspector (Window|Panels|Layers or F2). Select the image and then click the lock on the Background to lock the layer.

3. Open the Stroke inspector (Window|Inspectors|Stroke or Ctrl+Alt+L/ Cmd+Option+L) and set the Stroke size to 1 (this example uses a Stroke size of 2 for illustrative purposes). In the Toolbox, click the Stroke color box and choose red from the color palette.

4. Zoom in on the side view of the car. Select the Bezigon tool and click the bottom of the car to the right of the front wheel well. Press Alt/Option and click the top of the curve around the wheel. Click once more to place an anchor point at the bottom of the wheel well. Figure 1.22 shows the front wheel well traced. It's not a bad fit; you can adjust the handles later.

5. Select the Pen tool and click and drag around the front curves as needed. Don't worry about tracing perfectly; you can adjust the curves later. Continue placing points around the straight areas until you reach the bottom of the car, just before the back wheel well.

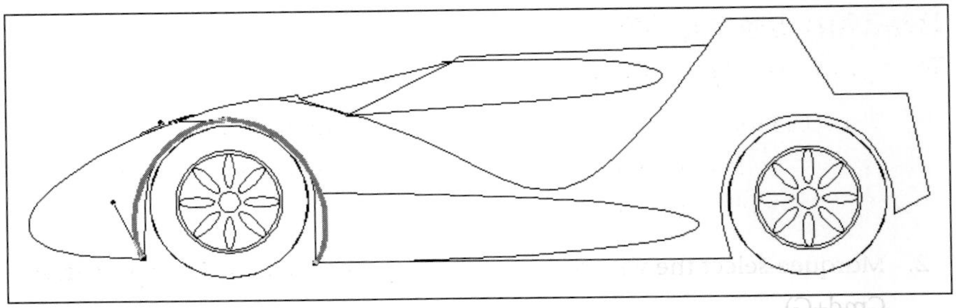

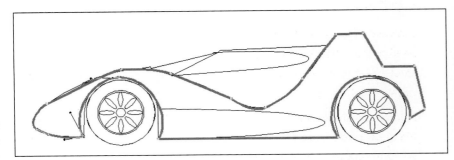

Figure 1.22
The front wheel well, traced
using the Bezigon tool.

6. Select the Bezigon tool and click a point at the bottom of the back wheel well area. Press Alt/Option, click at the top of the wheel well curve, click at the bottom of the left side of the wheel well, and click the beginning anchor point to close this path. Figure 1.23 shows the traced path.

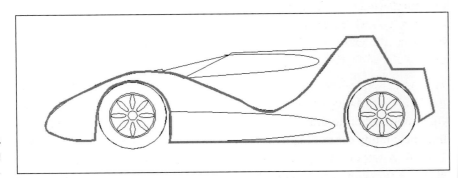

Figure 1.23
The traced main path of the side
view of the electric car.

7. Select the path and use the Subselection tool to pull the control handles to adjust the curves to fit the original drawing. In particular, you need to adjust the curves around the wheel wells. All I had to do was pull up slightly on the control handle and pull toward the wheel well. Figure 1.24 shows the path traced with the control handles adjusted.

Figure 1.24
The path with the control
handles adjusted.

8. Finish tracing the rest of the car using the same techniques. You'll draw the wheels in Chapter 2.

Drawing the Top View

To draw the top view of the car, follow these steps:

1. Trace the top view of the car using the Pen tool and the Bezigon tool. Drag a guide line to the center of the car and trace only the left half of the car. Don't trace the console in the center.

2. Marquee-select the whole car and then group (Modify|Group or Ctrl+G/ Cmd+G).

3. Double-click the Reflect tool to open the Transform panel. Enter "90" into the Reflect Axis box, enter "1" in the Copies box, and click the Reflect button.

4. Using the Pointer tool, select and move the flipped duplicate to match the left side.

5. Marquee-select the whole tracing and choose Modify|Join. You may need to join a few areas separately, depending on how carefully you traced; just be sure all the lines are connected so you can fill the drawing with color.

6. Figure 1.25 shows a rough tracing with no alterations. To break this file apart and see what it looked like before, choose Modify|Split; now you can separate the two halves. To ungroup each half, choose Modify|Ungroup.

7. To finish the top view, trace the center objects and place them in the car.

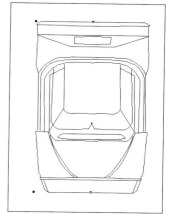

Figure 1.25
A rough tracing of the top view after it has been reflected, grouped, and joined.

The Pencil Tool

The Pencil tool offers much more control in FreeHand than in Fireworks. It is an unrestricted drawing tool, but you can also add controls such as straight and constrained line segments. To draw a straight-line segment, you press and hold the Alt/Option key. To constrain the straight line to 45-degree angles, press Shift+Alt/Option.

You can customize the Pencil tool by double-clicking its icon in the Toolbox. In the Pencil Tool dialog box (Figure 1.26), select the FreeHand option in the Tool Operation section to draw a line of uniform weight. The Precision option defines how many control points are placed on the path, based on settings from 1 to 10: A setting of 1 places fewer control points, whereas a setting of 10 places many points on the path. The Draw Dotted Line option shows the line you are drawing as a dotted line; when you release the mouse button, the line appears as a solid line. If you draw a closed shape, a small solid box will appear when the cursor is in the correct position to close the shape.

Figure 1.26
The Pencil Tool dialog box.

LYIT
006·6869
LIBRARY
S 0 0 2 2 7 6 5
LETTERKENNY

If you're drawing with the Pencil tool and you don't like something you drew, don't release the mouse button—simply press Ctrl/Cmd and drag backward to erase. When you have removed the offending part of the path, release the Ctrl/Cmd key and continue drawing.

When you select Variable Stroke in the Tool Operation section, several other controls become available. The "line" produced when Variable Stroke is selected is a closed path consisting of an inner and an outer line, plus a fill. This multipart line lets FreeHand generate lines of varying widths. And, you can draw a line that is one color on the edges and a different color between the lines. In the Width section of the Pencil Tool dialog box, Minimum and Maximum slidebars control the width of the line when you are using a pressure-sensitive tablet. When you exert more pressure on the pen, a wider path results. You can also use the arrow keys on your keyboard to accomplish this variation: The right key makes the line wider, and the left key makes the line narrower.

The Calligraphic Pen option in the Tool Operation area of the Pencil Tool dialog box provides controls that are similar to those of the Variable Stroke option, except you can produce a fixed width in addition to the minimum/maximum line widths. The Angle selection controls the angle of the FreeHand tool to produce the effect of drawing with a calligraphic pen.

PROJECT Tracing a Map Line Drawing

The map you'll trace in this project will be used in the Atlantis interface (designed by Jeffrey Roberts of jefargrafx) in Chapters 11 and 12. Of course, it isn't a real map, or even a detailed one. When I draw real maps, I usually start with a line drawing I drew on paper. Depending on how you work, you may need to scan in your drawing. For this exercise, the mapdrawing.gif file is provided for you to trace. At the end of this project you will find tips on how to add roads and bushes. Follow these steps:

1. Open the mapdrawing.gif file from the Chapter 1 resources folder.

2. If you have a drawing tablet, now would be a great time to use it; I used one to do this tracing. You can trace the map with a mouse, but doing so is much tougher.

3. Double-click the Pencil tool icon to access the Pencil tool options; choose FreeHand and a Precision value of 5. Select the Draw Dotted Line option to see a dotted line as you draw; it will turn solid as soon as you release the mouse.

4. Open the Layers inspector (Window|Panels|Layers or F2), select the image, and click the lock on the Background to lock the layer.

5. Open the Stroke inspector (Window|Inspectors|Stroke or Ctrl+Alt+L/ Cmd+Option+L) and set the Stroke size to 4. In the Toolbox, click the Stroke color box, and from the color palette choose a bright blue.

6. Start drawing around the line; you may need to zoom in. You don't need any width sensitivity settings for this particular drawing, but you might want to experiment with them as you draw. If you are using a mouse, press the right arrow key to make the line wider and the left arrow key to make it thinner.

7. When you have completely traced the path, you will have far too many points. To remove the extra points, choose Modify|Alter Paths|Simplify, enter "2" (my personal choice), and click Apply. Continue applying the Simplify command with a low number until the path becomes unacceptable. If you go too far, simply choose Edit|Undo.

8. You will add this line drawing to the Atlantis interface in Fireworks, so you save it as a native FreeHand file.

Variations

If you'd like to add some additional effects to your map, try the next two sections, which will show you how to add bushes and roads to your map drawing.

Adding Bushes to a Map Drawing

If you need instructions on blending, refer to Chapter 3. This drawing tip comes from the Tips archive at Ian Kelleigh's Web site (**www.freehandsource.com**). The tutorial is called "Creating Cartographic Trees." This is the short version; for more information and images, check out Ian's site. At this point, I assume you know how to use the Stroke and Fill inspectors and the Color Mixer panel (refer to Chapter 4 for more information on the Color Mixer panel).

To add bushes to a map, follow these steps:

1. Using the Pencil tool, draw any shape to represent a bush.

2. Draw a small circle with the Ellipse tool—not too big, but large enough to make your bush outline lumpy.

3. Make a clone (Edit|Clone) of the circle and move it to the right.

4. Shift+select both circles and blend (Modify|Combine|Blend). You'll have to guess how many blend steps you need (in the Object inspector, the default is 25 steps).

5. Shift+select the blend and the path. Choose Modify|Combine|Join Blend To Path. With the blend still selected, adjust the number of blend steps so that the circles overlap each other slightly (I adjusted mine to 30 steps).

> **Note:** It's easier to trace an object with a contrasting color so you can see what you are doing. You can change the path to the color you want when you've completed the tracing.

> **Note:** You can save the tracing as a native FreeHand file if you are using FreeHand 9 or earlier, or as a FreeHand 10 file if Fireworks 5 and Flash 6 have been released when you read this. If the new versions aren't released or you don't have them (and you are using FreeHand 10), then export as a FreeHand 9 file.

6. Choose Modify|Ungroup. You now have two separate objects.

7. Marquee-select both objects and choose Modify|Combine|Union. In the Fill inspector, choose Basic and fill with green. The results look like a bush, as seen in Figure 1.27.

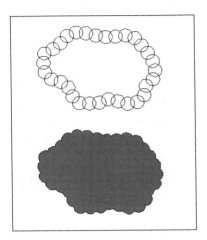

Figure 1.27
The bush shape with circles around it, and the finished bush.

Adding Roads to a Map Drawing

This is just one way to make a road with a dashed line. Follow these steps:

1. Select the Pencil tool and draw a curvy line.

2. Set the Stroke to 25 and fill with black.

3. Choose Edit|Clone two times. Move one copy to the side and change the fill color of the other stroke to yellow. This stroke will go behind the black stroke to make a yellow edge on the road.

4. The stroke for the edge should be 6 points. Because there are two sides, you need to add 12 points to the yellow stroke: the original 25 plus 12, which equals 37. With your yellow stroke selected, change the point size in the Stroke inspector to 37.

5. Drag the black stroke over the yellow stroke and center it. If you can't see the yellow stroke when you move it, choose Modify|Arrange|Move Forward.

Note: If any of the strokes you place on top of each other don't show or are in the wrong order, choose Modify|Arrange| Move To Front.

6. Select the clone of the black stroke that you moved to the side in Step 3 (or, copy one of the other strokes). In the Stroke inspector, choose the Basic stroke, 6 points, and white. From the preset lines drop-down menu, choose the large dashed line (last in the list). Place this white dashed line in the middle of your road. Figure 1.28 shows the result.

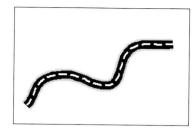

<figure>**Figure 1.28**
The completed road, with a yellow border and a white dashed line in the center.</figure>

Moving On

In this chapter, you got a close-up look at how to use the main drawing tools in FreeHand and the differences among them. You should now be able to choose which drawing tool will do the best job for you. In addition, you can now edit and manipulate your shapes. With these skills, you can produce great vectors for use in Flash.

In Chapter 2, you will use some of the special drawing tools FreeHand offers, such as lenses, envelopes, and bitmap tracing.

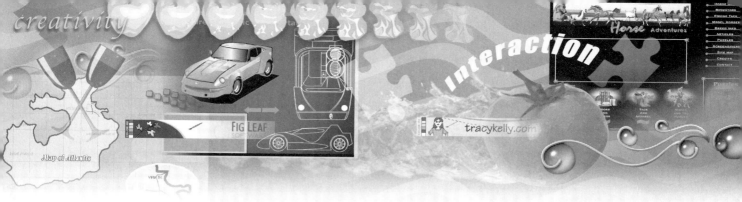

Chapter 2

Using Special Drawing Tools

In this chapter, you will use the Transparency and Magnify lenses. You will change the shape of objects using custom and preset envelopes, and you'll trace a bitmap.

Using Paste Inside

The Paste Inside technique is quite useful and can solve several limitations in FreeHand. For instance, the envelope you'll learn how to use later in this chapter can't be used on bitmap images. As an alternative to using envelopes for shapes, you can draw a shape and paste the contents inside of the shape. To paste an object inside a shape (vector or raster/bitmap), follow these steps:

1. For this exercise, you will use the Paste Inside command on a header for an Equine (Horse) bookstore. Open the hab.gif file from the Chapter 2 resources folder.

2. Select the Rectangle tool from the Toolbox. Draw a rectangle over the hab.gif (Horse Adventures Bookstore) image and then drag it off and above the hab.gif image. If you have a filled rectangle, open the Fill inspector (Window|Inspectors|Fill or Ctrl+Alt+F/Cmd+Option+F) and choose None for the fill. In the Stroke inspector (Window|Inspectors|Stroke or Ctrl+Alt+L/Cmd+Option+L), use a Basic stroke and 2 points with a color you can see.

3. With the rectangle selected, choose Modify|Ungroup. Select the Subselection tool and click the bottom right point. Press the Alt/Option key and drag to the left to form the curve you see in Figure 2.1. Click the bottom left point, press the Alt/Option key, and drag to the left to form the curve for the right side.

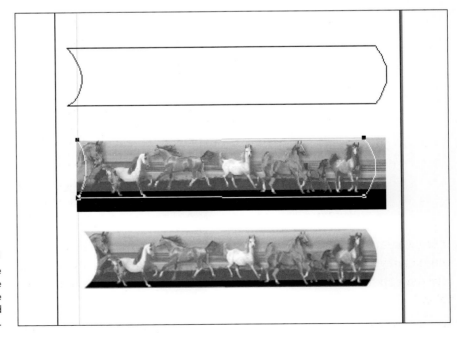

Figure 2.1
The two curves added to the rectangle shape on top, the position of the shape over the image (center), and the finished result on the bottom.

4. Drag the shape with the two curves on top of the hab.gif image. I changed the stroke color to white so you could see it. Place the image under the shape to the position you see in Figure 2.1 (center) with the right curve inside the image. You will need to move the left side points to within the image as well; the shape is a bit large.

5. When you have the image and shape in the right position, select the image only and choose Edit|Cut. To place the image in the shape, select the shape (if your stroke is white like mine, you'll have to click around until you find the shape) and choose Edit|Paste Inside. The bottom image of Figure 2.1 (bottom) shows the end result of the Paste Inside command.

Note: What you see inside of the shape is what will be pasted inside.

Using Lenses

FreeHand has six special lens effects you can apply to your art: Transparency, Magnify, Invert, Lighten, Darken, and Monochrome. A *lens* in FreeHand is an effect that is overlaid on an image; it causes an interaction between the image and the object you place on top of it. A lens effect will work even if the layer is locked.

Figure 2.2 shows the Transparency lens dialog box; it looks basically the same for all the lenses, with slight variations. You will only try the Magnify and Transparency lenses in this chapter, because they are the only ones suitable for Flash export.

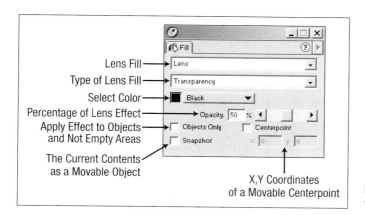

Figure 2.2
The Transparency lens dialog box.

When you first select the lens as a fill, a warning dialog box will open and tell you that any spot colors will be converted to CMYK. Click OK; this warning is relevant only if you are preparing a document for print and are using spot colors.

You can position the center of each lens by selecting the Centerpoint option and entering specific X, Y coordinates or by simply dragging. The Objects Only option applies the lens effect just to an object and not to empty areas. The Snapshot option takes a picture of the effect as seen through the lens. You can move this snapshot without affecting the original image. You will see another good use of the Snapshot option later in this chapter ("Magnifying Part of the Atlantis Map" project).

Transparency Lens

The Transparency lens is affected by the color you choose. If you choose white, you will get the illusion of transparency without changing the color of the object. If you choose a color, the effect will be of two colors overlapping, similar to a beam of colored light shining on the object. You determine the amount of transparency by choosing a percentage amount in the Fill inspector. An Opacity value of 0 yields a 100 percent transparent lens, and a value of 100 makes the lens completely opaque. The "Adding Transparency" project will add transparency to the windows of a car.

PROJECT Adding Transparency

In this project, you will add transparency to the front windshield and the driver's side window of a Z Car. To begin, follow these steps:

1. Open the zcar.FH9 file, which is in the Chapter 2 resources folder.

    Figure 2.3 shows the Z Car without any lens effects applied.

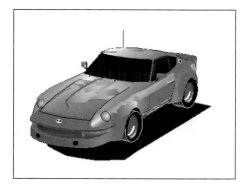

Figure 2.3
The Z Car without any lens effects applied.

2. Select the front windshield.

3. Open the Fill inspector (Window|Inspectors|Fill or Ctrl+Alt+F/ Cmd+Option+F), if it isn't already open. Click OK when the spot color warning opens.

4. The current fill is a basic black. Select the Lens fill type and the Transparency lens type.

5. In the Fill inspector, select the Objects Only and the Snapshot options (Figure 2.2).

Figure 2.4
The Z Car with a Transparency lens applied and the Fill inspector settings used.

6. Change the Opacity to 20 percent for this example. Figure 2.4 shows the Z Car with the Transparency lens applied and the Fill inspector with the settings used. Close this file without saving it. (You'll see why in a moment.)

You may wonder where that dog came from that you can see through the windshield. If you are doing transparencies, you'll need to have something below the object you apply the lens to in order to see something. In this case, I hid the "something" below the black windshield intentionally so you'd be surprised when you applied the Transparency lens fill. The steering wheel and seats could have been illustrated and added, but in this case I used a bitmap image and the Paste Inside command.

To make the object with the dog, follow these steps:

1. Open the Z Car file from the Chapter 2 resources folder.

2. With the Pointer tool, select the black windshield and move it to the left off of the car.

3. Select the dog image and delete it. Select the black windshield and choose Edit|Duplicate.

4. With the duplicate copy selected, change the fill to None in the Fill inspector. In the Stroke inspector, change the fill to Basic with 1 point (temporarily).

5. Open the dog.jpg file from the Chapter 2 resources folder. I have already cropped, scaled, and rotated it for you. Place this image behind the windshield outline and choose Modify|Arrange|Move Backward. Position the image where you want it to be in the shape (see Figure 2.5).

6. Choose Edit|Cut, select the outline, and choose Edit|Paste Inside. In the Stroke panel, change the stroke to None.

Note: You never know where or when inspiration will come. My daughter was getting riding boots from a tack shop when I saw this dog. It helps to carry a camera with you. The one used for this shot was a Kodak DC 3400.

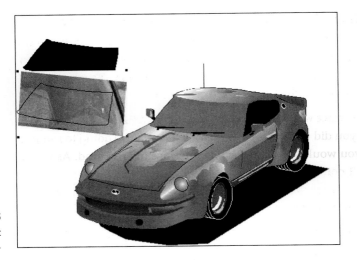

Figure 2.5
The dog image placed where it needs to be in the shape.

7. You can now position the windshield with the transparency applied back on the car and put the black windshield in place.

Magnify Lens

By applying the Magnify lens, you can magnify a portion of an image up to 20 times. The Snapshot option allows you to generate a close-up of a portion of an image and still maintain the original image.

The Magnify lens works very much like the Transparency lens. To magnify an area, follow these steps:

1. Open any image. Select the Ellipse or Rectangle tool and draw an area over an object on the canvas.

2. Open the Fill inspector (Ctrl+Alt+F/Cmd+Option+F). Choose Lens for the type of fill and Magnify for the type of lens.

3. Type in the amount of magnification you want; the value can range from 1 to 20.

4. Select Objects Only if you don't want blank areas affected. Select Snapshot.

5. If you wish, change the centerpoint by dragging or by typing in X, Y coordinates.

6. You can position what appears in the magnified section by dragging the ellipse or rectangle around the area you want to magnify.

7. Once the location and magnification are the way you want them, you can move the snapshot off to the side or to another area. You can also delete the original if you wish.

PROJECT Magnifying Part of the Atlantis Map

The Atlantis interface includes a rough map outline. If this were a real map, it would probably have more detail. For demonstration purposes, the Atlantis interface file has been modified to make a map page. You will find a file called AtlantisMap.png in the Chapter 2 resources folder; it is ready for use.

This particular interface was produced using Fireworks, and the map was drawn in FreeHand, as you did in Chapter 1. In reality, if you were going to magnify part of a map, you would make this whole interface in FreeHand. As you do this project, I will point out some workarounds that are included so you can use this Fireworks file for the Magnify lens example. To practice with the Magnify lens, follow these steps:

> **Note:** The map outline was drawn in FreeHand and placed in the Atlantis interface in Fireworks, and saved as a PNG file. When I opened the file in FreeHand, the layers were lost and the sharpness of the lines was not very distinct. If you add the map in FreeHand, it will look better when you magnify it.

1. Open the AtlantisMap.png file from the Chapter 2 resources folder.

2. Open the map.FH9 file from the Chapter 2 resources folder. You can either drag this map onto the AtlantisMap file or copy and paste it.

3. Place the map outline as shown in Figure 2.6.

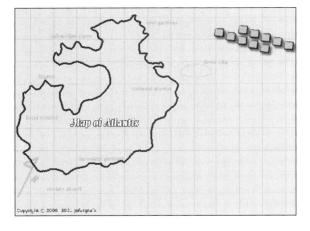

Figure 2.6
The map outline in place.

4. Select the Text tool, click the canvas, and type "water park". Highlight the text. In the Text inspector, change the font to 12-point Allegro BT. To change the text color, click the color box next to the Fill icon in the color portion of the Toolbox (bottom) and select a color (see Figure 2.7). Or you can mix your own colors by adding the RGB values in the Color Mixer (Window|Panels|Color Mixer).

5. Select the Pen tool and zoom in on the water park map area. Draw some additional lines for the map, using a Basic stroke with 1-point size and blue fill. Select the Type tool and type a couple of street names: "Vista Dr." and "Water St." respectively. In the Text inspector, choose a

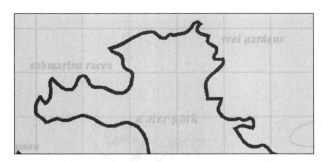

Figure 2.7
The words "water park" added
to the map.

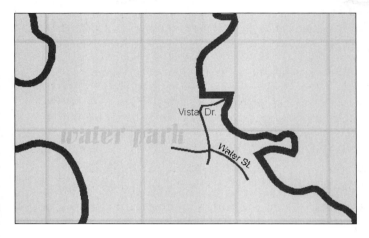

Figure 2.8
The map detail and street
names added.

4-point, black Arial font. Select the Rotate icon (more in Chapter 3 on
rotation) and place your cursor over the corner of the "Water St." text.
Click and drag to place the text at an angle (see Figure 2.8).

6. After all those steps, the magnification will be the easiest of all. Select
    the Ellipse tool and draw an ellipse around the water park area of the
    map. Figure 2.9 shows about how big you need to draw it to contain
    the magnified section of the map.

Note: To determine the
ellipse's size the way I did,
apply your magnification settings and then increase the size
of the ellipse until it encloses
the area you want to magnify.

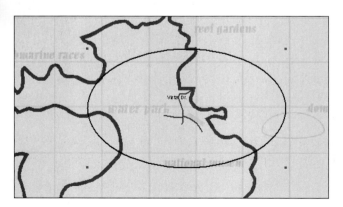

Figure 2.9
An ellipse drawn around the area
to be magnified.

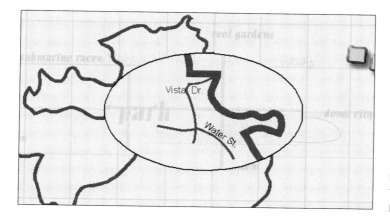

Figure 2.10
The magnified view of the water park area of the Atlantis map.

7. In the Fill inspector, choose Lens for the fill type and Magnify for the lens type. Type "2" for the magnification and select the Objects Only and Snapshot options. The result will look like Figure 2.10.

8. Select the Rectangle tool and draw a rectangle in the lower-right corner of the Atlantis map. Use a Basic fill and a dark orange color. Click and drag the magnified section over the orange rectangle. In the Stroke inspector, change the stroke color to white and the point size to 4 (see Figure 2.11).

Note: If you want to rearrange what is seen in the magnified area, you can use the Pointer tool to move the ellipse so it includes different areas, but do this before you select the Snapshot option.

Note: To see the effect of the Snapshot option, deselect it and then move the ellipse off the map. You will notice the ellipse is empty. Select Edit|Undo, select the Snapshot option, and move the magnified area. This time, the magnified area moved with the ellipse.

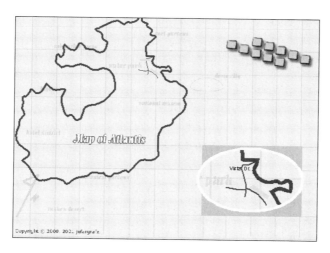

Figure 2.11
The magnified section moved into place on the Atlantis map page.

9. Choose Save and save your file.

Because I'm using FreeHand 10 and some readers may have version 9, this file is exported as a FreeHand 9 file and saved in the Chapter 2 resources folder as AtlantisMap2.FH9.

Using Envelopes

In FreeHand, you can enclose one or more objects in an envelope. You can reshape the contents by reshaping the envelope. You can use a preset envelope as is or modify it using the path tools, such as the Pen and Pointer tools. Or, you can use a custom shape you've made and convert it into an envelope.

To access the Envelope toolbar, choose Window|Toolbars|Envelope. Figure 2.12 shows the Envelope toolbar and its icons.

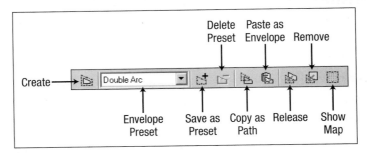

Figure 2.12
The Envelope toolbar and its icons.

Note: You can't place a bitmap image into an envelope. If you need to get around this limitation, you can trace the bitmap using the Trace tool and then put the resulting object in an envelope. You will use the Trace tool later in this chapter.

Note: When placing vector graphics into an envelope, be sure to group them first. Otherwise, you may get unexpected results.

You can copy envelopes as paths, paste paths as envelopes, or save any shape as a preset. If you wish, you can delete the presets that ship with FreeHand and add your own. It's also easy to release an object from an envelope.

Preset Envelopes

FreeHand 10 includes 21 preset envelopes, as does FreeHand 9. To use a preset envelope, follow these steps:

1. Open or draw an object.

2. Select the object and choose a preset from the drop-down menu on the Envelope toolbar.

3. Click the Create icon to apply the envelope to the object (see Figure 2.12 for the icon location).

4. To practice using some of the envelope features, click the Release icon. Your object will maintain the distortions of the envelope.

5. If you want to remove the envelope without applying the distortions, click the Remove icon.

Custom Envelopes

You can convert any shape into envelopes or alter one of the presets into a custom envelope by following these steps:

1. Draw a shape and copy it (Ctrl+C/Cmd+C). Click the Paste As Envelope icon, and an envelope will be made from your shape.

2. Click Save As Preset and give the envelope a unique name.

3. Select a graphic. Your new preset will be the selected preset; click the Create icon.

4. To alter a preset shape, select an object or graphic and a preset shape and click Create. Select the Pointer or Subselection tool and alter the shape of the preset. Click Save As Preset icon and name your new preset.

PROJECT Putting a Poem into an Envelope

In Chapter 8, you'll use Fireworks to make the ornament used in this poem's Web pages, and you'll insert the poem. To put the poem in an envelope, follow these steps:

1. Open a new file (File|New), choose File|Import, and locate the Poem.txt file in the Chapter 2 resources folder. Click your document. Figure 2.13 shows the poem in the FreeHand document.

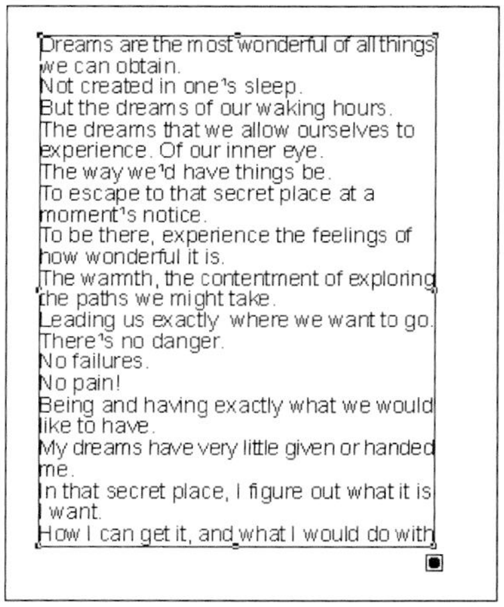

Dreams are the most wonderful of all things we can obtain.
Not created in one's sleep.
But the dreams of our waking hours.
The dreams that we allow ourselves to experience. Of our inner eye.
The way we'd have things be.
To escape to that secret place at a moment's notice.
To be there, experience the feelings of how wonderful it is.
The warmth, the contentment of exploring the paths we might take.
Leading us exactly where we want to go.
There's no danger.
No failures.
No pain!
Being and having exactly what we would like to have.
My dreams have very little given or handed me.
In that secret place, I figure out what it is I want.
How I can get it, and what I would do with

Figure 2.13
A poem imported and placed in a FreeHand document.

2. With the text selected, choose Rectangle from the Envelope Preset drop-down menu and click the Create icon.

3. Select the Pointer tool and pull the center points on the right and left sides outward, as shown in Figure 2.14.

4. If you look closely at the new shape, you'll see that some of the poem is cut off. Click the Remove icon and use the Pointer tool to pull down the black rectangle on the bottom-right corner of the text until you see the line "If only in Life's Dream". Click the Create icon to reapply the Rectangle envelope.

5. Using the Subselection tool, pull out the sides again. Because this text will be used on a black background, the text needs to be white. In the Toolbox, select the Stroke color box and choose white from the color palette.

Figure 2.14

The new preset shape.

6. Choose File|Export and export your envelope as a FreeHand 9 file. Because this file will be imported into Fireworks, it needs to be a FreeHand 9 file (FreeHand 10 was released after Fireworks 4). If Fireworks 5 is released by the time you're reading this book, you can use a FreeHand 10 file.

Using the Tracing Function

There are many things in FreeHand that you can't do with bitmap images. For example, you can't put a bitmap into an envelope or on the perspective grid. To overcome this drawback, you can use the FreeHand Trace tool. Of course, this tool has many other uses, as well—one of the most popular is to trace line art that you drew, scanned, and brought into FreeHand. By tracing the art, you can make it into a scalable vector object suitable for use in Flash and/or print. Traced bitmaps are often used to convert company logos into vectors.

The Tracing function offers you a lot of control and flexibility. To get really good at using the tool, you will need to practice to see how each setting affects your drawing and/or file size. Of course, if the file's destination is the Web, file size is a very important consideration.

If you use the Trace tool often or are tracing a complex bitmap (like the jukebox in the next project), be sure to go to Edit|Preferences and allow plenty of RAM. In FreeHand 10, you can choose the Redraw tab and type in a RAM amount or use the default Dynamic setting. I have 512MB of RAM, which was enough to trace the jukebox; but when I tried to simplify paths, I got a message warning that I didn't have enough RAM. (You may not get a similar warning. FreeHand 10 seems to have different problems on different machines. I'm using the first release so maybe these things will be fixed by the time you receive this book.)

The Trace tool is not limited to bitmaps; you can also trace FreeHand objects and text. You may wonder why you'd want to trace an object that is already a vector. The answer is that you can use the tracing as a clipping path and then paste a bitmap inside it.

The Trace Tool

You have a lot of flexibility when you use the Trace tool. Figure 2.15 shows the Trace Tool options.

To achieve the best trace, you will need to have a good understanding of the options available as well as plenty of practice.

Color Mode

When you select the number of colors you'd like in your traced image, remember that the more colors you choose, the more RAM is required. You will never get a trace that is as good as a vector you drew. If you are tracing a black and white line scan, choose 2 from the Colors drop-down menu. You can have FreeHand trace in different color modes such as RGB, CMYK, or Grayscale. If your image has more than 256 colors, the extra colors will be converted to the nearest available color.

Resolution

You have three choices in the Resolution drop-down menu: High, Normal, and Low. Low uses the least RAM.

Trace Layers

The Trace Layers drop-down menu allows you to decide if you want to trace a particular layer, all layers, or Background. It's a good idea to use Background and lock the layer; that way, your bitmap is on the Background layer and won't move or be altered, and your traced image is on a foreground layer.

Path Conversion

The Path Conversion drop-down menu determines how FreeHand generates the path. The possible choices are as follows:

- *Outline*—The outer borders of all the graphic elements are traced, the objects are closed, and the paths are filled. When you choose Outline, the Path Overlap option just below it becomes available. When you're tracing continuous-tone images, Loose works well. For color tracing with precision, use Tight; and for logos and text, use None.

- *Centerline*—Use this option to trace things like technical drawings, which have no fills. FreeHand traces at the center of the graphic strokes and produces an outline only with no fills. When you choose Centerline, the Uniform option appears. Select Uniform if you want all your strokes to be the same size, regardless of the size in your scan or drawing.

- *Centerline/Outline*—When you choose this option, the Open Paths Below option becomes available. In the Open Paths Below box, you enter a number from 1 to 10 pixels that determines which attributes will be given to each traced path. The Open Paths Below value determines the value below which FreeHand will draw an open and stroked path or if the path will be closed.

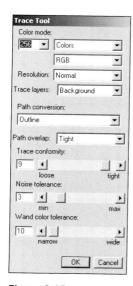

Figure 2.15

The Trace Tool options.

Note: If you are accustomed to using other wands, such as Photoshop's, you may find the Trace tool a bit awkward for selecting colors. For instance, you click to select a color, and the amount of detail you get will depend on the Wand Color Tolerance you have set. The problem comes when you hold the Shift key to add to the area. Sometimes doing so adds to the area, and sometimes it subtracts—and then you click again to get the dialog box. A minus or plus sign appears next to the wand cursor; but when you're tracing an image with a lot of dark colors, these symbols can't be seen.

- *Outer Edge*—Only the edge of the graphic is traced, producing a clipping path into which you can paste the original graphic.

Trace Conformity

You can enter a Trace Conformity value from 0 to 10 by using the slider or by typing it in the dialog box. This number determines how close to the original path the traced path will conform. The higher the setting, the more points you'll have.

Noise Tolerance

You can enter a Noise Tolerance value from 0 to 20, which determines how noise is handled in the trace. The higher the setting, the more noise is ignored.

Wand Color Tolerance

A Wand Color Tolerance color range from 0 to 255 is available, where 0 is the most sensitive to color changes and 255 is the least sensitive. The Wand tool's tolerance setting determines the tool's sensitivity in selecting areas of contiguous colors. To use the Trace tool to select just areas of color, click in the area of the color you want to trace and hold the Shift key to add to the color selection. When your selection is made, release the Shift key and click once with the Trace tool in the selection. A dialog box will open in which you have the option to trace the selection or convert the selection edge.

PROJECT Tracing a Juke Box and a Photo

You will trace the jukebox in both FreeHand and Flash. You can use the one you like the best in the final project where you will add music (Chapter 17).

Tracing the Jukebox

To practice tracing the jukebox, follow these steps:

1. Open the corvette.jpg file from the Chapter 2 resources folder. This image was donated by The Game Gallery at **www.homegameroom.com**.

2. Double-click the Trace tool to open the options dialog box. Feel free to experiment with the settings. The ones I settled on are as follows:

   - *Color Mode*—64, Colors, RGB
   - *Resolution*—Low
   - *Trace Layers*—Background
   - *Path Conversion*—Outline
   - *Path Overlap*—Loose
   - *Trace Conformity*—10
   - *Noise Tolerance*—1
   - *Wand Color Tolerance*—133

3. Lock the Background layer in the Layers inspector by clicking the open lock; it will close.

4. With the Trace tool, make a selection by dragging around the top half of the jukebox, to just below the pages area. Be patient; you now have to wait while FreeHand renders the trace.

5. Select the Pointer tool and place it in an area of the traced image that doesn't have many points. Drag the traced part off to the side. Figure 2.16 shows the result. You can also find this image in the Color Studio.

Figure 2.16
The trace of the top part of the jukebox.

6. With an image as complex as this one, I use the Modify|Alter Path| Simplify command. I applied Simplify with a setting of 5 successfully three times.

7. I didn't want the center part of the jukebox, so I began tracing the bottom; the rectangle in Figure 2.17 shows the part that is being traced.

Figure 2.17
The bottom trace area of the jukebox.

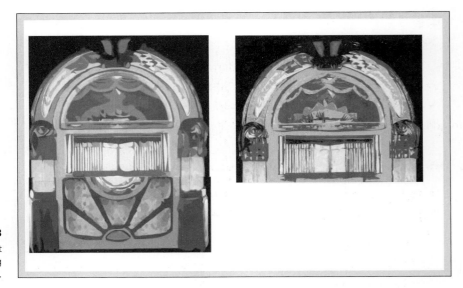

Figure 2.18

The Flash tracing on the left and the FreeHand tracing on the right.

Figure 2.18 shows the jukebox traced in Flash on the left and the one traced in FreeHand on the right. I cut out the middle of the jukebox and did a quick patch of the Flash trace (it's not complete yet; the gradient will be fixed in Flash as well as other enhancements) and optimized it in Fireworks using a JPEG setting with 50 percent quality. The file size is 28.8KB. The image on the right is what was done in FreeHand. I optimized it in Fireworks using the same settings as for the Flash image. The size of just the top portion is 26.9KB. It's up to you to decide which is better.

Photo

You'll trace a picture of a horse, not because it's needed as a vector for use in Flash, but because the image will go on a puzzle box using the perspective grid. The perspective grid does not work with bitmap images. To trace a photo, follow these steps:

1. Open the horseimage.jpg file from the Chapter 2 resources folder.

2. Double-click on the Trace tool and use the following settings:

   - *Color Mode*—128, Colors, RGB

   - *Resolution*—Low

   - *Trace Layers*—Background

   - *Path Conversion*—Outline

   - *Path Overlap*—Loose

   - *Trace Conformity*—3

- *Noise Tolerance—3*

- *Wand Color Tolerance—156*

3. Click the Background layer in the Layers inspector and lock it.

4. With the Trace tool, make a selection by dragging around the whole photo.

5. Select the Pointer tool and place it in an area of the traced image that doesn't have many points. Drag the traced part off to the side.

6. Choose Modify|Alter Paths|Simplify, enter "10", and click OK. Repeat this step once. Select the Pointer tool, draw around your traced image, and then group the image (Modify|Group).

7. You can now export your image (File|Export). I exported it as a FreeHand 9 file, opened it in Fireworks, and optimized it using a JPEG setting and a quality of 40.

8. To get a better feel for how the Trace tool works, you can perform two more tests and then compare the results. Repeat Steps 2 through 7, but in Step 2, change the Color Mode to 256. Notice how much green appears in this trace; it doesn't look very good.

9. To improve the previous trace, repeat Steps 2 through 7, but in Step 2, change the Wand Color Tolerance setting up to 255. The resulting trace has much better color.

Results

The results of these three traces can be found in the Color Studio as well as here. You won't see the full impact unless you look at the Color Studio or do it yourself. The first photo was traced using 128 colors and optimized as a JPEG at 40% quality; the file size is 19KB. The second photo used 256 colors and was optimized with the same settings; the file size is 18.9KB. The third photo changed only the Color Tolerance, and the file size is 19.9KB. Figures 2.19, 2.20, and 2.21 show the results.

Only you can determine the tradeoff of file size versus quality—your priority will depend on the use of the trace. For my purposes, the third trace with the higher Color Tolerance setting will do the trick.

As you've seen in these projects, considerable trial and error is involved in determining which trace settings will work for you. We tested only three; for a critical project, you may need to test many more times.

Figure 2.19
Trace using 128 colors.

Figure 2.20
Trace using 256 colors.

Figure 2.21
Trace using a Color
Tolerance of 255.

Moving On

You should now be comfortable using some of the special tools at your disposal in FreeHand, such as envelopes, Paste Inside command, and different lenses. You now know how to trace a bitmap to convert it into a scalable vector image.

In Chapter 3, you will learn how to blend and transform objects.

Chapter 3
Manipulating Objects

This chapter explains the order of objects within a drawing and how to transform objects by using the transform tools. You also will learn how to blend objects that can be used as animations in Fireworks and in Flash.

Arranging Objects

Your art can become disorganized quite quickly when a lot of objects are involved. Layers help keep your files in order. Each layer can contain many objects stacked on top of each other. Even if objects don't overlap, they are still in a stacking order, which is determined by the object that was drawn first. Each new object you draw is put on top of the previous one.

Stacking Order

Layers are prioritized from the top of the Layers list to the bottom. The item on the top layer is the foremost item in a piece of art. The items on the bottom layer come after everything else in the priority order. Figure 3.1 shows how FreeHand handles layers and stacking within the layers.

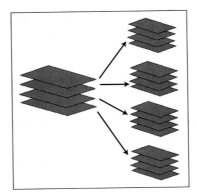

Figure 3.1
The stacking order of layers and the objects on each layer.

Each object has its own properties, its own X, Y coordinates, and its own stacking order. You can move the position of an object by choosing Modify|Arrange|Bring To Front, Move Forward, Move Backward, or Send To Back.

Aligning

Objects can be aligned in reference to each other and to the page. Figure 3.2 shows the Align panel (Modify|Align or Ctrl+Alt+A/Cmd+Option+A) with a drop-down menu open. The drop-down choices are the same for the Horizontal and Vertical options.

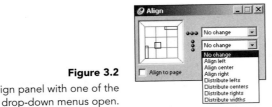

Figure 3.2
The Align panel with one of the drop-down menus open.

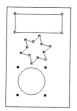 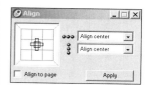

Figure 3.3
Three objects aligned using the Align panel visually.

You can easily use the Align panel visually for multiple objects. On the left side of Figure 3.3, three objects are drawn and selected. In the Align panel, you can click the center of the diagram or use the drop-down menus to specify where each object will be placed. In this example, I clicked the center of the diagram and clicked the Apply button. The result is the object shown in the center image of Figure 3.3.

If you are new to aligning objects using the Align panel, then draw a few shapes and practice with each of the different options available in the Horizontal and Vertical drop-down menus. Remember to click the Apply button so you can see the changes each option makes.

Grouping

You can group multiple objects together by Shift+selecting them and choosing Modify|Group (Ctrl+G/Cmd+G). Grouping helps keep design elements orderly. Grouped objects also can be released to layers for use in animations. Grouped objects are much easier to move around, as well. I often group objects just to change their location and then ungroup them when they are in place.

> **Note:** If you try to edit an object and you can't access any of the edit options, you may be trying to modify a group. Choose Modify|Ungroup then proceed with the edit.

Locking

You can lock an object or group by choosing Modify|Lock. Locking objects has various uses. You can lock an object and use the Align panel to align with reference to the locked object. If you need to select objects near the bottom of a large stack, locking the top object makes it easier to select other objects. Or, if you are done with an object, you can lock it so that no alterations can be made accidentally. A locked object can still be selected, but you can't move or transform it.

To practice locking, follow these steps:

1. Open a new document (File|New), choose the Spiral tool, and drag a spiral in the center of your canvas. Open the Stroke inspector (it's probably already open; but if it isn't, choose Window|Inspectors|Stroke or Ctrl+Alt+L/Cmd+Option+L) and change the Width amount to 4 points.

2. Select the Rectangle tool from the toolbar. Drag a rectangle over the bottom portion of the spiral. Click the Fill inspector tab (in the inspector set with the Stroke inspector) and choose Basic.

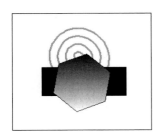

Figure 3.4
Three objects stacked on each other.

3. Select the Polygon tool and draw over the rectangle. In the Fill inspector, choose a gradient fill. Figure 3.4 shows the order of the objects.

4. Select the rectangle and choose Modify|Lock. Select the Pointer tool, marquee-select all the objects, and move them by clicking and dragging down. As you can see in Figure 3.5, the locked object does not move.

Figure 3.5
The group of three objects selected and moved: The locked object remains in place.

Transformations

FreeHand includes a powerful set of transformation tools. These tools allow you to move, rotate, scale, skew, and reflect objects. You can make transformations using the icons in the Toolbox or numerically using the Transform panel (Window|Panels|Transform or Ctrl+M/Cmd+M). To access transformation options for the individual transform tools, you can double-click one of the transform icons in the Toolbox or use Modify|Transform and select the one you want. Once the Transform panel is open, you can select the options for the transform tools from the icons that run along the left side (see Figure 3.6). Figure 3.7 shows the icons in the Toolbox. The Move tool is accessed in the Transform panel.

Figure 3.6
The Transform panel.

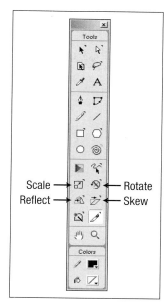

Scale
Reflect
Rotate
Skew

Figure 3.7
The Toolbox showing the transform tool icons.

Rotate

When you select the Rotate icon in the Toolbox, your cursor will change to a crosshair. The spot where you place the cursor will be the origin of transformation or the *point of origin*, around which rotation occurs. You can rotate manually or using the Transform panel. To rotate manually, click your cursor where you want the origin point and then drag.

Note: When you enter positive degrees of rotation angle in the Transform panel, the object will rotate to the left; negative degrees will make the object rotate to the right.

To rotate an object using the Transform panel, follow these steps:

1. Select the Ellipse tool and draw a circle. Use the Rectangle tool to draw a small rectangle, as shown in Figure 3.8.

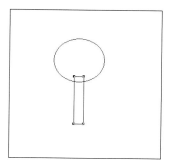

Figure 3.8
The shape to use for a rotation.

2. Shift+select the circle and rectangle. Choose Modify|Combine|Union to make one shape.

3. Select the Rotate icon from the Toolbox. (If the Transform panel isn't open, double-click the Rotate icon to open it.)

4. In the Transform panel, enter the degrees of rotation you want in the Rotation Angle box (45 is used here).

Note: If your object has a fill (basic, gradient, etc.) or a clipping path with contents, you can specify in the Transform panel exactly what you want to rotate. You can also set the X, Y coordinates for the origin point.

5. In the Copies box, type "7".

6. Click the Rotate button. Figure 3.9 shows the result. Note that you did not set an origin point; this example used the default.

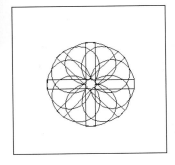

Figure 3.9
The object rotated 45 degrees and copied 7 times.

7. Choose Edit|Undo. You will now set your own origin point. Press the Alt/Option key and click below the shape, as shown in Figure 3.10.

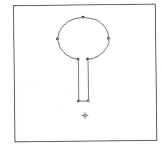

Figure 3.10
The combined shape with the crosshair to set a new origin point.

8. Enter "45" for the Rotation Angle and "7" for the Copies value. Click the Rotate button. Figure 3.11 shows the result. This example demonstrates the power and flexibility you have by simply changing the origin point.

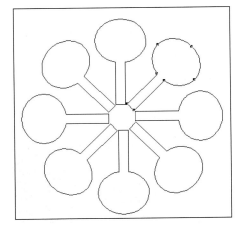

Figure 3.11
The 45-degree rotation applied using the new origin point.

Scale

The Scale tool allows you to resize an object. You can choose whether to resize proportionally. Figure 3.12 shows the Scaling options in the Transform panel.

To use the Scale tool, follow these steps:

1. You can scale one object or a group of objects by selecting them.

2. Select the Scale icon in the Toolbox. To scale and still maintain the original proportions, press the Alt/Option key and drag one of the corner points in or out.

3. To scale using the Transform panel, double-click the Scale icon in the Toolbox if the Transform panel isn't open. Select the Scale icon in the Transform panel to access the options for scaling. Enter the X, Y values or, if you want a uniform scale, select the Uniform option and enter a percentage of scale you'd like.

4. If you want to scale and add a copy or copies, enter the number in the Copies box.

5. Click Scale when you are done.

Figure 3.12

Scaling options available in the Transform panel.

PROJECT Making Car Tire Centers

The side view of the Z Car you learned to draw in Chapter 1 has tires that were made using the Rotate tool. Follow these steps to make the tire centers:

1. Open a new document (File|New), select the Ellipse tool, and drag an oblong ellipse onto your canvas.

2. Click the Stroke inspector tab (Ctrl+Alt+L/Cmd+Option+L), select a Basic stroke, and select Hairline for the stroke size.

3. Double-click the Rotate tool icon if the Transform panel isn't open; if it is open, just select the Rotate tool icon.

4. Press the Alt/Option key to place the origin point below the bottom of the elongated ellipse, as shown in Figure 3.13.

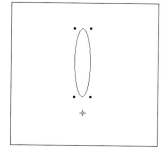

Figure 3.13

The origin point set for the elongated ellipse.

5. Enter "45" for the Rotation Angle and "7" in the Copies box. Click the Rotate button.

6. Select the Ellipse tool and draw a circle in the center of the rotated ellipses, as shown in Figure 3.14.

Figure 3.14

The elongated ellipse rotated and duplicated, forming the center for the tires.

7. With the Ellipse tool, draw a large ellipse around all the shapes. If your ellipse is too large or too small, select the Scale tool. While holding the Shift key (to constrain proportions), drag the bottom-right point in to make the ellipse smaller or out to make it larger. Position the ellipse so it touches the edges of the tire center. The arrow keys are helpful when positioning objects like this ellipse.

8. Select the Scale icon in the Transform panel to access its options. Select the Uniform option. Type in "110" for the Scale % value, specify 1 copy, and click the Scale button. Figure 3.15 shows an additional circle applied.

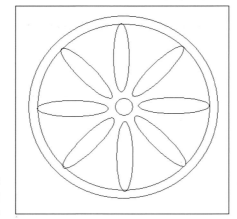

Figure 3.15

The large ellipse scaled and copied, forming two ellipses.

9. For the rest of the tire, repeat Step 8, changing the Scale % value to 150. Figure 3.16 shows the completed tire.

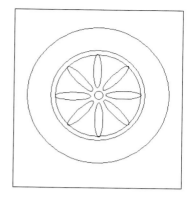

Figure 3.16
The completed tire.

10. Using the Pointer tool, marquee-select the whole drawing and choose Modify|Group.

11. Select the Scale tool. Holding the Shift key, drag to the proper size to fit in the drawing of the car.

Reflect

The Reflect tool is great when you're working with symmetrical designs or if you want to make a reflection of an image. You can set the Reflect Axis value either in the Transform panel or manually by pressing the Alt/Option key and clicking where you want the reflect axis to be. To try the Reflect tool, follow these steps:

1. Draw half of a wine glass or any symmetrical shape. (This glass will be used in the Bar Wars scene in Chapter 5; it's colorized in Chapter 4.) Figure 3.17 shows the wine glass's left side.

2. Double-click the Reflect tool icon in the Toolbox.

3. Move the crosshair cursor to the center of the top of the glass. Hold the Alt/Option key and click at this point, as shown in Figure 3.18.

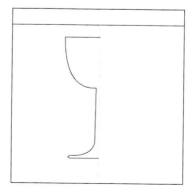
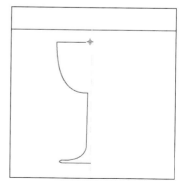

Figure 3.17
(Left) Half a wine glass.

Figure 3.18
(Right) The position of the Reflect Axis being set.

Figure 3.19
The wine glass half reflected and
in position.

Note: You can make a reflection of an object by selecting
the Reflect tool and simply
clicking the crosshair cursor
where you want to reflect.
However, this method does
not make a duplicate—it acts
more like a vertical flip.

Note: The Reflect tool was
used to duplicate half of the
top view of the Z Car in
Chapter 1.

Note: You don't have to skew
by clicking and dragging a
point. Place the crosshair
anywhere you want and drag
with the mouse to get a feel
for the different skew effects.

4. In the Transform panel, enter "90" for the Reflect Axis (a value of 180 causes a horizontal flip) and specify 1 copy. Click the Reflect button. Figure 3.19 shows the result.

5. To complete the wine glass, Shift+select both halves and choose Modify|Join. Click the Option inspector tab (Window|Inspectors|Object) and select the Closed option if it isn't already selected.

Skew

You can use the Skew tool to distort an object. Select the Skew tool from the Toolbox and select the Skew icon in the Transform panel to access its options. You can set numeric skew angles, centers, and copies from within the Transform panel. But the easiest way, if you aren't mathematically inclined, is to skew visually.

Figure 3.20 is the result of skewing the tire.FH9 file (in the Chapter 3 resources folder) using the Skew tool. Select the Skew tool and drag the bottom-right point to the right. The Transform panel changes to reflect the skew values.

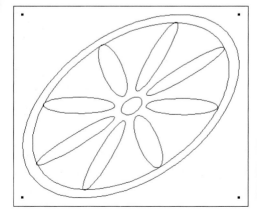

Figure 3.20
The tire skewed to the right using
the Skew tool.

Using the Blend Function

In a blend, you have at least a beginning and an ending object, and FreeHand generates the steps in between. The results get interesting when you blend two or more different shapes. To make a blend, follow these steps:

1. Select the Rectangle tool and draw a square on the left side of the canvas.

2. Select the Ellipse tool and draw a circle on the right side of the canvas, as shown in Figure 3.21.

Figure 3.21
A square and a circle ready to be blended.

3. Shift+select the square and the circle and choose Modify|Combine|Blend (Ctrl+Shift+B/Cmd+Shift+B). Figure 3.22 shows the blend.

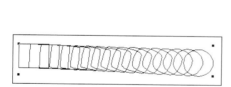 

Figure 3.22
The square and the circle blended.

4. You can control the number of intermediate steps in the Object inspector. Leave the blend selected, change the Steps value in the Object inspector, and press Enter/Return. Figure 3.23 shows the same blend with Steps reduced to 10.

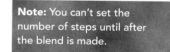

Note: You can't set the number of steps until after the blend is made.

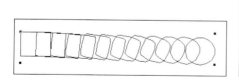 

Figure 3.23
The blend with the intermediate steps reduced to 10.

As mentioned in the introduction of this section, you can blend more than two objects. Figure 3.24 shows the beginning objects on the left and the resulting blend. As you can see, you can come up with some pretty interesting blends.

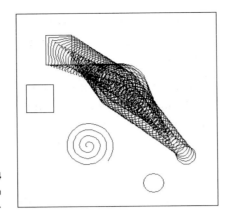

Figure 3.24
Three objects that yield an
interesting blend.

PROJECT Blending a Whole Apple into an Eaten Apple

This apple will be used as an animation in the children's Web site named Horse Adventures. You will export this blend and turn it into an animation in Fireworks in Chapter 12. To make a blend, follow these steps:

1. Open the apples.FH9 file from the Chapter 3 resources folder.

2. Using the Pointer tool, place the whole apple on top of the eaten apple, as shown in Figure 3.25.

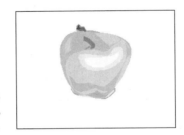

Figure 3.25
The whole apple placed on top
of the eaten apple.

3. Shift+select the top apple and the lower apple.

4. Choose Modify|Combine|Blend (Ctrl+Shift+B/Cmd+Shift+B).

5. In the Object inspector, change the Steps value to 7 and press Enter/Return.

6. To prepare this blend for use as an animation in Fireworks, you will now put each of the blended objects onto its own layer. Choose Xtras|Animate|Release To Layers, and the Release To Layers dialog box opens (see Figure 3.26).

Figure 3.26
The Release To Layers dialog box.

7. Choose Sequence from the Animate drop-down menu and select the Reverse Direction option. If you didn't reverse the direction, the eaten apple would appear first and blend to the whole.

8. Save your file. If you are using version 10 and want to make your file available to users of earlier versions, you'll have to export. To export to an earlier version, choose File|Export and choose the version of FreeHand you are exporting to.

Blending to a Path

Blending to a path is very similar to making a regular blend, except that the blend will conform to the shape of a path. This is a good feature to use to put text on a curved path for uses such as logos. To blend to a path, follow these steps:

1. Draw two shapes with any attributes you'd like. This example uses a Basic stroke of 4 for both objects. The stroke color on the star is red, and the rectangle is bright blue. The fill is basic, light blue in the star and light green in the rectangle.

2. Shift+select each shape and choose Modify|Combine|Blend (Ctrl+Shift+B/ Cmd+Shift+B). In the Object inspector, enter a Steps value of 25.

3. Draw a path. Here is a quick path to try: Select the Spiral tool and drag a large spiral. I used a Basic stroke of 4 and a color of bright blue (see Figure 3.27).

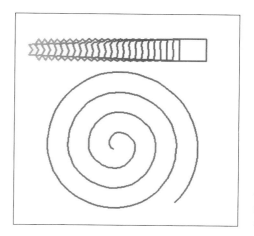

Figure 3.27
The filled and stroked objects blended with 25 steps, and a spiral path.

4. Shift+select the blended objects and the path. Choose Modify|Combine| Join Blend To Path. Figure 3.28 shows the result. You can do some really interesting things with this feature.

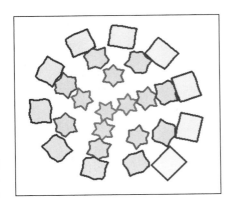

Figure 3.28

The blend of a star and a rectangle attached to a spiral path.

![PROJECT]

Blending a Logo on a Path

This project demonstrates one way to make a title for the Bar Wars scene you will start in Chapter 4. To make a title that is on a path, follow these steps:

1. Open a new document (File|New), select the Type tool, and click the canvas. Type "BAR WARS" in all capital letters. Select the text and change the font. The font used here is 24-point Arial. You can change these settings in the Text inspector or from the Text toolbar (Window|Toolbars|Text).

2. To change the stroke or fill, you have to click away from the text to get rid of the bounding box, then select the Text tool, and highlight the text to select it. Click the Stroke tab and use a Basic stroke with a size of 4. In the Color Mixer (Shift+F9), click the bottom icon (on a PC, it's a Windows logo) and select red for the color. Click OK. Click and drag the red color and drop it onto the color box in the Stroke panel.

3. Click the Fill tab and change the color to white using the method from Step 2.

4. Using the drawing tool of your choice, draw a curvy path. I used the Pen tool and Shift+dragged the second and third points, as shown in Figure 3.29.

Figure 3.29

Text with a fill and stroke with a path drawn.

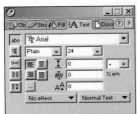

5. Shift+select the text and the path and choose Text|Attach To Path (Ctrl+Shift+Y/Cmd+Shift+Y).

6. Click the Object inspector tab. In the Orientation area, select Skew Vertical. The result can be seen in Figure 3.30. Experiment with some of the other orientation options; a couple of them give a "drunken" look, which could also work in this case.

Figure 3.30
The text attached to the path and the orientation changed.

7. Save the file. You can use this title in the Bar Wars Scene project in Chapter 15, or you can use another option you will see in Chapter 15.

Symbols

Symbols in FreeHand are like symbols in Fireworks and Flash. When you convert any object, text, or group into a symbol, it is stored in the Library. You can make symbols several ways:

- With the Library panel open (Window|Library or F11), you can drag the object into the List View area of the Library.

- You can choose Modify|Symbol|Convert To Symbol or Copy To Symbol.

- Select the right-pointing arrow in the Library panel and choose New Graphic from the Options pop-up menu.

- Click the plus (+) sign in the lower-left corner of the Library panel.

When you save your file, the symbol will import to Flash as a symbol and will appear in the Library. To edit a symbol, double-click the symbol name to open a separate edit window. After you make your changes, leave the Auto-Update option selected (it is by default) to update all instances of the symbol. (An *instance* is a copy of the original object, which is stored in the Library.)

Symbols are useful because multiple symbols in a document do not add weight to the file size. They are great for repeating items such as logos. If you need to change a logo or other repeating item that you've made into a symbol, all you do is change the original and you are done. To totally replace one symbol with another, simply drag the replacement object onto the name of the old symbol in the Library panel. A prompt will open, giving you several choices: New Symbol, Replace, Convert, or Cancel. To replace, simply select Replace.

PROJECT Converting the Horse Adventure Bookstore Header into a Symbol

Converting objects into symbols is probably one of the easiest things you'll do in FreeHand. You make the Horse Adventures Bookstore header in Chapter 9 and adjust its colors in Fireworks. You paste it inside a shape in Chapter 2. To convert it into a symbol, follow these steps:

1. Open the habheader.FH9 file from the Chapter 3 resources folder.

2. Select the header.

3. Choose Modify|Symbol|Convert To Symbol.

4. If Flash 6 is released and you have FreeHand 10, you can export the symbol by choosing Export from the Options pop-up menu (right-point-ing arrow) in the Library. Otherwise, export as a FreeHand 9 file and import into Fireworks or Flash.

The symbol will open in Flash and Fireworks as a symbol. Open the Library panel, and it will appear as a symbol.

Moving On

In this chapter, you have learned how to manipulate and arrange your objects. Using layers and stacking gives you tremendous control over how your objects are arranged. You can manipulate objects in multiple ways, such as rotating, skewing, and blending.

In Chapter 4, you will see how to use the color tools as well as the new Contour Blend tool.

Chapter 4

Adding Color

In this chapter, you will learn how to use the color functions in FreeHand. You'll work with swatches, the Color Mixer, and the gradient tools.

Working with Color

Over the next few pages, we will take a quick look at some of the color tools available in FreeHand so you are familiar with them before you begin the projects. You will also use the new Contour gradient tool. You will use the Transparency lens and transforms tools discussed in previous chapters, as well.

Color Modes

In FreeHand, you have the option of selecting which color mode to use. The choices are:

- *CMYK*—Cyan, magenta, yellow and black. Used for four-color process ink printing.

- *RGB*—Red, green, and blue. Your monitor uses this color mode.

- *HLS*—Used for choosing colors based on their hue, lightness, and saturation qualities.

- *System Color picker*—The choices are your *operating system colors*.

This book uses the RGB color mode, because the focus is on Web production rather than print. It is especially important to be sure your colors are RGB when importing into Flash. Flash is a Web-only tool, and it automatically converts your CMYK colors to RGB. You'll get better and more predictable results if you convert to RGB before importing into Flash.

You can change modes in the Color Mixer, as you will see in the next section.

Color Mixer and Tints Panel

You can open the Color Mixer several ways; for example, you can choose Window|Panels|Color Mixer, use the keyboard shortcut (Shift+F9), or select the icon (paint palette) from the Toolbox. In the Color Mixer, you can define custom colors, enter RGB (or CMYK) values, and select the color mode you want to use.

The Swatches panel (Window|Panels|Swatches) provides easy access to the colors you want to use in your document. To add a new color to the Swatches panel, drag the color and drop it in the panel, or click the button to the left of the color area. The Add To Swatches dialog box will open, in which you can name your color; the name must be different than currently named colors.

Figure 4.1
The Color Mixer panel and the Add Swatches button.

If you click the Options pop-up menu (right-pointing arrow), you can select from a number of color options, including a Web Safe palette. You also can choose if you want a process color or spot color. This choice is irrelevant for the Web, but it's very important if you are designing for print; process color uses four colors (CMYK), and spot color uses one color (which is great for two-color printing). Figure 4.1 shows the Color Mixer; the arrow is pointing to the Add Swatches button. Figure 4.2 shows the Add Swatches dialog box.

Figure 4.2
The Add Swatches dialog box.

In the Tints panel, you can make percentage tints of a color you made in the Mixer panel. Simply click one of the percentage boxes, use the slider, or type in a percentage value. After you define a color in the Color Mixer or in the Tints panel, you can add it to the Swatches panel by dragging the color and dropping it on the panel or by clicking the Add Swatches button to the left of the color area. Figure 4.3 shows the Tints panel.

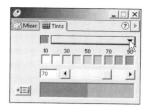

Figure 4.3
The Tints panel.

Swatches Panel

The Swatches panel is your color control center. Here, you determine which palette to use and organize the colors needed for each document or project. You add custom mixed colors and tints to the Swatches panel as needed. You can view the colors two ways: with the names showing or with just the color swatches. Figure 4.4 shows the Swatches panel with the names showing, and Figure 4.5 shows just the swatches; you choose which works best for you.

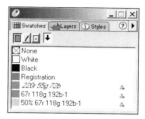

Figure 4.4
The Swatches panel with the color names visible.

Swatches Panel Options

If you click the right-pointing arrow in the Swatches panel, the Options pop-up menu opens; it provides all kinds of color options (see Figure 4.6). For Web design, you'll probably want to choose the last item, Web Safe Color Library. Figure 4.7 shows the Web Safe Color Library dialog box.

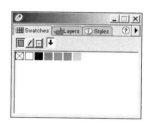

Figure 4.5
The Swatches panel with the color names hidden.

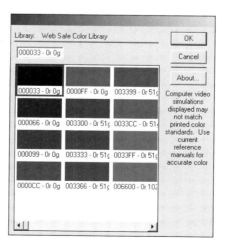

Figure 4.6
(Left) The Options pop-up menu in the Swatches panel.

Figure 4.7
(Right) The Web Safe Color Library dialog box.

Figure 4.8
A Web-safe color added to the Swatches panel.

Photoshop ACT Files

Although there are not many ACT color files that ship with Photoshop 6, you can import Photoshop ACT color tables if you'd like, but not through the Options pop-up menu. Choose Xtras|Colors|Import RGB Color Table and navigate to the folder in which you keep your ACT files. In FreeHand 10, one ACT file already is available; it's called Greys.

Figure 4.9
The list of color files that ship with FreeHand 10.

Below each color box are six numbers and/or letters followed by sets of two numbers and letters. The first six characters are Hexadecimal numbers, which are used in HTML coding to identify colors. The three sets of two numbers/letters (you can only see two sets in the figure) are the RGB values. Figure 4.8 shows the whole default name of a Web-safe color, which includes the Hexadecimal number and the RGB value with three sets of letters/numbers.

Also notice the icon to the right of the Web-safe color in Figure 4.8. The three little circles indicate an RGB color. The colors above this color are also RGB, but they are not necessarily Web safe. The first color below Registration is *1c 80m 59y 0K*; it has no icon, because it is a CMYK color added only to demonstrate the difference to you. Another way to identify CMYK versus RGB is that the CMYK color names are italicized and RGB names aren't. (Web-safe color names are italicized, though.)

Import and Export Color Tables

FreeHand 10 ships with quite a few custom color tables that you can choose from by selecting the Import option from the Options pop-up menu (see Figure 4.9).

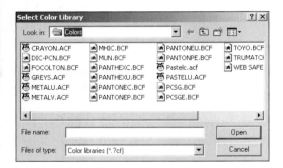

To export your current swatches for use in other documents or to share them, choose Export from the Options pop-up menu. A dialog box will open in which you can choose which colors you'd like to export. When you click OK, the Create Color Library dialog box opens, as shown in Figure 4.10. Name the Library and the file, and select how you'd like the colors displayed.

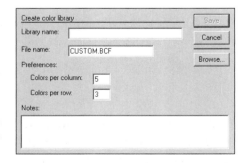

Figure 4.10
The Create Color Library dialog box.

Applying Color

Many options in FreeHand give you several ways to accomplish the same task. Applying colors is no exception. To apply color to an object, you can select the object and click a color name or a color in the Swatches panel, or you can simply drag the color on top of the object (whether it's selected or not). With a selected object, you can also use the fill and stroke icons found at the bottom of the Toolbox (see Figure 4.11). When you click the color box next to either the stroke or the fill, you will see either the color cubes (Figure 4.11) or your color swatches from the Swatches panel. To change color swatches to color cubes or vice versa, click the color box, click the right-pointing arrow (your cursor will still be the dropper, but that's fine), and choose the appropriate option.

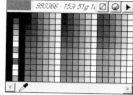

Figure 4.11
The stroke and fill icons with the color cube options open.

Changing Stroke and Fill Colors

In the Stroke panel, shown in Figure 4.12, you can change the color of the stroke by clicking the arrow next to the color box and selecting a color. The only colors available will be those you put in the Swatches panel. You can also select an object and change the stroke via the stroke color box in the Toolbox, or you can use the Color Mixer and drag the color on top of the color box in the Stroke panel. The fill color is changed the same way as a stroke color. Figure 4.13 shows the Fill panel with the Basic fill option selected.

Note: To change the color of just the stroke by dragging a color, you have to drag the color to the Stroke panel and not to the object. If you drag the color to the object, the fill will be changed rather than the stroke.

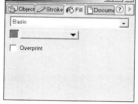

Figure 4.12
(Left) The Stroke panel.

Figure 4.13
(Right) The Fill panel.

Using Gradients

Although gradients are available in the Fill panel, using a gradient isn't the same as simply changing a fill color. With the Gradient fill option, you have not only a choice of colors but also a choice of what type of gradient. Figure 4.14 shows the Gradient dialog box.

The three icons at upper left are (from left to right) Graduated, Radial, and Contour; a sample of each type (default angles) appears in Figure 4.15. To change the type of gradient, simply select the appropriate icon; you can see the changes in realtime in your document.

Figure 4.14
The Gradient dialog box with the Graduated gradient selected.

Gradient Color Changes

To change the color of the gradient, select the color icon and choose the color you want. To add a new color, just drag a color swatch onto the color ramp (the area that has the color boxes below the gradient preview) of the Gradient

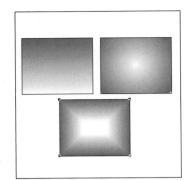

Figure 4.15

Graduated, Radial, and Contour gradient samples.

dialog box. You can drag swatches from the Color Mixer, Tints panel, and fill area in the Toolbox or from the Swatches panel. To duplicate a color, click a color that is currently on the color ramp, press the Alt/Option key, and drag a duplicate copy to the location where you want it to appear.

Graduated Gradient

The Graduated gradient provides two Taper options: Linear (color tapers in equal increments) or Logarithmic (color tapers in increasingly wide bands). You can change the direction of the gradient by entering a number for the angle; or, easier yet, click and drag the circle until the gradient is where you want it.

Figure 4.16

The Radial gradient options.

Radial Gradient

The options for the Radial gradient are a bit different than the Graduated gradient. Because it's radial, it has a center point. You can move the center to any location you'd like. The radial options appear in Figure 4.16.

Contour Gradient

The Contour gradient is a new addition to FreeHand 10. It's great for things like buttons, but it can be difficult to use for complex drawings. You will use it on a car later in this chapter, and it works out pretty nicely. However, the contour is based on the shape of the object, and the contour is split strangely at times.

You can move the center point for Contour gradients the same as for Radial gradients, but you have an additional option: Taper. You can use the slider to adjust the size of the taper, or you can enter a value. The lower the number, the wider the center color will be.

PROJECT Making a Wine Glass

In this project, you will make a wine glass that will be imported into Flash. In Flash (see Chapter 14), you'll finish the glow, make a duplicate, apply rotation, and make the glasses into a symbol. You'll then use the file in a Flash movie called Bar Wars. You will use gradients in this project, along with many of the tools from previous chapters. I will reference the other chapters in case you began reading here and need review of some of the techniques. To make the wine glasses, follow these steps:

1. You drew this glass in Chapter 3. The starter file wineglass.FH9 is in the Chapter 4 resources folder, in case you didn't save the glass drawing or you haven't done it. This file contains the outline shape of the glass as well as a finished glass for your reference, which will make things easier if you need the extra help. Open (File|Open) the wineglass.FH9 file.

2. Open the Color Mixer, select the RGB icon, and enter a red value of 7, a green value of 77, and a blue value of 145. Click the Add To Swatches icon. You can name the color if you want, but I used the default names with the RGB values, leave the Process radio button checked (or select it).

3. Select the glass outline and click the color name (7r 77g 145b) to fill the glass. In the Fill inspector, choose Lens, Transparency, and 50% (the Transparency lens is discussed in Chapter 2). Click OK in reply to the lens warning; it applies to print. Figure 4.17 shows the result so far.

Figure 4.17
The glass shape (left) with a transparency fill.

4. Choose Edit|Clone. Select the Rectangle drawing tool and draw a rectangle that is about two-thirds the height of the glass top and that extends beyond the sides. Figure 4.18 shows the size and placement of the rectangle.

Figure 4.18
A clone and a rectangle added to the glass.

5. In the Color Mixer, select the RGB icon and enter a red value of 153, a green value of 0, and a blue value of 0. Click the Add To Swatches icon. Select the Pointer tool, select the rectangle you added to the glass, and then click the red color you just added to the Swatches panel to fill the rectangle. In the Stroke inspector, change the Stroke to None.

6. To place the red wine into the glass, you will do a Paste Inside (discussed in Chapter 2). With the wine in position as shown in Figure 4.18, choose Edit|Cut. Select the glass with the Pointer tool. In the Fill inspector, choose None (this won't work with the lens applied) and choose Edit|Paste Inside. Figure 4.19 shows the wine in the glass. Notice the cloverleaf in the center; it indicates that the file contains a Paste Inside.

Figure 4.19
The wine placed in the glass.

7. Select Edit|Clone, select Edit|Cut Contents, and delete the red rectangle; you won't need it on the clone (you'll still see the wine from the previous copy). Select the Pointer tool and select the clone copy. To verify you have the correct copy, drag it to the side (if it is the right copy, it will have no fill) and choose Edit|Undo Move. Now you have the correct copy selected. Select the Pen tool and place the mouse pointer over the stem base points; you will see a minus (-) sign. Click to remove. As you pass over the next points, they will have a little inverted V. Click each point, and the minus sign will appear; click again to delete (deleting points is discussed in Chapter 1). Remove all the points until only the glass top remains, as seen in Figure 4.20.

Figure 4.20
The duplicate glass with the stem and base removed.

8. This next part is a bit tricky, but if you follow the instructions carefully, you'll be thrilled with the result. The glass top will still be selected but if for some reason you deselected, select just the glass top. You can check to be sure it's the right selection the same way you did in Step 7. Choose Edit|Cut. In the Layers panel, choose New from the Options pop-up menu. Choose Edit|Paste. Move the pasted outline above the glass so you can work on it. You added this shape to a new layer because it's difficult to select otherwise.

9. Choose Edit|Clone. Select the Pointer tool and drag the top-left point in to about the inside of the white highlight on the sample. Move the upper-right point in to the inside of the blue highlight. See Figure 4.21 for placement; the line is white so you can see it. This step is tough to explain, and you may need to experiment to get it just right.

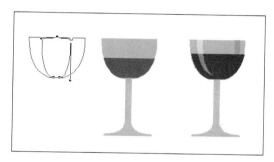

Figure 4.21
The duplicate glass top (with a white stroke for visual purposes only) dragged to a new shape and location.

10. Select the inside cloned shape (the smaller one) and Shift+select the full-sized clone of the glass top just under it. Choose Modify| Combine|Blend. In the Object inspector, change the Steps value to 12. Your blend should look like Figure 4.22. If it doesn't and it's a skewed blend, you may have moved your points above the large shapes top. Just delete the small one, choose Edit|Clone again, and try again. Once it looks like Figure 4.22, drag it on top of the glass.

Figure 4.22
The two glass tops blended with 12 steps.

11. Change the Stroke to None. You will add a Lens fill now, but you can't add it to a group. The blend is a group, so choose Modify|Ungroup.

Note: It's important that you do not deselect your blend until you are told to do so.

12. In the Fill inspector, add a Lens fill, set Lighten to 5%, and press Enter/ Return. Choose Modify|Group. You can now deselect. Your glass looks like Figure 4.23.

Figure 4.23
The glass tops blended with a Lens Lighten fill applied.

Note: When you finish, if your wine is a different color than the sample, the difference is due to the stacking order of the objects. Don't be concerned just yet about that; the order will need to be adjusted in Flash anyway.

13. All that is left to finish the glass is to add the two highlights. Using the Pen tool or the drawing tool of your choice, draw the white highlight shape and then the blue (you can select the highlights from the finished sample and clone or duplicate them, if you'd like). When the white highlight is drawn, use a Stroke of None and a Lens fill, Lighten 70%. For the blue highlight, use a Stroke of None and a Lens fill, Transparency, color 0r 77g 145b, and 20% Opacity. Put each highlight in place. If you don't see the highlight, choose Modify|Arrange|Bring To Front.

Adding a Neon Effect to the Stem of the Glass

Because this project is a pun on *Star Wars*, I wanted the glass stem to glow like a light saber (the weapon used by fighters on both sides of "the force"). If you are new to designing illustrations, you will do well by visiting The FreeHand Source (**www.freehandsource.com**). Once you understand the principles, tips, and techniques found there, you can apply them to other projects. At The FreeHand Source, this technique was used to demonstrate a glow around a sun; I used the idea to produce the neon effect for this glass stem. To make the stem glow, follow these steps:

1. Open the stem.FH9 file from the Chapter 4 resources folder to use as a reference. It shows how the stem will look when finished.

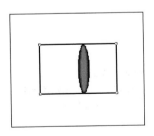

Figure 4.24
A rectangle drawn around the stem sample.

2. Select the Rectangle tool and draw around the stem, as shown in Figure 4.24. Drag the rectangle below the stem to work on it.

3. Select the Oval tool and draw an oval about the size of the sample stem. Move it to the center of the rectangle. It is important that the oval be exactly the same height as the rectangle. Select the stroke icon in the Toolbox and select a yellow color. Double-click the Scale tool to open the Transform panel. Select Uniform, 50%, and 1 Copy, and click the

Scale button. Pull the top points up and the bottom points down to make the smaller ellipse reach almost the top and bottom of the larger ellipse (see Figure 4.25). You want the large ellipse to be slightly larger—but not too much. You'll see why later in the project.

4. The project doesn't make much sense yet. I had you make the drawings so you can see what you are doing. Because the background of the glasses will be black, you need to fill the rectangle with black. In the Stroke inspector, give it a Stroke of None. If you can't see the yellow ellipses, then with the rectangle selected, choose Modify|Arrange|Send Backward. Select the large ellipse; in the Stroke panel, choose None (it was yellow so you could see to select it). In the Fill panel, select a Basic fill of black. This fill will blend in to the rectangle's color.

5. Select the small ellipse. In the Stroke inspector, choose None. In the Fill inspector, choose a bright blue and deselect. Select the Subselection tool, select the small ellipse, Shift+select the large ellipse (you'll have to guess or change the view to keyline—Drawing Mode pop-up menu in the Status toolbar for Windows or in the lower left of the Document window for Macintosh—to make selecting easier), and choose Modify|Combine|Blend. In the Object inspector, change the Steps value to 40 and press Enter/Return. A nice glow should now appear around the blue area. You can delete the black rectangle. You just blended the blue into the black, producing the glow.

6. Choose Edit|Copy and open the wineglass.FH9 file. Choose Edit|Paste. Place the stem on the finished glass, as shown in Figure 4.26.

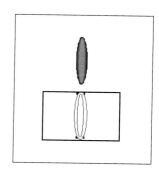

Figure 4.25
The rectangle and large and small ellipses.

Note: If you don't see a slight glow, the center ellipse may be too large. You can choose Edit|Undo until you undo the blend; then make the smaller ellipse a tiny bit smaller and repeat the blend.

Figure 4.26
The glowing stem added to the wineglass.

Adding a Glow

The wineglasses will have a white glow around them so they stand out from the black sky background they will be on. You will finish the glow in Flash. To begin making it, follow these steps:

1. Select the finished wineglass on the blue base only (so you get the whole glass, not the glow), choose Edit|Duplicate, and choose

Figure 4.27
A large stroke added to the
duplicate glass.

Modify|Arrange|Send To Back. Select the fill icon in the Toolbox and choose yellow; do the same for the stroke. (This step is only so you can see what you are doing.) In the Stroke inspector, change the stroke size to 12. Figure 4.27 shows the size of the stroked duplicate.

2. Move the duplicate to the side, away from the glass. Marquee select it and choose Modify|Join. Move the shape back over the wineglass and choose Modify|Arrange|Send To Back. Change the stroke and the fill to white.

Fixing the Angle of the Wine

In Flash, you will duplicate this wineglass, rotate the two glasses, and crisscross them like swords. The wine is at the wrong angle when the glasses are rotated; it needs to slant so it doesn't defy physics. Figure 4.28 shows how the glasses would look if we didn't fix the angle. Figure 4.29 shows the corrected angle, but the drawing isn't quite finished; the glow isn't added to this sample until the Flash section of the book.

Figure 4.28
(Left) The wineglasses
crisscrossed with the wine
at the wrong angle.

Figure 4.29
(Right) The crisscrossed
wineglasses with the
wine angle changed.

To change the angle of the wine, follow these steps:

1. Open the wineglass.FH9 file. Select the blue part of the bottom of the glass and move it to the side (see Figure 4.30). Select near the invisible base of the wine object or use the keyline view (remember, you changed the Fill and Stroke to None on that object). You'll know the correct option is selected when you see the cloverleaf in the center. Choose Edit|Cut Contents and select the red rectangle.

2. Choose Modify|Transform|Activate Handles. Place your cursor in the corner until you see the rotate icon. Rotate to the position shown in Figure 4.31.

3. Choose Edit|Cut, select the invisible glass, and choose Edit|Paste Inside. Move the blue glass back into position and choose Modify|Arrange|Move Backward. The result will look like Figure 4.32.

Figure 4.30
The blue glass object moved to the side.

Figure 4.31
The wine object rotated in position.

Figure 4.32
The rotated wine and glass reassembled.

4. Export the glass as myrotatedwine.FH9. Of course, you can save it as a FreeHand 10 file if Flash 6 is released or if you have upgraded to both FreeHand 10 and Flash 6.

The wineglass is ready for use in Flash.

PROJECT Adding Color to the Electric Car

You drew an electric car shape in Chapter 1 for the Point of Purchase drawing. Jeffrey Roberts did the Point of Purchase and rendered the Z Car in a 3D program, which then is placed on the pedestal to be rotated in Flash. The electric car wasn't rendered, so you won't be able to put it on the pedestal for rotating, but you can color it in FreeHand 10 to practice using the gradient tools. We are going to use the Contour gradient, which is a new feature of FreeHand 10. It's a bit difficult to really see how nice this car looks in black and white; you can also see it in the Color Section. To add color to the electric car outline, follow these steps:

1. Open the electric.FH10 file from the Chapter 4 resources folder. There is also a copy of electric.FH9, but the Contour gradients will be converted into a Paste Inside blend because FreeHand 9 doesn't have a Contour gradient. This starter file contains the completed car and some extra shapes for you to fill in. The entire drawing is in electriccar.FH9, if you want to use it. Figure 4.33 shows the starter file, electric.FH10.

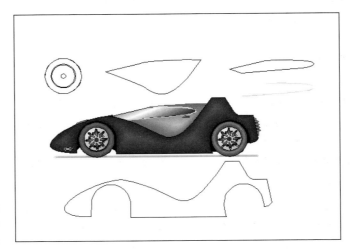

Figure 4.33
The finished, colored electric car and practice outlines.

2. Select the car body. In the Fill inspector, select Gradient for the fill and select the Contour Gradient button. Figure 4.34 shows the color swatch positions and the center point position. Because I've included a finished car, you can also select its body and check the Fill inspector to see what settings were used. The colors used, from left to right, are 0r 27g 99b, 0r

106g 181b, white, and white. For the RGB colors, add the values in the Color Mixer and drag each color to the Swatches panel. To add the color to the gradient, click the first color swatch on the left and then select the dark blue (0r 27g 99b) from the Swatches panel to select it. To add a new swatch to the gradient, click and drag a copy of the light blue (0r 106g 181b) swatch from the Swatches inspector onto the gradient, as seen in Figure 4.34. Repeat for the next white swatch; the last swatch is probably already white.

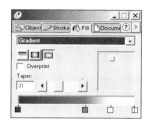

Figure 4.34
The Contour gradient settings used.

3. Set the center point according to the position shown in Figure 4.34. I noticed on my practice copy that the white part of the Contour gradient wasn't as bright as the example, even though I used the same settings. If you need to adjust the placement of the center, move the center point. To adjust the color, click and drag the color swatches until you get the look you want. Figure 4.35 shows the finished body gradient.

Fast Fill

If you are in a hurry and you want to copy a fill, you can select the original body fill and choose Edit|Copy Attributes. Select the body outline and choose Edit|Paste Attributes.

Figure 4.35
The body of the car with the Contour gradient applied.

4. The top of the car uses the same type of gradient and is done the same way, but it only has two colors. Select the original to see the placement of the center point. The blue used is 0r 106g 181b. Remove the stroke when you are done filling the top.

5. The window is a Graduated gradient. Select the original to see the placement of the color swatches. The left swatch is 45r 164g 217b, the second is white, and the last swatch is 0r 40g 95b. The Taper is Linear and the angle is 291 degrees, with a black stroke that has a point size of .25. A highlight is added below the window outline; it's a Graduated gradient, as well.

6. Select the tire. Give it a Contour gradient fill with black for the left color swatch, white for the right, and an additional white to the left of the right swatch (select the original tire to see the placement of the swatches). Change the Taper to 36 and the center point to the top center.

7. The blue tire center, the spokes, and the little circles between the spokes all are filled with a Radial gradient.

Moving On

In this chapter, you learned how to apply color to strokes and use the various gradients including the new Contour gradient.

In Chapter 5, you will use perspective grids and start a project with *Star Wars*-type text effects to be completed in Flash.

Chapter 5

Using the
Perspective Grid

In this chapter, you will learn how the perspective grid works and practice with the unusual techniques required to put objects in perspective. You also will discover how to make your own custom grids suitable for background elements.

Perspective Grids

Perspective in illustrations gives the illusion of 3D in a 2D environment. When objects are placed on the perspective grid, the foreground is larger than the part going toward the vanishing point, making the object appear nearer or farther away depending on its perspective placement.

A FreeHand perspective grid is a non-printing grid with one, two, or three vanishing points; the grid includes horizontal and vertical grid lines. You can customize your own grid and save it. The grids in FreeHand are plotted at a set size, but you can alter the settings.

Showing and Hiding Perspective Grids

To show or hide the perspective grid, you can toggle the view on or off by choosing View|Perspective Grid|Show (the view is off by default). If you turn off the view, just select the Show option to toggle it back on (a checkmark).

Customizing the Grid

You can customize the view by choosing View|Perspective Grid|Define Grid. Select 1, 2, or 3 from the Vanishing Point drop-down menu. Change the Grid Cell Size or the various grid color options. Click OK when you are satisfied. You can see the Define Grids dialog box in Figure 5.1.

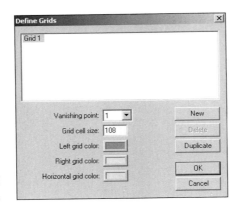

Figure 5.1
The Define Grids dialog box.

To see the grids using the defaults, choose View|Perspective Grid|Show. To define a grid with one vanishing point, choose 1 from the Vanishing Point drop-down menu in the Define Grids dialog box and click OK. One vanishing point has the perspective of a right or left wall and a floor (see Figure 5.2). Choose View|Define Grids again, choose two vanishing points, and click OK. Using two vanishing points displays a floor and left and right walls (see Figure 5.3). Repeat, and this time choose three vanishing points to add the dimension of height (see Figure 5.4).

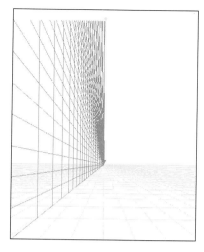

Figure 5.2

A perspective grid with
one vanishing point.

Figure 5.3

A perspective grid with
two vanishing points.

Figure 5.4

A perspective grid with
three vanishing points.

Figure 5.5
The Perspective tool
in the Toolbox.

Note: If you hold the arrow key instead of a tap you will not be able to align to the grid properly.

To practice using the Perspective tool (Figure 5.5), follow these steps:

1. Choose File|New, choose File|Import, and navigate to the Chapter 5 resources folder on the companion CD-ROM. Select the testingperspective.FH9 file and click Open.

2. Choose View|Perspective Grid|Show (the grid is turned off by default on a new document). A perspective grid with one vanishing point is the default, so you don't have to define the grid just yet.

3. Select the Perspective tool from the Toolbox.

4. Using the Perspective tool, select the text you imported.

5. Here is the tricky part, which will take a bit of time to get used to. Press and hold the mouse button on the selected text or object. Tap the left arrow key once and move the text/object into position on the grid. To attach the text to the perspective grid, release the mouse button when the text/object is where you'd like it to be.

For a perspective grid with one vanishing point, you tap the left or right arrow key to attach your text/object to the vertical grid, or the up or down arrow to attach to the horizontal grid. When you have two or three vanishing points, the left arrow attaches to the left vertical grid and the right arrow attaches to the right vertical grid (see Figure 5.6). If you select text or an object and tap the up or down arrow, the object attaches aligned with the right or left vanishing point.

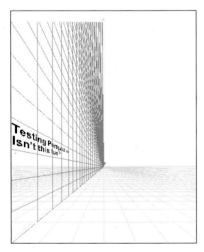

Figure 5.6
The text in perspective on the left wall.

6. Once you have the object/text you can move it on the grid by simply dragging the text (as long as you are using the Perspective tool to move). Try moving it down to the left corner of the left wall; it looks like

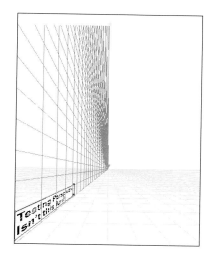

Figure 5.7
The text applied to the
perspective grid near the floor.

your text is standing up on the floor (Figure 5.7). Experiment with different positions; you will notice that the closer to the vanishing point you place the text, the farther away it appears.

7. Before you move on, try customizing the grid. You can use the Perspective tool to click and drag any part of the perspective grid. Select the vanishing point and drag to the right. Note that the text is still in the perspective where you placed it. You must select the text and tap the appropriate arrow key to reposition the text. But if it's an object, you can Shift+select both the object and the portion of the grid you are moving if you want the attached object to change perspective as you alter the grid.

PROJECT Text for the Bar Wars Scene

Ian Kelleigh of The FreeHand Source (**www.FreeHandSource.com**) contributed this project. His site has plenty of tips for using FreeHand, so be sure to check it out. This project concentrates on getting text ready for use in a Flash movie; you'll add other components, such as the title and logo and the scrolling action, in Chapter 15.

One of the most-requested features for Flash is the ability to create and animate 3D objects. Lots of third-party applications will produce these kinds of effects (at an extra cost, of course), but none do it as quickly and easily as FreeHand. If you have FreeHand 9 or later, you can produce some nifty 3D perspective objects and import them into Flash very easily. In fact, you can even animate them.

This tip describes the first steps in how to produce scrolling text like that at the beginning of the movie *Star Wars* and animate the text in Flash. Yes, this is a strange technique to write a tutorial about, but several members of the Flash community asked how to do it. I thought, "What better way to demonstrate how to animate perspective text objects using FreeHand?"

Follow these steps:

1. In a new FreeHand document (File|New), select the Text tool and drag a text box. Enter the following text to animate: "In a small town far away, a young stranger appeared in a local pub with a cue stick. Little did the locals know, this stranger was the best pool player in the galaxy. Meanwhile, the town's law enforcement was planning a big rebellion against the Mayor who was about to close this pub forever." For this particular example, the text should simulate the *Star Wars* opening scroll. Choose a bold, sans-serif font, such as black, 20-point Arial Black. You'll color it later.

2. To make the perspective grid visible, choose View|Perspective Grid|Show. The default grid will work fine for this example, although you may want to experiment with different grids later.

3. Select the Perspective tool and drag the text block onto the grid. While you are holding down the mouse button, press the down arrow key to map the text to the bottom plane, as shown in Figure 5.8. Exact placement on the grid isn't important, but you should keep the text near the bottom of the document and near the center of the grid's middle line.

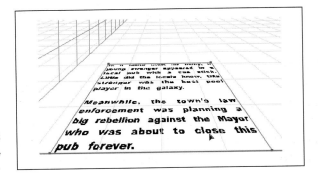

Figure 5.8
The text block attached to the bottom plane.

4. Select the Pen tool and draw two lines from the perspective grid intersection point on the horizon. These lines should extend all the way down the sides of the text box (see Figure 5.9). These lines will act as guides later in the Flash movie.

5. Shift+select the lines and the text box and copy them (Edit|Copy) to the Clipboard. If you wish, you can continue now to the Flash section (Chapter 15) to finish this project. If you'd rather wait, choose File|New and Edit|Paste (Edit|Paste Special in FreeHand 10).

If you decide to go ahead and finish this project and you are using FreeHand 10, then you must use the Copy Special option found under the Edit menu in FreeHand. From here (Figure 5.10), choose FreeHand 9 as the format.

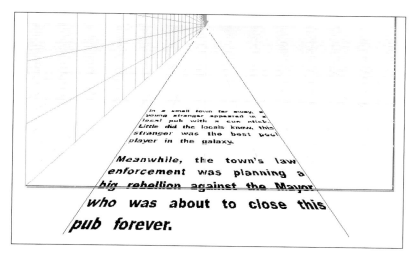

Figure 5.9
The guide lines, drawn with the Pen tool.

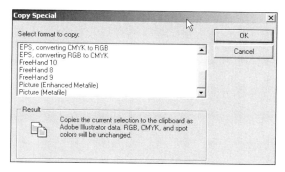

Figure 5.10
The Copy Special dialog box.

PROJECT Drawing Special Grids

Grids are very popular for use in Web page designs and are frequently used for decorative purposes and background elements in collages. The grids I will show you are not perspective grids or FreeHand grids; they are custom grids, made using the Pen tool and the blend function. The credit for these neat grids goes to Ian Kelleigh of The FreeHand source. I have modified the instructions a bit.

Corner Grid

To make a grid like the one shown in Figure 5.11, follow these steps:

1. Open a new document (File|New). Select the Pen tool from the Toolbox and draw a straight horizontal line (hold the Shift key).

2. Select the Pointer tool and click in any blank area to deselect. Select the Pen tool again and draw a straight vertical line just below the horizontal line, as shown in Figure 5.12.

3. Depending on the size of the grid you are making, you may want to change the stroke size. For the example in Figure 5.11, I used 1.5 points and a color of black. The Color Studio shows an example I did using a bright blue and bright green line. Play around with the different settings—they can be quite interesting.

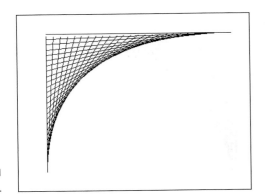

Figure 5.11
A corner grid shape.

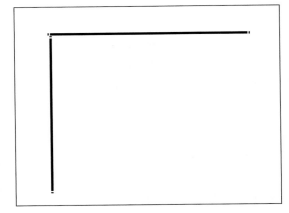

Figure 5.12
A vertical line drawn below the
horizontal line.

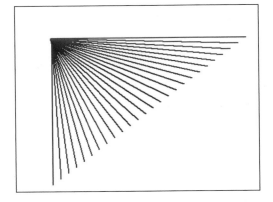

Figure 5.13
The result of undoing and then
repeating the blend.

4. Select either line and choose Modify|Alter Path|Reverse Direction.
   Shift+select both lines and choose Modify|Combine|Blend. If you don't
   reverse the path of one of the lines, the result is shown in Figure 5.13.

5. If you want to change the look of the grid, you can do so by opening
   the Object inspector (Window|Object) and changing the number of
   blend steps to 15. Figure 5.14 shows the grid with fewer steps.

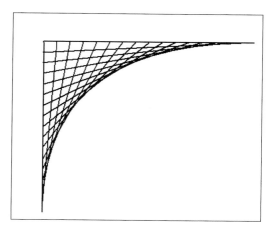

Figure 5.14
The same corner grid with the blend steps reduced to 15.

6. You can edit your blend after it's done. Select the Subselection tool and select one of the lines. You can change the stroke size and/or color. If a slight gap appears in your blend where the two lines meet, use the Subselection tool to move one of the lines.

Sphere Grid

This is a quick way to make a spherical grid, which shows both shape and dimension. Follow these steps:

1. Open a new document (File|New). Choose the Ellipse tool, hold the Shift key to constrain to a perfect circle, and drag a circle in your document. You need a stroke to see the circle, but don't use a fill.

2. Choose Modify|Ungroup (Ctrl+Shift+G/Cmd+Shift+G).

3. Shift+select a point on the right side and a point on the left side (you can choose any two points that are opposite each other). Choose Modify|Split. Figure 5.15 shows how the circle looks so far.

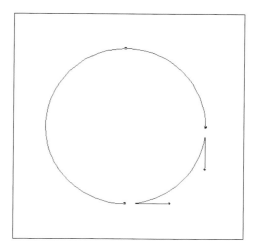

Figure 5.15
The circle after it's split.

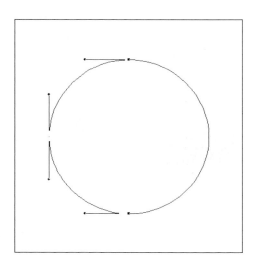

Figure 5.16
The left side point selected.

4. Click anywhere in a blank area of the document to deselect. Using the Pointer tool, drag a selection around one of the points in the split area. (Figure 5.16 shows the left side point selected.)

5. Choose Modify|Combine|Blend and leave the default of 25 steps (the blend options are changed in the Object inspector). Figure 5.17 shows the sphere after the blend.

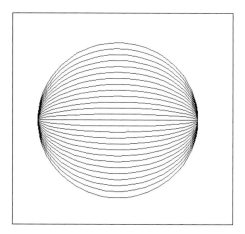

Figure 5.17
The sphere after the blend.

Note: In FreeHand 10, you can skip the clone step (Step 6) and enter "1" in the Copies area of the Transform panel when you are setting the values for rotating (Step 7).

6. Your sphere should still be selected. Choose Edit|Clone.

7. With the sphere still selected, double-click the Rotate tool in the Toolbox. The Transform panel will open. Enter "90" for the rotation and click the Rotate button. Figure 5.18 shows the finished sphere grid. You can edit it by changing the blend steps.

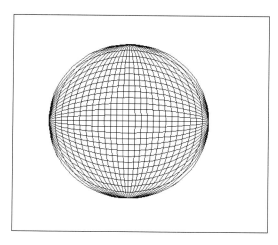

Figure 5.18
The finished sphere grid.

Moving On

In this chapter, you learned how to use and edit the perspective grid. You also learned a couple of tricks for making corner and spherical grids.

In Chapter 6, you will learn how to export FreeHand files for use in Flash. You'll also see what items import well and what don't.

Chapter 6

Importing and Exporting

In this chapter, you will learn how to avoid exporting pitfalls and how to prepare your art for export for use in Flash. You will learn to export FreeHand documents as HTML or PDF documents. We also will look at importing from other applications.

Importing

Because this book focuses on using FreeHand with Fireworks and with Flash, we won't do a lot of comparison of other Application formats in this section of the chapter; the FreeHand manual and online Help cover this topic quite well if you need additional information.

Here are brief descriptions of the FreeHand import functions:

- *Fireworks PNG Files*—Fireworks PNG files open in FreeHand as bitmap images, which means you cannot edit the original objects and the layers are lost.

- *SWF Files*—You can't import SWF (Flash) files into any version of FreeHand. If you'd like FreeHand to include this functionality, send your request to the FreeHand Wish list at **wish-freehand@macromedia.com**.

- *Photoshop PSD Files*—To import Photoshop PSD files, choose File|Import and locate the file. Photoshop files import as bitmaps, which means you lose editability. If the image is masked, the mask is maintained, but you can't edit it. On the other hand, Fireworks will import a PSD file with layers intact, and the mask is editable. If you need editable PSD files, then Fireworks is the better tool for the job.

- *PDF Files*—You can open and edit Adobe Acrobat Portable Document (PDF) files, including multipage documents, in FreeHand.

- *Other File Types*—FreeHand is quite flexible in opening files from other applications. For instance, you can import EPS, TIFF, and Illustrator AI files. GIF and JPEG files import into FreeHand as bitmap images. Illustrator files maintain a lot of editability, depending on comparable features.

Exporting

This section discusses how to export your work from FreeHand primarily for use in Flash. I also explain how to save or export files for use in Fireworks. You will discover the advantages of the tight integration among FreeHand, Flash, and Fireworks. You also will learn which items export properly. In addition, you will embed a Flash movie into an HTML file from within FreeHand.

Because I assume you will be exporting for use on the Internet, you need to change a couple of preferences. Choose File|Output Options. Figure 6.1 shows the Output Options dialog box; deselect the Convert RGB To Process option. Choose Edit|Preferences and select the Export tab. At the bottom of the Preferences dialog box (Figure 6.2) in the Convert Colors To drop-down menu, choose RGB.

Figure 6.1
The Output Options dialog box.

Exporting for Use in Fireworks

Chapter 12 compares the various export options in FreeHand and how they import into Fireworks. You also can open native FreeHand files in Fireworks

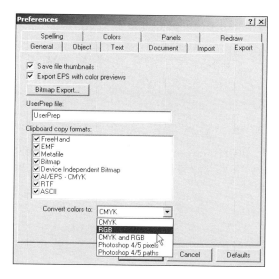

Figure 6.2
The Preferences dialog box.

without exporting; just be aware of version compatibility. For instance, FreeHand 10 files won't open in Fireworks 4 (unless a fix or patch is made available by the time you read this), because FreeHand 10 was released after Fireworks 4.

Exporting in PDF Format

Most things you can do in FreeHand will export to PDF format. However, some things can't be exported, such as:

- Alpha channel transparency

- Overprinting

- Special text effects

- EPS images

- PostScript fills, custom fills, textured fills, strokes, and arrowheads

To export a FreeHand document to PDF format, choose File|Export and choose PDF from the Save As Type drop-down menu. Click the Setup button. Figure 6.3 shows the options available for exporting as a PDF document. Choose the options you want and click OK. In the Export dialog box, browse to where you want to export your file, name the file, and click Save.

Exporting in HTML Format

If you have a mockup that you've done in FreeHand or another document that you'd like to automatically make into an HTML page, it's easy to do. Choose File|Publish As HTML. Figure 6.4 shows the HTML Output dialog box. If you want to accept the default setup, click Save As HTML; otherwise, click the Setup button. Figure 6.5 shows the HTML Setup dialog box. Choose where you'd like your file saved, whether you want the layout to be in layers or in tables, and which format you'd like for the images.

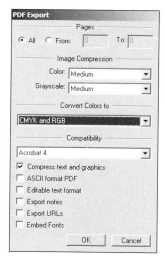

Figure 6.3
The PDF Export dialog box.

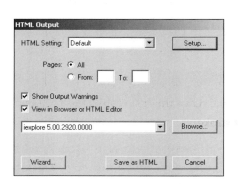

Figure 6.4
(Left) The HTML Output
dialog box.

Figure 6.5
(Right) The HTML Setup
dialog box.

PROJECT Point of Purchase Layout

Jeffrey Roberts (**www.jefargrafx.com**) designed the Point of Purchase Flash movie. The final version has a red 3D car, which will be rotated in Flash. For this example, you will use the Point of Purchase design as a Web page instead of a Flash movie. You will use the blue Z Car that you drew in Chapter 1 and colorized in Chapter 4. To lay out this design as a Web page, follow these steps:

1. Figure 6.6 shows the finished layout; you can refer to it for placement. Open the electric car.FH9 file from the Chapter 6 resources folder. Select the top view and choose Modify|Transform|Activate Handles. Shift+drag the bottom-right point to scale the image down a little. Repeat for the side view.

2. Place the car drawings according to Figure 6.6. Open the bluecar.FH10 file to place in the layout. There is also a copy of bluecar.FH9 in the Chapter 6 resources folder. The Contour gradient is transformed into a Paste Inside blend in the FH9 file.

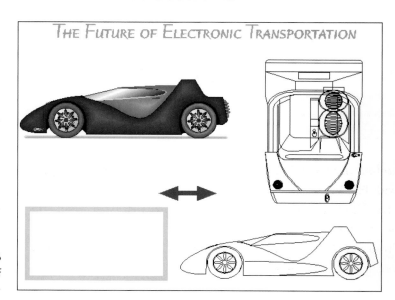

Figure 6.6
The layout of the Point of
Purchase Web page.

3. Select the Text tool and type "The Future of Electronic Transportation" at the top center of the document. In the Text inspector (Ctrl+T/ Cmd+T), choose your font; I used 36-point italic Ruzicka Freehand Roman. Change the fill and stroke to orange.

4. Select the Rectangle tool and draw a rectangle to the left of the side view drawing, as shown in Figure 6.6. Give the rectangle a Basic fill of white and a 6-point Basic yellow stroke.

5. For the arrow, select the Pen tool and draw a very short line. In the Stroke panel, choose the first left-pointing arrowhead from the left drop-down menu and the first right-pointing arrowhead from the right drop-down menu. Adjust the length of the line until it's the size you want. In the Stroke panel, change the color to blue and the Width to 8 points.

6. Choose File|Publish As HTML and click the Setup button. For this export, choose the Layout option Positioning With Tables, select the location to save the file, click OK, and click Save As HTML. Figure 6.7 shows the layout as viewed in Internet Explorer 5.

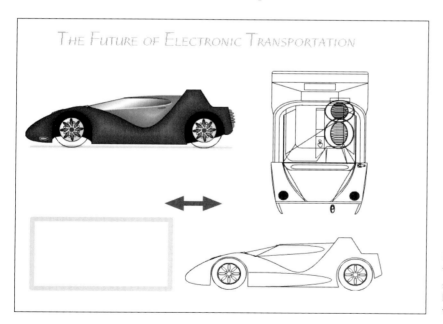

Figure 6.7
The Point of Purchase design as seen in the Internet Explorer 5 browser after being exported from FreeHand as HTML.

7. A warning window will inform you that some effects are not compatible with IE5. Take a close look at Figure 6.7; the tires have lost their gradient. The Contour gradient had no problem exporting, but the tires did. To rectify this problem, marquee-select the car and choose Modify|Group. Choose File|Publish To HTML and click Save As HTML. Figure 6.8 shows the car as it should look.

Naming the HTML File

Save your document prior to publishing as HTML; otherwise it will be called Untitled.

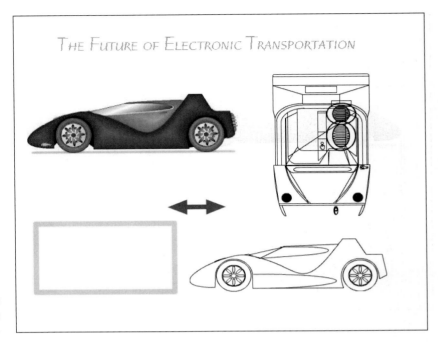

Figure 6.8
The car after rasterizing it
before export.

8. Choose Publish As HTML using the Layers option. You will see the differences in Dreamweaver at the end of this project. Save the file as pointofpurchase2.FH10 (or your version); a file is already saved for you in version 9 and 10 in the Chapter 6 resources folder. Choose File|Publish As HTML, click the Setup button, change the Layout option to Positioning With Layers, click OK, and click Save As HTML. The use of tables versus layers does not change the appearance of the layout in a browser.

Comparing Layers and Tables in Dreamweaver

I published the pointofpurchase file in tables and layers into the Chapter 6 Pop folder and the pointofpurchase2 file into the pop2 folder inside the Pop folder. Figure 6.9 shows the HTML with the table view on, as seen in Dreamweaver UltraDev 4. (A demo version of Dreamweaver 4 is on the companion CD-ROM.) UltraDev just happens to be what I use; the Dreamweaver portion is the same as the demo. Figure 6.10 shows pointofpurchase2 using layers. In Dreamweaver, you can select each layer individually and place it where you'd like.

Note: The Layers option is not compatible with version 3 and earlier browsers.

You need to check one more thing: the file sizes. The pointofpurchase file using tables is nearly double the size of the file using layers.

Exporting for Flash

It's easy enough to do the actual exporting of a FreeHand document for use in Flash; but to save time later, you should be aware of some things prior to exporting. I've compiled a list of what needs to be done to achieve the best compatibility with Flash for different effects in FreeHand. You will see firsthand many of the exporting pros and cons in the project at the end of this section.

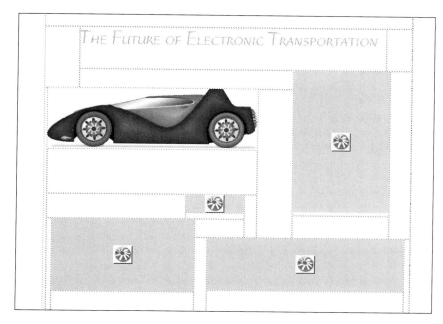

Figure 6.9
The tables that are generated when published as HTML using table positioning.

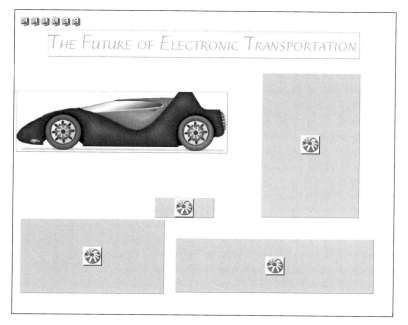

Figure 6.10
The layout as seen in Dreamweaver using the Position Using Layers option.

Assigning Flash Actions

Before we look at exporting a Flash movie, we'll take a quick tour of how to assign actions and view Flash movies in FreeHand. The ability to assign actions in FreeHand is very limited; only six actions are available:

- *Go To*—The movie goes to the frame or scene that the Go To action assigns.

- *Play And Stop*—Tells a movie when to play or when to stop.

- *Print*—Allows a user to print from a specified frame.

Note: The FreeHand manual lists seven actions, including Tell Target, which is from Flash version 4. However, the actions available within FreeHand do not list Tell Target.

- *Full Screen*—Displays the Flash movie in the whole screen of the user.

- *Start/Stop Drag*—Allows you to drag specified movie clips.

- *Load/Unload Movie*—Specifies when a movie should be loaded or unloaded when there are more than two pages.

You can see more in-depth discussion of all these actions in the Flash section of this book, with the exception of Tell Target, which we will not use. But if you'd like to make a simple movie and add actions in FreeHand, you can do so by following these steps:

1. Select the object you want to assign an action to.

2. Choose Window|Panels|Navigation (see Figure 6.11).

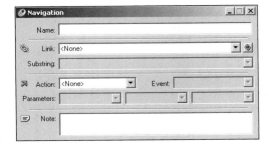

Figure 6.11
The Navigation panel.

3. From the Action drop-down menu, choose the action you'd like.

4. From the Event drop-down menu, choose the event that will trigger the action.

5. Select the Parameters for the action. You can add a link as well, if you'd like.

6. You can add additional actions by repeating Steps 3 through 5.

7. To test your movie, choose Control|Test Movie or choose Window|Toolbars| Controller. The Controller toolbar, shown in Figure 6.12, lets you easily export, change the export settings, and use the VCR-like play controls.

Figure 6.12
The Controller toolbar.

Flash Export Tips

This section gives a brief summary of what you can do to get better results with your FreeHand files in Flash, as well as what does and doesn't export for use in a Flash movie.

Type

Limit the number of embedded typefaces used. Instead of embedding your text, you can convert the fonts to outlines (they won't be editable, though). To convert text to paths, select the text and choose Text|Convert To Paths.

If the text is editable in FreeHand, it will be editable in Flash. There is one exception: If you use a custom horizontal scale on the text in FreeHand, it won't be editable in Flash. Type effects are also not compatible in Flash.

Color

Flash is a Web-only tool; therefore, it only understands and uses RGB color. At the beginning of this chapter, you changed your preferences to convert all colors to RGB.

Gradients

Up to eight gradient colors display properly in Flash. You can use more than eight, but the additional colors will be broken into separate shapes, which will add to your file size.

EPS Graphics

Embedded EPS graphics will not import into Flash.

Lens Fill

All the Lens fill options (with the exception of the monochrome fills) will export into Flash. If you convert a Transparency Lens fill into a symbol, you will loose the transparency. The Transparency Lens fill in Flash is called an Alpha channel.

Fills

The PostScript fills—custom, texture, and pattern—are intended for print only and will not export into Flash.

Placement

You will save yourself a lot of time and headaches if you design in FreeHand for the final result in Flash. In other words, use the same size bounding box you want in Flash and draw and/or place your elements in the position you'd like them to be in a Flash movie. It's more difficult to position elements in Flash. You should be aware that Flash import aligns to the top left of original placement.

Layout

In the Document inspector (Window|Inspectors|Document), click the Landscape icon to change your layout; most Flash movies are wider than they are tall.

Symbols

Symbols import into Flash and appear in the Flash Library panel.

Guides

FreeHand guides import into Flash as Flash guides.

Clipping Paths

When you use the Paste Inside function in FreeHand (Chapter 2), the object becomes a clipping path when exported to Flash. The clipping path is a graphic symbol in Flash that contains the clipping object on a mask layer and the clipped artwork on a nested layer. If the clipping path has a stroke, it will have its own Flash layer. This approach is a great way to use a mask in Flash—it works better than the way Flash handles masks.

Layers

FreeHand layers import into Flash. If you locked layers in FreeHand, they remain locked in Flash. If you choose Keyline view in FreeHand, the Keyline view imports into Flash.

Dashed Strokes

Dashed strokes do import; but if you use kerning, leading, and/or tracking, you'll need to convert to paths first.

SWF

You can only export as SWF format in FreeHand version 8.01 or later.

Image Formats

Use only image formats supported by Flash: JPEG, PICT, BMP, GIF, and PNG.

Exporting to SWF

To export a single page or multipage document as layers, pages, or both, choose File|Export and choose Macromedia Flash (SWF) from the Save As Type dropdown menu. (If you prefer to use the Controller toolbar, click the middle icon to export as SWF.) Click the Setup button. Figure 6.13 shows the Movie Settings dialog box. As you can see, it contains quite a few options. You can choose the image and path compression and the type of animation, if any. Once you have made your selections, click OK. Any actions you have assigned will export and work in Flash.

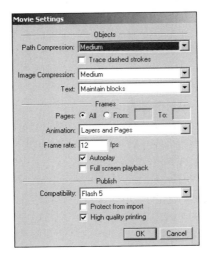

Figure 6.13
The Movie Settings dialog box.

Exporting to Flash

PROJECT

This project is contributed by Ian Kelleigh of The FreeHand Source (**www.freehandsource.com**). I have put it in the book's format and added notes occasionally, but the sample image, discussion, and instructions are Ian's.

For a long time, Flash users have wanted the ability to produce 3D or perspective effects easily inside Flash. Until that functionality is built in, users will have to rely on third-party applications. Fortunately for them, there's FreeHand. Macromedia has worked hard to make it easy for Flash users to bring in FreeHand art while keeping their artwork's colors, formatting, layers, and special effects intact. As a result, they can use FreeHand to make neat effects such as perspective objects and custom envelopes—things they normally couldn't do in Flash.

On the flip side, FreeHand users had to wait until Flash 5 was released to gain the ability to bring their art into Flash without having to bend over backward to keep layers, colors, and other effects intact.

File Conversion Tips and Troubleshooting

When Macromedia first announced that Flash 5 could now open native FreeHand 7 through 9 files, I thought, "Finally, now we FreeHand users won't need to go through all those workarounds to get our beloved art into Flash." Although Flash 5 can open native FreeHand files, you should be aware of several things regarding how Flash converts those files. In the following sections, I detail several steps that will help you get through those conversions without too many problems.

Keep in mind that Macromedia released FreeHand 10 after Flash 5, so Flash 5 doesn't understand the FreeHand 10 format. If you are working in FreeHand 10, you'll have to export your art to FH7 through 9 formats until Macromedia releases either an update to Flash 5 or a completely new upgrade to Flash 6.

I'm going to show you first how easy it is to import your FreeHand art into Flash 5 and keep everything intact.

Flash 5 Conversions

Flash 5 can now open native FreeHand files from versions 7 through 9 with near perfection. This ability means no more exporting as SWF or Adobe Illustrator files to retain layers and object information. Figure 6.14 shows the sample image for this project. I've tried to include all kinds of different objects—including layers, symbols, Lens fills, Paste Insides, and dashed strokes—to show how they convert into Flash 5. The colors are all CMYK mixtures. To begin, follow these steps:

> **Note:** If you changed your preferences and output options to convert to RGB at the beginning of this chapter, your results will vary from Ian's. To duplicate the export, change your preferences and output options back to CMYK.

1. Open the Logo Sample.FH9 file from the Chapter 6 resources folder on this book's companion CD-ROM.

Figure 6.14
The sample logo used in
this project.

2. Open Flash 5 and choose File|New (or click the New icon). Choose File|
   Import and select the Logo Sample.FH9 file in the Chapter 6 resources
   folder. Flash 5 will open the FreeHand Import dialog box (Figure 6.15).
   As you can see, you have a great deal of control over how the art is imported. Most of these options are self-explanatory, and I won't go over
   them in detail. One thing I like is that you can choose to keep layers
   intact, turn them into keyframes, or flatten the whole image. You can
   also choose to turn pages into scenes—a very handy option for producing larger Flash sites, which you may have worked on in FreeHand.

Figure 6.15
The FreeHand Import dialog box
as seen in Flash.

3. Click OK when you are done selecting your import options. Figure 6.16
   shows the result of the import in Flash (if you have the View|Guides
   option checked to Show). Those colors don't look too great, but they are
   easy to fix, as I'll explain later. As you can see, everything came in
   perfectly. The Lens fills show up fine, and even the Paste Insides at the
   top of the logo are intact. It's extremely nice that the dashed stroke
   came in as a dashed stroke and not as a solid line. I will cover what
   happened with each object later, as well as how some of these objects
   were converted.

Note: You can see Figure 6.16
and the logo with correct
colors in the Color Studio.

Figure 6.16
The logo with CMYK color, as it appears imported into Flash 5.

Page Placement and Guides

Flash will import your art aligned with the top-left corner of its original placement. If you have a special page size, then get the X, Y coordinates from the Document inspector in FreeHand (see Figure 6.17) and write them down. Also note what measurement system you are using (see Figure 6.18).

Note: The measurement system is Points by default (see Figure 6.18). You can change the units of measure by selecting another option from the Units pop-up menu located in the Status bar. Pixels are used in this example.

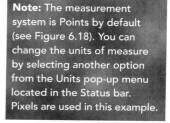

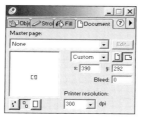

Figure 6.17
The Document inspector in FreeHand.

Figure 6.18
The Status bar.

Guides will also be imported exactly the way you have them placed from the top-left corner; this fact is good to remember when you're creating art and plan to bring it into Flash later. To check page placement and guides in Flash, follow these steps:

1. In Flash, open a new document and choose Modify|Movie. The Movie Properties dialog box will open, as shown in Figure 6.19. Enter the page size you wrote down in FreeHand from the Document inspector and select the Ruler Units value that you used in the FreeHand document.

Note: You need to have Guides turned on in FreeHand and in Flash to view them when imported into Flash.

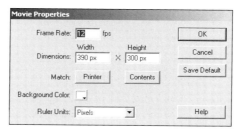

Figure 6.19
The Movie Properties dialog box with the pixel settings added.

2. Choose File|Import and import the Logo Sample.FH9 file. Once it imports, you can see that the guides are in the same location and the Guides layer was imported as a true Flash Guides layer. The Guides layer that appears in Flash (Figure 6.20) can safely be removed, because Flash has its own built-in Guides layer that isn't really visible in the Layers panel. Very nice!

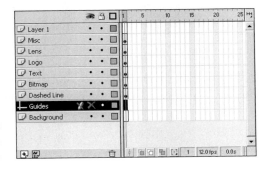

Figure 6.20
The Guides layer in Flash, which you can delete.

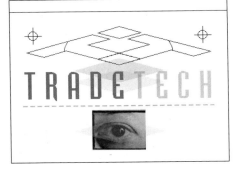

Figure 6.21
The Layers inspector showing the Logo layer in Keyline view and the Logo and Text layers locked.

In this exercise, you will see that the art is sitting on various layers. You will lock the Logo and Text layers, as you can see in the Layers panel in Figure 6.21. The Logo layer also will be set to be in Keyline view. To test locked layers and Keyline view, follow these steps:

1. Open the Logo Sample .FH9 file in FreeHand. Click the circle to the left of the Logo layer name to select Keyline view. (The solid circle will turn into a circle outline with a dot indicating Keyline view.) Click the open lock next to the Logo and Text layers to lock them.

2. Save or export the logo in FreeHand as Logo Sample2.FH9. A copy of Logo Sample2.FH9 is also provided on the companion CD-ROM.

3. Open a new Flash movie and choose File|Import. Select the Logo Sample2.FH9 file you just saved and accept the import defaults. Flash 5 is so smart about the layer import, it keeps layers locked as well as in Keyline view, as seen in Figure 6.22. Note that Flash keeps its default layer, Layer 1. You can safely remove it if you don't want it.

Note: When you have a numbered file such as Logo Sample2.FH9, you will get a dialog box in Flash that says, "This file appears to be part of a sequence of images. Do you want to import all of the images in the sequence?" Click No. Flash thinks that because there is a number you may have a series of files for an animation you want to open.

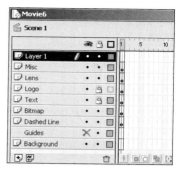

Figure 6.22
The layers portion of the Timeline in Flash showing that the layers are locked and in Keyline view.

Color Conversion

Remember that yucky color conversion? It's very easy to fix in FreeHand before you import. The colors I used are CMYK mixtures, as shown in the Swatches panel in Figure 6.23. Flash isn't very smart about converting CMYK colors, so you have to give it something it does understand: RGB colors. To fix the colors, follow these steps:

1. You can convert your colors to RGB from within the Swatches panel. In FreeHand 9 or 10, Shift+select all your colors and quickly convert them in one step by choosing Make RGB from the Options pop-up menu (right-pointing arrow). Figure 6.24 shows the Swatches panel after you change the colors to RGB. Don't be alarmed by any color shifting you see in FreeHand—the colors will look just as you intend in Flash.

Figure 6.23
(Left) The CMYK colors as seen in the Swatches panel.

Figure 6.24
(Right) The Swatches panel showing the colors converted to RGB.

2. Save or export as Logo Sample3.FH9. Once you've done that, choose Edit|Undo to get back your CMYK colors.

3. In Flash, open a new document, choose File|Import, and select Logo Sample3.FH9. Once imported into Flash 5, the colors look exactly how you want them to. Compare them with the FreeHand drawing.

Note: Because this is a logo, you'll probably want to print it, as well. So, it's a good idea to have a copy saved using CMYK and one saved using RGB.

I don't think the color conversion problem can be considered a bug, because Flash works in an RGB-only color space. Just remember this quick workaround before you bring FreeHand art into Flash 5.

> **Note:** Figure 6.26 shows the gradient that was pasted inside each part of the logo shape. I moved the gradients below the shapes they're pasted into so you can see them.

Clipping Paths

Now it's time to look at some of those objects one at a time to see how they were converted. Figure 6.25 shows the Paste Inside or clipping paths. They are just simple gradient fills clipped (Edit|Paste Inside; see Figure 6.26) in the polygon shapes.

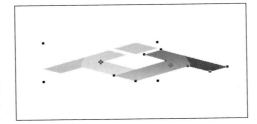

Figure 6.25
The gradient fills pasted inside the logo shapes.

Figure 6.26
The gradients that were pasted inside the logo shapes.

Figure 6.27
The Paste Inside as a clipping path and two symbols in Flash.

To see how the clipping paths appear in Flash, follow these steps:

1. In Flash, open a new document, choose Edit|Import, and import any one of the Logo Sample files.

2. Choose Window|Library in Flash. In Flash 5, these clipping paths are added to the Library panel as symbols, as shown in Figure 6.27. They are automatically put into a FreeHand object group, in a subgroup called Clip Paths. This is just Flash's way of keeping everything organized for you.

3. When you edit one of these symbols (double-click the icon next to the symbol in the Library), you'll notice that Flash converted this clipping path using its own method, which is to use masks to accomplish the same result as the clipping path (see Figure 6.28). The clipping path has actually turned into a Masking object, and the gradient sits on the layer underneath the mask. How smart is that?

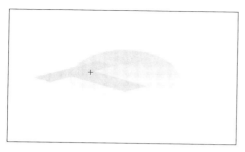

Figure 6.28
The edit mode of one of the clipping path symbols and Layer 2, indicating a mask.

Dashed Lines

The dashed stroke that I used is a basic 2-point stroke with a predefined dash, as shown at left in Figure 6.29. It has a squared cap, which is very important, as I'll explain in a bit.

Figure 6.29
The dashed stroke as seen in FreeHand.

To see how it imports into Flash, follow these steps:

1. Open a new document, choose Edit|Import, and choose the Logo Sample.FH9 file.

2. In Flash, the stroke comes in as a native dashed stroke, as shown at right in Figure 6.29, keeping the spacing and width. Remember, this was a basic dashed stroke, and Flash still has problems with certain dashed strokes from FreeHand.

3. Zoom in close to the line. You'll notice that the dashes are now rounded, as shown in Figure 6.30. Be aware of this issue when trying to import really fat strokes with dashes—they won't look very good. Also, be careful with strokes that have custom spacing, like the examples shown in Figure 6.31. Flash 5 only allows a custom spacing with two options. Any strokes like those in Figure 6.31 will be imported as solid in Flash. If you need squared or custom dashes, then the best thing you can do is to export the line as an SWF file and turn on the Trace Dashed Strokes option.

Figure 6.30
(Left) A closeup of the dashed line in the sample logo.

Figure 6.31
(Right) Custom strokes in FreeHand.

Symbols

FreeHand 9 introduced the ability to make symbols and place multiple instances of them in your art, as shown in Figure 6.32. FreeHand 10 now has a Library panel much like the Flash version. Before Flash 5, FreeHand symbols didn't import as native Flash symbols.

I'm happy to say that Flash 5 now keeps FreeHand symbols intact when you import them, adding them to the Library panel as shown in Figure 6.33.

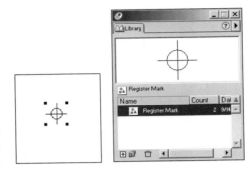

Figure 6.32

The register mark in FreeHand and in the Library panel.

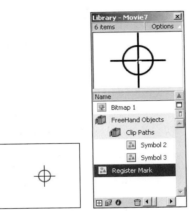

Figure 6.33

The register mark in Flash and in the Library panel.

Text Conversion

Any editable text from FreeHand also will be completely editable in Flash 5. Point sizes, leading, and kerning all come over fine. Be aware that Flash 5's letter kerning (or spacing) is defined quite a bit differently than FreeHand's.

Here's another thing to watch out for. If you have any text with a custom horizontal scale, you should be careful. Flash 5 doesn't recognize this kind of formatting and will import it like regular text. However, when you import the art, deselect the Maintain Text Blocks option in the FreeHand Import dialog box. The text will come in fine as an object, although the text will not be editable.

Also remember that text effects applied in FreeHand will not convert to Flash; be careful with them.

Other Fills and Effects

Lens fills are always a fun addition to art in FreeHand. Upon inspection of Figure 6.34, you can see that the top fill is a Transparency Lens with 20% Opacity applied. When imported into Flash, Lens fills retain their transparency. In Flash, this transparency is called Alpha, as shown in Figure 6.35.

Tile fills would not import correctly into previous versions of Flash. In Figure 6.36, I've made a simple Tiled fill containing star shapes.

> **Note:** To fill with a tile, first draw what you'd like to tile, and then choose Edit|Copy. Select the object you want to fill. In the Fill inspector, choose Tiled and click Paste In.

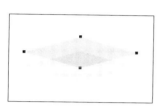

Figure 6.34
Transparency as seen in FreeHand.

Figure 6.35
Transparency as seen in the Color Mixer in Flash.

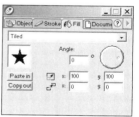

Figure 6.36
A circle filled with a star tile.

Imported into Flash 5 (tiledball.FH9), the fill takes on the form of a series of symbols in the Flash library. If you were to further edit it, you'd notice that in fact it's a mask/symbol combination that mimics the Tiled fill, as shown in Figure 6.37.

Not all fills will import into Flash. Pattern fills, PostScript fills, texture fills, and custom fills will not be converted; be aware of them when producing art for Flash.

Curve Path Problem

With all these great conversion features, a few odd things can always happen to your art. This one is especially important.

Figure 6.37
The tiled object in Flash and the Library.

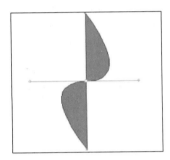

Figure 6.38
A path drawn in FreeHand.

Figure 6.38 shows a simple path drawn in FreeHand. It has quite an extreme curve point in the middle, as shown with the control handles extended.

The curve in Figure 6.39 is the same path after being copied and pasted into Flash 5. It may be hard to distinguish the problem just by glancing at it.

Figure 6.39
The FreeHand path as seen when copied and pasted into Flash 5.

In Figure 6.40, I placed the FreeHand shape under the Flash version (shown as a red outline in the Color Studio). This is a significant bug, and no real explanation has been offered as to why it happens. It only seems to occur with extreme curves, and it has to do with how Flash draws them with its own Bezier controls. Watch carefully when your art imports to see how curves are affected.

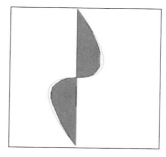

Figure 6.40
The FreeHand curve placed
under the Flash curve.

With FreeHand's Flash Anti-Alias view mode, you could see how certain objects would look when converting to Flash. I'm happy to say that it's now out of date with the release of Flash 5, as I've shown you. I hope many of the other little wrinkles will be ironed out in future updates to help make these types of conversions even easier and more trouble free.

You may be pleasantly surprised by how quickly and accurately Flash 5 imports even the most complex art you can throw at it. With all you've learned in this chapter, this process will give you fewer headaches.

Moving On

In this chapter, you have experimented with many different FreeHand features that import beautifully into Flash as well as a few that don't. You also saw the difference between exporting to HTML using layers or tables.

You will now move on to Section II, Fireworks, where you will learn the ins and outs of slicing, optimizing, and working with bitmap images.

Part II

Fireworks

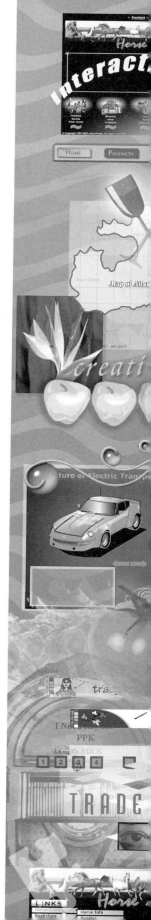

Chapter 7

Fireworks Essentials

This chapter is the first one in the Fireworks section. In this chapter you will work with the most essential, commonly used tools in Fireworks. You will perform some stunning text effects that are often used for logos and titles, as well as produce a realistic sphere using the gradient and transform tools.

Fireworks Introduction

In this next section of the book (Chapters 7–12), the focus is on Fireworks' strengths in the context of Web development workflow. Although you will learn techniques that may be performed in FreeHand as well as in Fireworks, you will see where Fireworks' strengths lie. When you have bitmap work to perform, such as slicing and optimizing, Fireworks is the application to use. Text effects with bitmap fills are also best designed in Fireworks. In the following pages, you will see how FreeHand and Flash cooperate well with Fireworks. At the end of the section, you will see a summary of what you accomplished in this section and what needs to be done or has been done in FreeHand and Flash.

Transforming Text

To *transform* means to convert or change your object into something different. Fireworks 4 makes transforming text a snap. In this chapter, you'll learn how to add strokes, fills, and effects, but you won't use any ordinary preset effects. You'll be amazed at how much flexibility you have in altering or transforming text. And, as long as you don't convert your text into an image or a bitmap, it remains fully editable—even after you twist it, turn it, and make it do all sorts of transforming contortions.

The text-transformation process is quite intuitive. First, you need to decide which type of font to use in your project. This decision isn't as easy as it sounds—have you noticed lately how many fonts you can choose from? Just go to any search engine and look for fonts, and you'll find thousands. The use of the appropriate font is as important as the effects you apply. As you work on the examples and projects in this chapter, you may not have the font I use installed on your computer. In that case, a dialog box will open giving you two options: You can change the font or select No Changes. The particular font does not affect the projects; it's a matter of choice and available fonts.

I'm assuming that you have used the Text Editor before and are familiar with its basic functions. You'll be pleased to discover that in Fireworks 4 you can move text in your document with the Text Editor open. What a timesaver! You can resize text and make any font corrections in real time as you see the text onscreen.

Putting Text on a Path

Making your text do acrobatic feats around a path doesn't require any special training. Text doesn't have to conform to rectangular blocks, but it can be attached to any path that you draw and still remain editable. Keep in mind that while text is attached to a path, the path will lose its stroke, fill, and any attributes attached to it; but, if you detach the text from the path, all the path's attributes return (of course, the text will no longer follow the path). To attach text to a path, follow these steps:

1. Open a new document (File|New) 300 pixels wide by 200 pixels high, with a canvas color of white. Leave the resolution at the default setting of 72 dpi.

2. Select the Pen tool or the Brush tool from the toolbar. Draw a curvy path that is open; don't close it by connecting the first and last points.

3. Select the Text tool from the Tools panel. Click the canvas, and the Text Editor will open. Choose your font: This example uses 22-point Arial Black and a color of dark blue. Leave everything else at the default settings. Type your text (for this example "Text on a Curve") and click OK when you are done. Figure 7.1 shows the Text Editor and the completed text on the path.

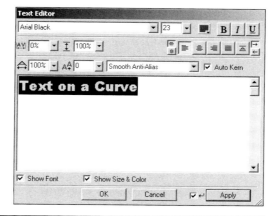

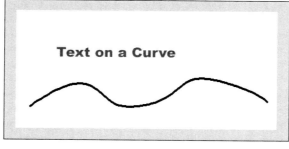

Figure 7.1
The curvy path and the added text.

4. To make the text wrap around the curve, select the text and Shift+click to select the path as well.

5. From the menu bar, select Text|Attach To Path (Ctrl+Shift+Y). Figure 7.2 shows the result.

6. To edit the text, double-click it to open the Text Editor. Trying the different options for alignment and orientation is the best way to see the resulting effects. Change the alignment—for instance, center the text on the path by clicking on the Center Alignment button on the left side of the Text Editor dialog box. Click OK when you are done. Figure 7.3 shows the text aligned to the center and the text color changed to black.

Figure 7.2
Text wrapping along a curve.

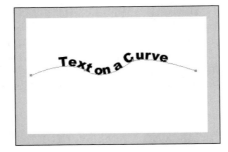

Figure 7.3
Text color edited and text centered on the path.

7. To familiarize yourself with some of the other orientation options, choose Text|Orientation and try each alternative. For example, the text we are using looks interesting if you choose Text|Orientation|Skew Vertical, as seen in Figure 7.4. If your text wraps upside down, choose Text|Reverse Direction.

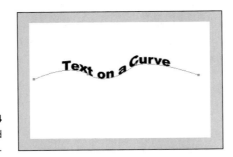

Figure 7.4
Skew Vertical orientation applied to the text/path object.

You may wonder what happens if the text is too long for the path. Some programs bunch the text at the end on top of itself, but Fireworks 4 is much more intuitive. Text that won't fit on the length of the drawn path will wrap itself around the underside of the path, following the same curve.

The results and settings for the text alignment will vary depending on the shape around which you are wrapping the text. The best way to get the right look is to experiment with the alignment, offset, horizontal scale, baseline shift, leading, and kerning. Experiment away—after all, the changes won't take effect until you click OK in the Text Editor. Even if you click OK and accept the changes, you can always go to the menu bar and choose Edit|Undo (Ctrl+Z) if you change your mind.

Change the Flow of the Text

Text begins to wrap at the first point you drew. If this placement isn't to your liking, you can alter the position of the text on the path in numerous ways:

- From the Text Editor, choose the alignment you want, such as Center, Right, Left, Justified, Stretched, Horizontal, or Vertical.
- From the menu bar, choose Text|Orientation. Then, select one of the options: Rotate Around Path, Vertical, Skew Vertical, or Skew Horizontal.
- For the most control, use the Offset option in the Objects panel. Here you can use both negative and positive values to position the text. This option requires trial and error. You can press the Enter key after each change and see the result, which makes it easy to try different settings.
- Choose Modify|Transform|Numeric Transform from the menu bar. The choices in this dialog box are Scale, Resize, and Rotate. You choose the percentage of change you want to occur; and, if you want only the height or width to change, be sure to deselect Constrain Proportions.

Editing Text on a Path

If you want to change the text on a path, or to change the path that the text wraps around, then follow these steps:

1. Select the text and the path object. From the menu bar, choose Text|Detach From Path.

2. Double-click the text to open the Text Editor. Make the necessary alterations and click OK.

3. Click the Subselection tool and then click the text and/or path you want to alter. The Subselection tool lets you click and drag the individual points to alter the path. The path for the text or the curve can be either horizontal or vertical; this option can produce some interesting effects.

4. When you are done, Shift+click the text and the path and choose Text|Attach To Path (Ctrl+Shift+Y).

It's easy to experiment with the look and feel of text on a path when you can make changes this quickly. Try adding a couple of different curves to your design in both horizontal and vertical positions and place text on them. The best way to learn is to experiment, experiment, and experiment. Be sure to save any material you want to keep (File|Save As).

PROJECT Placing Text on the Top and Bottom of an Ellipse for a Web Page

As you have just seen demonstrated, placing text on a path is quite simple. But have you considered putting text on the top and bottom of an ellipse? In this project, you'll add text to the top and bottom independently. To do this, you must cut the path in half to form two arcs and then reverse the direction of the bottom type. You will add the title of a poem and the author's name to a

Viewing Settings

If you want to view the settings for any text or object, open the PNG file from the chapter folder and double-click the text. The Text Editor opens with the settings intact. To see which effects have been added, simply select the text and click the Effect panel, Fill panel, and/or Stroke panel. To see the specifics of the effects added, double-click the effect name, and the current settings will be listed.

Web page. In Chapter 2, you add the envelope to the poem using FreeHand; and you make the ornament in Fireworks in Chapter 8. You'll make the little spheres later in this chapter. The completed file is in the Chapter 7 resources folder and is called lifesdream.png. To add text to the top and bottom of an ellipse, follow these steps:

1. Open the lifesdream.png file from the Chapter 7 resources folder.

2. To help draw the ellipse to fit around the image, go to the menu bar and choose View|Rulers. Select Rulers if it isn't already selected.

3. To add guides that will help you draw the path for the ellipse, click and drag from the vertical ruler (you will see a green line as you drag) and place the line near the right edge of the text image. Repeat for the other side.

4. Click and drag a horizontal guide line down from the horizontal ruler and place it on top of the text image; leave a little space so the title you'll add won't touch the text image. Repeat this step for the bottom of the text image. Figure 7.5 shows the guides.

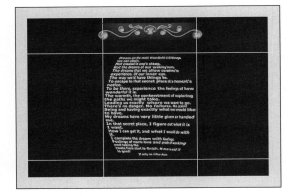

Figure 7.5
Guides in place for drawing the ellipse.

5. Select the Ellipse tool, place the cursor in the top-left corner of the guide intersection, and drag an ellipse to the bottom-right corner. If a fill appears, change it to None in the Fill panel. Add a white stroke in the Stroke panel so you can see the ellipse.

6. Too much text shows outside the border of the ellipse; you need to alter the size of the ellipse some. Select the Subselection tool and click and drag the two side (center) points (see Figure 7.6). Drag out the points to surround the text. It's OK if some of the text around the edges isn't surrounded, because the path will be moved lower later in this project.

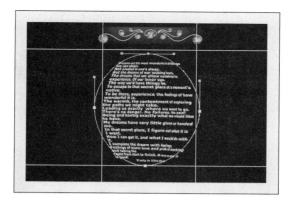

Figure 7.6
The ellipse with the sides pulled out to surround most of the text.

7. Drag a guide from the horizontal ruler to the center of the ellipse (near the center points you just pulled out).

8. Select the ellipse path with the Selection tool. From the toolbar, select the Knife tool. Because this exercise uses guides, you can easily make this slice. Go to View|Guides|Snap To Guides and be sure Snap To Guides is selected. Click and drag the Knife tool along the center guide you placed to cut the ellipse in half.

9. Select the Type tool and click the canvas. In the Text Editor, type the text for the top of the ellipse: "If Only in Lifes Dream". This project uses bold, 36-point Ruzicka Freehand RomanSC with a Smooth Anti-Alias edge and a color of Hex #D89495 (see Figure 7.7).

> **Note:** If you are not using guides with Snap To Guides turned on, you can make a straight cut by holding the Shift key as you slice horizontally.

> **Moving Cut Paths**
>
> If you want to move the path you just sliced, click in your document to deselect the path. Now, select the path you'd like to move, and click and drag it wherever you'd like. Notice that you now have two open paths instead of one closed path.

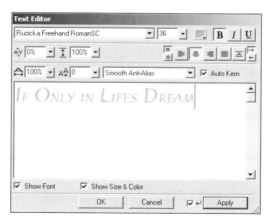

Figure 7.7
The Text Editor dialog box with the text settings for the title.

10. This text doesn't use any effects; but if you wanted to add them, now would be the time. When you are ready to attach your text to the ellipse path, select the text and Shift+select the ellipse. Figure 7.8 shows the text and only the top half of the ellipse selected.

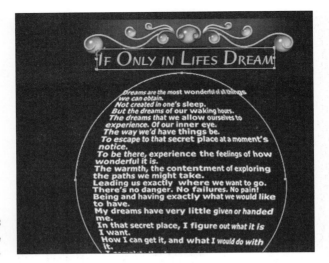

Figure 7.8
The title text and top half of the ellipse selected.

11. Choose Text|Attach To Path (Ctrl+Shift+Y).

12. If your text isn't centered on the ellipse, choose Text|Center Horizontally. Click the title and move it above the poem text.

13. Repeat Steps 8 through 11 using the words "by Arvita Mott". You'll notice that the text is upside down. Choose Text|Reverse Direction to place the text on the inside of the ellipse.

14. You can leave the text where it is and just move the path below the poem, or you can move the text to the outside of the ellipse by adjusting the Baseline Shift value in the Text Editor. Double-click the text "by Arvita Mott", and the Text Editor will open. Use the slider near the Baseline Shift area until the text is where you want it; this example uses a value of -25 (see Figure 7.9). Figure 7.10 shows the finished project.

Note: When you use your Text Editor again, the Baseline Shift will still be at the new value; be sure to change it.

Figure 7.9
Baseline Shift adjusted to move the bottom text (the arrow is pointing to the new value).

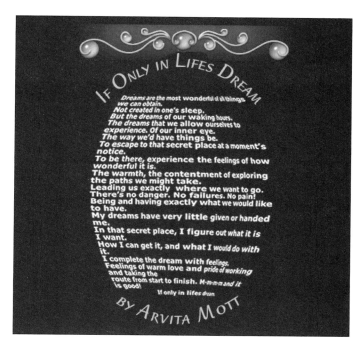

Figure 7.10
The finished title and author name on a path.

Editing Text with Transform Tools

Four transform tools are available in Fireworks 4: Skew, Rotate, Distort, and Scale. You can apply them to any text object. Using these transform tools, text can be resized, rotated, slanted, and pulled out of shape—and still be fully editable.

You can transform text either as a path object or as a pixel image. The Transform As A Path option is the default; it produces much smoother edges that look less jaggy. Of course, in some instances you may prefer the rough, jagged-edge look.

Skew

Before skewing text, be sure the bounding box is the same size as the text. The Skew tool affects the entire text object, including the excess area in the bounding box. To skew an object, follow these steps:

1. Select the object to be skewed.

2. Click the Skew Transform tool in the Tools panel (Figure 7.11). Or, choose Modify|Transform|Skew.

3. You now have access to the points. By dragging them, you alter the shape. To add perspective, click and drag a corner point.

Figure 7.11
The Skew Transform tool.

Rotate

Objects rotate around the pivot point, which is in the center by default. If you want to change the point of pivot, simply move the center point by clicking and dragging. You can apply clockwise (CW) or counter-clockwise (CCW) rotation, either manually or with preset settings from the menu bar. Follow these steps:

1. Select the object to be rotated.

2. To Rotate 180 percent or 90 percent, choose Modify|Rotate Canvas|180%, 90%CW, or 90%CCW.

3. To rotate visually, select any of the transform tools.

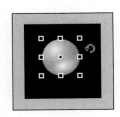

Figure 7.12
The Rotate tool visible.

4. Move the cursor outside the area with the points, and you will see the rotation tool, as shown in Figure 7.12. Simply click and drag in the direction you'd like to rotate. To constrain the rotation to 15-degree increments relative to the horizon, Shift+click and drag.

Distort

Distorting text is similar to using the Skew tool, except that the points react a bit differently. For instance, with the Skew tool if you drag a corner point out, both top points, left and right, expand. With the Distort tool, the point moves independently:

1. Select the object you want to distort.

2. Click the Distort tool.

3. Drag points to adjust the shape.

Scale

The Scale tool works by simple dragging the points. If you drag the corner points in or out, the object is scaled proportionately. You can also pull the center top and bottom points to enlarge vertically or the center side points to stretch horizontally.

Numeric Transform

Instead of dragging to make your transformations, you can transform numerically:

1. Select the object to transform.

2. From the menu bar, choose Modify|Transform|Numeric Transform (Ctrl+Shift+T). In the resulting Numeric Transform dialog box, shown in Figure 7.13, you can scale, resize, or rotate. If you deselect Scale Attributes, any of the effects or strokes added won't scale with the object you are scaling.

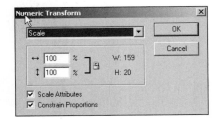

Figure 7.13
The Numeric Transform dialog box.

Info Panel

When you need to make precise adjustments to an object's size and/or location, using the Info panel can save you a great deal of time. In the Info panel, you can make numeric adjustments to objects.

To use the Info panel to determine the X, Y coordinates of the width and height of a particular object, select the object and read the results in the panel. To see the color or X, Y coordinates under your cursor, look at the bottom half of the Info panel—it changes as you move the cursor.

To make numeric adjustments, double-click the parameter you want to change and enter the new number. After each entry, press the Enter/Return key to activate the change.

The right-pointing arrow lets you change the way the Info panel displays results. For instance, you can make the color HSB instead of RGB.

Effects

Fireworks uses *Live Effects*, which can be edited even after you've saved the file and open it at a later date. The Effect panel even lets you see exactly what effect has been applied and the settings used. This is a great way to learn how an effect was achieved when someone shares files with you, or if you forgot how you produced a certain effect.

Adding Effects

You will find yourself returning to the Effect panel often. It contains a variety of effects to enhance almost any project you design.

To add effects, follow these steps:

1. Select the object you want to add an effect to.

2. Click the Effect tab. From the drop-down menu, choose the effect to apply. This menu contains items similar to the Xtras menu. The difference is that the effects on the Effect panel are applied to vector objects, whereas the Xtras menu converts vectors into bitmaps first. When you use a plug-in from the Effect panel, it remains fully editable. You will see that the Shadows And Glow and Bevel And Emboss categories appear in the Effect panel. You may find yourself returning to these two categories often.

3. Assume you make a selection of Shadows And Glow|Drop Shadow. You will be presented with a dialog box to set the distance of the shadow, the softness amount, the angle, and the opacity. The settings are similar for most effects.

4. Press Return/Enter to apply the changes.

> **Note:** For ease of use, you may want to leave the multitabbed panel containing the Effect panel, Stroke panel, and Fill panel open in your workspace. To open it, choose Window|Effect.

Editing Effects

If you want to go back and change an effect or if you want to see how you achieved a certain look, all you have to do is open your PNG file and follow these instructions:

1. Click the object that contains the effect you would like to view or alter. If you have a hard time selecting the proper object, try selecting from the Layers panel.

2. Click the Effect tab (the Fill And Stroke tab works the same way). You will see a list of used effects. To view what the object would look like without a certain effect, click the checkmark to deselect the effect. If you decide you don't want a particular effect, select it and click the Trashcan icon in the lower-right-hand corner to delete it.

3. To view the specific settings of any effect, double-click the effect name. You now have access to the settings and can make any alterations.

The ability to see the effects applied to any object and change the settings is a great timesaver. If you have produced a project but you didn't write down how you did it (haven't we all), you can reconstruct the entire object by clicking the various effects, strokes, and fills to see exactly what you did.

Strokes

The Stroke panel provides 48 built-in strokes, but you can produce an infinite number of variations. Options such as color, strokes, patterns, textures, width, edge, softness, and so on, can change the text effect slightly or drastically, to produce a unique new look. You probably know that to apply a stroke, you select your object and choose a stroke selection from the Stroke panel. Modifying a stroke requires a few more steps, but is still quite simple.

Modify a Stroke

You will now modify the stroke of a preset style that has been applied to some text. If you would like to follow along with the example, you can find the modify.png file in the Chapter 7 folder on the CD-ROM. Follow these steps:

1. Open the modify.png file and select the text. If your Stroke panel isn't open, choose Window|Stroke.

2. The strokes, effects, and fills applied appear in the Stroke, Effect, and Fill panels, respectively.

3. To modify the stroke color, select the color change you want from the color well.

4. The edge softness slider changes how the stroke blends. Change this value if you want a softer edge.

Note: The stroke techniques we will be performing on text work the same way for any object.

Hex Numbers

If you know the Hex number, you can type it in at the top of the color well. Remember, if you type anything into any of the dialog boxes, you need to press Enter/Return.

5. To change the stroke's thickness, simply click the down arrow next to the thickness number or type a number and press Enter/Return.

Gradients

A gradient is a blend of two or more colors. Gradients often are used to produce lighting effects to give the illusion of depth. They also are used as terrific backgrounds and as a fill for transparency masks when working with bitmaps (see Chapter 9). In this section you will learn how to use gradient fills and how to edit them to suit your needs.

Filling with Gradients

You can add unique colorization to a graphic with the use of a gradient fill. Fireworks 4 ships with 11 types of gradients and 13 preset gradient color patterns. However, the number of alterations and variations is almost endless. The best way to describe the 11 types of gradients is to show you samples. In Figure 7.14, you can see a representation of each gradient using the Copper preset. From left to right and top to bottom, they are Linear, Radial, Ellipse, Rectangle, Cone, Starburst, Bars, Ripples, Waves, Satin, and Folds.

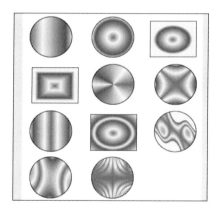

Figure 7.14.
A representation of the gradient options.

To apply a gradient, follow these steps:

1. Select an object you want to apply a gradient to.

2. From the Fill panel, choose one of the gradient options.

3. Choose the color combination you like from the Preset gradient color sets. Or, use the default gradient. The default is a combination of whatever color the stroke is and the color of the fill tool.

4. You can adjust the edge attributes in the Fill panel as well. The choices are Anti-Alias, Hard, or Feather. If you choose Feather, you have the option to type in how many pixels you want the edge of your gradient to be feathered.

If your object is selected, it is automatically filled with the gradient. Test each of the presets and all the different gradient types to get an idea of how each one looks and performs.

Altering Gradients

You can customize gradients by adjusting the pattern's center, width, and/or skew. This is where the real power of the gradient tool becomes evident. The colors can be changed, as well, as discussed in the next section. To change the gradient fill's direction or location, follow these steps:

1. Follow the steps from the previous section to fill an object with a gradient.

2. Select the Pointer tool and select your gradient-filled object. As soon as it is selected, you will see the gradient handles.

3. Drag on the circular handle to adjust the gradient's starting point.

4. Move the cursor over the control handles until you see the rotate cursor. You can now drag the handles by using the Rotate tool or by simply dragging the square or round handle to a new location.

5. By dragging the square handle, you change the direction of the gradient, as seen in Figure 7.15.

Moving the Gradient Handles

A gradient's control handles do not have to be constrained within the object. You can drag the round or square handles outside of the object area to achieve the desired effect; in fact, you can drag both handles completely off the object.

Figure 7.15
Using gradient handles to alter the gradient's look.

Editing Gradient Colors

You can change, delete, or move around existing colors in a gradient, or add new colors with ease. To alter the colors of a gradient, follow these steps:

1. Draw a rectangle to fill with a gradient style.

2. Click the Edit button in the Fill panel. You will see color swatches below the gradient representation. A swatch appears for each color in the gradient and at the position each color begins. You can see the options in Figure 7.16.

3. To change any of the colors, simply click the color box and choose another color from the Swatches. Or, use the Eyedropper and sample from an image you have open in the workspace.

Figure 7.16
The gradient fill editing options after you click the Edit button.

4. To add another color, place your cursor anywhere in the row containing the current color markers, where you want another color added. You will see a plus (+) sign next to your cursor; click to place another color box. Select a color by clicking the color box.

5. To move the position of any of the colors, click and drag the color box to the new location.

6. To delete a color, click and drag the color box toward the bottom of the panel.

You have a lot of control when it comes to gradient colors. You can sample colors from other images with the Eyedropper tool—just as you can when selecting solid fills—to produce some interesting color combinations.

PROJECT | Make Small Spheres with Highlighting

In this project, you will make a sphere and alter it for use in an ornament that you will design in Chapter 8. To make this sphere, follow these steps:

1. Open a new file (File|New) with a size of 130 pixels by 130 pixels with a canvas color of black.

2. Select the Ellipse tool. Press the Shift key to constrain to a perfect ellipse and drag an ellipse on your canvas. Don't worry about the size; you can open the Info panel (Window|Info) to check it. The size used in this example is 64 by 64 pixels; type the numbers in the Info panel and press Enter/Return to activate the change.

3. Open the Fill panel (Window|Fill) and choose Radial from the Fill category. In the Gradient Preset area, choose black, white. (You are choosing this option so that only two color boxes appear in your gradient; otherwise you'd need to delete the extras.) Click the Edit button. Figure 7.17 shows the edit options.

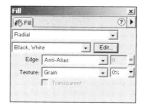

Figure 7.17
The Gradient Edit dialog box.

4. Click the first color box (it looks like a little white house) and select the white swatch. Click the second color box (on the right), which opens a panel of color swatches. You can choose any color you'd like, but for this project, type in Hex #D89495 and press Enter/Return. Figure 7.18 shows the sphere so far with the gradient added.

5. Select the Pointer tool and select the sphere; you will see the gradient handles. Click and drag the circle to move the white area to the upper portion of the ellipse. See Figure 7.19 for placement.

6. Select the Ellipse tool again and draw another, smaller ellipse inside the larger ellipse, as shown in Figure 7.20. You can set the size in the Info panel: Enter "37" for the Width and "21" for the Height and press Enter/Return.

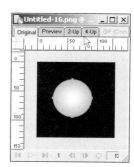

Figure 7.18
Sphere with the gradient added.

Figure 7.19
(Left) The placement of the white highlight.

Figure 7.20
(Center) A smaller ellipse added to the larger ellipse.

Figure 7.21
(Right) The second ellipse rotated and placed at the bottom of the large ellipse.

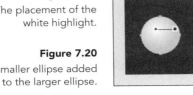

Figure 7.22
The ellipse with the inside ellipse altered.

Figure 7.23
The completed ellipse with a stroke added.

7. You need to move the second ellipse so it's at an angle on the bottom of the large ellipse. Refer to Figure 7.21 for placement. To place the ellipse at an angle, choose Modify|Transform|Free Transform. Hover your cursor on the outside of the ellipse, and you will see the Rotate tool. Click and drag to the position you want.

8. This second ellipse is another highlight area, but it is not white enough. Click and drag the square handle out just a little, leaving a bit of pink. From the Fill panel's Edge area, select Feather from the drop-down list; choose 10 for the amount using the slider. You can experiment with the slider to see if you prefer more or less feather. Figure 7.22 shows the nearly completed ellipse.

9. You may not notice, but the edges are not as smooth as they could be. Even though the background is black, a small black stroke can help define this sphere. Be sure only the large sphere is selected. From the Stroke panel, choose Basic from the Stroke Category list and Soft Rounded from the Stroke Name list, with a tip size of 2 and a color of black. Now the sphere is finished (Figure 7.23). The completed sphere is in the Chapter 7 resources folder.

Variation

For a sphere that has more depth and a glassier look, try these steps:

1. After you draw your ellipse (Steps 1 and 2 from the previous section), fill it with a solid fill instead of the gradient. From the Fill panel, choose Solid and a color of Hex #874A4A.

2. In the same position where you moved your white highlight (Figure 7.19), place a tiny white circle with a feather of 1.

3. Repeat Steps 6 through 9 from the previous section, with one exception—edit the gradient color and change the pink to a dark burgundy, Hex #874A4A. The results can be seen in the Color Studio. The finished variation, glassysphere.png, is also included in the Chapter 7 resources folder.

   The variation of this sphere will be used to make a Web page ornament in Chapter 8. All you need to do is save this file as a Fireworks PNG file.

Filling with Patterns and Textures

Using patterns and textures is a technique that is commonly used to add depth and detail to objects. Fireworks 4 ships with some preset patterns and textures, but the real variety comes from the ability to use almost any pattern or texture you have.

Filling with Patterns

Using a pattern in an object will increase the range of options you have as a designer, making flat, uninteresting objects come alive. Fireworks 4 ships with a small selection of over 30 patterns; the Other option in the Fill panel opens the door to tremendous variety. You are limited only to what you can hold on your hard drive or on CD-ROMs. Any 32-bit image in a BMP, PNG, GIF, JPEG, TIFF, or PICT (for the Macintosh) file format can become an instant pattern. Follow these steps:

1. Select the object you want to fill.

2. From the Fill panel, choose Pattern from the Fill category.

3. In the Patten Name box, choose Other. Browse to an image file, select it, and click Open.

Patterns can be altered the same way as gradients, by moving the handles and rotation symbol.

Adding Textures

You can add textures to any fill, modifying the brightness of the fill but not the hue. Texture files use the grayscale value of an image; you can also use any PNG, GIF, JPEG, BMP, TIFF, or PICT file as a texture. To add texture, follow these steps:

1. Select any object containing any fill, gradient, or pattern.

2. From the Fill panel, click the Texture drop-down list and choose one of the included texture files.

3. Adjust the percentage of opacity; this value will determine the amount of the texture that is seen. In Figure 7.24, a coffee bean texture and a cloth texture have been applied to two rectangles with a 50% Opacity value.

Figure 7.24
Textures applied to rectangles at 50% Opacity.

PROJECT Making a Web Page Title

In this project, you will make the title for the Horse Adventures children's Web site. This is a copyrighted logo and can't be used as is on any other site. However, you can use the pattern fill with different words and font. To begin, follow these steps:

1. Open a new canvas (File|New) with a size of 400 pixels wide by 100 pixels high. The canvas color doesn't matter, but, for visual appeal while you are designing this title, a tan color looks good.

2. Select the Text tool and click the canvas. In the Text Editor, type "Horse" and select any font and size. The font used for this particular Web page was 80-point Staccato222BT. Choose black for the color. Click OK.

3. This first text object will be used as the edge of the text. To fill the text, open the Fill panel (Window|Fill) and select Pattern from the Fill category. In the Pattern Name area, scroll down and choose Other. A dialog box will open allowing you to locate the pattern to fill with. In the Chapter 7 resources folder is a pattern named metalpatina.jpg; select it and click Open (PC).

4. In the Texture area, choose Line-Horiz 1 from the drop-down menu and select 100% for the Amount Of Texture. Notice how the texture has a metallic look at this point (Figure 7.25).

> **Opening Files Containing Fonts You Don't Have**
>
> The source file for Horse Adventures is included in the Chapter 7 resources folder. If you open this file or any other that contains a font you don't have installed on your computer, a dialog box will open giving you the option to change the font. Either make a new selection or click No Change.

Figure 7.25
The text with a texture applied, giving it a metallic look.

5. To bring back a bit of the color that was lost by applying the texture, open the Effect panel and choose Adjust Color|Hue And Saturation. Enter "6" for the Hue, "-35" for the Saturation, and "-44" for the Lightness. Figure 7.26 shows the Hue/Saturation dialog box, and Figure 7.27 shows the result.

6. Select Edit|Clone (Ctrl+Shift+D). Because the effects added for the bottom text object are not needed for this copy, open the Effect panel and delete the Hue/Saturation effect. In the Fill panel, change the Texture Amount to 0%. Figure 7.28 shows the cloned text object with the effects deleted.

7. Using the keyboard arrow keys, click the up arrow three times to nudge the cloned copy up by 3 pixels and click the left arrow three times to move to the left by 3 pixels. This placement allows the edge object to be seen a bit.

> **Note:** The amount you nudge the top text object will depend on the size of the text. For instance, the word "Adventures" (in Step 12) is nudged up 2 pixels and to the left 2 pixels.

Figure 7.26
The Hue/Saturation dialog box with the changed settings.

Figure 7.27
The texture object after hue and saturation adjustments have made it darker.

Figure 7.28
The cloned text object with the effects deleted.

Figure 7.29
The top text object (the clone) has been moved and a stroke has been added.

8. In the Stroke panel, choose Charcoal for the Stroke Category and Soft for the Stroke Name. The tip size is 1. Figure 7.29 shows the top text object moved and a stroke added.

9. In the Effect panel, choose Adjust Color|Brightness And Contrast and enter "20" in the Contrast area. Click OK.

10. Select both text objects. The easiest way is to use the Pointer tool to drag a selection around the first letter, and then group by choosing Modify|Group or by using the keyboard command Ctrl+G/Cmd+G. You also can select both objects from the Layers panel by Shift+selecting each object and then grouping them (Ctrl+G/Cmd+G).

11. The final touch is to add a shadow. From the Effect panel, choose Shadow And Glow|Drop Shadow. Change the Distance to 10, the Softness to 6, and the Opacity to 50%. Figure 7.30 shows the finished text.

Figure 7.30
The finished text effect for the word "Horse".

12. Repeat the previous steps for the word "Adventures", except you should use Century Gothic with a size of 26 points. The other exception is that you only need to nudge the clone two times. Use the default Drop Shadow option with a Distance of 7 and Softness of 4. Change the Opacity to 50% (Figure 7.31).

The Horse Adventures logo will be added to a collage in Chapter 9.

Figure 7.31
The finished title for the Horse Adventures Web page.

Editing Text

If you try to edit text or click on text to see which font was used or its settings and the Text Editor doesn't open, you probably have to ungroup the text. In the horses.png file, if you were to click on "Adventures", the Text Editor would not open because it's a group. Select the text and either choose Modify|Ungroup or Ctrl+Shift+G/Cmd+Shift+G.

Note: The dimensions used in this header are not a standard banner size. The size was determined by the current Web site the header is a part of. To distinguish the book support area from the Web design area of the site, the header was changed as well as the background color and logo color of the page.

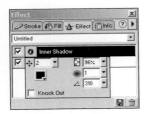

Figure 7.32
The inner shadow settings.

PROJECT Designing the *Fireworks 4 f/x & Design* Web Page Header

In this project, you will use text and effects to design the title header for the *Fireworks 4 f/x & Design* Web page, which supports the book of the same title. This technique works equally well on any background. The background used on the Web page is copyrighted and is supplied for practice only. If you would like to visit this site, you'll find it at **www.je-ideadesign.com/fireworksbook.htm**. To begin making this title, follow these steps:

1. Open a new file (File|New) 480 pixels wide by 58 pixels high. Or, start with the background supplied by opening the Fireworkstitle.png file.

2. If you don't start with the Fireworkstitle.png file, choose the Rectangle tool and draw a rectangle to cover the canvas area. In the Fill panel, choose Pattern and then select any pattern fill you would like to use. Or, use a bitmap sized as you want (the Fireworkstitle.png file is a bitmap).

3. Select the Text tool and click the document. In the Text Editor, type "Fireworks" and choose the font and size you'd like to use. This example uses 65-point Calfisch Script Web. The color used here is Hex #FFCC33, Bold is selected, and the Edge is Crisp Anti-Alias. Click OK when you are done making your selections.

4. To add an effect to the text, open the Effect panel (Window|Effect) and choose Shadow And Glow|Inner Shadow with a Distance of 2, Opacity of 96%, and a Softness of 1. Figure 7.32 shows the settings.

5. Add a stroke from the Stroke panel. Choose Air Brush from the Stroke Category and Basic for the Stroke Name with a Tip size of 3 and a Color of white.

6. To add a drop shadow, choose Shadow And Glow|Drop Shadow with a Distance of 9 and a Softness of 4. The settings can be seen in Figure 7.33. The results so far can be seen in Figure 7.34.

When you delete a frame, you delete all of its content, with the exception of a frame that has been distributed to individual frames (see the section "Distribute to Frames). The deleted frame containing a shared frame will not affect other frames that are using the shared frame. To delete a frame or frames, click the frame or Shift+click multiple frames and use any of the following options:

- After you make your selection, click the Trashcan icon to delete.

- Click and drag the frame(s) on top of the Trashcan icon.

- Click the right-pointing arrow in the Frames panel and choose Delete Frame from the pop-up menu.

> **Note:** The name of the New/Duplicate Frame icon is misleading. You will not get a duplicate of the previous layer with this option; a new blank frame will be added. To produce a duplicate, click the right-pointing arrow and choose Duplicate Frame, or you can drag the frame you want to duplicate onto the New/Duplicate Frame icon.

Moving and Duplicating Frames

Moving frames works the same way as moving layers: You click and drag the frame to the desired position. If you double-click the frame name, you can rename it; this is a change from Fireworks 3. In Fireworks 3, when you moved a numbered frame, the number changed to the new position it was moved to. In Fireworks 4, you can give your frames unique names, and moving the frames does not change the names or numbers assigned.

Duplicating frames is a good way to save time by altering only the elements that change in each frame. Duplicating frames also makes it easy to reverse an animation. When you Shift+select multiple frames and duplicate them, the duplicates automatically begin with a duplicate of the last frame in the selection.

To duplicate a frame, click the right-pointing arrow to access the pop-up menu and choose Duplicate Frame.

Distribute To Frames

You use the Distribute To Frames option when you have multiple objects on one layer that you want in individual frames. Shift+select each object and click the Distribute To Frames icon; each object will be placed automatically in its own frame. For instance, when you make a blend in FreeHand, you can bring it into Fireworks (see Chapter 12) and distribute the blended items onto frames.

Sharing Layers across Frames

The ability to share layers across frames is important. When you have a repeating element, such as a background image, it would be very inefficient and time consuming to have to insert it into every frame. Sharing layers across frames automatically places the contents of the selected layer onto every frame present and all frames added. There is one caveat, though: It is an all-or-nothing proposition. To share a layer across all frames, follow these steps:

1. Double-click the layer you want to share.

2. Name the layer in the Layer Name dialog box and select Share Across Frames. Click anywhere on the screen to close, or press Enter/Return. You also can click the right-pointing arrow and choose Share This Layer.

3. Repeat for any other layer you want to share.

4. To disable sharing of a particular frame, double-click the layer and deselect the Share Across Frames option.

Onion Skinning

The Onion Skinning option comes in handy when you need to place an object in one frame in alignment with an object in another frame, or if you need to add to or subtract from an object appearing on another frame. Using Onion Skinning is like placing tracing paper over the individual frames—you can see through to the other frames. One advantage of using the Onion Skinning feature is that you can select the faded objects on frames other than the selected one and edit them. To use Onion Skinning, click the Onion Skinning icon (the far-left icon on the bottom of the Frames panel). Figure 7.40 shows the Onion Skinning options.

Figure 7.40

The Onion Skinning options.

Looping

Looping sets the amount of times your animation will repeat. You can make it play over and over again indefinitely, choose a specific number of times to loop, or not loop at all. No looping simply means the animation plays one time and stops. To set the looping options, click the GIF animation looping icon (next to the Onion Skinning icon) and select No Looping, a number, or Forever. No Looping is the default.

Frame Delay

The frame delay determines how long each frame is visible before the next frame appears. The delay settings are specified in hundredths of a second. A setting of 10 means 10 one hundredths of a second (or $1/10^{th}$ of a second), and a setting of 100 causes a one-second delay before the next frame appears. To set the delay, double-click the last column in the Frames panel where you see a number. Enter the delay time and click outside the dialog box to close it.

Note: The types of tweening available in Fireworks are position, opacity, scale, rotation, and effects. You cannot do shape tweening, which gradually changes one graphic into another (as you can in FreeHand and Flash). However, you can achieve a type of shape tween by using the Transform option and altering a shape by choosing Modify|Transform|Skew.

Tweening

Tweening in Fireworks is performed on two or more instances of the same symbol. The *same symbol* is a key factor; but you can trick Fireworks, as you will discover in the next section.

Tween Live Effects

Tweening Live Effects is a method that cannot be produced using the Animated Symbol dialog box. This is a little known, undocumented feature, and it can produce amazing results. You can also use Alienskin's Eye Candy 4000 (demo on the companion CD-ROM) filters as Live Effects. To tween Live Effects, follow these steps:

1. Open a new document (File|New) with a size of 300 pixels by 300 pixels.

2. Select any of the drawing tools and draw an object, such as a circle or star.

3. With the object selected, choose Insert|Convert To Symbol. The symbol is added to the library, and an instance appears in your document, as indicated by the little arrow in the corner.

4. To create the second symbol, press Alt/Option, click the symbol and drag a copy to the desired location. Doing so produces a duplicate instance and the ending point of the tween.

5. Select the beginning instance and open the Effect panel. From the drop-down list, choose Adjust Color|Color Fill; select a color different from that of the ending symbol. You may wonder how you can do this, given that tweening can be performed only on two instances of the same symbol, and you just altered one. If you were to try and tween these two instances right now, it would not work. To make the two instances the same, you must apply the same effect to both.

6. Select the ending instance and choose Adjust Color|Color Fill from the Effect panel. This action fools the symbols into thinking they're the same. The same effect is added (with a different setting); just move the opacity slider to 0, and no visible effect is applied.

7. Shift+select the beginning and ending symbol instances and choose Modify|Symbol|Tween Instances. Accept the default frames, select the Distribute To Frames option, and click OK. Play your animation, and you will see the gradual color change.

Using More Than Two Symbols

You can use more than two instances of a symbol when tweening. If you place instances in other locations, the tween will follow a path according to the stacking order; the closest to the canvas is the beginning point of the tween. Just remember that when you tween Live Effects, you must apply the effects—whether they are invisible or not—to every instance. You can make transformations such as width, height, and skew, or opacity and blending modes separately to individual instances to produce what appears to be two different instances.

Moving On

You should now be comfortable with all the basic tools of Fireworks. Now that you are able to add effects, perform special text applications, and use the fill tools (most importantly, the Gradient tools), you should be ready to tackle almost any project.

In Chapter 8, you will master the vector tools, which also include effects and fills you have used in this chapter. You will complete the ornament for which you made the spheres in this chapter, and you'll draw specialized shapes for the Eyeland Studio interface, the Atlantis interface, and more.

Chapter 8

Working with Vector Tools

This chapter describes the Vector tools, which are used to draw paths that you can manipulate and enlarge to any size without losing image integrity. You'll learn to draw objects for Web pages and will draw the components for an interface that you'll animate in Flash.

Understanding Paths

In Fireworks, an object is also a *path*—a vector graphic. Whereas bitmap images use a grid of colors called *pixels* (more in Chapter 9 on using bitmaps), vectors use mathematical calculations. A path starts at X, Y and ends at A, B. Every path has at least two points, yielding a line segment. A path can be open (a line) or closed (lines connecting).

A line in Fireworks that does not connect to itself to make an enclosure is considered an open path. To end an open path that you are drawing, double-click the last point. To end a closed path, click the first point added; the beginning point and the ending point are the same. If you close the path by going beyond the first point, the path won't be closed, even though it looks like it is. That could affect your drawing, because a path that is not closed will not fill how you expect, and usually won't fill at all.

Because of the mathematical nature of vectors, they are very flexible. A vector object can be stretched to a larger height and width and still maintain its image integrity. As the object increases or decreases in size, Fireworks recalculates as necessary to render a great-looking image. This quality makes vector objects popular for use in animations and especially important for use in Flash. The ability to scale a vector drawing is also beneficial if you design a logo—it can be scaled down for Web use and scaled up for print.

Vector Tools

To use all the Vector tools in Fireworks, you need to be in Vector mode. If you are currently in Bitmap mode (indicated by a blue-striped outline) and you select a vector-only tool, such as the Pen tool, you will automatically be switched to Vector mode. But, if you choose a tool such as the Rectangle tool, which can be used in either mode, you will need to switch modes manually. The easiest way to switch to Vector mode is to click the red circle with a white X (the Exit Bitmap Mode button) at the bottom of your document window. An arrow is pointing to the icon in Figure 8.1.

The Vector tools include the shape tools: the Rectangle tool, Ellipse tool, Rounded Rectangle tool, and Polygon tool. Freeform Vector tools also are available, including the Pencil tool, Brush tool, and Pen tool. Every vector path object can have a stroke, effects, and fill applied to it. If you aren't familiar with the Stroke panel, Fill panel, and Effect panel, please refer to Chapter 7.

Using the Vector Shape Tools

The vector shape tools are some of the easiest to use. You will probably use tools such as the Rounded Rectangle tool on a regular basis for making buttons. Every object drawn with a vector shape tool contains a starting point and

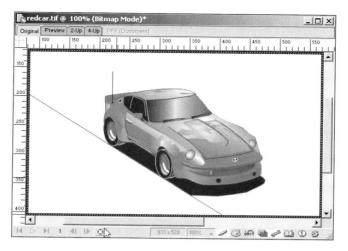

Figure 8.1
The Exit Bitmap Mode button.

an ending point, which plot the path of a line. The vector shape tools automatically place those points. You can control how the points are placed by editing them.

Ellipse Tool

You can use the Ellipse tool in both Vector and Bitmap modes. To draw an ellipse, follow these steps:

1. Open a new document, File|New; a size of 300×300 pixels with a white canvas will do for this example. Select the Ellipse tool from the Tools panel.

2. Click and drag an ellipse on your canvas.

3. To set a specific size for your ellipse, open the Info panel (Window|Info), enter the specific Height and Width measurements you want, and press Enter/Return.

4. Add any strokes, fills, or effects you'd like.

5. Notice that four points are automatically added to the ellipse you just drew. These points control the shape of the object. To edit the shape, select the Subselection tool (white arrow) from the Tools panel. Click and drag down on the bottom point of the ellipse. An egg shape is the result. As soon as you began pulling down the point, you probably noticed lines appear on the other points. These are control handles, which we'll discuss later in this chapter.

Rectangle Tool

You can use the Rectangle tool in both Vector and Bitmap modes. To draw a rectangle, follow these steps:

1. Select the Rectangle tool from the Tools panel.

2. Click and drag a rectangle on your canvas.

3. To set a specific size for your rectangle, open the Info panel (Window|Info), enter the specific Height and Width measurements you want, and press Enter/Return.

4. Add any strokes, fills, or effects you'd like. To apply strokes, open the Stroke panel (Window|Stroke). If you need more information on strokes, fills, or effects, refer to Chapter 7.

5. To edit the shape, notice the four points that were automatically added to the rectangle. Select the Subselection tool from the Tools panel. Click and drag out the point in the lower-right corner. An error dialog box will open stating, "To edit a rectangle's points, it must first be ungrouped. OK to ungroup the rectangle and turn it into a vector?"

   A rectangle in Fireworks is a group of four points, and the rectangle must be ungrouped so that you can manipulate just one point. The second half of the error message, which asks if it's OK to ungroup the rectangle and turn it into a vector, may lead you to think that you are not in Vector mode, but you are. Click OK, and click and drag out the lower-right point.

Polygon Tool

In Fireworks, you can draw an equilateral polygon from a triangle with 3 sides to a polygon with 360 sides. The Polygon tool also works in both Vector and Bitmap modes. To make a polygon, follow these steps:

1. Double-click the Polygon tool to access the Tool Options panel, shown in Figure 8.2.

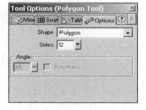

Figure 8.2
The Polygon Tool Options panel.

2. Select the shape you want: Polygon or Star. If you select the Star shape, an Angle option is also available. If you choose the Automatic option, the Angle varies according to how many sides you have selected. The closer to 0 the Angle is, the thinner the point is. The closer to 100 the Angle is, the thicker the point is. To demonstrate, choose Star with 12 sides and an Angle of 10.

3. Drag and draw a star on your canvas, as shown in Figure 8.3.

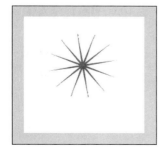

Figure 8.3
A star with 12 sides and an Angle value of 10.

4. If you left the Tool Options panel open (if not double-click the Polygon tool), change the Angle value to 90.

5. Drag and draw a star on your canvas. See Figure 8.4.

Figure 8.4
The star with 12 sides and a new Angle of 90.

The Polygon tool always draws from the center out. To constrain the shape to a 45-degree angle, hold down the Shift key and drag the shape.

Vector Path Freeform Drawing Tools

The freeform drawing tools enable you to draw any shape. If you have a digital drawing tablet, now would be the time to use it. It's much easier to draw freeform lines with a drawing pen than with a mouse.

Pencil Tool

The Pencil tool has a default stroke of 1-Pixel Hard. Unlike some of the tools that retain the last setting used, the Pencil tool must be reset each time you use it if you want something other than the default stroke. You can use the Pencil tool in both Vector and Bitmap modes.

To see the Pencil tool options, double-click the Pencil tool icon in the Tools panel. The options can be seen in Figure 8.5.

- *Anti-Aliased*—Puts a smooth edge on the lines you draw; this feature is particularly important if the lines are curved. Transitional colors are used along the edge of the object, blending the background color with the stroke color.

- *Auto Erase*—Macromedia describes this function as drawing the fill color over the stroke. It does, but only if you draw over the stroke after you've drawn it. This is a very strange feature; it works the same way as drawing a new path and applying a stroke.

- *Preserve Transparency*—Works only in Bitmap mode. This feature enables you to draw only in areas containing pixels, not in transparent areas with no pixels.

Changing the Angle or Sides

You must change the Angle and/or Sides of a polygon shape or star *before* you draw the shape—you cannot change the settings for the drawn shape after the fact. If you want a different Sides or Angle value, double-click the Polygon tool icon to access the Tool Options dialog box and change the value before you redraw.

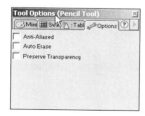

Figure 8.5
The Pencil Tool Options dialog box.

To draw with the Pencil tool, follow these steps:

1. Select the Pencil tool from the Tools panel.

2. Click and drag to draw with the Pencil tool.

3. If you want an open path, release the mouse when you are done drawing.

4. If you want a closed path, draw to the beginning of your line and release the mouse.

Brush Tool

The Brush tool looks like paint or ink, but the result is still a path containing points—you can edit it like any other path. Strokes, fills, and effects can be added, as well. You can use the Brush tool in both Vector and Bitmap modes. The Brush Tool Options dialog box opens when you double-click the brush icon. You will see a Preserve Transparency option, but it is available only in Bitmap mode; no options are available in Vector mode.

To draw with the Brush tool, follow these steps:

1. Select the Brush tool from the Tools panel.

2. Click and drag to draw with the Brush tool.

3. If you want an open path, release the mouse when you are done drawing.

4. If you want a closed path, draw until you see a small dot on the bottom right of the cursor, which indicates the line is closed, and release the mouse.

Pen Tool

With the Pen tool, you don't actually draw the line. Each time you click, you put down a point (dot). Fireworks automatically adds a line between the points, thereby completing a line segment. The Pen tool is available only in Vector mode. If you are in Bitmap mode and choose the Pen tool, Fireworks will automatically change to Vector mode.

The Pen tool has two kinds of points: a Corner point, which has at least one straight segment; and a Curve point, which has at least one curved segment. To see first-hand the difference between these two types of points, follow these steps:

1. Open a new document (File|New) and use a size of 300×300 pixels. Check to be sure you have a fill color selected for the stroke (the pencil icon in the Color section at the bottom of the Tools panel).

2. Select the Pen tool and click the canvas; go straight across the page a few inches and click again. A line connects the two points. Continue clicking anywhere on the canvas. No matter where you click, the lines keep connecting the dots.

3. When you are done practicing, delete your lines. Select the Pen tool and click the canvas; click again a few inches away, and then go down the page a bit and click and drag. As you drag, the line is curved, as shown in Figure 8.6. It takes practice to get used to working with a curved line.

When you draw with the Pen tool and drag to form Curve points, Bézier control handles are added to the path. Control handles control the shape of the object. Later in this chapter you'll learn how to manipulate these handles.

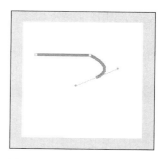

Figure 8.6
A path with Corner points and a Curve point.

Using the Control Handles of a Bézier Curve

A Bézier curve (pronounced "bezz-ey-aye") is based on mathematical calculations. The name comes from Pierre Bézier, who in the 1970s formulated the principles on which most vector objects are now based. The theory is that all shapes are composed of segments and points. A segment can be straight, curved, or a combination of both straight and curved. A combination of two or more points joined by a line or a curve is referred to as a *path*.

After you've drawn a Bézier curve, you may want to make adjustments to it. You work with the control handles by using the Subselection tool and clicking a point on the path. The points are hollow squares; when you click them, they turn into solid squares and are ready to manipulate. Bézier handles are usually visible when you select a Curve point. To practice manipulating Bézier curves using Bézier control handles, follow these steps:

1. Select the Pen tool, click three points in a row, and then double-click the ending point of the path (see Figure 8.7).

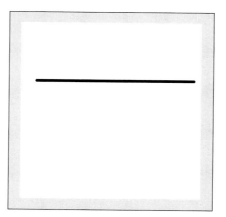

Figure 8.7
A practice line for adding a Bézier curve.

2. Select the Subselection tool. Click any point on the path. If no handles appear (they won't on a straight line), click the middle point, then press the Alt/Option key, and click and drag the point down. When you release the mouse button, a control handle will be visible. Figure 8.8 shows what your curve should look like as a result of holding the Alt/Option key and pulling down on the middle point.

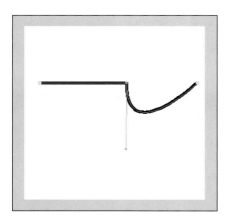 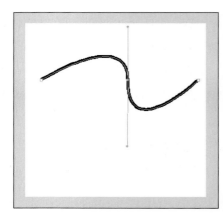

Figure 8.8
(Left) A Bézier curve added to the middle point of the practice line.

Figure 8.9
(Right) Two handles on the Bézier curve.

Change a Curve to a Straight Line

To change a straight line into a Bézier curve, select the point, hold down the Alt/Option key, and drag a point. It's important to remember that you must click the point before you click and drag; otherwise, the point will move and no control handle will be evident. To change a Bézier curve back into a straight line, select the Pen tool and click the point of the curve you'd like to be a straight segment; the curve segment of that point will become straight.

Cursor Preferences

If you are using the Precise cursor, you will not see the little icons, such as the *x*, which offer visual clues when using the Pen tool. You may want to change your preferences by choosing Edit|Preferences and unchecking the Precise cursor option.

Note: If the end points you want to connect are not close together, you may need to add one or more points before you connect the ends. See "Continuing a Path."

3. Click the same point, press the Alt/Option key, and drag straight up. Figure 8.9 shows the results.

You'll need practice to get a feel for which direction to pull and turn to get the desired shape when you're working with Bézier curves. Practice by clicking and dragging the top control handle up, down, and all around.

Editing with the Pen Tool

Earlier in this chapter, you learned how to draw paths and how to connect their beginning and ending points. Sometimes, you will need to join multiple paths, or you may want to break apart a path. You can use the Pen tool to join multiple paths, close a path, or continue a path.

Closing a Path

If you try to fill a path object and nothing happens, or the fill isn't confined to the area inside the path (thereby producing very strange results), your path most likely is not closed. You need to join the path, or join multiple points to close the path. To close a path, follow these steps:

1. With the Pointer tool, select the path you want to close.

2. Select the Pen tool, move your cursor over one of the end points of the path (when you are near the end point, a little *x* will appear in the lower-right corner of the cursor), and click the end point once. A little arrow appears in the corner of the cursor, indicating that you can select a closing point.

3. Move your cursor to the end point you want to connect to and click once. The path is now closed.

Continuing a Path

Adding to a previously drawn path is similar to closing a path, but you don't have to close a path to add to it. To continue a previous path, follow these steps:

1. With the Pointer tool, select the path you want to add to.

2. Select the Pen tool, move your cursor over one of the end points of the path, and click the end point once.

3. Move your cursor to the next location at which you want to add a point and click once. Continue clicking to add points as desired.

Joining Paths

After you draw multiple paths, you can join them together using the Pen tool. This technique may sound the same as closing paths, and it is almost the same; the difference is that you don't have to close the joined paths. To join paths, follow these steps:

1. With the Pointer tool, select one of the paths you want to join.

2. Select the Pen tool, move your cursor over one of the end points of the path, and click the end point once.

3. Move your cursor to the end point of the segment you are connecting to and click once. You can combine as many paths as you like in this way.

Adding and Deleting Points

If you want a path to change direction, you need to add points to make it do so. You could use the Bézier tool to make a curve to change the path's direction, but you may not want a rounded curve. If you need to change direction but want a sharper turn, then you need to add points using the Pen tool. See the "Eyeland Studio Interface" project later in the chapter for a good example of adding points. To add points to an existing path, follow these steps:

1. With the Pointer tool, select the path you want to add points to.

2. Select the Pen tool and click once on the path's line to add one point (you will see a little plus sign next to the Pen tool). If you want a curved segment with Bézier control handles, click and drag.

3. Repeat for as many points as you need. When you are done, select any other tool to stop adding points.

When you use the freeform tools, they often add more points than necessary to maintain the design's shape. The extra points don't hurt anything, but you may want to clean up the object some. Sometimes, the extra points can make a design look choppy or not as smooth as it should. To remove points, follow these steps:

1. With the Pointer tool, select the path you want to delete points from.

2. Select the Pen tool. As your cursor passes over the point, you will see a minus sign on the right corner of the cursor. Select the point you want to delete by clicking it one time.

Note: You could skip Step 1 and not use the Pointer tool to select the point and select the point using the Pen tool. To delete a point, you select a point by clicking it once with the Pen tool, which causes the – sign to appear; then you click again to delete the point. You will also notice that while you move the Pen tool, it appears attached to the end point (this line clinging to the cursor is why I don't care for doing it this way). Don't worry; as soon as you click, the delete action continues as it should.

Note: The number portion of the Simplify option can be difficult to understand. It isn't a point amount nor is it a percentage. Simplify looks at more than the number of points: It will get rid of points that are on top of each other and redraw the path with a similar curvature. The larger the number you specify using the Simplify option, the fewer points will remain on your path. If you use a number that's too low, the path's shape may be altered. For example, a simple half-circle requires only two points, but if you drew it with the Pencil tool, you'll have many points. You can use Simplify to reduce it to two points.

3. Another way to remove unwanted points is to choose Modify|Alter Path|Simplify, type in a number Amount and click OK. Although this option doesn't give you precise control, it is a fast way to make simple changes.

Join

The Join operation isn't the same as connecting paths into one continuous path using the Pen tool. The results of the Join operation can be seen in Figure 8.10. This example shows overlapping areas being joined with a fill added. However, you can also select multiple shapes and join them into one path without overlapping, as you will see in the "Making a Decorative Ornament" project later in this chapter.

To join paths together, follow these steps:

1. With the Pointer tool, Shift+select all the objects you want to join.

2. Choose Modify|Join.

3. If you don't like the result or if you want to split the join apart at a later time, choose Modify|Split.

Figure 8.10
The Join operation demonstrated on two circles.

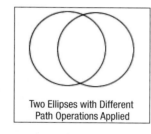
Two Ellipses with Different Path Operations Applied

The Join Command Applied

Punch

Punch is probably the most fun of all the path operations, especially if you like to punch holes in things. Figure 8.11 shows the results of using the Punch operation.

Figure 8.11
Two circles with the Punch operation applied.

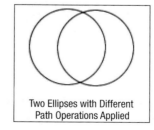
Two Ellipses with Different Path Operations Applied

Punch with Drop Shadow Applied

To use the Punch operation, follow these steps:

1. Open a new document (File|New) 300 pixels wide by 200 pixels high, using White for the canvas color.

2. Select the Rectangle tool and drag a rectangle to cover the canvas. Fill with any color you'd like. (I used blue.)

3. Select the Ellipse tool and drag to draw three ellipses. Change the fill to something other than your rectangle's color and not white (the background color). My ellipses are red (see Figure 8.12).

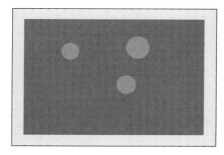

Figure 8.12
A blue rectangle with red ellipses ready to be punched out.

4. With the Pointer tool, Shift+select the object you want to punch and the object you are punching it out of—in this case, one of the ellipses and the blue rectangle.

5. Choose Modify|Combine|Punch. Repeat for the other two ellipses.

6. If you really want to see the punched effect, open the Effect panel, choose Shadow And Glow|Drop Shadow, and accept the defaults. Figure 8.13 shows the final result. You can see that holes have been punched through the rectangle. This is a great effect if you want to make a pegboard or add detail to an interface.

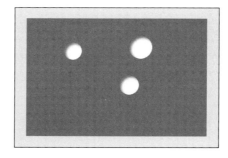

Figure 8.13
The ellipses punched out of the rectangle with a drop shadow added.

Knife Tool

The Knife tool is in the same location as the Eraser tool. In Bitmap mode, it is the Eraser tool; in Vector mode, it is the Knife tool. The Knife tool works only on paths, not on bitmaps. You can use the Knife tool to cut an open path in pieces or slice a closed path apart.

As with the majority of the other Vector mode editing tools, you can double-click the Knife tool icon to access its Tool Options panel. However, you won't get the options you expect. Macromedia didn't change the tool options for the Knife tool, so the Eraser Tool Options panel opens—Fireworks doesn't include any options for the Knife tool. To use the Knife tool, follow these steps:

1. Open a new document (File|New) 300 pixels wide by 300 pixels high, using White for the canvas color.

2. Select the Rectangle tool and draw a rectangle; fill it with any color you'd like.

3. Select the Knife tool. Beginning at the top of the rectangle, click and drag all the way through. The slice won't be apparent when you are done. Select the Pointer tool and click anywhere other than the rectangle to deselect the rectangle. Click one side of the rectangle and drag to separate the piece you just cut.

PROJECT Making a Decorative Ornament

The ornament you are making is included on a Web page containing a poem. This Web page started in FreeHand, where the poem was converted to an envelope shape (see Chapter 2); then the title and author name were added in Chapter 7. This project demonstrates the use of the Vector tools in Fireworks to produce intricate designs such as this ornament.

The following project is an adaptation of a Photoshop PSD file, demonstrating how you can convert many of the Photoshop tutorials available on the Internet into useable Fireworks techniques. This particular ornament did not have a tutorial, but the PSD file was enough to reproduce the ornament. I'm using the pattern with the permission of original designer, Shafqat Ali. His Web site is at **www.designwithphotoshop.com**. This is one of my favorite Photoshop sites; he does beautiful and very intricate work. Be warned: the pages take a long time to load, but it's worth the wait.

The finished ornament can be seen at the end of the project.

Preparing All the Spheres

As you can see in the final figure of this project, this design uses quite a few spheres. You will make, change the color of, and resize all the spheres needed in this section. The sphere we're using is a variation of the sphere you made in Chapter 7, when I demonstrated how to use gradients. A copy is provided in the Chapter 8 resources folder in the file glassysphere.png. To begin, follow these steps:

1. Choose File|Open. Navigate to the Chapter 8 resources folder on the companion CD-ROM and select glassysphere.png. Click Open.

2. This ellipse consists of three pieces, and you need to group them to move the ellipse and to change its color. Use the Pointer tool to marquee-select the pieces; or, Shift+select each piece in the Layers panel and group (Modify|Group).

3. Open a new canvas (File|New) with a Custom canvas of black. A size of 200 pixels by 200 pixels is more than enough room to work on. Drag the glassy sphere you grouped in Step 2 onto your new canvas.

4. Open the Info panel (Window|Info). Enter "31" for both the Width (W) and the Height (H) and press Enter/Return.

5. The glassy sphere is already the right color (burgundy). You will need three burgundy spheres, so press the Alt/Option key and drag two copies. Place the three completed spheres at the top of your document, out of the way. Make one extra copy and move it to the center of the canvas to make alterations.

6. Select the extra copy of the burgundy sphere. In the Info panel, change the Width and Height to 17. Open the Effect panel and choose Adjust Color|Hue And Saturation. In the Saturation box, type "-100". In the Lightness box, type "0" if any other value appears. Leave the Hue as is. Click OK. You've produced a gray sphere.

7. Alt/Option+drag three copies of the gray sphere. Move two of them out of the way; the other two are the same size needed for the gold spheres in the final ornament, so you will just change their color. In the Effect panel, click the little icon next to the effect already applied or double-click the Hue/Saturation name to open the Hue/Saturation dialog box. In the Hue box, type "41"; in the Saturation box, type "17"; and in the Lightness box, type "11". Click OK. Move your finished gold spheres out of the way.

8. Alt/Option+drag a copy of the gold sphere into your work area. Select it and, in the Effect panel, choose Adjust Color|Hue And Saturation. In the Hue box, type "86"; in the Saturation box, type "11"; and in the Lightness box, type "–8". Click OK. You now have a green sphere.

9. The green sphere needs to be a bit smaller. Select it and, in the Info panel, change the Width and Height to 11. Alt/Option+drag one copy of the green sphere.

10. The last two spheres are the little ones in the center of the ornament. Alt/Option+drag a copy of one of your burgundy spheres into your work area. In the Info panel, change the Width and Height to 11 and press Enter/Return. Alt/Option+drag a copy of the resulting small sphere.

11. You are now done with the spheres. Save the document for use when you complete the ornament. A copy called spheres.png has been saved for you in the Chapter 8 resources folder, if you'd rather skip this part.

> **Note:** The original Photoshop file has shadows with all the spheres, but because this project uses a black background, they are not necessary.

Making the Basic Shape

The ornament basic shape is shown in Figure 8.19. To draw it, you could use the Pencil tool, the Brush tool, or the Pen tool. The tool you use depends on the way you want to draw. You can draw the shapes freehand using the Pencil or Brush tool. The easiest way to do that would be to draw your design on paper first and then trace it using a drawing tablet, such as Wacom. Another option, which worked better for me, is to use the Pen tool and trace around the shape. This is the technique that will be discussed in this project. (Be sure to check out **www.designwithphotoshop.com** to become inspired about all the designs you can produce using spheres and curly patterns.) A movie tutorial is included for this technique because it may be difficult to grasp. It is in the movie folder and is called ornamentshape.mov. If you are more comfortable using FreeHand, the Bezigon tool would be great for this technique as well. To begin drawing the shapes using the Pen tool, follow these steps:

1. Open the ornamentbasicshape.png file. Because you could begin with this file, you won't want to destroy it. In the Layers panel, click the right-pointing arrow and choose Lock All. Click the yellow folder icon at the bottom of the Layers panel to add a new layer. Now you can work without affecting the original layer.

2. Because the technique is the same for drawing the various swirly lines, we'll give instructions for the bottom, large one. Select the Pen tool. In the Stroke panel, choose Basic, Soft-Line, a Tip size of 2, and a color that will be visible, such as red. Figure 8.14 shows where to place the first point by clicking with the Pen tool. When tracing a design, you may need to select the Zoom tool and click on the area on the canvas you'd like to make larger.

Figure 8.14
The first point placed.

3. Figure 8.15 shows where to place the second point. To place this point, make it a curve segment by clicking and dragging to fit the curve the best you can. Don't worry about making it perfect.

Figure 8.15
The second point placed by clicking and dragging with the Pen tool.

Figure 8.16
The third point placed by clicking and dragging with the Pen tool.

4. Click and drag to place the third point as shown in Figure 8.16.

5. Figure 8.17 shows the next three points. Simply click to add them. You could probably use fewer points; I used too many to demonstrate the Simplify command later.

Figure 8.17
Three points added by clicking with the Pen tool.

6. Add the last two points by clicking and dragging to conform to the curves. Because the stroke is a different color, you can see how close your design lines up with the original. Using the Subselection tool, you can pull the handles in either direction to make alterations.

7. When you are done and the shape pleases you, choose Modify|Alter Path|Simplify. For this path, enter an amount of 2 and click OK. Figure 8.18 shows the result. A setting of 2 maintained the shape's integrity and reduced the total points to only four.

Figure 8.18
The path simplified to four points.

8. Repeat this process for all the shapes on one side of the design, and then draw the center shape. When you are done and satisfied with all the shapes, Shift+select each shape (not the center) and choose Modify|Join.

9. To make the second side, select the joined portion you just made, choose Edit|Clone, and then choose Modify|Transform|Flip Horizontal. Move the clone into position. Now Shift+select the first section you made, the center, and the right section. Choose Modify|Join. In the Stroke panel, change the color to Gray (Hex #999999). Figure 8.19 shows the basic shape.

Figure 8.19

The basic shape path drawn and joined together.

10. You can now unlock the original layer by clicking the lock. If you'd been tracing a bitmap file, you could now delete the layer. You can delete it anyway, if you'd like, and save your own drawing.

Adding Depth to the Basic Shape

To give some depth and dimension to the basic shape, follow these steps:

1. Open the drawing you saved or open the ornamentbasicshape.png file from the Chapter 8 resources folder.

2. Select your basic shape, click the right-pointing arrow in the Layers panel, and select Duplicate Layer. In the dialog box that opens, choose At The Top Or Before Current Layer. Double-click the name and change it to Color.

3. In the Stroke panel, change the color to Hex #B0987C and press Enter/Return.

4. Zoom in so you can see what you are doing. With the Color layer selected, press the down arrow on the keyboard one time and the right arrow one time. Deselect so you can see the result. Just a little of the gray shows.

5. To add dimension to the bottom of the shape, select the Color shape. Click the right-pointing arrow in the Layers panel and select Duplicate Layer. In the dialog box that opens, choose At The Top Or Before Current Layer. Double-click the name and change it to Shadow.

6. In the Stroke panel, change the Color to white and leave everything else as is. In the Effect panel, choose Shadow And Glow|Drop Shadow, with a Distance of 7, Softness of 6, Angle of 323, and Opacity of 100%. Select the Knockout option. Place the shadow as shown in Figure 8.20. You will notice a bit of white highlight, as well.

Figure 8.20
The shape with color, shadow, and highlight added.

7. Choose Modify|Canvas Color. Select Custom, choose black, and save. The sample file is saved as finishedbasicshape.png.

Putting the Ornament Together

You'll need to open two files to complete this ornament: finishedbasicshape.png and the spheres file. To complete the design, follow these steps:

1. Make the finishedbasicshape.png file active and select Layer 1. Drag a large burgundy circle to the canvas. In the Layers panel, drag the sphere below the basic shape. Position the sphere on the bottom-left curl (see Figure 8.21) so that the top highlight remains white. If you move the sphere too close to the shape, the shadow will dull the highlight. Repeat for the right side. You may want to double-click each object's name in the Layers panel and change it to a distinctive name.

Figure 8.21
The first sphere positioned on the basic shape.

2. Repeat Step 1 for the gray, gold, and green spheres.

3. From the spheres canvas, drag a large burgundy sphere to the center of the ornament.

4. The two tiny spheres for the center go on top of the curly ends. Select the Color layer, and then drag the small burgundy spheres from the spheres canvas into place. The finished ornament can be seen in Figure 8.22 and in the Color Studio.

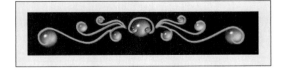

Figure 8.22
The finished ornament.

PROJECT Eyeland Studio Interface

The Eyeland Studio interface is provided to you compliments of Scott Hamlin of EyelandStudio.com. This interface is currently being sold at **www.eyewire.com**. You can alter, customize, and generally do what you'd like with it, but you can't distribute or sell the Flash file. If you were designing a new interface, you would probably begin with a drawing passed on by a designer, draw your own, or simply experiment on screen. For this project, you can pretend that a designer handed you this image of Eyeland Studio and said, "Make it happen." Because many pieces need to be drawn to produce the entire interface, in this project you will draw a few representative shapes to learn the techniques involved. After that, you will be given basic instructions for similar tasks. If you'd rather not do this project but want to go right to the Flash section, the completed shapes are included in the Eyeland.png (resources folder) file and exported as an Illustrator AI file into the Eyeland folder. All the AI files in the Eyeland folder (on the companion CD) are ready for Flash.

Tasks Used throughout This Project

Please remember that when you enter anything in a panel or a dialog box via the keyboard (such as a Hex color number, size, and so on) you need to press the Enter/Return key to activate the change. Any setting you adjust using the slider function is automatically applied.

As a quick review, to avoid repeating each command many times in this project, you change a color by clicking the Color box and either typing a Hex number or using the Eyedropper to sample. To adjust the size of an object, use the Info panel (Window|Info). To group, choose Modify|Group or Ctrl+G/Cmd+G; to ungroup, choose Modify|Ungroup or Ctrl+Shift+G.

Depending on how you like to organize your objects, you may want to add a new layer for each new element you add. To add a new layer, open the Layers panel and click the yellow folder icon at the bottom of the panel.

Producing the Top Title Area

Figure 8.23 shows a screen shot of the finished Eyeland Studio interface. You will redraw the elements needed using the Eyeland.tif file as a tracing reference.

> **Timesaving Tip**
>
> Positioning objects exactly where you want them is not a strong point of Flash. To alleviate this problem and to save a lot of time, position your elements in Fireworks as you want them to appear in Flash. Draw a rectangle the size of the Flash bounding box. By doing so, you can easily line up your elements in Flash.

Figure 8.23
The Eyeland Studio file that you will reproduce.

You will begin by tracing all the basic shapes. Then, you will prepare them for Flash. To begin preparing EyelandStudio.tif for use in Flash, follow these steps:

1. Open Eyeland.tif, which can be found in the Chapter 8 resources folder on the companion CD-ROM. In the Layers panel, click the yellow folder icon to add a new layer. Select the Rectangle tool and drag a rectangle to fill the entire canvas. In the Fill panel, add a black fill. This rectangle will serve as the bounding box area.

   Note: If you want to be sure that you don't accidentally draw on the tracing file, then lock the layer by clicking the area to the right of the eye icon on the background layer.

2. Select the Rectangle tool and drag a rectangle over the whole top title area (the light green area). In the Info panel, change the size to a Width of 640 and a Height of 95, set the Color to white (for visibility; if you used the correct fill, you would not be able to see the outline below), and change the Opacity to 70%. Double-click the object name in the Layers panel and change it to "Main title background".

3. Select the Subselection tool and click the bottom-right point of the rectangle. A warning dialog will open, saying "To edit a rectangle's points, it must first be ungrouped. OK to ungroup the rectangle and turn it into a vector?" Click OK. Select the point again and move it to the left, making a diagonal line as seen in Figure 8.24.

Figure 8.24
The Main title background area with a shape adjustment.

4. Select the Pen tool and add three points (see Figure 8.25 for placement). Select the Subselection tool and move the two inside points you added up on a diagonal, as shown in Figure 8.26.

5. The point closest to the button area may need to move to the right just a bit after you pull up the other point. Draw a rectangle around the small light-green area containing the three little circles (Opacity at 70%). With the

Figure 8.25
Three new points added to the
Main title background area.

Figure 8.26
Two of the new points adjusted
to conform to the tracing shape.

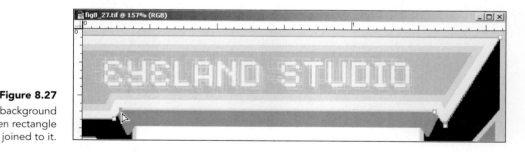

Figure 8.27
The Main title background
with the small green rectangle
joined to it.

Subselection tool, move the top-right point to conform to the shape below. Shift+select the little rectangle and the large one (Main title background) you just made and choose Modify|Combine|Union (see Figure 8.27).

6. Add a new layer, draw a rectangle around the white area, and set the size to 122 by 78. Leave the color white and be sure no stroke is applied. Set the Opacity to 50% for easier visibility. Move the points to conform to the lower shape using the Subselection tool. Rename the object "Top white area" (see Figure 8.28).

Figure 8.28
The Top white area of the title area has been traced.

7. Add a new layer and draw a rectangle (503 by 78) over the dark green area below the black title area, as shown in Figure 8.29. Change the Opacity to 50% and the color to light yellow for visibility, and name the object "Center background".

Figure 8.29
The dark green title area and Center background beginning to be shaped.

8. Select the Subselection tool and click the lower-right point of the rectangle you just drew. Click OK in response to the warning. Move the point on a diagonal to the lower edge; then select the top-left point and move in on a diagonal, as shown in Figure 8.30.

Figure 8.30
The lower-right point and the upper-left point of the Center background area are moved.

9. You need to add some points to the bottom to conform this shape to the shape below it. Select the Pen tool and add three points, as seen in Figure 8.31. Select the Subselection tool and move the two inside points up on a diagonal to match the design (see Figure 8.32).

10. For the black center area, just click points at each corner and the angle using the Pen tool. Name this object "Black center". Use the Pen tool to trace the green area above the text area (name it "Dark Green"), as seen in Figure 8.33.

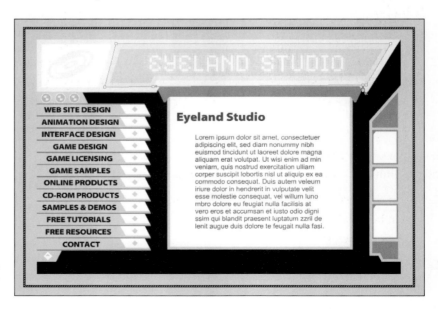

Figure 8.31
Three points added to the bottom of the Center background shape.

Figure 8.32
The Center background adjusted to the shape below it.

Figure 8.33
The Pen tool used to trace the shape of the Dark Green object.

Center Text Area

The center text area contains only two elements: the light green background and the white text area. To trace them, follow these steps:

1. Select the Rectangle tool and draw a rectangle that covers the light green border. Set the Opacity to 70% so you can see through to the green area below.

2. With the Subselection tool, move the top point up a bit into the dark green area above it.

3. Change the fill color to light yellow and set the Opacity to 50%. Name this object "Light green background".

Figure 8.34

The center text area being drawn
and raised a bit into the dark
green area above it.

4. Drag a rectangle over the white area. Using the Subselection tool, pull the
   right corner up a bit as well (see Figure 8.34). Name this "Center text".

5. Make a copy of the white text shape and move it out of the area.
   Shift+select the light green rectangle and the white rectangle and
   choose Modify|Combine|Punch. Name it "Light green background".
   Move the white copy back into position over what is now a light green
   outline. Name it "Text box".

Right Side Elements

You make the elements of the right side bar using instructions similar to those
in the previous sections, so the instructions here will be brief. To begin, follow
these steps:

1. For the right side, trace the main light green shape using whichever technique works best for you—either use the Rectangle tool and adjust with
   the Subselection tool, or use the Pen tool. Name it "Right green box".

2. Use the Rectangle tool to drag a shape over the small dark green areas
   below the white boxes. In the Info panel, set the size to 46 by 63.

3. Use the Pen tool to trace the white boxes, as shown in Figure 8.35.

4. Make an extra copy of the white center and move it to the side. Center the
   original white box you traced over the dark green rectangle. Shift+select
   both and choose Modify|Combine|Punch. Name it "Right green border".
   Move the white box back into place over the resulting dark green outline.
   Shift+select both and group. Make two copies and place them according to
   the tracing pattern. Ungroup all when you are finished. Name the white
   boxes, "Top white", "Center white", and "Bottom white".

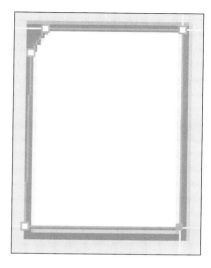

Figure 8.35
The small white box traced using the Pen tool.

Logo

The logo is made a bit differently than the rest of the tracing. You can trace it by following these steps:

1. Select the Ellipse tool and draw an oval the approximate size of the logo. In the Fill panel, choose None for the Fill; and in the Stroke panel, use a Tip size of 1 and a Color of black. (This fill is for visibility only; you'll remove it later.)

2. Choose Modify|Transform|Free Transform and rotate until the angle is right. Pull out the corner squares until the oval fits the logo.

3. You may have areas that are too large. In Figure 8.36, you can see white where the arrow is pointing. Use the Subselection tool, click the bottom-left point near the arrow, and pull up the handle a bit to tighten the ellipse around the logo.

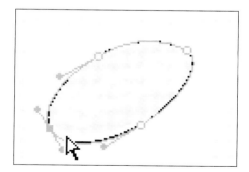

Figure 8.36
The logo shape showing an area that needs to be adjusted to fit.

4. Use the Pen tool to trace the moon-shaped center object on the left. Use the Bézier handles to adjust the shape. Select a point, click again, hold the Alt/Option key, and drag a curve handle if you didn't add a curved point while drawing.

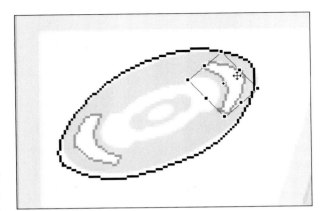

Figure 8.37

An enlarged view of the moon shape rotated and in position.

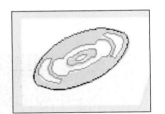

Figure 8.38

The logo shape completely traced.

5. Select Edit|Duplicate or press Alt/Option and drag a copy. Choose Modify| Transform|Free Transform and rotate and move over the top-right moon shape, as seen in Figure 8.37.

6. Use the Pen tool to trace the remaining centerpiece. Choose Duplicate and, in the Info panel, change the size to 25 by 15, change the color to the light green, and position in the center of the logo.

7. Add the white oval and use Modify|Transform|Free Transform to position it. Figure 8.38 shows the traced logo.

8. Name each of the elements you traced. These names will be especially important when you are ready to fill and combine the parts of the logo. The names used in this example are "Logo background", "Half moon left", "Half moon right", "Center shape", "Small center", "White center".

9. Select the Logo background. In the Fill panel, choose Solid for the Fill Category and Hex #66CC00 for the Color. In the Stroke panel, choose None. Choose Modify|Arrange|Send To Back.

10. Fill the half moons, logo center, and White center with a Color of white and a Stroke of None. Fill the Small center with Hex #66CC00 and a Stroke of None. You can now Shift+select all the logo elements and group.

Three Little Circles

To draw the three circles on the left beneath the top white area, follow these steps:

1. Add a new layer, draw a 17-by-17 circle, and add a white stroke. In the Object panel, select the Draw Stroke Outside Path option. Fill the circle with a Color of Hex #66CC00.

2. Open a new document that is 50 by 50. A diamond is made for the buttons which you can find in the Eyeland folder. The file is called buttonstuff.png. Copy the diamond in the Free Tutorials button and paste it into the new document. Pull a guide to the center of the

diamond, select the Knife tool, and cut across the center. Click the canvas, select the top half of the diamond, and choose Modify| Transform|Flip Vertical. Repeat this step for the bottom half, and then Shift+select and group. Fill with a Color of Hex #CCFF99 and resize to 10 by 10.

3. Drag the little diamond shape to the circle area. Choose Modify| Transform|Free Transform and use the Rotate option until the rotation lines up. Copy the circle and little icons two times (Alt/Option+drag a copy) and place over the remaining two circles on the tracing layer.

Buttons

To draw the buttons for an interface that will be animated in Flash, you need to know what you will do with the buttons in Flash. This particular button slides when the mouse cursor passes over the button. See the emerald.swf file (Eyeland folder) to see the buttons in action.

Drawing the buttons and diamonds is an easy task and uses the techniques we've already taught. The buttonstuff.png, buttonslide.png, and diamondmotion.png files in the Eyeland folder in Chapter 8 let you see how the buttons were drawn or try the technique for yourself.

You need to make dark green lines that appear at the bottom of every button. Using the Pen tool, draw a line 200 by 1 pixel. Make a 190-by-1 pixel line for the top button in the Stroke panel, using a Tip size of 2 and Color of Hex #339900.

Preparing for Export

How you export depends on how you work in Flash. All the traced objects are on separate layers, ready for use in Flash. However, not everyone likes to use everything on separate layers.

If you were to look at emerald.fla (Flash source file), you would see that some of the non-interactive elements are grouped together for easier placement in Flash. You will do the grouping now; adding color to the traced objects also will be easier once they are grouped. Because we used a color and opacity that are easy to see for tracing, you will need to change them. Follow these steps to group the stationary non-interactive elements in this file:

1. Open Eyeland.png. Shift+select all the light green objects from the Layers panel: "Main title background", "Bottom light green", "Green frame", and "Ltgreen side". Check the Stroke panel and be sure that the Stroke is None.

2. Group the selected objects. Change the Opacity to 100% and the Fill to Hex #33900 or any color you'd like (Fill panel).

3. Shift+select all the dark green areas: "Center background", "Dark green", "Dkgreen top", "Dkgreen bottom", "Dktop", "Dkcenter", and "Dkbottom",

Note: When you're drawing with the Pen tool, it is easier to get a perfectly straight line by pulling down a guide and clicking your points on it. This works better and more consistently than holding the Shift key as you draw.

Note: Because there are so many layers, it may be difficult to locate all the specific names. It is easier to select the object you want in the document, and then check the Layers panel to verify that you have the correct file.

Note: After you group, if you can't see the logo or center elements, just drag the grouped layer to the bottom of the Layers panel. You may need to do this with other grouped objects, as well.

as well as the dark green lines between each button. Group the selected objects (Modify|Group). Fill with Hex #339900 (or whatever fill you prefer) and change the Opacity to 100%.

4. Shift+select the white objects: "Top white area", "White text", "Whitetop", "Whitecenter", and "Whitebottom". Group them (Modify|Group). Fill them with white (be sure Opacity is set to 100%).

Exporting

You could simply save the PNG file and import it into Flash. Many people prefer to import a vector image as an Illustrator AI file. You can compare these options in Figures 8.39 and 8.40.

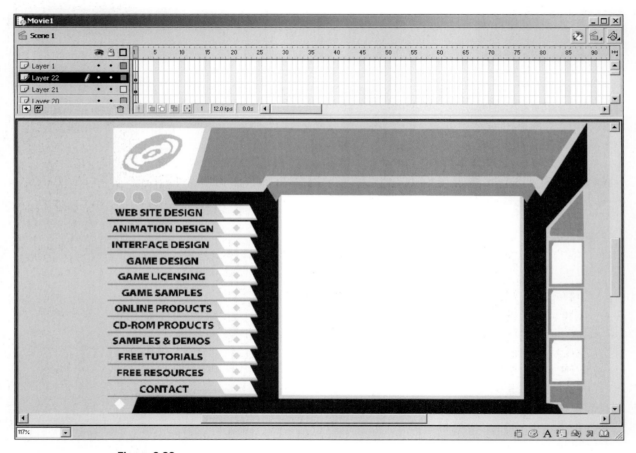

Figure 8.39

The Eyeland Studio interface saved as a PNG file and imported into Flash as a PNG.

The PNG file in Figure 8.39 has lost the center elements in the three little grouped circles. The bottom rectangle below the buttons also has lost its center element. The text has imported very poorly. In addition, this file took quite some time to import into Flash. On the other hand, the AI file (Figure 8.40) imported perfectly and almost instantly. To export as an Illustrator AI file, simply choose File|Export, choose Illustrator 7 in the Save As Type area, and click Save. Export the Eyeland.png, buttonslide.png, buttonstuff.png, and diamond_motion.png files as Illustrator 7 files. If you need more help on exporting, see Chapter 12.

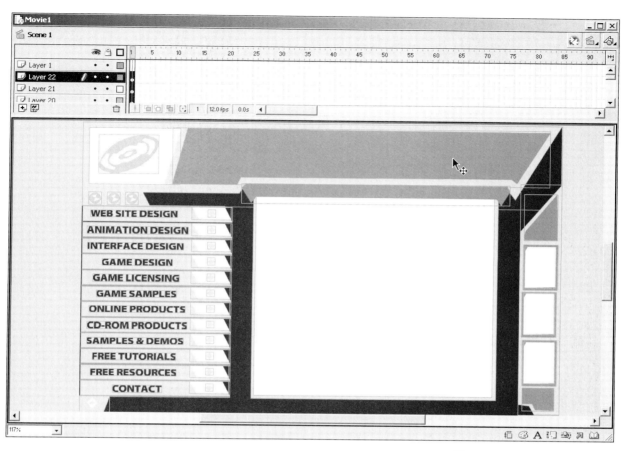

Figure 8.40

The Eyeland Studio interface exported as an Illustrator AI file and imported into Flash.

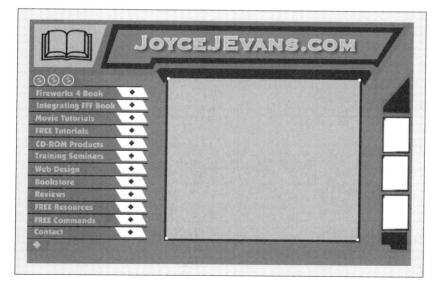

Figure 8.41

The Eyeland Studio interface customized with new colors, logo, and text.

Because this interface is yours to do with as you please (for your own use), you can alter the colors, text, and so on. Figure 8.41 shows an example of the interface with custom colors, logo, and text.

Moving On

You should now be comfortable working with the various Vector tools. You have an arsenal of different shapes and freeform tool techniques with which to draw custom objects and line drawings.

In Chapter 9, you will learn about working with bitmaps. You will use the selection and image editing tools of Fireworks 4 to manipulate photographs (bitmapped images).

Chapter 9

Bitmap Drawing and Editing

This chapter describes using the selection and image editing tools of Fireworks 4 to manipulate photographs (bitmapped images). Discover how to apply transparency expertly, achieve seamless compositions, and produce images without halos or jagged edges.

Bitmap Mode

Digitized photographs are composed of a grid of colors called *pixels*, the smallest component of a bitmapped image. (A bitmapped image is also known as a *raster* image or, in Fireworks, an *image object*.) Editing bitmaps involves adding, removing, or coloring individual pixels.

Pixels distinguish a bitmapped image from a vector image, which consists of paths. (A *path* is a line with at least two points.) Because vector objects (called *objects* in Fireworks) are produced using a mathematical calculation, they are fully scalable. Conversely, pixel images lose detail as they are scaled up, because each image contains a fixed number of pixels. When you scale up a bitmapped image in Fireworks, Fireworks has to guess which pixels need to be resampled to "fake" the detail in the increased space. This stretching of pixels most often results in what is known as a *pixelated image*. You can identify pixelated images by the obvious squares you can see or by the blurred details. The more an image is stretched, the worse it looks. On the other hand, if a bitmapped image is larger than necessary, you can scale it down; this process resamples the pixels into a smaller area and produces a sharper image with more detail.

Fireworks has a separate environment called Bitmap mode in which you work with bitmap images. Bitmap mode includes tools that you use only for editing bitmapped images, such as the selection tools and filters on the Xtras menu. Although you must be in Bitmap mode to edit bitmapped images, you usually do not have to make a conscious effort to open this mode. As soon as you click a bitmap tool, such as the Magic Wand or a Marquee tool, you are automatically in Bitmap mode. Plenty of visual clues alert you that you are using Bitmap mode. The most obvious is the blue-striped border around your image; others include a red circle with a white x at the bottom of your document window, and the document's Bitmap Mode title bar. To manually activate Bitmap mode, simply select one of the Marquee tools.

Working with Selection Tools

The selection tools are available only when you're editing bitmap images. The bitmap selection tools include the Rectangle Marquee, Oval Marquee, Polygon Lasso, Lasso, and Magic Wand. The selection tools let you isolate problem areas or select an area in which to apply effects, correct colors, or give other special attention. They are also used to select specific areas to copy or cut from an image. Each selection tool has a specific function and works in a specific way.

In this chapter, you will learn how to use each selection tool to its full advantage. The ability to make a specific selection will enable you to alter an area of an image without the fear of going over the lines and harming other areas not intended for editing. When you make a selection (indicated by a moving dotted line), only that area will be affected by anything you do or apply.

With all the selection tools, if what you selected is close to the shape you want and just needs a bit of cleaning up (a few stray pixels here and there), you can smooth the selection by choosing Modify|Marquee|Smooth and then choosing the number of pixels you'd like to smooth. You can also expand or contract the selection by choosing Modify|Marquee|Expand or Contract.

Rectangle and Oval Marquee Tools

The Rectangle and Oval Marquee tools make selections according to their respective shapes. Click the tool of your choice and click and drag over an area of the image. To move a selection made with a Marquee tool, hold down the Alt/Option key and drag to another location in your document. To draw a constrained shape (a perfect circle or square), hold down the Shift key while dragging.

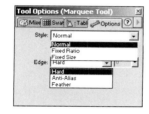

Figure 9.1
Marquee Options panel.

You can also set constraints on both the Rectangle and Oval Marquee tools by double-clicking the marquee icon. Figure 9.1 shows the options included on both Marquee Options panel submenus.

After you make a selection, it is surrounded by a moving dotted line, sometimes referred to as "marching ants." This area is isolated from the rest of the image. Within the selection area, you can colorize; add effects, fills, textures, and gradients; and perform a number of other alterations.

Changing the Shape of a Selection

If you've made your selection using a rectangle or a circle, but you want to add details that are outside of this shape, you can easily do so. To add to the selection, put your cursor just inside the selected area, hold down the Shift key, and drag with the Rectangle, Oval, or Lasso tool to enclose the new area, ending inside the current selection. To add a totally new selection, simply press the Shift key and make the selection. Subtracting from a selection works the same way, but you press the Alt/Option key instead of Shift.

Modifying a Selection

You can choose from a number of options when you need to modify a selection. To make a modification, choose Modify|Marquee and select any of the options, such as Expand, Contract, Smooth, Border, Feather, Select Inverse, or Select Similar. The other options are to Save Selection or Restore Selection; you use these options in the Selective JPEG function of optimizing images (discussed in Chapter 11).

Magic Wand

The Magic Wand tool works differently than all the other selection tools. The Magic Wand tool makes selections based on color. You determine the range of color in the selection by setting the tolerance. To set the tolerance of the Magic Wand tool, you use the Magic Wand tool's Options tab, shown in Figure 9.2. The higher you set the Tolerance, the more colors that will be added to the selection; 0 means one pixel, one color.

Figure 9.2
The Magic Wand tool's Options tab.

Polygon Lasso

The Polygon Lasso tool makes precise selections of irregular-shaped areas. To use the Polygon Lasso tool, select it and click where you want to begin the selection. Keep adding points by clicking around the area you are selecting until the selection is complete. Double-click at the starting point to close the selection. You will see blue lines as you click another point; if the line isn't conforming to your shape, then add another point (click) a bit closer to the last point.

Applying Feathering to a Marquee Edge

Feathering the edges of a selection helps you move a portion of one image and make it part of another image, avoiding sharp, distinctive edges. The feathered edge transitions from opaque to transparent. Vignettes are also produced using feathered edges. Follow these steps to apply feathering to any marquee edge:

1. Open the background image called HAbackground.png from the Chapter 9 resources folder.

2. Double-click the Oval Marquee tool to open its Options panel. Change the Edge to Feather and use 30 for the amount of feather (the larger the number, the larger the area affected). Drag a selection in the background, as shown in Figure 9.3.

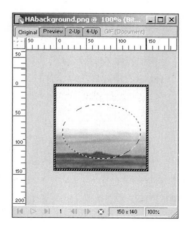

Figure 9.3
A selection made using the Oval Marquee selection tool.

Note: The surrounding area is black because the canvas color is black on the Habackground.png file (see Figure 9.5).

3. Choose Modify|Marquee|Select Inverse and press Delete (this deletes the surrounding area); the selection will look like Figure 9.4 with the selection still active. Figure 9.5 shows the feathered selection with the marquee selection off (Ctrl+D/Cmd+D).

The background for the icons on the bottom of the Horse Adventures Web site was produced using this technique. Figure 9.6 shows this background with an image on top of it.

Figure 9.4
The selection inverted and the inverse area deleted.

Figure 9.5
The feathered selection after the unwanted background areas that are part of the inverse selection have been deleted.

Figure 9.6
The finished feathered selection used as an icon.

Repairing and Altering Images

Old photos are great candidates for repair, but almost any image you use probably will need something fixed. You need to take special care when repairing an image with texture, patterns, or shadows. Scanned images usually need some kind of adjustment. The quality of digital images has improved greatly in the last couple of years, but some will still require adjustments or repairs using the tools described in the following sections.

Using the Rubber Stamp

The Rubber Stamp tool works the way you would expect a rubber stamp to work: You press it in the ink (over a part of the image) and then press the stamp's impression in another area. The Rubber Stamp tool works only on bitmap/raster images. It is similar to the Brush tool, except you are painting with an image.

The Rubber Stamp tool excels at covering blemishes and removing small items (or large items, if you are adventuresome) from a photo. It gets really challenging when you try to repair a highly textured or patterned area. You'll find a movie tutorial called RubberStamp.mov demonstrating some of the basic steps in the Movie Tutorials folder on the companion CD-ROM. To learn how to stamp, where to stamp, and how to get the stamping samples, follow these steps:

1. Open the whitehorse.png file from the Chapter 9 resources folder. (This horse photo was donated by Darryl Larson Productions, **www.darryllarson.com**.) The horse has a brown spot on its forehead (it may be a natural mark, but for demonstration purposes, you will remove it) and a scratch on its belly. In Figure 9.7, arrows point to the two areas that you will repair.

Figure 9.7
Arrows pointing to the problem areas to be repaired.

2. Zoom in to 400%; you will need to be able to see the detail. Double-click the Rubber Stamp tool to access the Tool Options panel. Set the Source to Aligned and the Sample to Image with a Tip Size of 5. To set the sampling point, hold the Alt/Option key and click with the Rubber Stamp tool. See Figure 9.8, which shows where the sampling point is being taken as well as the Rubber Stamp Tool Options panel.

3. Click the white scratch using the sample point as paint, and then move the sample point for the center of the blemish and the right side. See Figures 9.9 and 9.10 for the other sample points necessary to cover the scratch. After each sample point has been set, click the scratch with the Rubber Stamp tool (see the rubberstamp.mov movie tutorial). Figure 9.11 shows the image with the scratch removed.

Rubber Stamp Options

Double-clicking on the Rubber Stamp tool accesses the Rubber Stamp options. For the Source, you have the option of Aligned or Fixed. Aligned moves in correspondence to your mouse movements. When you release the mouse, you can again begin to touch up with the sampling point in the same position in relation to your mouse. Fixed puts the sampling points in one spot, and it stays there. If you release the mouse and click again in a different area, you will still copy the same sample area—it does not move as your mouse moves.

Sample determines if the sampling point is being derived from inside the image itself only. Document allows you to sample from anywhere in the document. For instance, you could sample from a vector object into the bitmap image object.

The Stamp area determines the softness of the edges. The box with a number in it is the Tip size.

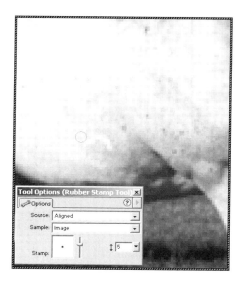

Figure 9.8
The first sampling point and the Tool Options panel.

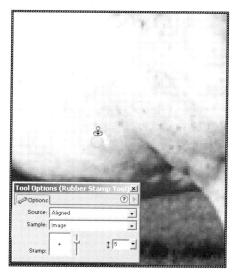

Figure 9.9
A sample point taken from beneath the center of the scratch.

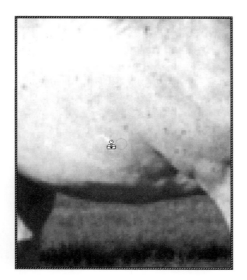

Figure 9.10
A sample point taken from the outside right edge of the scratch.

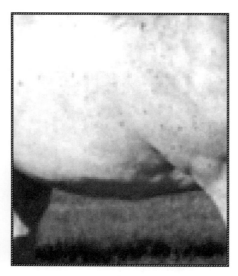

Figure 9.11
The scratch removed.

Note: You can use the Rubber Stamp by clicking and dragging, but that technique usually yields a pattern.

4. Zoom in to 800% to better see the blemish on the head. This part of the image has more shading, so you will need to sample multiple times from the areas around the head to get a good, clean repair. Figure 9.12 shows the sampling points needed. Click often, or you may get a distinct pattern.

You can see a sample of a major repair done entirely by using the Rubber Stamp tool and the Brush tool in the Color Studio. The original image is a white horse with a rider. The rider as well as the bridle was removed. It was particularly challenging to avoid patterns; I used many, many sample points, as you've seen in this section. I used the Brush tool at different opacity settings to add shading back to the jaw once the bridle was removed.

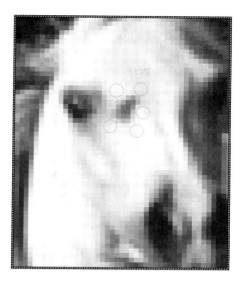

Figure 9.12
The many sample areas needed to get a good repair.

Adjusting Hue and Saturation

The Hue and Saturation filter changes the color hue of a selected image or a selection. This filter works great to add subtle color or to totally change the color of an image or object. This is the filter to use when you want to change the overall color of an image. You've seen Web sites that use the same image header throughout the site, except that different sections utilize different colors; this tool is often used to achieve that effect.

You can use the Hue and Saturation filter on the collage used for Horse Adventures. (You will see how to make this collage later in the chapter.) The same collage of horses is used for the Horse Adventures bookstore. To distinguish the bookstore from the game, the header was changed to what looks like a duotone. The collage.jpg image is copyrighted and is for your practice only. To get this effect, follow these steps:

1. Open collage.jpg from the Chapter 9 resources folder.

2. Choose Xtras|Adjust Color|Hue/Saturation. Select the Colorize option and type "15" for the Hue, "28" for the Saturation, and "51" for the Lightness. When you have the look you like, click OK. Figure 9.13 shows the result.

Note: To determine which color you want, be sure the Preview option is selected. Then, you can just move the sliders and see onscreen the effect of the changes.

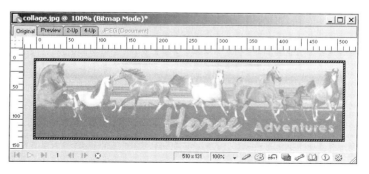

Figure 9.13
Hue and Saturation applied to the horse collage.

Masking Images

Fireworks 4 enables you to combine an image with a path or use an image as a mask object. You don't apply a mask directly to the image—you apply it to a mask object, which resides above the image to be masked. A mask object contains a fill, which affects the pixels of the image or object that is being masked.

A mask distinguishes the boundaries of an image that you want to cut out to a specific shape. The fill color or texture determines how much of the image will show through the mask. In the areas of a mask that are white, the underlying area will be totally invisible. In the areas of a mask that are solid black, the image will be totally visible. The varying degrees of gray determine the amount of transparency.

Using a Bitmap Mask

You can draw a bitmap mask by using the bitmap tools, such as the Paint Brush, Pen, Rectangle, Oval, or Polygon (using the drawing tools is discussed in Chapter 8). You can produce some pretty detailed masks using the bitmap drawing tools. To demonstrate using an existing image (made using the bitmap drawing tools), follow these steps:

1. Open the horsetocutout.png file from the Chapter 9 resource folder on this book's companion CD-ROM. Figure 9.14 shows the horse you will remove from its background. (This horse photo was donated by **www.platinumarabians.com**.)

Using Bitmap Objects

In the example of cutting a horse out of its surroundings, the bitmap happens to be a black mask. You could use any image to achieve the same results. You may get an image to be used as a mask from a client, or you can use a mask produced in another program. For instance, Photoshop masks are importable into Fireworks, where they remain intact.

Figure 9.14
A horse that needs to be extracted from its surroundings.

2. Open the horsemask.png file from the Chapter 9 resource folder. Figure 9.15 shows the bitmap object that you will use to remove the horse.

3. Drag the horsemask image on top of the horsetocutout image and position it perfectly over the horse. You may need to zoom in to see better.

4. Shift+select both the horsemask and the horsetocutout images.

Figure 9.15
The bitmap object used to remove the horse from its surroundings.

Figure 9.16
(Left) The horse has been removed from its surroundings.

Figure 9.17
(Right) The Layers panel with the horse mask applied.

5. Choose Modify|Mask|Group As Mask; Figure 9.16 shows the result. Figure 9.17 shows the masked object in the Layers panel.

Adding Transparency to a Mask

Adding transparency to a mask is the most frequently used technique for seamlessly blending images or for removing parts of an image. You achieve transparency by using a black and white gradient fill in the masking object or image. Wherever there is black, the underlying image will be visible; wherever there is white, the underlying image will be invisible. The shades of gray render the transparency according to the lightness or darkness of the gray. To add transparency to a mask, follow these steps:

1. Open the rearinghorse.png file (a photo of Shah Azim, donated by **www.paragonarabians.com**) and the sky.png file from the Chapter 9 resources folder. You will cut out this horse later in this chapter, but you can borrow the finished version to demonstrate masking and transparency.

2. Drag the horse onto the sky and position it as seen in Figure 9.18.

3. To add a mask object to the horse, click the yellow folder icon in the bottom of the Layers panel to add a new layer.

4. Select the Rectangle drawing tool and drag a rectangle over the whole horse.

Figure 9.18
The horse added to the sky image.

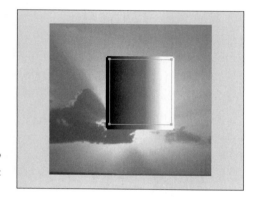

Figure 9.19
A rectangle filled with a gradient to be used as a mask.

Note: If you want to preserve the transparency mask or Alpha channel (the transparent areas of a bitmap image) from Fireworks to be used in other applications, use the PNG32 format for export and set the Matte color to Transparent in the Optimize panel.

To open a PNG file that contains an Alpha channel in Photoshop, use the Magic Wand tool to select the dark area containing the transparency, and then delete the selected area to return to the correct display of the image.

5. Open the Fill panel (Shift+F7), select Linear from the Fill category, and choose white, black from the Preset Gradient Color Sets. Figure 9.19 shows the result so far.

6. Shift+select the rectangle and the horse image (select from the Layers panel, because you can't see the horse to select it on the canvas) and choose Modify|Mask|Group As Mask. Notice that where the rectangle is black, you can see the image, and where the rectangle is white, the horse image fades into the image below; see Figure 9.20. However, this gradient needs to be altered—the horse is too faded. In the next section, you will see how to edit the gradient. Save the image as MYhorseinsky (File|Save As). There is a copy of horseinsky.png in the Chapter 9 resources folder if you'd rather use it.

Editing a Masked Group

With the release of Fireworks 4, editing a masked group is easier than ever. After you apply a mask, a pen icon appears in the Layers panel in the mask icon. To edit the horse in the sky, follow these steps:

1. Open the MYhorseinsky.png file you saved, or open the horseinsky.png file in the Chapter 9 resources folder.

Figure 9.20
The mask applied to the horse image.

2. Click the pen icon in the Layers panel (located in the bitmap mask icon).

3. The gradient handles are now apparent. Click and drag the circle handle to just under the horse's jaw, and drag the square handle down toward the bottom of the horse. The exact position of the gradient is visible in Figure 9.21. It's great to be able to alter the mask visually, even after it's been applied. Figure 9.22 shows the end result.

Figure 9.21
(Left) The gradient handles in the new positions, altering the gradient.

Figure 9.22
(Right) The horse rising from the clouds.

PROJECT Cutting a Horse from Its Background

If you make a lot of collages or image compositions, you will most likely use this technique often. To cut a horse from its background, follow these steps:

1. Open zim.jpg from the Chapter 9 resources folder on the companion CD-ROM. The photo of Shah Azim was donated by **www.paragonarabians.com** for use in this book and for the collage for the Horse Adventures Web site.

2. Double-click the Polygon Lasso tool. In the resulting Tool Options panel, choose Feather, using a 3-pixel width.

3. Select the edges of the horse. If your selection is overinclusive or underinclusive, use the Shift key to add to the selection or the Alt/Option key to subtract. Figure 9.23 shows the selection. Figure 9.24 shows the little area between the front legs that you need to remove from the selection. When you hold down the Alt/Option key, a little minus sign (-) appears next to the Polygon Lasso tool, indicating you will be taking away from the selection.

Figure 9.23
(Left) The horse is selected.

Figure 9.24
(Right) The Polygon Lasso tool displays a minus sign when you hold down the Alt/Option key to subtract from the selection.

4. Once your selection is the way you want it (zoom in to check the edges), choose Modify|Marquee|Select Inverse. Press the Delete key to remove the background. Figure 9.25 shows the cut-out horse.

Figure 9.25
The horse cut out from its background.

5. To test your edges, choose Modify|Canvas Color and select white. Figure 9.26 shows the horse on a white background. It looks pretty good. You might want to take the brush tool and sharpen the edges around the hoof, depending on the application you will use the image for. In this case, it's part of a collage, and the edge sharpness isn't vital. Choose Modify|Canvas Color and select Custom and black for the color. Figure 9.27 shows the horse on a black background.

Figure 9.26
(Left) The cut-out horse on a white background.

Figure 9.27
(Right) The cut-out horse on a black background.

6. For this particular example, the horse will be part of a collage. So, simply save it as horse.png. If you want to use this image as is, you need to export it. Because this particular image is a photo, it is best suited to the JPEG format. Select JPEG in the Optimize panel with a Quality of 80. If the background on which you are placing this image is anything other than white, select the background color from the Matte settings (or type in the Hex number) and export (discussed in Chapter 12).

> **Note:** If neither background looks good, just choose Edit|Undo until you get back to the selection. Add or subtract as necessary and repeat Step 4. The black background in Figure 9.22 initially had a slight lighter edge; I went back and altered the selection and lowered the feather to 2, to help sharpen the hoofs a bit in the white background.

PROJECT   A Composite Image

A *composite image* is a composition containing pieces of other images or compositions. Composite images often combine elements to convey an idea, thought, or concept. Putting together all the pieces can be challenging, because you want each item to blend seamlessly and appear to belong in the composition. In this project, you will add the horse you cut out in the "Using a Bitmap Mask" section to a composite image and make it blend into the edge of the header. Because this is a real Web site header and copyrighted, I don't provide all the images; but I give all the instructions. To begin, follow these steps:

1. Determine the size you want your composition to be. In this project, the background is an image of a sunset. If you are using a photo background like this one and are not concerned about image detail, open the image and choose Modify|Image Size, deselect the Constrain Proportions option, and type in the dimensions you want: 510×131 for this sunset background. The distortion in this case is a desired effect; you're primarily interested in the color.

2. Prepare each image that you are going to use in the composition. The horse you masked in the "Using a Bitmap Mask" section is used in this composition. In fact, all the horses used in the composition (except the horse you cut out using the selection tools) were produced this way.

> **Note:** The other horses in the collage were cut out by masking them with a bitmap and were then placed on the collage. These horse photos were donated by Darryll Larson Productions and Paragon Platinum Plus Arabians; you can find out more about each company in Appendix A.

Note: You may have images that you want to cut out exactly, such as the horses; or you may have loose selections that a mask will cover, or possibly a selection you cut out using the feather techniques. All the masking and selection techniques discussed in this chapter can be used to prepare your images for a collage.

3. Once you have prepared the images, you are ready to assemble the collage. Open the collage.png file and the rearinghorse.png file from the Chapter 9 resources folder on the companion CD-ROM. The horse is cut out, and no mask is applied to this version.

4. Drag the horse into the left corner of the header, as shown in Figure 9.28.

Figure 9.28
The horse added to the collage.

5. The cut-off edge of the horse doesn't look nice against the background. To make it fade into the black area, add a new layer in the Layers panel. Select the Rectangle tool and draw a rectangle to be used as the masking object over the horse. In the Fill panel, add a linear fill with the preset gradient of white, black. You can see the result in Figure 9.29.

Figure 9.29
The mask object added to the horse.

6. Shift+select the rectangle and the horse from the Layers panel and choose Modify|Mask|Mask As Group. Figure 9.30 shows the result, which is definitely too light.

7. With the Pointer tool, select the masked horse. Click the pen icon with the mask icon in the Layers panel. Move the gradient handles until the horse blends into the black area. Figure 9.31 shows the gradient position.

Figure 9.30
The added mask is almost totally transparent.

Figure 9.31
The gradient position to make the horse blend into the black area.

Moving On

You should now be comfortable making selections and using masks. You are now able to cut out any image and blend it seamlessly into any other image you'd like. You learned in this chapter how to alter the color of an image, how to cut out a portion of an image, and how to make a feathered selection and use masks.

In Chapter 10, you will learn how to make several different kinds of navigation aids, including the new pop-up menus and disjoint rollovers.

Chapter 10

Navigation Magic

This chapter provides you with several Web page navigation solutions. You will learn how to make the popular new pop-up menus, as well as navigation bars, disjointed rollovers, and simple rollovers, which can be made interactive even if you don't know any JavaScript code.

Navigation Solutions

Navigation is the single most important part of any Web site, enabling the user either to have an enjoyable experience or—if the navigation is not well planned—to have a frustrating experience. Although Fireworks can't plan effective navigation for you, it can make the buttons and elements you need for the navigation.

Using the Button Editor

The Button Editor is one of the easiest editors to use. Don't let its simplicity fool you, though, because it significantly streamlines your workflow by enabling you to give the same button up to four different states in one location.

The majority of Web navigation buttons on the Internet (such as rollovers) are made interactive using JavaScript. By using the Button Editor, you can design interactive JavaScript buttons without having any knowledge of JavaScript code; Fireworks generates the necessary JavaScript code for you. You can produce up to four states for a button simply by changing the appearance of each state. Any button produced with the Button Editor automatically is made into a symbol. If you want more than one button, you simply drag another instance onto the canvas from the Library panel.

The following are the four different states of a button:

- *Up*—The default appearance of the button as first seen by the user.

- *Over*—The way the button looks when the user passes the mouse pointer over it. The Over state alerts users that this button is "hot," meaning that it leads to another page of the Web site or to an anchor on a Web page, when clicked.

- *Down*—The appearance of the button after it has been clicked. This state often looks as though the button has been pressed down.

- *Over While Down*—The appearance of the Down state button when the mouse pointer moves over it.

Another important feature of the Button Editor is that when you alter the text on the Up state button, the text is automatically updated for the other states as well, eliminating the need to change the text on all four buttons.

Making a Button Symbol

You can make a button directly in the Button Editor or convert an existing button into a button symbol and edit it in the Button Editor. A button symbol encapsulates up to four different button states and moves as a unit. Instead of spending lots of time reproducing similar buttons, you can simply place a symbol onto your canvas and edit the text and link. To use the Button Editor to make a button for the Horse Adventures Web page, follow these steps:

1. To make a button from scratch, open a new document (File|New); a size of 200×50 pixels will work here. Choose Custom and select black for the canvas color. Then choose Insert|New Button to open the Button Editor.

2. The Button Editor has several different tabs. When you click each one, Fireworks gives you a description of what the corresponding state does. The Up state tab should be the active one. Select a drawing tool and draw your button anywhere in the Button Editor. For this example, choose the Ellipse tool and drag a circle in the Button Editor. In the Info panel, change the button size to 9×9 pixels. In the Fill panel, choose Red for the Fill.

3. Select the Pen tool. Click a starting point and an ending point to draw a horizontal straight line. In the Stroke panel, choose Pencil from the Stroke Category, 1-Pixel Hard for the Stroke Name, a Tip size of 1, and a Color of white. In the Info panel, make the line 138 pixels long (W) and press Enter/Return. Using the Pointer tool, place the line next to the red circle, touching its right edge.

4. Click the Over tab and click the Copy Up Graphic button (see Figure 10.1) to put a copy of the Up state in the Over state's editing box. Now you can change the fill of the Over state, and you can add a stroke or Live Effect to the button, to the text, or to both. Be sure the button (and text, if any) is selected so that the effects are added. For this example you will draw a little yellow flare to use for the rollover effect.

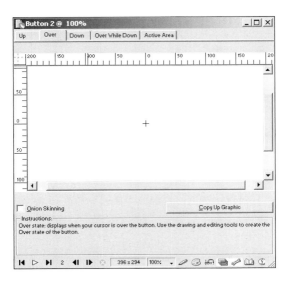

Figure 10.1
The Copy Up Graphic button in the Button Editor.

Note: If you want to convert a button graphic into a button symbol, choose Insert|Convert To Symbol, select Button as the animation type, and click OK. If you double-click the button, the Button Editor will open.

Specific Sized Buttons

You can use the Info panel (Windows|Info or Alt+Shift+F12/ Option+Shift+F12), which is housed with the Stroke and Fill panels by default, while you are in the Button Editor. To produce a button of an exact size, type the dimensions in the Height and Width boxes in the Info panel and then press Enter/ Return to activate the changes. If you click on the canvas or elsewhere and do not press the Enter/Return key, your changes will not be activated.

Note: If you're only making a button or two, select the Text tool and type the text you want on the button. Remember that the text is fully editable and can easily be changed later. Use the center-text alignment from the Text Editor so that the text maintains its centered position. If you are making multiple buttons, the technique I show for the navigational bar is much better than the one for making individual buttons.

Custom Buttons

For any of the button states, you can import a button, draw a unique button, or drag a button from another document, instead of using the Copy Graphic Up/Down button.

Figure 10.2
The flare blown up and the stokes highlighted.

5. The little yellow flare that you'll use for the Over state was made visually using a blown-up view. We used the Brush tool with a stroke using Air Brush, Basic, Tip size of 2, and Color of yellow. The highest concentration of color appears in the center. For the lighter edges, double-click the Tip image. In the Options tab, lower the Ink Amount to 50%, and then paint short lines on the ends of the darker ones. A small dot was made with the brush for the little piece of yellow to the right side. You'll see in a moment what it's for. Figure 10.2 shows the lines highlighted so you can see them. The file named flare.png, which you can open and zoom in on, is also supplied in the Chapter 10 resources folder.

6. Using the Pointer tool, drag a selection around the entire flare and group it (Modify|Group or Ctrl+G/Cmd+G). Line up the flare and the red circle so that the little yellow section on the right is in the center of the circle; see Figure 10.3.

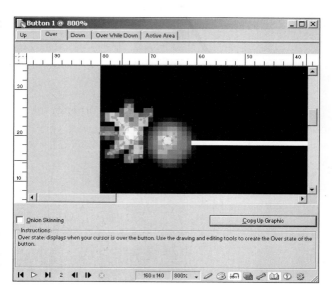

Figure 10.3
The flare lined up with the rest of the button.

7. The Down and the Over While Down states are not used in this example. Click the Active Area tab; you will see a slice added to your document automatically. The Active Area is set to Automatic by default and generates a slice large enough to cover all the button states. There is one slice for all four button states; you can change the size by dragging the slice points.

8. If you want to add links to your buttons, click the Active Area tab and then the Link Wizard button. See the "Link Wizard" sidebar for the details.

Link Wizard

This image shows the Export Settings tab of the Link Wizard; you can select a preset, or click the Edit button to have access to the full range of optimization options.

In the Link tab, you add the URL you want to link to, the alternate text, and any text you'd like to appear in the status bar of the browser.

The other two tabs in the Link Wizard are the Target tab, where you set a target window or frame for the link to open in, and the Filename tab, where you name the button either manually or by using Fireworks' auto-naming feature.

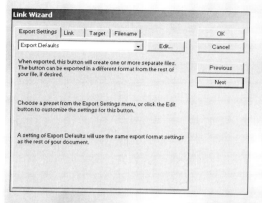

The Link Wizard's Export Settings tab.

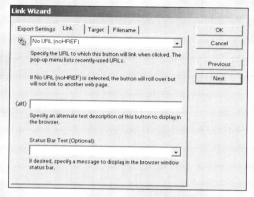

The Link Wizard's Link tab.

9. Close the Button Editor by clicking the X in the top-right corner of the editor. An instance of the button is automatically placed in your document, indicated by the little arrow in the corner. Figure 10.4 shows the instance of the symbol in your document.

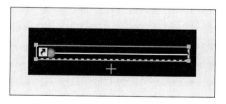

Figure 10.4

An instance of the button made in the Button Editor on the document.

10. The symbol is automatically added to the Library panel (Window|Library). If you want to add more buttons to your document, you drag them from the Library panel by clicking and dragging either the button symbol or the name of the symbol onto your document. (You don't need any more symbols for this example.) Figure 10.5 shows the symbol in the Library panel.

11. To save this symbol for use in making a navigation bar, you need to export the symbol. In the Library panel, click the right-pointing arrow and choose Export Symbols. In the Export Symbols dialog box, select the symbol you want to export and click Export. A window will open in which you name and save your symbol. This symbol has been saved as HAbuttonsymbol.png in the Chapter 10 resources folder.

Figure 10.5

The button symbol added to the Library panel.

12. You can easily preview your new button by clicking on the Preview tab in your document window, passing your mouse over the button, and clicking the button to see the different states.

Editing Button Symbols

Editing the buttons you have made is quite simple. The following is a list of the different portions of your buttons and the steps for editing each portion:

- *Text*—Select the text you want to edit, open the Object panel (Window|Object or Alt+F2/Option+F2), and type in the new text. This technique works only if the button symbol has text on it.

- *Button Characteristics*—Double-click to open the Button Editor, click the tab for the state(s) you'd like to alter, and make your changes. Close the Button Editor when you are done.

- *Imported Symbols*—When you edit an instance of a button, you break the link with the original object, allowing you to make changes in the new document without affecting any documents containing the original symbol. To update an imported button, click the right-pointing arrow in the Library panel and choose Update from the pop-up menu.

- *Active Area*—If you want to change the active area of the button slice, you must do so from within the Button Editor.

Using the Library Panel

Libraries are timesavers, because they enable you to use symbols over and over again. Because buttons are used frequently, managing them through the Library panel not only is convenient but also helps your workflow. All you have to do is drag and drop a symbol from the Library panel into your document or share a library with a co-worker.

Two types of libraries exist: the type that a document contains by default, and the type that you can generate and save. The default library is generated as soon as you convert an object into a symbol and includes the symbols the Button Editor adds. This library is saved along with the document; when you reopen the document, the library is available. For instance, if you'd like a set of buttons to be available for other projects, you can save the library for use in any document. The next section explains how to do this.

Exporting Libraries

If you have a series of symbols that make up a navigation system, you may want to save the set as a library. To save a library of symbols in your current document to use again or to share with someone else, follow these steps:

1. Open the HAbuttonsymbol.png file from the Chapter 10 resources folder. Open the Library panel by choosing Window|Library.

Note: When you edit an original symbol, if it's been used in other documents, you can update all instances simultaneously by choosing Update from the Library Options (F11) pop-up menu. If you try to edit an imported symbol, a warning will open telling you that an edit will break the link to the original symbol.

Button Changes

Any change you make to an individual button produces a new symbol. For instance, if you change the text, a new symbol is placed in the library with the new text; if you change the button color of just one button, a new symbol is placed in the library. To learn how to keep all the buttons of a Web page as one symbol, see the "Navigation Bars" section later in the chapter.

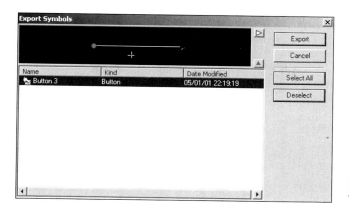

Figure 10.6
The Export Symbols dialog box.

2. Click the right-pointing arrow and choose Export Symbols from the pop-up menu to open the Export Symbols dialog box (see Figure 10.6).

3. Select the symbols you want to export (only those in the current document will be available). If you want to export them all, choose Select All; if you want several in a row, Shift+click to select the group; if you want to pick and choose, press Ctrl/Option and click the desired symbols. When you are done, click Export.

4. Name your library, choose where you want to save it, and click Save. A library can be saved anywhere you like—but when you import it, you must be able to remember where you saved it.

Importing Libraries

To use a library that you have saved in your current document or to use a saved library from another document, you need to import it. To import a saved library, follow these steps:

1. Open the Library panel (if it isn't already open) by choosing Window|Library.

2. From the Options pop-up menu, choose Import Symbols.

3. Locate your saved library; select it, and click Open.

4. The Import Symbols dialog box opens with the list of symbols in the library you saved. Choose the symbol (or symbols) that you want and click Import.

Navigation Bars

A navigation bar, also called a *nav bar*, contains a series of buttons that usually appears on every page of a Web site. In this section, you will see how to make an entire navigational system into an editable symbol.

Frequently Used Libraries

If you think you will use a library often, save it or move it to the Fireworks Library folder: Macromedia\Fireworks 4\Configurations\Libraries. By placing your files there, you can easily access them by choosing Insert|Libraries.

Using Editable Button Symbols for Navigation

In this exercise, you will make buttons with Up, Over, and Down states and combine a series of buttons with different text to use as a navigation bar. Normally, if you change text on a symbol, Fireworks makes a new symbol; if you want to change the button itself, you must edit each individual symbol. This exercise will show you how to produce symbols with different text and still be able to edit the button properties only once to update all the other symbols in the nav bar.

Making a Button

To make a navigation system with editable buttons, you need a button to start with. To make a button, follow these steps:

1. Open a new document that is large enough to hold a button. A size of 200×75 pixels and a white canvas color will work fine for this example.

2. Choose Insert|New Button and make a button with three or four states. Select the Rectangle tool and draw a rectangle in the Button Editor. In the Info panel, set the size to 100 pixels wide by 30 high and center the best you can over the cross. In the Fill panel, select a dark blue fill. In the Effect panel, choose Shadow And Glow|Drop Shadow and accept the defaults.

3. Click the Over tab. Click the Copy Up Graphic button. You will now see the same graphic you have in the Up state. To change the color for the Over state, click the color well in the Fill panel and change it to a bright green.

4. Click the Down tab. Click the Copy Over Graphic button. Make the changes you'd like to see when someone clicks your button. For this example, go to the Effect panel, select the Drop Shadow, and click the Trash icon to delete the shadow. Choose Bevel And Emboss|Inset Emboss. Close the Button Editor. Figure 10.7 shows the blank button symbol in your document.

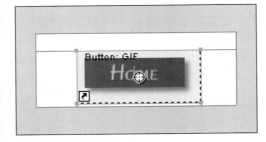

Figure 10.7
The button symbol in the document.

5. A symbol for the new button is now in the Library panel. You will need to open this panel (Window|Library or F11).

Adding the Text

Adding the text as follows will allow you to edit the appearance of the button one time and have the changes appear in the entire nav bar:

1. Double-click the instance of the blank button to open the Button Editor.

2. The first and most important thing to do is add a new layer. Click the yellow folder icon in the Layers panel to do so.

3. Select the Type tool. In the Type Editor, type "Home". The font used in this example is Ruzicka Freehand RomanSC, 24-point, gold. Select the Center Alignment button. Click OK. Center the text on your button.

4. To get the text for the other states in the same position as the Up state, select the text and copy (Ctrl+C/Cmd+C), click the Over tab, and paste (Ctrl+V/Cmd+V). While the pasted text is still selected, change the fill color to a dark blue, select the Down tab, and repeat the copy and paste and fill color. Although it is a bit more work initially, you'll be glad you did it this way if you ever need to edit the buttons' appearance. Close the Button Editor. You will see how to use this button and change the text in the next section.

5. Save this button as samplebutton.png (also in the Chapter 10 resources folder).

Making the Nav Bar

You will be making a fully editable nav bar with buttons and individual text all as one symbol. To assemble the nav bar, follow these steps:

1. Open a new document to begin building the navigation bar. Choose File|New, enter a size of 600×80 pixels, and specify a white canvas.

2. Open the bar.png file from the Chapter 10 resources folder. Open the samplebutton.png file you made in the previous section or from the Chapter 10 resources folder.

3. Select your new document to make it active, choose Insert|New Symbol, and choose Graphic. Drag the bar into the Symbol Editor.

4. Select the samplebutton document to make it active, open the Library panel, and drag four instances of the button symbol from the Library panel on top of the bar in the Symbol editor. Position the first and last buttons where you want them; don't worry about the middle ones. To align all the buttons, Shift+select them, choose Modify|Align|Distribute Widths (if the buttons are horizontal), and choose Modify|Align|Center Horizontal. You can see the horizontal alignment in Figure 10.8. We placed a guide line near the top to help line up the buttons.

Note: You didn't need to close the Button Editor before adding the text; I had you close it only to show you the symbol in the document. You will edit it next to add the text.

Note: Double-check to be sure that the text is in Layer 2. Sometimes, even if you select one layer, you are returned to the first layer mysteriously. The text *must* be on a layer that is not shared.

Note: The bar.png file is simply a large button. If you want to make it yourself, select the Rectangle tool and draw a rectangle. Change the size in the Info panel to 494×60 pixels. In the Fill panel, choose a bright green color. In the Effect panel, choose Bevel And Emboss|Outer Bevel with a Bevel Edge Shape of Frame 1, a Width of 6, a Softness of 3, and a color of dark blue. Leave the other settings at their default. Remember, you can check the settings used in any PNG file made in Fireworks by selecting the object and checking the various panels.

Figure 10.8

A series of buttons
aligned horizontally.

5. Open the Layers panel (Window|Layers or F2). Select the current layer, which is probably called Layer 1. Click the right-pointing arrow, and from the Options pop-up menu choose Share This Layer. Doing so adds the large background graphic to the other states of the buttons and avoids the appearance of white boxes around the buttons when the mouse hovers over them. If you want to change the text on the buttons *do not* close the Symbol editor but continue to the "Editing the Text" section. If you did close the Symbol editor, you can simply double-click the symbol to open the editor.

Editing the Text

I'm sure you don't want all your buttons to say "Home". To change the other buttons, follow these steps:

1. If your Symbol editor is still open, select the second button symbol. (If it isn't, double-click the symbol in your document to open the Symbol editor.) Open the Object panel (Window|Object or Alt+F2/Option+F2). Highlight the Button Text, which is "Home", and type in "Products". Press the Enter/Return key. A window will open asking if you want to edit all instances of the button or just the current; select Current.

2. Repeat for button three and change the text to "Company", and repeat again using "E-mail" for button four.

3. Close the Symbol editor when you are done. Test your nav bar by selecting the Preview button and mousing over the buttons. Figure 10.9 shows the completed navigation bar as a symbol in your document.

Figure 10.9

The completed navigation bar as
a single symbol in the document.

Editing the Navigation Buttons

Editing the buttons' appearance on this sample navigation bar is now very easy to do. To begin editing, follow these steps:

1. Open the SampleNavigationBar.png file from the Chapter 10 resources folder if you've closed it.

2. Open the Library panel (F11). You will notice a symbol for the blank button and the navigation bar.

3. Double-click the blank button symbol to edit it. The warning in Figure 10.10 will appear; it simply lets you know that the link will be broken from the original button you started with. Click OK.

4. Select the button and change the color or apply a style. In this example, I applied a glass style that I made. You can find two styles in the file called glass.stl in the Chapter 10 resources folder.

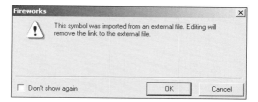

Figure 10.10
The warning dialog box that opens when you edit the blank button symbol.

5. In the Up state, select the blueglass style (click it in the Styles panel); in the Fill panel, change the color to a brighter blue. In the Effect panel, choose Shadow And Glow|Drop Shadow and accept the defaults.

6. For the Over state, select the button and apply the greenglass style (click it in the Styles panel). In the Effect panel, add a drop shadow.

7. For the Down state, select the button and apply the greenglass style. In the Effect panel, choose Bevel And Emboss|Inset Emboss and accept the defaults.

8. Close the Button Editor. Figure 10.11 shows the changed nav bar in the Up state, and Figure 10.12 shows it in the Over state. To better see the glass effect, you can find this sample in the Color Studio.

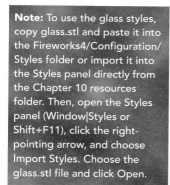

Note: To use the glass styles, copy glass.stl and paste it into the Fireworks4/Configuration/Styles folder or import it into the Styles panel directly from the Chapter 10 resources folder. Then, open the Styles panel (Window|Styles or Shift+F11), click the right-pointing arrow, and choose Import Styles. Choose the glass.stl file and click Open.

Figure 10.11
The edited nav bar in the Up state.

Figure 10.12
The edited nav bar in the Over state.

PROJECT Designing the Horse Adventures Navigation

Planning your Web site and layout in advance can save you a lot of time. The Horse Adventures site is an instance where that lesson is particularly true. Because I knew the general layout of the site and the final size, I knew how large of an area was devoted to the navigation. By knowing the size in advance, I could make the buttons and the defined area for the navigation bar the proper size to fit the site.

The Horse Adventures Web site is copyrighted by Idea Design (**www. je-ideadesign.com**) and is not available for your personal use. This project is for your learning and inspiration only. To make a navigation bar for the Horse Adventures Web site, follow these steps:

1. For a navigation bar, you need a blank button if you want to edit its appearance easily. You made the button for this Web site in the "Making a Button Symbol" section earlier in this chapter. Or, open the HAbuttonsymbol.png file from the Chapter 10 resources folder.

2. Open a new document that is 172×275 pixels with a black canvas color.

3. Select the new document you opened to make it active. Choose Insert|New Button. You are now working in the Button Editor—no matter what panels, layers, and so forth you use, *do not* close the Button Editor until the instructions say to. The steps will not work if you perform them outside the Button Editor.

4. Select the HAbuttonsymbol.png file to make it active. In the Library panel (F11), drag the button symbol (graphic or text) from the Library into the Button Editor. Figure 10.13 shows where the guide line is placed as well as the position of the first button.

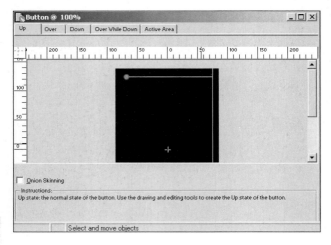

Figure 10.13

The HAbuttonsymbol in the Up state as seen in the Button Editor.

5. Select the layer you are currently using (probably called Layer 1). From the Options pop-up menu, choose Share This Layer.

6. Drag 10 more button symbols into the Button Editor (or copy and paste or clone). Place the first button near the top, the last button at the bottom, and nine others anywhere in between. Shift+click to select all the buttons (or use the Pointer tool to marquee select) and choose Modify|Align|Distribute Heights. Figure 10.14 shows the nav bar so far.

7. To add the text to each button, you need to add a new layer. Click the yellow folder icon in the Layers panel to add a new layer.

8. Select the Type tool. In the Type Editor, type "Horse Game". The font used in this example is CopprplGoth BD BT 14-point, bold, and white. Click OK. Center the text on your first button.

9. If you want plenty of practice adding text, repeat Step 8 for the words "Bookstore", "Equine Tack", "Model Horses", "Breed Info", "Articles", "Puzzles", "Screensavers", "Site Map", "Credits", and "Contact". Position all the text where you want it on your buttons.

10. To get the text on the other states in the same position as the Up state, select and copy (Ctrl+C/Cmd+C), click the Over tab, and paste (Ctrl+V/Cmd+V). Repeat this process for each word.

11. Before you close the Button Editor, click the Active Area tab and drag the top-left point down to below the Contact button. Doing so removes the large single slice that Fireworks adds. Figure 10.15 shows the completed navigation bar as a symbol in your document. Figure 10.16 shows the navigation added to the Horse Adventures Web page.

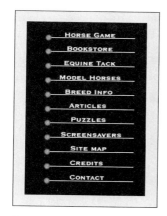

Figure 10.14
The navigation bar with all the buttons added.

Shortcut

You can Shift+select each word in the Up state and paste it into the other states.

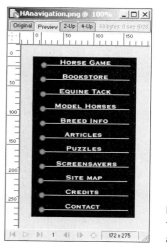

Figure 10.15
The completed navigation bar as a single symbol in the document.

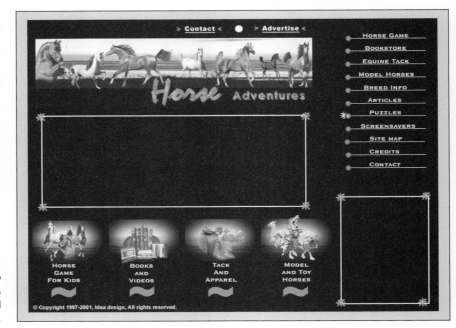

Figure 10.16
The completed Horse Adventure navigation added to the Web page.

Rollovers

JavaScript rollovers all work the same way: When a cursor passes over one graphic, a trigger is activated. A number of behaviors or actions can be assigned to this trigger, such as replacing the current image with another or displaying a graphic or text in another location of the Web page. The trigger is always a hotspot or a slice. Hotspots can be used only to trigger events such as Set Text Of Status Bar and cannot perform events such as swapping an image. They can, however, be used to trigger an event in another slice object, which you will see in "Making Disjointed Rollovers."

Making Disjointed Rollovers

When you use a *disjointed rollover*, a mouse pointer moves over or clicks the trigger area and an image is displayed in a different part of the Web page. You'll see disjointed rollovers used quite often on buttons, wherein the trigger area is a button and the target area displays a text description. In this exercise, you will use a new Fireworks 4 feature, the drag-and-drop behavior, which is a fantastic timesaver. To produce a disjointed rollover for the reef gardens text on the Atlantis interface that Jeffrey Roberts designed, follow these steps:

1. Open the AtlantisSliced.png file from the Chapter 10 resources folder.

2. In the Tools panel at the bottom is a section called View. Be sure the Hide/Show Slices (2) button is selected; this is the slice view.

3. In the Frames panel (Window|Frames or Shift+F2), select Frame 2. You will see a rectangle in the AtlantisSliced.png window that says "Your Image Goes here"; delete it two times (the first time you delete the slice, the second time the image).

4. Open the reef.png file. (This image was found at **www.flowergarden.nos.noaa.gov**, and the site says the information can be copied and shared.) Drag the reef image into the white area. Choose Insert|Slice (Alt+Shift+U/Option+Shift+U). Click Frame 1, and you will see a blank white box; click Frame 2, and you will see the reef image.

5. Click on Frame 1 and then select the object that will be your trigger. In this exercise, the trigger is the text "reef gardens". You will see a little round circle in the center of the slice. Click and drag the circle to the white rectangle (the reef picture will appear here). A Swap Image dialog box opens with Frame 2 as the default; in this instance, click OK. (If you are doing multiple disjointed rollovers, your images will be on different frames; you will need to specify which frame to access for the rollover.) Figure 10.17 shows the squiggly line that adds the OnMouseOver Swap Image behavior to the reef gardens slice. If you want to see the behavior that has been added, open the Behaviors panel (Window|Behaviors). Figure 10.18 shows the disjoint rollover in action.

> **Note:** This particular file happens to have a Frame 2 added. If you are working with a file that doesn't have any added frames, then you need to select Frame 1 and drag it onto the New/Duplicate Frames icon. The image you are going to display on the rollover will be in Frame 2.

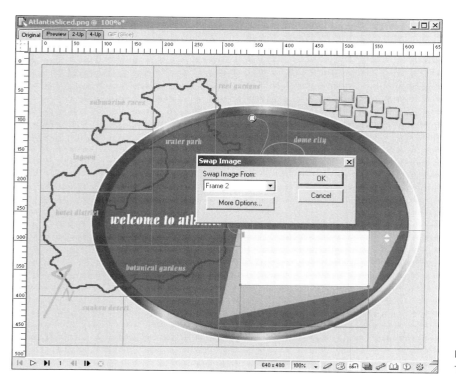

Figure 10.17
The Swap Image dialog box.

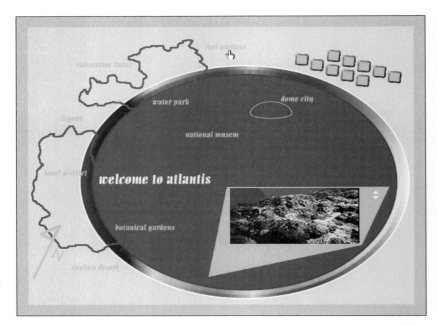

Figure 10.18
The disjointed rollover as seen in Preview mode.

Long Links

Depending on which build or version of Fireworks 4 you have, you may discover that you can't type really long links in the Link box. If this is the case, an upgrade is available at Macromedia (**http://www.macromedia.com/support/fireworks/** —click the Download option on the right) to fix the problem. The alternative is this workaround. Before you begin your pop-up menu, open the URL panel (Window|URL). In the Current URL box (you don't need to have a file open), type a URL address and click the + to add it to the URL Library. No additional steps are necessary. Now, when you click the down arrow next to the Link box in the Set Pop-Up Menu Wizard, any links in the URL Library will be available.

Pop-Up Menus

The Set Pop-Up Menu Wizard is one of the newest additions to Fireworks 4. It certainly has gained the most attention in the user groups. This section shows you the basics of how to use the Set Pop-Up Menu Wizard in the way it is intended to be used. You also will get a look at some of the shortcomings of using an automatic tool.

Making an Instant Pop-Up Menu

This section explains how to make a pop-up menu, which is a relatively easy process. The only part that may be a bit confusing at first is adding submenus. Thus, we take extra care to give you the exact steps and illustrations for adding submenus. After you understand the indent and outdent concept, the rest is pretty easy. To make your pop-up menu, follow these steps:

1. Open a new document (File|New) with a size of 300×300 pixels and a canvas color of white.

2. Draw a rectangle (any size and anywhere on your canvas, it's just practice) and choose Insert|Slice. With the slice selected, choose Insert|Pop-Up Menu. The Set Pop-Up Menu Wizard will open as seen in Figure 10.19.

3. In the Text box, type the name of a menu entry. ("Books" is used in this example.) If you want a link, type one in the Link box (books.htm is used here). Click the plus sign (+) next to Menu to add the menu item.

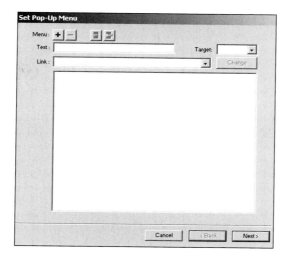

Figure 10.19
The Set Pop-Up Menu Wizard.

4. Type the next entry in the Text area, "Beginner". If you want a link, enter it (booksbeg.htm) and then click the plus sign (+) next to Menu.

5. The item you added in Step 4 is added to the menu, but you want it to be a submenu item. Select the second entry and click the Indent icon (see Figure 10.20).

Note: Menu items are not indented; when you want a submenu, click the Indent icon, which denotes an entry as a submenu. When you want an item that appears indented to be a menu item, click the Outdent icon. Submenu items should be placed under the menu they are attached to.

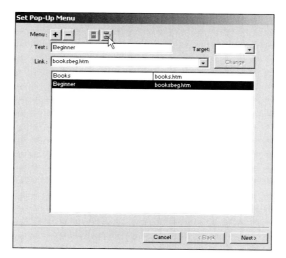

Figure 10.20
The Indent icon.

6. Continue adding menu and submenu entries. Click the Next button when you are finished.

7. Another Set Pop-Up Menu window opens (see Figure 10.21), in which you set the appearance of your menus. The choices are HTML and Image. (The Image option is a graphic instead of HTML code; it will be demonstrated in a project later in this section.) You can see a preview of how the menu will look at the bottom of the Set Pop-Up Menu dialog box. You can select the font, the point size, the Up state text and cell color, and the Over state text and cell color. Experiment a bit here until you get the look you like.

Note: The fonts included in the Set Pop-Up Menu Wizard are the ones most likely to be on everyone's computer. If you are using the Image option, only the graphic is exported, not the text—the browser renders the HTML text.

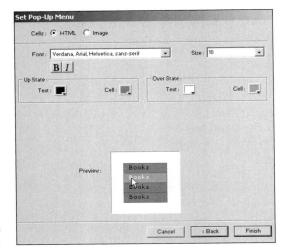

Figure 10.21
Set Pop-Up Menu Wizard's
appearance dialog box.

Alternatively, you can use an image for the menu, by clicking the Image option. Now, you have additional choices. Instead of just text and cell color options, you can choose from a list of styles. They look very much like the styles you've used before, because they are the same styles—they're just stored in a different place. See the section "Using Custom Styles for Pop-Up Menus" for more information on this feature. Select a style and experiment.

8. Click the Finish button. To preview a pop-up menu in a browser, choose File|Preview In Browser.

Exporting a Pop-Up Menu

After you complete the pop-up menu, you are ready to export it. For this exercise, choose File|Export|HTML And Images. Select the Images In Subfolder option so your images are saved in an images folder. Save when you are done.

Fireworks will generate all the JavaScript for the menu in a file called fw_menu.js, which is placed in the same folder as the HTML file. Be sure to upload the fw_menu.js file to your server, or your menus won't work. Only one fw_menu.js file exists, no matter how many menus are included. If you have submenus, then an Arrow.gif image file is produced, as well.

Using Custom Styles for Pop-Up Menus

If you want to use an image menu design that isn't available in Fireworks, you can make your own style. You can make absolutely any design you want (graphic only, no text) for your image menu and save it as a style.

To make a custom style, design your button, click the right-pointing arrow in the Styles panel, and choose Export Styles. Give your style a distinctive name and save it in the Fireworks 4\Configuration\Nav Menu folder.

Dreamweaver Library Item

You can't export the Fireworks pop-up menu as a Dreamweaver library item. But, there is a workaround at the Macromedia Fireworks Support site. Get online, and in Fireworks, choose Help|Fireworks Support Center; you will be taken to the Fireworks Support page. Search for "Dreamweaver library of a pop-up menu" or "pop-up menus" and you will find the workaround.

Your custom styles can now be used for pop-up menus. The styles for menus are not stored in the same location as the regular Style panel styles. If you have saved other styles for use in Fireworks, they are in the Fireworks 4\ Configuration\Styles folder. To use any of these styles with pop-up menus, copy the file you want and paste it into the Nav Menu folder, which is also in the Configuration folder. Every style file in the Nav Menu folder will automatically be available in the Set Pop-Up Menu Wizard.

Editing a Pop-Up Menu

Using the Set Pop-Up Menu Wizard, you can edit the options within the wizard and the physical location of the menu in your document. To edit anything within the Set Pop-Up Menu Wizard, double-click the menu outline; when the wizard opens, make any changes you want.

To change the location of the menu, select the slice to which the pop-up menu is attached and drag the outline to a new position. If you want to practice moving the menu, open the file you saved in the "Making an Instant Pop-Up Menu" and the "Exporting a Pop-Up Menu" exercises. Click and drag the bottom of the menu outline to line up with the bottom and left side of the Fireworks button. You may need to preview a few times to get the position where you want it. Figure 10.22 shows the moved position of the menu.

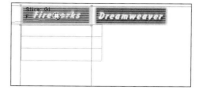

Figure 10.22
The pop-up menu lined up and in position.

Advanced Editing of Pop-Up Menus

Editing a pop-up menu involves editing the JavaScript file the menu generates. This subject is beyond the scope of this book, but it is covered in depth in *Fireworks 4 f/x & Design*. By editing the JavaScript, you can eliminate borders or change their color and size, change the size of the buttons, and adjust many other physical attributes of the menus.

Note: You can't preview a pop-up menu in Fireworks; you have to use the browser preview (File|Preview In Browser).

Limitations of Pop-Up Menus

A few of the problems you may encounter using Fireworks 4 pop-up menus include the following:

- Pop-up menus do not span frames in a Web page layout. If you have a menu in a top or side frame, the only part of the menu that will show is whatever fits in the current frame. If you must use frames, this probably isn't the menu solution for you.

- Customization of any serious nature involves knowing how to hand-code JavaScript.

- The absolute positioning of pop-up menus causes several problems when placing the code into other editors. Editors that don't handle layers can't place pop-up menus without hand-coding.

- Pop-up menus cannot be used in a centered table in your layout. Other layout workarounds must be used, such as layers that have absolute positioning.

Limitations aside, the pop-up menu feature of Fireworks 4 is a terrific timesaving addition.

PROJECT Making a Pop-Up Menu Using Images

You will make a pop-up menu for the Horse Adventures Web site as an alternative to the navigation bar you added earlier in this chapter. Pop-up menus save a great deal of space on a Web page. The horsecollage.png file is supplied in the Chapter 10 resources folder for your practice. Follow these steps:

1. Before you begin this project, you need to make a style that can be used for the image pop-up menu as well as for the link graphic. Open the horsecollage.png file in the Chapter 10 resources folder.

2. Select the Rectangle tool and draw a rectangle in the lower-left corner of the horse collage. In the Info panel, enter 94×24 for the dimensions of the rectangle and press Enter/Return. In the Fill panel, choose a Fill Category of Linear and click the Edit button. Click inside the first color box and enter Hex #FFFF00. Click in the color box on the right side and enter Hex #FF9900.

3. In the Stroke panel, select Basic for the Stroke Category, Hard Line for the Stroke Name, a Tip size of 4, and a color of black. To change the direction of the gradient, click the Pointer tool and move the circle handle to the top center of the rectangle and the square handle to the bottom center, as shown in Figure 10.23.

Figure 10.23
The gradient position of the link graphic and the graphic placement in the collage.

Note: The gradient's new position will not be part of the style.

4. Select the new link graphic and open the Styles panel (Shift+F11). From the right-pointing arrow, choose New Style. In the New Style dialog box, name your new style "Hacustom" for this example. Accept the default settings and click OK to add the new style to the Style panel.

5. To save the style for use in the pop-up menu, click the right-pointing arrow again and choose Export Styles. In the Save As dialog box, name the style again and browse to your Fireworks 4 folder. Locate Fireworks 4\Configuration\Nav Menu and save your style there.

6. Select the Type tool and click the link graphic. In the Type dialog box, type the word "Links". Highlight the word and select a font; this example used CopprplGoth BD BT, 30-point, and black. (We're using a larger than normal font because this is a children's site.) Click OK. Center the text. Figure 10.24 shows the link graphic in place.

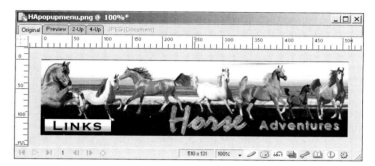

Figure 10.24
The link graphic complete and in position on the Horse Adventures Web page.

7. Select the link graphic and choose Insert|Slice, or draw a slice using the Slice tool, or right-click and choose Insert Slice. Choose Insert|Pop-Up Menu. The Set Pop-Up Menu Wizard opens, as seen in Figure 10.25.

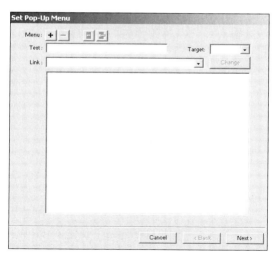

Figure 10.25
The Set Pop-Up Menu Wizard before any entries are made.

8. In the Text area, type "Horse Game". In the Link area, type "Hahome.htm". Click the plus sign (+) to add the menu item. In the Text area, type "Horse Info" and click the plus sign to add the menu item. Because Horse Info is a submenu of Horse Game, select its name and click the Indent Menu icon (the last icon on the right on the top row).

Note: The same link is being added to this example. Of course, if this were for use on a Web page, you would add the appropriate links in the Link area.

9. Type "Puzzles" in the Text area and click the plus sign. It is probably already indented as a submenu; but if not, select its name and click the Indent Menu icon. Repeat for the word "Screensavers". Type "Bookstore" in the Text area and click the plus sign. Select the word "Bookstore" and click the Outdent Menu icon (to the left of the Indent Menu icon) to make the word "Bookstore" a main menu item. Repeat this technique for the rest of the menu items. The complete list of names appears in Figure 10.26.

Figure 10.26
The Set Pop-Up Menu dialog box with the menu items added.

10. Click Next when you are finished adding the menu items. Figure 10.27 shows the next Set Pop-Up Menu dialog box with the Image choice selected instead of the HTML choice. This example is using a 12-point Verdana, Arial, Helvetica, sans-serif font. The only other choices that work for the Image selection, other than the style you want to use, are the Text Color options for the Up state and the Over state. In this case, use black text for the Up state and a medium green for the Over state. In the Style area, choose the custom gradient you exported as a style at the beginning of this project. Click Finish when you are done.

11. The pop-up menu is outlined in blue. To move it into position, click the blue lines and drag to below the link graphic, as seen in Figure 10.28.

12. To preview the pop-up menu, choose File|Preview In Browser and select your browser of choice. Figure 10.29 shows the pop-up menu as viewed in Internet Explorer 5.

13. To export your menu, choose File|Export|HTML And Images and select the Put Images In Subfolder option. Browse to the folder you want to save in. The fw_menu.js has now been generated. If you need more help or explanation on exporting, refer to Chapter 12.

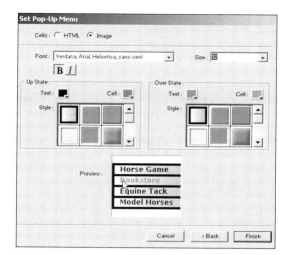

Figure 10.27
The second Set Pop-Up Menu dialog box showing the Image options.

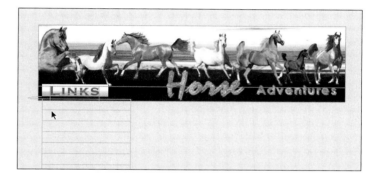

Figure 10.28
The pop-up menu moved into position under the link graphic.

Figure 10.29
The pop-up menu as viewed in Internet Explorer 5.

Moving On

You should now be able to implement a variety of different navigational interfaces for your Web sites. You have learned how to produce the popular disjointed rollovers and automatic navigation bars. Add to this mix the new pop-up menu skills, and you are ready to tackle any navigational challenge.

In Chapter 11, you will learn how to slice and when to slice, as well as how to best optimize your images for quick Web page loading.

Chapter 11
Slicing and Optimizing

This chapter explores how to intricately slice complicated designs. It also teaches how to use a new feature of Fireworks 4 that enables you to optimize parts of your document with different settings— even within the same slice!

Slicing

Of the three programs we are working with—FreeHand, Fireworks, and Flash—Fireworks is the one to use for slicing images or whole documents. Slicing an image is one of the most important things you will do in Fireworks. The decisions of whether to slice your image or document, where to slice, and how to slice all contribute to how (and sometimes whether) users will view your Web pages. Slicing, when needed, allows for better and specialized optimization to decrease the file size. Using slicing techniques, which ultimately reduce the file size, is vital to the final display of your project. The following section will help you decide if your image fits the profile of images that need to be sliced.

To Slice or Not to Slice

Before beginning to slice your images, you need to understand why it needs to be sliced, or whether it needs to be sliced. Many people mistakenly believe that slicing always increases the loading speed. This usually isn't so; in most cases, the page actually takes longer to load with sliced images, because of the increased hits to the server (every slice is requested from the server). Slicing does make the page appear to load faster, because the user can see parts of the image before the whole thing loads. This perception is important—it beats staring at a blank page.

Some of the many reasons to slice an image are as follows:

- If you need to export some slices as JPEGs and some as GIFs or GIF animations within the same document, then slicing is the best way to go. That way, some of the slices can be a different format to suit your needs.

- If an image is over 20KB, it needs to be sliced to form the perception that it's loading faster.

- If you want to attach behaviors such as rollovers to an area, it has to be a slice or a hotspot object.

- Slices help your Web pages load faster when your site includes a logo or other repeating elements. Slicing helps loading for multiple uses because once an image is downloaded, it remains in the browser's cache and doesn't have to be downloaded the next time it is needed.

Using Repeating Elements

When a logo or element is repeated often within your site, be sure that the element or slice is linked to the same image file. That way, after the server retrieves it one time, it is in the browser's cache. If you use the same image and put it in different folders, then the server will have to fetch it each time.

Another wonderful advantage of slices is that if you need to update one section or slice, you don't have to redo the whole image. For instance, suppose you have a complicated navigation bar that you have optimized, sliced, exported, and incorporated into every page on a large site. You then discover that one of the major links is spelled wrong. You can simply fix a copy of the one image (or two or more images, if it's a rollover), optimize it, export it, and upload it to replace the incorrect image.

Working in the Web Layer

The Web layer is the special layer that contains Web objects. Web objects—hotspots and slices—allow you to add interactivity to your document. All the hotspot coordinates and slices that you've made in your document will appear in the Web layer. Everything on this layer is shared across all layers, meaning that if a slice or hotspot encloses elements that are actually on different layers, the slice or hotspot is active on each layer. The slice or hotspot as a unit, not as an individual piece of the unit, will activate whatever behavior you have assigned to it. For example, a button with text may be on two layers—the object or button shape on one layer, and the text on another. You make the button (including the text) a hotspot or a slice and add a rollover behavior to it (this process is explained in detail in Chapter 10). The action will be triggered anywhere on the button—not just on the text or just on the button shape, but anywhere on the slice or hotspot area.

Using the Guides

Before you begin to slice an image, you need to set up a few aids for yourself. Using guides is an efficient way of defining your slices. Guides not only provide a visual aid, but they also help with your selection if you have the Snap To Guides option selected (View|Guides|Snap To Guides); this option allows selections within a set amount of pixels (determined by you) to automatically snap to the guide. To set up guides, follow these steps:

> **Note:** You can set your own preferences regarding how the Snap To Guides function responds. Choose Edit|Preferences and click the Editing tab. In the Snap Distance dialog box, enter the number of pixels from the guide your object needs to be before it is snapped to the guide.

1. Open a new document, choose File|New, and set the width and height to any size. To pull guides onto your document, the rulers have to be visible. From the menu bar, choose View|Rulers.

2. Choose View|Guides|Snap To Guides.

3. To place guides, click a horizontal or vertical ruler and drag a guide into your document. Figure 11.1 shows guides in place on a document.

The guide will not be visible until you begin to pull it onto your document, at which point you will see a green line (the default color).

Slicing Tools

The slicing tools are the Rectangle Slice tool and the Polygon Slice tool. The Rectangle Slice tool works the same way as the other Rectangle tools in Fireworks; click and drag over the area you want to define. The Polygon Slice tool also works the same way as the other Polygon tools in Fireworks; click a starting point and click to add points to define a shape.

Figure 11.1

Guides in place on a document.

What often confuses Fireworks users is the fact that you can define a polygonal shape with the Polygon Slice tool, but you can't export the polygonal shape as a polygon. All slices are rectangular, without exception. The polygonal shape will be cut into a series of rectangles that will fit together with the polygon shape enclosed. The polygon will have extra areas around it defined as rectangular slices. The benefit of using the Polygon Slice tool may seem dubious, because it's cut into rectangles anyway; but it can be much easier to cut the shape if you define it and have Fireworks cut it up appropriately. On the other hand, if your shape is large and contains other slices within it, you could end up with a lot more slices than necessary. In such a case, defining your own slices would be better than allowing Fireworks to generate them for you.

Defining the Slices

Once you place guides on your document, you could just export your whole image without ever manually defining a slice. Fireworks would automatically slice it for you following the placement of the guides. To do this, you would choose File|Export, choose HTML And Images under the Slices option, and then choose Slice Along Guides.

Although this technique is easy, it doesn't provide you with any ability to add interactivity to the document or the image. Plus, this technique usually produces far too many images; in many instances, it defeats the purpose of slicing the image. Another drawback to slicing using the guides is that you will most likely slice through areas you'd rather not have sliced.

To slice an image with control and precision, follow these steps:

1. Select the Rectangle Slice tool (to the right of the Hotspot tool; see Figure 11.2) from the Tools panel.

2. Drag a rectangle around the area you want to slice.

3. Repeat Step 2 for the rest of the slices.

4. If you want to adjust the size of the slice, use the Pointer tool to move the boundaries. You can copy and paste a slice selection, as well.

5. After you complete the slicing, save your file.

Every time you define a slice, Fireworks automatically places red lines where you could make additional slices to slice the whole page. As you make additional slices, the red lines change. In Figure 11.3, you can see two slices made using the Rectangle Slice tool. The rest of the lines (red) are automatically added by Fireworks and can be used as automatic slicing guides. You can stop slicing after a few slices and allow Fireworks to use its own guides (the red lines) to slice the rest of the image, or you can continue to slice the entire image. You also can export just the slices you made.

Naming Slices

Slices are named in the Optimize panel (Window|Optimize). Auto-Name Slices is the default setting. Auto-Name uses the root name of your document plus the row number and column number. With Auto-Name, the file names for the

Note: A green overlay will appear when a slice is drawn. You can toggle this view on and off by using the icons in the Tools panel section located at the bottom section, labeled View.

Figure 11.2
The Rectangle Slice tool.

Slice Overlaps

If one slice overlaps another, a behavior, action, or optimization settings will attach to the top slice.

Note: The best way to learn what gets exported with the different options is to make a practice folder to export into. Try making a few slices and then export them (File|Export) using the HTML and Image settings, or just the Images selection. Then, export with the Export Using Guides option.

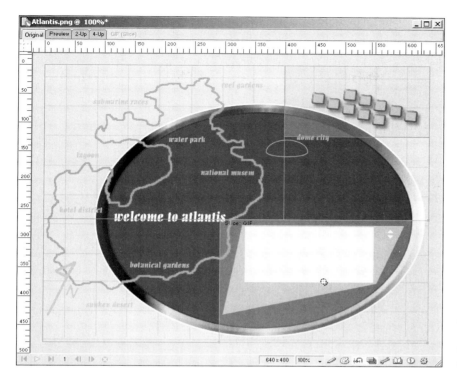

Figure 11.3
Two slices made using the Rectangle Slice tool, and the red lines that Fireworks adds automatically.

slices in Figure 11.3's Atlantis image would look like this: atlantis_r2_c4.gif. To name your own slices, follow these steps:

1. After you make a slice, open the Object panel if it isn't already open (Alt+F2/Option+F2).

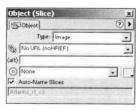

Figure 11.4
The Object Panel with Auto-Name Slices selected.

2. Figure 11.4 shows some of the options available for your slice. For now, deselect the Auto-Name Slices option and type in your own slice name. Don't type the file extension, just the name (no spaces or invalid characters).

3. If you'd like to customize the Auto-Name feature, select File|HTML Setup and click the Document Specific tab. Figure 11.5 shows the options with the current default settings. You can set up a default any way you'd like. For instance, you could put the word "slice" where it currently says "row/column" in the first row. The drop-down menus give you some options to choose from. When you are done, click the Set Defaults button to save your settings.

Adding URLs and Alt Tags to Slices

Many designers believe that every image on a Web page should contain an Alt tag. Valid reasons exist for this opinion. The alternative text appears before an image is fully loaded. So, while the image is loading, the user can see what is

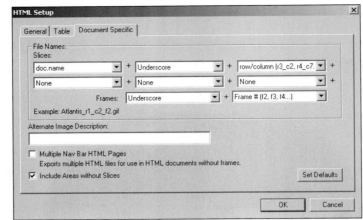

Figure 11.5
The Document Specific tab of the HTML Setup dialog box, where you can set a naming system for auto-naming slices.

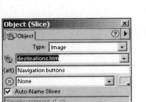

Figure 11.6
The Object panel.

Note: If you don't have any URLs in the drop-down box, it is because you haven't entered any yet. Open the URL panel (Window|URL), type in commonly used URLs, and press the plus (+) sign to add them to the URL Library. Any URL placed here will be available in the Object panel as well as in the pop-up menu.

coming; or, if they have images turned off, they can read a description of the image. Many users utilize the alternative text to speed their search time, because you may find a link via the Alt tag and click it before the page finishes loading.

Accessibility issues are a very good reason to include alternative text. Many visually impaired users have readers that read the alternative text—and if you don't include it, those users won't know the purpose of the image. Of course, your images should all serve a purpose and be worthy of alternative text. To add alternative text or URLs to your images, follow these steps:

1. Click the object to which you want to add a URL and/or alternative text. If the Object panel isn't open, select Window|Object (see Figure 11.6).

2. In the URL box, type the link or choose it from the drop-down list (the arrow next to the URL box), as seen in Figure 11.6.

3. Type a Target, if you have one. The targets choices are:

   - *_blank*—Loads the linked document in a new, unnamed browser window.

   - *_parent*—Loads the linked document in the parent frameset or window of the frame that contains the link. If the frame containing the link is not nested, then the linked document loads into the full browser window.

   - *_self*—Loads the linked document in the same frame or window as the link. This target is implied, so you usually don't need to specify it.

   - *_top*—Loads the linked document in the full browser window, thereby removing all frames.

4. Add the alternate text in the Alt box.

5. You can also deselect the Auto-Name Slices option and give your slice a unique name.

Object Slicing

Object slicing is great if you have individual objects on your page, such as buttons or a logo. Using object slicing is a quick and easy way to add a slice, especially if you are not slicing the whole page but just certain parts of it. To slice an object, follow these steps:

1. Select the object you want to slice.

2. On a PC, right-click (on a Mac, Ctrl+click) and choose Insert Slice.

Not only is object slicing easy, but you have choices, as well. This tool does have some drawbacks, however, especially if you are slicing buttons and the area behind them. Using the Add Slice feature will most likely produce extra slices unless your buttons are literally touching each other. The area between the buttons will be made into additional slices.

Text Slices

The purpose of text slices is to have a slice area in which you can enter HTML text. Small amounts of text are frequently made into images; but if you want to change the text, you will have to change the image. Another potential problem is that small text often appears murky when it's an image. HTML text solves these problems. You can type this text either within Fireworks or in your HTML editor. A text box is transparent and uses the canvas color.

To define a text slice, follow these steps:

1. Select the slice you want to be reserved for text.

2. In the Object panel, click the drop-down menu and choose Text. If you want to add text from within Fireworks, enter it in the white box under the Text selection (see Figure 11.7). You can add special HTML formatting from within Fireworks, but it isn't necessary. You can also add the text later in an HTML editor.

That's all there is to it. The slice color will turn a darker green, and a Text Slice label will replace the Slice label.

Adding Alternative Text

Alternative text entered in the Alternate Image Description box via the Document Specific tab found in the Export panel (File|Export|Options|Document Specific) applies to the entire image, not just a slice. Use this option for the document name or when you have no slices. To add alternative text to slices (or to hotspots), enter it in the Object panel for the individual slices.

Note: Fireworks 4 provides other ways to add a slice. With the object selected, you can choose Insert|Slice or use the keyboard command Alt+Shift+U/Option+Shift+U.

Figure 11.7
The slice defined as a Text object with HTML coded text added.

Text Background Image

If you would like the text box to blend into the color of a slice and not the canvas, export a copy of the slice *before* you change it to a text slice. Save the exported image with a distinctive name. When you open the finished HTML document (after you do your slicing and exporting) in an editor such as Dreamweaver, you can use the exported slice as a background in the text cell. This background is entered in the Properties Inspector in Dreamweaver.

More on Text Boxes

Text boxes have no border, cell padding, or cell spacing, so your text is placed right up against the edge of the area. If the text box has a bordering image or background, it will be quite unsightly. The problem can be solved by inserting blank images before and after the text box, or by inserting slices before and after the text box. You can then fill the extra text boxes or slices with the background color or background image in your image-editing program.

PROJECT Slice the Atlantis Document

To continue with the Atlantis document that has been built throughout this book, you will now slice it; you'll optimize it later in this chapter. The completed Atlantis.png document, prior to slicing, is in the Chapter 11 resources folder. The AtlantisSliced.png sample of the document is already sliced. Figure 11.8 shows the Atlantis document prior to slicing.

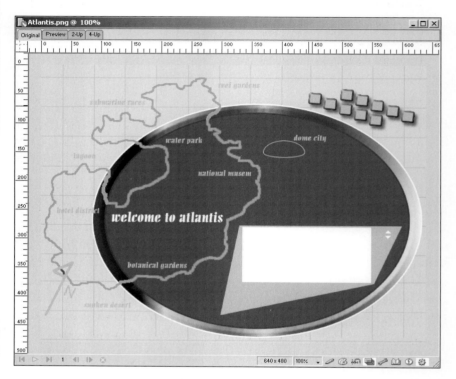

Figure 11.8
The Atlantis document ready to be sliced.

To slice the Atlantis document, follow these steps:

1. Open the Atlantis.png file, choose File|Open, and navigate to the Chapter 11 resources folder on this book's companion CD-ROM. If you don't have the same fonts used in the sample documents, a dialog box will open, asking about a replacement; either select one or choose No Change.

2. It helps if you know how you will use an interface—what objects need to be links, and so on. For this document, the text headings or names will all be links. The buttons will be rollovers and will also have a disjoint rollover attached, meaning that when a mouse cursor moves over the button, an image will appear in the white area. This same behavior will be attached to each text link, as well. Knowing this, you need to slice each text area, the buttons, and the white box.

3. Select the Rectangle Slice tool and drag a selection around the text "submarine races", beginning in the top-left corner. You can line up the next two text areas with this slice. Keep in mind that your goal is to have as few slices as possible to achieve your desired results.

4. With the Rectangle Slice tool, drag a selection around all the buttons beginning in the top-right corner. You can open the AtlantisSliced.png file for reference. Figure 11.9 shows what would happen if you used the Rectangle Slice tool to individually slice each button—you would have a ridiculous number of slices. For this reason, you will add hotspots to this area later in the chapter.

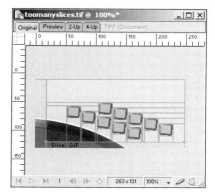

Figure 11.9
The buttons sliced separately, resulting in far too many slices.

5. The white box area needs to be a slice in order to receive the swap images. The up/down buttons to the right of the white box need to be a slice in order to receive a behavior, as well.

6. The rest of the document can be sliced, or you can leave it unsliced and Fireworks will automatically slice it later. If you think that any area will require special optimization, then you should slice it. Figure 11.10 shows the Atlantis document after it is sliced.

7. Once you have the slices the way you want them, you need to add alternative text to each one. Select one slice at a time and, in the Object panel, add the alternative text in the Alt area. Add a URL or target if the slice has one. You also can give a slice a custom name by deselecting the Auto-Name Slices feature.

> **Note:** In this document, you should slice all areas because of the gradient fill around the black center. This gradient poses a problem, which you will see in the optimization section of this chapter. If you are using the AtlantisSliced.png file, you will also notice that the buttons have blue squares on them; you'll add these squares in the "Adding Hotspots" section of this chapter.

Adding Hotspots

Hotspots are used to mark a region to enable browser interactivity. Hotspot information is stored in the Web layer. When you produce an image map to which you want to attach a URL link, you need to add a hotspot to the area

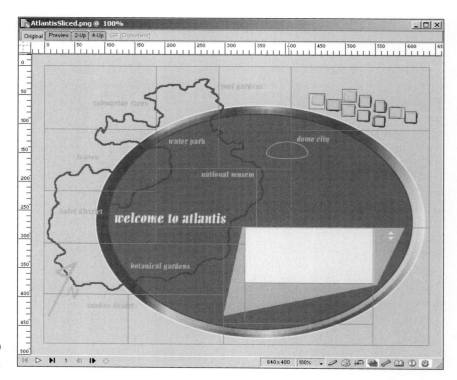

Figure 11.10
The sliced Atlantis document.

Note: Image maps are normally an image in which certain areas are "hot," meaning that if the user passes the mouse over those certain areas, they can click and go somewhere. These "hotspots" are what makes an image interactive and are what the URL gets attached to. Image maps produce a map code like **<map>** in your HTML document. It's important to understand that the map coordinates are not attached to a particular image but are embedded in the source code. Each image map in your document produces another map code which may be <map2>.

Hotspots Shapes

Hotspot shapes can be moved and resized with the transform tool or using numeric positioning in the Info panel.

that takes the user to another page when they click the hotspot. Hotspots don't require slicing, but they offer limited functionality. (You can't do much more than attach URLs.) The buttons from the Atlantis layout would produce a ridiculous number of slices; in this instance, it is more beneficial to the loading time to add hotspots. To add a hotspot, follow these steps:

1. Open the Atlantis.png file, which is in the Chapter 11 resources folder.

2. Select the Rectangle Hotspot tool and draw over each of the little buttons in the right corner. You will see a blue semitransparent box over each button.

3. Select one hotspot at a time and set its attributes in the Object panel (see Figure 11.11). Figure 11.12 shows the buttons on the Atlantis layout with hotspots added. The Layers panel shows the Web layer with the hotspots.

You can use the three hotspot tools to define different shapes for hotspot areas: the Rectangle Hotspot tool, the Circle Hotspot tool, and the Polygon Hotspot tool. To access hotspot tools, hold your cursor over the Hotspot icon in the toolbar. A pop-out will appear with rectangle, circle, and polygon shapes; choose the one you want to draw with. Your newly drawn hotspot will be ready to receive an event or a URL.

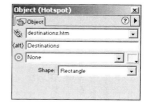

Figure 11.11
Setting the hotspot attributes.

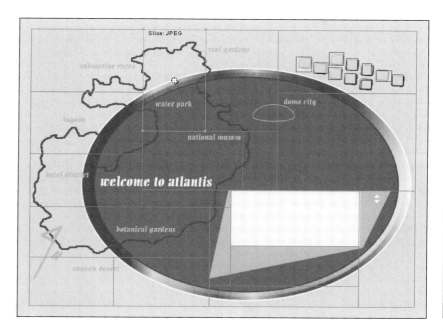

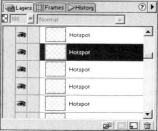

Figure 11.12
The Layers panel shows the Web layer with the hotspots.

Optimization

Optimizing your images has a tremendous impact on how fast your Web page will load in the user's browser. Even though many people in the USA have fast Internet connections, most rural areas and other countries do not. It may be easy for a developer with a high-speed connection to lose site of the fact that the majority of Internet users are connecting with a modem. Keep in mind that the larger the file or combination of files on a Web page, the longer the page will take to load. The connection speed determines how long each file takes to load.

Optimization, or making your image the smallest possible size while retaining an acceptable quality, is one of the most important factors in how quickly your Web page loads or appears to load. With the release of Fireworks 4, you can now export with GIF, JPEG, and PNG images in the same document, and you can apply different settings to specific areas of a JPEG image. The file types currently available for the Web include the PNG format, but not all browsers support this format yet; so, you may not want to use that one just yet.

Activate Hotspot Options

If you are working on a vector or text-type image map, the hotspot tools will be available to you. If you are defining a hotspot on a bitmap image, the choices may be grayed out; to activate them, click on the Web layer.

The 2-Up and 4-Up Tabs

The 2-Up and the 4-Up tabs let you view the effects of the optimization you are applying to an image or slice. The 2-Up tab shows you the original image and another image alongside it with the optimization settings you have chosen in the Optimize panel prior to clicking the 2-Up tab. The 4-Up tab is the most useful; it allows you to view the original and three other possible optimization settings at the same time, enabling you to compare different optimization settings to see which offers the best quality in relation to file size. To alter the optimization settings, you select the preview option you want to change and modify the setting in the Optimize panel; you can do this for each of the three views. If you look at the bottom of each view, you can see the file type, quality (or dither and colors for GIF), file size, and approximate time required to load the image in a browser. You can view both GIF and JPEG formats, if you desire. Figure 11.13 shows the 4-Up view with the original, the GIF settings, then with JPEG settings used in the fourth example. (This example doesn't use the fourth window.) The first pane or the original view is green showing the slice view. The other panes are a light peach with the selected slice showing the true color.

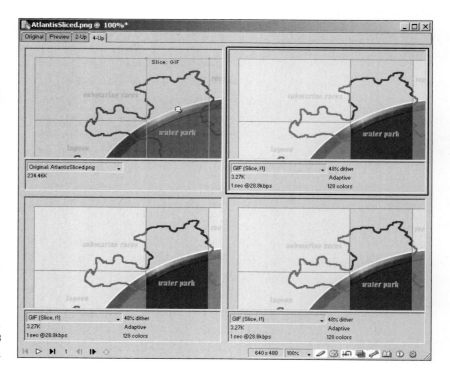

Figure 11.13
The 4-Up view.

GIF Optimization

GIF stands for Graphic Interchange Format. It's pronounced either "Jiff" or "Giff" (hard g), according to the Webopedia online encyclopedia. But regardless of how you say the word, the function of a GIF image remains the same. Some of the advantages of a GIF image are its small file size, animation capabilities, transparency, and interlacing. The biggest disadvantage is that it utilizes a maximum of 256 colors.

The GIF compression algorithm works best for line art and images with large areas of flat color. If you are optimizing photographs or images with gradients, JPEG is usually a better choice. You will not experience a loss of quality using the GIF format for an image with 256 or fewer colors, because of the lossless compression scheme of the GIF format. A *lossless compression scheme* (more on this in the "JPEG Compression" section) looks for patterns of data; when a new color is detected, the file size increases, which is why the GIF format is best for images with a lot of flat color areas.

Before you set the optimization settings, you should familiarize yourself with the Optimize panel (Window|Optimize) shown in Figure 11.14. As you can see, the Optimize panel provides a lot of options. The boxes you see on the panel are representations of the various pop-up menus and drop-down menus.

The first white-boxed area is the Settings area. When you select GIF from the Export File Format drop-down menu just below the Settings area, you will see that GIF WebSnap128 is the default saved setting.

The time to set the optimization settings is before you export. Some of the options in the Optimize panel for the GIF format require a bit of explanation.

Figure 11.14
The Optimize panel.

The Indexed Palette

Nine preset color palettes appear in the Indexed Palette drop-down menu (just below the Export File Format drop-down menu), plus Custom. Each option makes available a different palette of colors. Here are just a few of the most-used palettes:

- *WebSnap Adaptive*—The default palette for indexed color in Fireworks. Any color that is not Web safe will be evaluated automatically and snapped to the closest Web-safe color, plus or minus seven values. This option doesn't guarantee that all the colors will be Web safe, but it's close.

- *Adaptive Palette*—Finds a maximum of 256 colors. It's not a preset color set, but the best 256 colors for your image. This technique may contain a mixture of Web-safe and non-Web-safe colors. Fireworks eliminates colors from the standard palette of 256 based on how often the color appears in your image, allowing more specific colors that your image requires.

- *Web 216*—Converts all colors in the image to the nearest Web-safe color.

Dithering

Dithering repositions colors to try and simulate colors that don't exist in an image. Dithering gives the illusion of new colors by varying the pattern of dots of color. Sometimes, dithering an image or slice can help improve the appearance of image quality. You will see the results of dithering a GIF image to improve the appearance of a gradient in the "Optimize the Atlantis Document" project in this chapter.

Check for Web-Safe Colors

If using all Web-safe colors is important to you, you can use the Find And Replace (Window| Find And Replace) feature to locate any color that is not Web safe. Once the non-Web-safe colors are identified, you can change them.

Reduce Colors Further

When you optimize a slice or image, you can select a color amount from the Optimize panel for GIFs. If you want to reduce the colors even further, open the Color Table (Window|Color Table) and deleted additional colors.

Interlacing

Interlacing is an option for GIF files you are exporting for use on the Web. When a file is interlaced, it appears "blockie" or blurry until it loads, enabling the user to see a blurred copy while the image is loading. The alternative is not to use the interlacing object, in which case the user will see nothing until the entire image loads. The drawback with an interlaced image is that it needs to load fully before it becomes clear.

Transparency

Transparency is one of the most useful benefits of a GIF or PNG file. When you make the background of an image transparent, it remains transparent on a Web page, allowing you to see through to the Web page's background color. Not only can the background be transparent, but you can add colors to the transparency, as well. Figure 11.15 shows the transparency options in the Optimize panel.

No Transparency
Index Transparency
Alpha Transparency

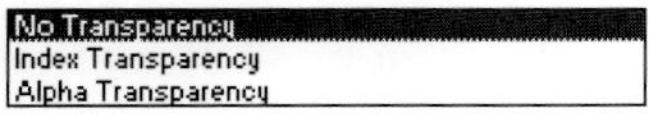

Figure 11.15
Transparency options in the
Optimize panel.

In Figure 11.15, you can see the three choices for transparency: No Transparency, which is self explanatory; Index Transparency, which makes the background color transparent, as well as anything else in your image that is the same color; and Alpha Transparency, which makes just the background color transparent.

The transparency options don't stop with these three choices. You can also use the three eyedroppers at the bottom of the Optimize panel to add more than one color (in addition to the canvas color) to the transparency, to subtract color from the transparency, and to set the index transparency color by sampling with the eyedropper (this technique lets you choose a color other than the background color to be transparent).

Matte

On the right side of the Optimize panel is the Matte box. You can probably tell by looking at it that it's a color box; the gray and white checks indicate that it is set to transparent by default. The Matte option allows you to export with a background color of your choice—without changing the canvas background color. This option is particularly important when you want to use the exported image in an environment different than the one it was designed in.

By setting the Matte color to that of the destination background, you eliminate the halo effect that is present when you use an image from a different background. For instance, you have probably seen countless images with white remnants around the edges that were placed on a dark background, producing what is called a *halo* around the images. The halo is the result of exporting a GIF that was originally on a white background and then placing it on a dark background.

You will also get the halo effect (a bit of the background color surrounding the image) with effects such as drop shadows. By setting the Matte color to the color of the destination canvas, the halo will be the color of the canvas and will not be noticeable. To choose a Matte color, simply click the color box and select a color, or type a Hexadecimal number and press Enter/Return.

Animation

GIF animations have the benefit of not requiring any plug-ins. They're added to a Web page like any other image. Animated GIF files contain frames with different images that are all contained in one GIF animation. When you are ready to export a GIF animation, you must select Animated GIF in the Export File Format drop-down menu.

JPEG Compression

JPEG stands for Joint Photographic Expert Group. (It is pronounced "Jay-peg.") JPEG compression is best used for any color or gray-scale realistic image, for example, photographs or continuous-tone artwork, as well as artwork with gradients applied. JPEGs are made smaller by lowering the quality setting, which results in the elimination of pixels in the image. With JPEG compression, you can display millions of colors, but you have no transparency options.

The JPEG compression algorithms work better for photographs than line art. JPEG images deal with millions of colors. Figure 11.16 shows the options for JPEG in the Optimize panel. A few of the features and options for JPEG images follow, with brief descriptions of each function:

Figure 11.16

Optimization options for JPEG images.

- *Lossy Compression*—Removes information from an image. JPEGs are compressed and are then decompressed when viewed, which can result in a longer loading time. You have control over quality settings in the Optimize panel; the higher the quality, the less compression.

- *Progressive JPEG*—Similar to GIF interlacing: The image appears blockie and gradually clears as it loads in a browser. The drawback is that Progressive JPEG is not supported by older browsers (before Netscape 2 and IE 3); these browsers will show a broken image.

- *Selective Quality*—A new feature in Fireworks 4. It's such a good asset that it is being covered in its own section in this chapter, "Selective JPEG Compression."

Warning

Don't JPEG a JPEG image— it will lose information each time and become considerably worse after the second time. If you want to work on an image multiple times, it is always best to save the image in its original format.

To compress an image using JPEG compression, follow these steps:

1. Select the image or slice you want to optimize.

2. In the Optimize panel, choose JPEG from the Export File Format area. JPEG—Better Quality(default) or JPEG—Smaller File. You also can manipulate the quality setting to meet your needs.

3. If you want to see the image gradually load in a browser, instead of waiting for the whole image to load, click the right-pointing arrow and choose Progressive JPEG from the Options pop-up menu.

4. From the same menu (right-pointing arrow), choose Sharpen JPEG Edges if you have text on an image background or perhaps a gradient background.

5. To view the different settings and options and decide which choices are best for your image, click the 4-Up tab in the document window. You can view four different optimization settings at once. You can try sharpening the edges, or smoothing them (see Step 6), or compare different quality settings.

6. Select a Smoothing amount from the slider to help soften edges that may be blockie (blocks of color where too many pixels have been thrown out). The drawback with smoothing is that is applies a slight blur. This option may or may not be suitable. The new Selective Quality JPEG compression does a similar job without blurring.

PROJECT Optimize the Atlantis Document

In this project, you will begin with the sliced Atlantis document you made earlier in this chapter. The file is AtlantisSliced.png; it can be found in the Chapter 11 resources folder if you didn't do the earlier project. You will optimize this document two different ways and then compare the quality versus the file size.

Optimize Using GIF Compression

The first optimization settings that you will try are all GIF settings, but they will vary with each slice. To optimize the Atlantis document, follow these steps:

1. Choose File|Open and open the AtlantisSliced.png file from the Chapter 11 resources folder.

2. You won't do every single slice, but a good portion of them. Start with the top-left slice, with the text "submarine races" in it. Click the slice and then click the Preview tab to see the effect of the settings. Figure 11.17 shows how your document should look so far. Notice where the arrow is pointing in Figure 11.17, near the 4-Up tab; this area shows the file size of the selected slice. Right now it is 920 bytes.

3. Open the Optimize panel and select GIF from the Export File Format. WebSnap Adaptive should be selected by default; if not, select it. Change the number of colors to 16. The image looks fine. Now change the num-

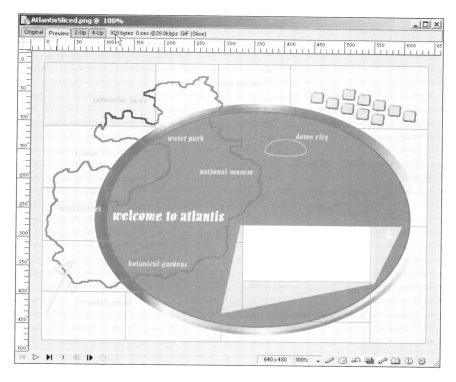

Figure 11.17
The Atlantis document with one
slice selected in Preview mode.

ber of colors to 4; it looks the same. If you want to experiment, try changing it to 2; the words disappear. Being able to preview while you make the adjustments is a helpful feature. Change the number of colors back to 4, and notice the file size of the slice: It's down to 675 bytes.

4. Select the slice to the right of the last slice, with the text "water park" in it. This slice contains a gradient, which will add the most weight to this document. Usually, gradients are best done using JPEG compression. You will see the difference in this case in the next part of this project. In the Optimize panel, choose GIF and try 64 colors; the gradient doesn't look good at all. Increase the colors to 128.

5. The next slice with "reef gardens" in it has even more colors in the gradient. Use the GIF setting with 256 colors. In some cases, you could also add some dithering. Dithering isn't a good choice for these slices, because of the text; the text is already on the borderline as far as visibility, and dithering would add a bit a blur.

6. Click the slice in the bottom-right corner, which has two white triangles. Set it to GIF and 64 colors. You can use fewer colors because the gradient has less color in this section.

7. Click the slice that has "dome city" in it. If you set it to 64 colors, you can see banding (lines) in the gradient; 128 works better.

8. As an experiment, click the bottom slice directly below the white box (mostly the gradient). 128 colors works pretty well on this slice, but choose 64 instead. It doesn't look as good as 128 colors. Move the Dither slider all the way to the top (100). The result looks considerably better, but it isn't really necessary for this slice. You can see how dithering can help in some cases, but it does add to the size. Optimizing is about making decisions and tradeoffs—it's up to you to decide which is more important: image quality or file size. For instance, you could lower the number of colors to 16 in this slice with a Dither of 100, and the quality would still be acceptable.

9. Continue to optimize following these guidelines. If you want to see which settings were selected for the rest of the document, open the AtlantisOptimized.png file from the Chapter 11 resources folder. If you look to the right of the 4-Up tab you will see the weight of the images only. For this document, it is 37.79KB, which isn't bad at all.

10. Some of the slices could be reduced further, if you really want to tweak them. Open the Color Table panel and manually eliminate any colors you don't want. For example, select the slice to the left of the white area (the vertical thin slice with a lot of orange in it). Look in the Color Table, and you will see that it contains a brown swatch. Select and delete the brown.

11. To export, choose Export|HTML And Images. For more on exporting, see Chapter 12.

Optimize Using GIF and JPEG

As a comparison, you will change some of the GIF slices in the Atlantis document to JPEGs. If you recall, gradients do better as JPEGs. This document is a bit challenging, because it is primarily large areas of flat color but the border of the center circle is a gradient. To test if some JPEG in this particular image is beneficial, you will change some of the slices:

1. Open the AtlantisOptimized.png file from the Chapter 11 resources folder.

2. Select the slice that says "water park" and click the Preview tab.

3. Open the Optimize panel. Change the File Format to JPEG and the Quality setting to 70. Figure 11.18 shows the selected slice in Preview mode with the Optimize panel settings.

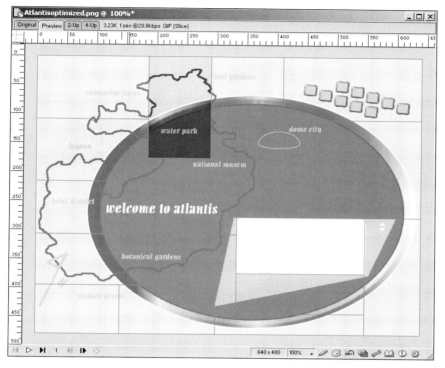

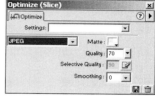

Figure 11.18

A slice selected in Preview mode and the Optimize panel with the new settings.

4. Change all the slices that contain the gradient to a JPEG at a Quality of 70. You won't be able to see the total file size in Preview mode as you could with the GIF document. Apparently, when the file formats are mixed, the total isn't reflected accurately. When I exported the file, the total file size was 57.7KB.

The Comparison

The GIF optimization settings' final image weight was 37.79KB, and the JPEG size was 57.7KB. The extra weight isn't always bad if the quality justifies it. Figure 11.19 shows the GIF results, and Figure 11.20 shows the JPEG results.

It is difficult to see much difference in these two figures. You can get a better idea of what has happened by looking at a blown-up view. The enlarged section is the gradient section at the top. Figure 11.21 shows the GIF enlarged, and Figure 11.22 shows the GIF and JPEG enlarged.

Now you can really see the true picture. In this case, the extra weight of the JPEG is not justified. Notice the blockies around the word and the buttons. The gradient looks nominally better. If this image was predominately a gradient, it would have been better as a JPEG; but because the dominant parts are large areas of flat color, it optimized better as a GIF, even with the gradient sections.

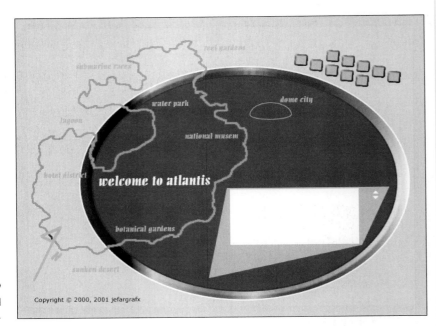

Figure 11.19
The Atlantis document optimized entirely in GIF.

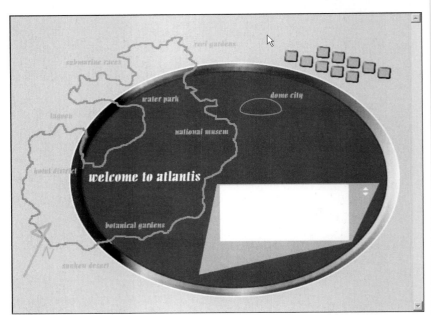

Figure 11.20
The Atlantis document optimized in JPEG.

Much of optimization is trial and error, and the Preview function of Fireworks is an invaluable tool. It's much easier to adjust the settings when you can see the effect in realtime without having to always check in a browser for each change.

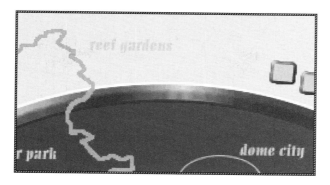

Figure 11.21

An enlarged section of the Atlantis document with GIF optimization.

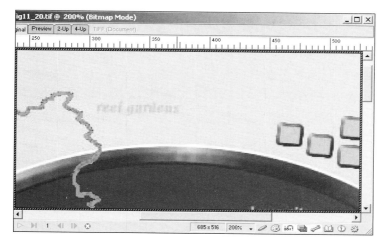

Figure 11.22

An enlarged section of the Atlantis document with GIF and JPEG optimization.

Selective JPEG Compression

Now that you know how to optimize your images, it's time to look at one of the newest features of Fireworks: selective JPEG compression. As you know, you can export images for the Web in GIF and in JPEG. Suppose you have an image with a gradient background; a gradient is best exported as a JPEG image. Because it's an image background, you will want to keep the file size down, so you export at maybe 70 percent to 80 percent, using the lowest possible setting that still yields an acceptable look. If you have text on this gradient, it may appear blockie or blurred if too much JPEG compression is applied. Using selective JPEG compression, you can now apply higher quality compression to specific areas, such as the text.

You can optimize the background of a JPEG image at a lower quality setting to emphasize the foreground image. Or, you can use a lower setting for most of a document and optimize the areas that have blockies (areas that appear a bit block-like and blurry when a JPEG image has been compressed too much) at a different setting.

Selective JPEG compression works in Fireworks by using a mask, but each document can have only one mask. If you are slicing a large image, you can apply selective JPEG compression to separate areas of the document, regardless of which slice it happens to be in. To try it for yourself, follow these steps:

1. Open the greetingcards.png file from the Chapter 11 resources folder.

2. Open the Layers panel (Window|Layers). You can see that the background and the center are both gradients. Because you know that you are going to optimize as a JPEG image, and that you are doing an exercise about selective compression, you need to convert the background into a bitmap image. Choose Modify|Convert To Bitmap. (If the background isn't a bitmap, you can't use the bitmap selection tools to make the necessary selections later.)

3. Open the Optimize panel (Window|Optimize) and change the format to JPEG with a Quality setting of 75. Click the Preview tab to see the optimization changes in realtime. The center portion shows a bit of banding, but other elements will be added to this center.

4. Select the Zoom tool and zoom in to 200%. Look at the text and the corners to evaluate the quality of the JPEG compression. Figure 11.23 shows the enlarged view of one corner and some of the text.

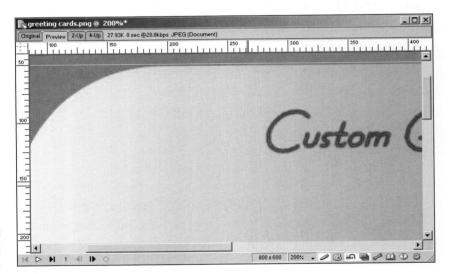

Figure 11.23
An enlarged view after JPEG settings have been made.

5. Scroll over to see all the text. In the Optimize panel, click the pencil icon to the right of Selective Quality. Figure 11.24 shows the Selective JPEG Settings dialog box. Select Enable Selective Quality and select the Preserve Text Quality option. Where you see a number, you can enter "90" (you will use that part later). Click OK.

Figure 11.24
The Selective JPEG Settings dialog box.

Figure 11.25
The text after applying Selective Quality with the Preserve Text Quality option.

6. Look closely at the text. Simply by selecting Preserve Text Quality, you've made it considerably better (see Figure 11.25).

7. To get rid of the blockies in each of the curved corners, you need to make a selection. Include the text in the selection as well. (The text could be left out of the selection because it is greatly improved; but it could be better, so include it.) Click the Original tab in the document window so you can make changes. Select the Lasso tool and make a selection around the corners. After you draw the first selection, hold the Shift key as you draw the next selection. Figure 11.26 shows the selections made.

Note: You can have only one JPEG mask per document. If you want to add to your current mask or subtract from it, you can make the mask active again by choosing Modify|Selective JPEG|Restore JPEG Mask As Selection. You can remove the mask in the same manner, but choose Remove JPEG Mask.

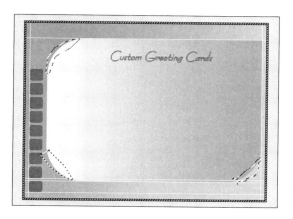

Figure 11.26
The selections made for the Selective Quality settings.

8. Choose Modify|Selective JPEG|Save Selection As JPEG Mask.

9. Click the Preview tab to see the difference; the blockies are gone. If you'd like an even better setting, change the Selective JPEG Settings by clicking the pencil icon in the Optimize panel or access the dialog box through the Modify menu (Modify|Selective JPEG|Settings). Choose Edit|Deselect or Ctrl+D/Cmd+D to remove the selection.

The PNG File Format

The World Wide Web Consortium has formally endorsed Portable Network Graphics (PNG). The PNG format was the result of developers who wanted an alternative to GIF. The problem was that the GIF format was free for many years, but then the patent holders began charging developers to use the GIF export technology. PNG is an exciting alternative, but at present it is only partially supported by Netscape and IE; thus it isn't a viable option at this point. PNG files support full alpha channel and graduated transparency, which the browsers do not support yet.

The PNG format uses a lossless compression and decompresses when viewed. PNG uses several different bit-depths: 8, 24, and 32. It has Gamma correction capabilities, which make an image view properly on both Macs and PCs. It will be a promising technology once it becomes fully accepted.

Moving On

In this chapter, you have learned how to slice and how to decide whether you should slice a document. You have also learned many things about the different file formats and the choices available to you when it comes to optimizing each slice for the best performance.

In Chapter 12, you will learn the best ways to import assests into Fireworks and how to export them either for Web delivery or in preparation for Flash or other applications.

Chapter 12

Importing and Exporting

This chapter provides in-depth information on how to import a variety of file formats into Fireworks and how to export in numerous formats for use in other applications. The focus is on importing images from FreeHand and exporting Fireworks images for use in FreeHand and Flash.

Note: Although Macromedia uses the term "style" in Flash, Fireworks, and FreeHand, the styles are not interchangeable.

Importing and Exporting Styles

When you make new styles, you can export just one or make several and export them as a set. Fireworks also ships with a couple different sets of styles. When you save a style, it can be used in other documents—not just the document you are currently working in.

To import or export styles in Fireworks, follow these steps:

1. Open the Styles panel (Window|Styles or Shift+F11).

2. Select the object with the style that you want to import or export. Click the right-pointing arrow and from the Options pop-up menu choose either Import Styles or Export Styles.

3. A window will open in which you can locate and choose the file to import or choose where to save the export.

4. Click Open or Save.

Importing and Exporting Libraries

You can import libraries you have saved from other documents. Or, you can save a library from your current document so you can use the elements in another document within Fireworks.

Note: Although Macromedia uses the same term "library" in Flash, Fireworks, and FreeHand, they are not interchangeable.

Exporting Libraries

If you have a series of symbols that make up a navigational system, you may want to save the set.

To save a library of symbols to use again or to share with someone else (for use in Fireworks only), follow these steps:

1. Open the Library panel (Window|Library or F11).

2. Click the right-pointing arrow. From the Options pop-up menu, choose Export Symbols (see Figure 12.1).

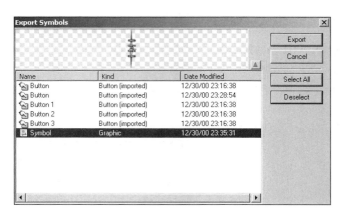

Figure 12.1
The Export Symbols dialog box.

3. Select the symbols you want to export. To select them all, click Select All; if you want several in a row, Shift+click; and to pick and choose, press Ctrl/Option+click. When you are done, click Export.

4. Name your library and choose where you want to save it. Click Save.

Importing Libraries

To use a library you have previously saved in your current document, you will need to import it. To import a saved library, follow these steps:

1. Open the Library panel; if it isn't already open, choose Window|Library.

2. From the Options pop-up menu, choose Import Symbols.

3. Locate your saved library and click Open.

4. The Import Symbols dialog box opens with the list of symbols in the library you selected to save. Choose the ones you want and click Import.

> **Note:** If you think you may use a library often, save it or move it to the Fireworks Library folder, which is in Macromedia\Fireworks 4\ Configurations\Libraries. By placing your file there, you can access it by choosing Insert|Libraries.

Importing Scanned Images

If you have a stack of photos collecting dust, you may want to scan them to preserve their color. Or, perhaps you have old heirloom photos you would like to restore. Pictures you've taken yourself can be used in image compositions, as backgrounds, or for a great personal Web site. No matter how you want to use your scanned photographs, Fireworks makes it easy to import them. You can use scanned images several different ways in Fireworks: You can import directly into Fireworks, open a scanned image, or place the image as an image object.

Using the Twain Function

You can import images directly by choosing File|Scan and using the Twain function. You have the option of using the Photoshop Acquire plug-in module or the Twain select option. (See your specific scanner instructions to learn how to perform the scan.) Scans made this way will open in Fireworks as a Fireworks document. You will notice a blue and black barber pole frame around the image, which indicates that the image is a bitmap.

Opening a Scanned Image

You can open a previously scanned image by choosing File|Open. The image will open at the same size and resolution at which you saved it.

Importing as an Image Object

When you import a scan as an image object, there are several ways to place the image in your document. You can choose File|Import or choose Insert|Image, locate the file, and click OK. Your cursor will change to a corner-shaped cursor, indicating an import is ready to be placed as an image object. You can simply

Note: When you place an image using the click-and-drag function, it is automatically resampled. In some cases, this resampling may not harm the image. But in many cases (especially if you have made the image quite a bit larger than the original), you will lose considerable image quality.

click the pointer to place the image at the original size and resolution, or you can click and drag the image to any size you'd like. In Fireworks, the image will be resampled automatically according to the size you drew.

Importing from Other Applications

The kind souls at Macromedia have made it possible to import many different file formats into Fireworks. In many cases, you can still edit vector images after you import them. This compatibility with other applications and their file formats makes the job of a designer much easier, especially when a client provides files from other programs—it's a hassle to have to use workarounds just to use a supplied file. Of course, sometimes you will still need to use alternative methods; but Fireworks will streamline your workflow by supporting many of the major application formats you are likely to encounter. Some of the most popular formats will be discussed in this section.

To avoid repetitive instructions, the basic step to import any file is to choose File|Import. The Import method allows you to place the image object anywhere on your open document window. File|Open applies to imported images, as well. The Open method opens the file without any extra canvas space, as seen in the bottom half of Figure 12.2.

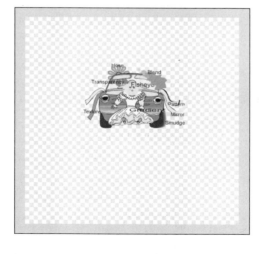
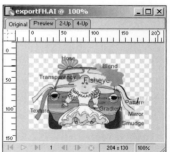

Figure 12.2
The image on the main canvas was brought into Fireworks using the Import option; the image in the exportFH.AI box was opened in Fireworks using the Open option.

Importing FreeHand Files

You can open and edit FreeHand files (including FreeHand 9 files) in Fireworks. At the time of this writing, FreeHand 10 was available; but, it came out after Fireworks 4, so FreeHand 10 files are not recognized. If you want to use FreeHand 10 files in Fireworks 4, you can export them as FreeHand 9 or earlier, Illustrator 88, or Photoshop AI files and then import them into Fireworks.

I made a test file with vectors in FreeHand 10 using gradients, blends, the Smudge tool, the Graphic Hose, and more, as shown in Figure 12.3. This piece

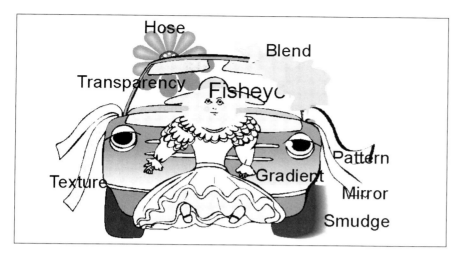

Figure 12.3

The original file in FreeHand 10 before being imported into Fireworks.

of EPS art that I added the labeled effects to comes from *ArtToday*. I exported the file as a FreeHand 9 file, an Illustrator 88 AI file, a Photoshop EPS AI file, a Photoshop 5 PSD file, an EPS file, and a PNG file. The results can be seen in the figures on the following pages. (You can see the differences better in the Color Studio of this book.) The breakdown of the results precedes each image.

With an active document open, you can choose to import (File|Import). In the Vector File Options dialog box all the images were scaled to 200 percent and the choices in the Render As Images area were all deselected, as seen in Figure 12.4. The Render As Images options were left deselected because you are testing the editability of FreeHand vector objects in these exercises. If the options were left selected, the image would open as a rasterized or bitmap image.

Of course, sometimes you will want to open an image as a bitmap—for instance, an object that will be used in a bitmap composition, which you will not need to resize or edit. Customized background images could be opened as bitmaps as well, because you probably wouldn't need to edit them in Fireworks.

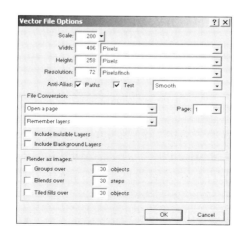

Figure 12.4

The Vector File Options dialog box with the settings used to import all the vector samples.

Importing Native FreeHand Format Files

In Figure 12.5, you can see that the pattern and texture were lost when the native FreeHand 9 file was imported. The mirror, Smudge, Fisheye lens, Transparency, blends, and gradients remained intact, although the blend is not as distinct as in the original file. The flower, which was made with the Graphic Hose, has lost some of its depth and size. The background is transparent (as long as the background you are importing into is transparent) because the Include Background Layers option was not selected in the Vector File Options dialog box.

Figure 12.6 shows the gradient handles in the editable gradient, along with a few of the vector paths selected. This image remained a scalable vector object.

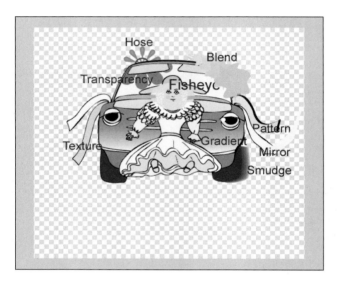

Figure 12.5

The native FreeHand 9 file imported into Fireworks.

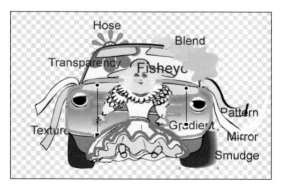

Figure 12.6

The native FreeHand 9 imported file showing some of the editable areas.

Importing an Illustrator 88 AI File Exported from FreeHand

The Illustrator 88 AI format had better results than the native FreeHand format in some cases and worse results in other areas, as seen in Figure 12.7. The blend is more distinctive and the Graphic Hose didn't loose its fullness. The biggest drawback is the gradient. The text is a bit strange—the word "Transparency" came in as three parts with odd spacing, and "Texture" came in as two parts with a space after the "T".

Figure 12.7
The FreeHand file exported as an Illustrator 88 AI format and imported into Fireworks.

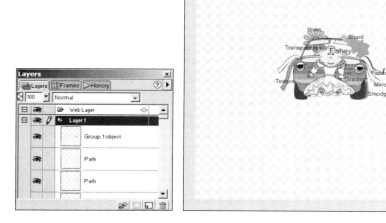

Figure 12.8
The Illustrator 88 AI file showing editability.

The gradient imported as a mask, as you can see in Figure 12.8, and it isn't editable unless you ungroup it. Once it's ungrouped you have a path with many points, which probably isn't what you want. If you wanted to, you could simply remove the old gradient and apply a new one.

Importing a Photoshop EPS AI File Exported from FreeHand

No image is shown for the sample file that was exported as Photoshop EPS AI, because it was identical to the Illustrator 88 AI format.

Importing a Photoshop 5 PSD File Exported from FreeHand

The image in Figure 12.9 was imported as a bitmap, which is a totally useless thing to do unless you want a flat image that you can't edit. This is not to say that all PSD files have the same flaw, as you will see in the next section. However, this is what happens to a FreeHand vector file exported as a Photoshop 5 PSD file.

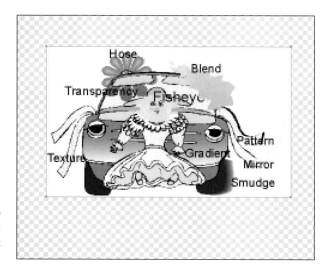

Figure 12.9
The file exported from FreeHand using Photoshop 5 PSD format and imported into Fireworks.

Importing an EPS File Exported from FreeHand

Programs such as FreeHand, Illustrator, and CorelDRAW all produce vector EPS files with special EPS headers that let the images be placed in layout programs such as InDesign or QuarkXpress. If you export a file from FreeHand as an EPS file, it will import into Fireworks as a rasterized EPS file. Figure 12.10 shows the EPS File Options dialog box that opens when you import an EPS file.

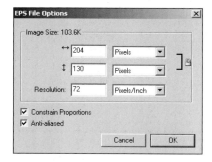

Figure 12.10
The EPS File Options dialog box.

You can see in Figure 12.11 that the EPS file did in fact open as a bitmap image. The background is transparent.

Importing a PNG File Exported from FreeHand

The PNG file exported from FreeHand opened as a bitmap image with a transparent background, as seen in Figure 12.12.

Importing GIF Files

Animations can be opened directly in Fireworks. Each image frame of the animation will appear on a separate Fireworks frame, as seen in Figure 12.13.

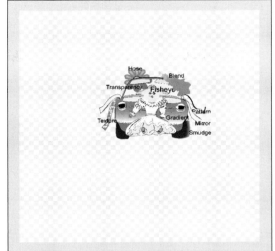

Figure 12.11
The imported EPS file.

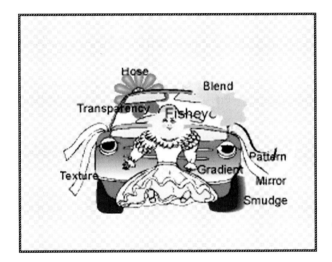

Figure 12.12
A PNG file exported from FreeHand and opened in Fireworks.

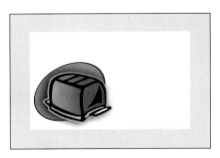

Figure 12.13
Opening a GIF animation with layers and frames.

GIF animations can also be imported into Fireworks. When you import an animation, it comes into Fireworks as a symbol. Figure 12.14 shows the animation symbol and the Library panel. For more information on using symbols, refer to Chapter 7.

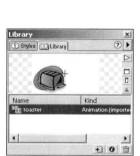
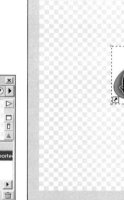

Figure 12.14

Importing a GIF animation, which imports as a symbol.

PROJECT Importing a Tweened Object from FreeHand and Making It an Animation in Fireworks

Tweening objects means that you have a starting graphic and an ending graphic, and the intermediate steps between the two are generated automatically by software. In Fireworks, you can only tween the same object. This object in Fireworks can be sized differently and have Live Effects applied (see Chapter 7), but it is still the same object. FreeHand does not have this limitation. In FreeHand, you can tween objects of different shapes; this process is called a *shape tween* in many applications, but in FreeHand it is referred to as a *blend*.

Because this project's primary purpose is to demonstrate importing FreeHand graphics suitable for a GIF animation into Fireworks, you will use a simple blend produced in FreeHand (see Chapter 3) and released to layers. We discussed a frame-by-frame animation in Chapter 7. Figure 12.15 shows the finished steps: Using blended objects, a whole apple changes into an eaten apple.

Figure 12.15

A FreeHand blend turned into an animation.

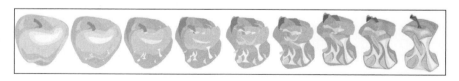

To import a blended object from FreeHand and make it into an animation, follow these steps:

1. To place this animation into your document, choose File|Import and locate the apples2.FH9 file in the Chapter 12 resources folder (accept the defaults in the Vector Option dialog box). Look in the Layers panel, and you will see the layers holding the steps of the blend performed in FreeHand.

2. Choose Edit|Select All. Open the Frames panel (Window|Frames), click the right-pointing arrow, and choose Distribute To Frames from the Options pop-up menu. This action distributes each layer to a frame.

3. Click on each frame to determine if each frame is in the position you want it to be. If not, then click and drag to the appropriate location. The frame numbers will change according to where you place them.

4. The number 7 in the Frames panel is the delay time between frames. At this setting, the apple will be eaten very quickly. To change the delay time, Shift+select Frame 1 through Frame 9, double-click (or click the right-pointing arrow and choose Properties from the Options pop-up menu), and type "15" (or any number you'd like) for the delay time.

5. To preview your animation, click the Play/Stop button.

Importing Photoshop PSD Files

Macromedia has done a great job of remaining compatible with Photoshop. This is an important fact, because many Fireworks users also use Photoshop or obtain Photoshop files from clients. Fireworks not only opens Photoshop PSD files (including Photoshop 6) and maintains their editability for features that are compatible with Fireworks, but it also gives you the option of maintaining features of the imported file.

Before you import Photoshop files, you need to set your file conversion preferences. Choose Edit|Preferences and click the Import tab. Figure 12.16 shows the Photoshop file conversion preferences.

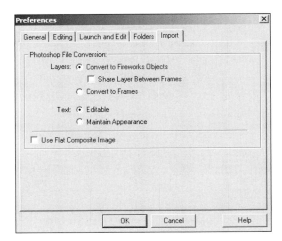

Figure 12.16
The Preferences dialog box for Photoshop files.

Photoshop 6 Files

Although Fireworks has great support for Photoshop files, it will discard Photoshop 6 features that Fireworks doesn't contain. For instance, Fireworks does not have adjustment layers, so they will not import into Fireworks. Other Photoshop 6 effects have no equivalent in Fireworks, such as Gradient Overlay and Stroke layer effects, and are also discarded.

Note: Photoshop 6 PSD files open only in Fireworks 4—not in earlier versions of Fireworks.

Note: Photoshop text is editable only in Photoshop 5.5 and earlier; text imported from Photoshop 6 is not editable and opens as a bitmap image. If you would like to perform the test yourself, use the photoshop6text.psd file in the Chapter 12 resources folder.

The default setting of Convert To Fireworks Objects is the most common way to import a Photoshop file. This option maintains the Photoshop layers in Fireworks. The other layer options are suitable if you are going to use the file for an animation. If you don't need the layers but simply want to import the file as a flat image, select the Use Flat Composite Image option at the bottom of the Preferences window. You could also use the Open command to open a Photoshop PSD file with layers and effects (ones supported in Fireworks) intact.

If you select Editable in the Text section of the Preferences dialog box, the text remains editable. If you choose Maintain Appearance, the text will be imported or opened as a bitmap image.

Importing Illustrator and CorelDRAW Files

You can import CorelDRAW 7 and 8 files into Fireworks and edit them, but many of the blends and effects applied in CorelDRAW will be lost. Illustrator files are limited to Illustrator 7 and 8. Illustrator 9 files will not open or import into Fireworks 4.

Exporting

You must optimize your images and documents prior to exporting them. In Chapter 11, you learned how best to optimize your images; now it's time to export them for use on the Web. Fireworks will not only export the image or images for you, but generate all the HTML code for a complete layout, if you so choose. Special export options make it easier to use your images and code in Dreamweaver, Director, and Flash. Macromedia developed an application that plays nicely with its own compatible applications, and also realized that many people use other popular applications such as Photoshop, Illustrator, and CorelDRAW. With this in mind, Fireworks provides support for those applications and more.

Caution

Always save your original PNG file in a safe location. All exports will turn your PNG file into a non-editable rasterized (bitmap) file. The editability of text, effects, paths, and layers will all be lost. It's much easier to make changes when necessary to the original file. Some formats, such as JPEG, cause you to lose more image detail and image integrity every time you edit them. You can export as a vector and maintain a degree of editability, but many of the editable details will still be lost.

It's important (or, at least, easier) to have your site structure set up before you begin exporting. If you set up your folders locally in the same way that they will be uploaded, you will save yourself many headaches. You will find it much easier to do some planning at the beginning of your project and save your files in the same folder they ultimately will be in.

When you choose to export images as well as the HTML code of a Fireworks document, the images and the HTML file (containing a table that places all the image slices back together) are generated. This HTML file and the images must be saved in the same folder as the file you will insert the Fireworks code into (for use in Dreamweaver), or all your image links will be broken. For example, a simple site structure might consist of a site folder called atlantis with an images subfolder and an assets subfolder.

If your site's HTML/HTM files are kept in the root folder named atlantis, you should export your Fireworks document containing the HTML document into the atlantis folder and designate that the images be exported to the images subfolder.

Export Preview

The Export Preview dialog box is an ideal way to proceed if you are exporting an image using only one format—in other words, if you have no slices that use different settings. Figure 12.17 shows the Options tab of the Export Preview dialog box, which you access by choosing File|Export Preview.

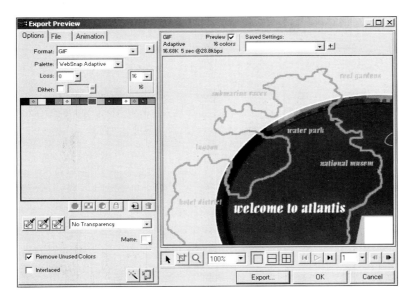

Figure 12.17
The Export Preview Options tab options.

The Export Preview Options tab contains the Format, Palette, and other optimization settings found in the Optimize panel. You can also edit colors, transparency, and many other options. At the bottom of the image window, you can choose to view the whole page, 2-Up, and 4-Up. If the file is an animation, you can play it from this preview. This window works well and has all the controls you need in one location. However, it isn't the best choice for a file such as the Atlantis image, because several slices in this layout have only 16 colors, and a couple have only 2 colors. If an image has different color settings or even different file formats for each slice, then do your optimizing in the Optimize panel, not the Export Preview dialog box.

Figure 12.18 shows the File tab of the Export Preview dialog box. You can scale your image if you'd like, or specify a specific area to export using X, Y coordinates and a specified height and width.

Export Wizard

Because I assume you know the basics of using Fireworks, I won't discuss the Export Wizard in detail. Actually, there isn't much detail to it. Basically, the wizard helps you choose an export format for your image.

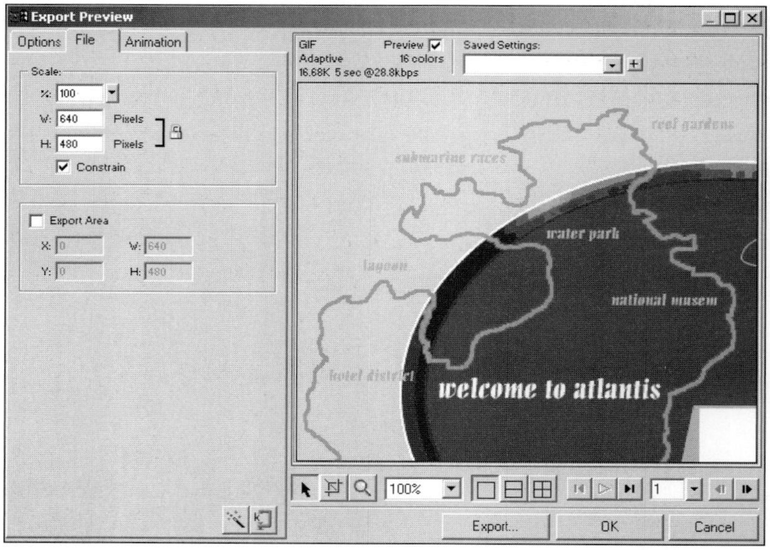

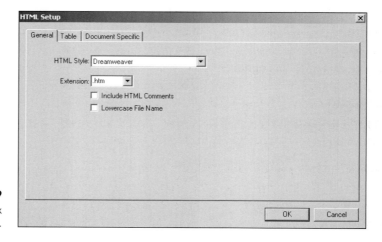

Figure 12.18
The File tab of the Export Preview dialog box.

HTML Preferences

If you ever plan to export images and the HTML code that puts all the pieces together, you will need to set your HTML preferences. You may as well do it now so you understand your options before you begin to export anything. You can access the HTML preferences two different ways. When you choose File|Export, click the Options button in the resulting dialog box. This method is a great choice if you are exporting and want to make a last-minute change. To set up your HTML preferences for the first time, choose File|HTML Setup. Both options give the same results.

HTML Preferences General Tab

From the HTML Style drop-down menu in the HTML Setup dialog box (see Figure 12.19), you can choose Dreamweaver, GoLive, FrontPage, or Generic. From the Extension drop-down menu, choose the file extension you'd like to use. To include HTML comments, select the option; select Lowercase File Name if you want to.

Figure 12.19
The HTML Setup dialog box showing the General tab options.

HTML Preferences Table Tab

The HTML Setup dialog box's Table tab, shown in Figure 12.20, provides some important options. One of the Space With options is 1-Pixel Transparent Spacer; this is probably the most-used choice, because it generates a transparent image as a space holder. After you export, you will notice a file called spacer.gif in the folder you exported to. This 1-pixel-by-1-pixel transparent file is used as a spacer to maintain a table's structural integrity in multiple browsers. This spacer is known by several names, and is frequently called a *shim* or a *transparency.gif* file.

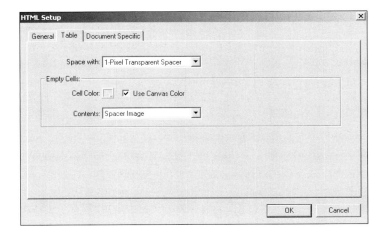

Figure 12.20
HTML preferences Table tab options.

You can also choose to export using a nested table; this method places one table into another table. This sort of table layout does not require spacers. Or, you can choose to export just a table with no spacers at all. This option will work fine in Internet Explorer, but Netscape Navigator often will not hold the table's integrity if empty cells exist. To help prevent the presence of an empty cell, you can choose Non-Breaking Space instead of Spacer Image for the Contents option. If your table has content in every cell, then Single Table—No Spacers will work fine.

The other option in the Table tab lets you control the appearance of empty cells (generated when you deselect Include Areas Without Slices) or text slices. If you deselect the default Use Canvas Color option, then you can select a color for the cell or text table. The last option specifies what you want to put in the empty cell. A spacer image uses the 1-pixel spacer.gif in the cell, and the non-breaking space inserts the HTML code (** **) for a space tag. If you choose None, nothing will be added to the cell. Although this option produces the smallest file, you may have problems with the table's integrity.

HTML Preferences Document Specific Tab

In the Document Specific tab, you change the default auto-naming of your slices. Of course, if you deselect the Auto-Name Slices option in the Object panel, this information will not apply. You may find it easier to set some

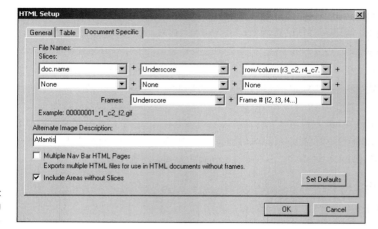

Figure 12.21

HTML preferences Document Specific tab with the naming parameters.

parameters for naming so you don't have to name each file individually. To follow along with the instructions that follow, refer to Figure 12.21, which shows the auto-naming options.

Auto-naming uses the root name of your document plus the slice's row number and column number. The atlantis file names would be as follows: atlantis_r2_c4.gif. You can set up a default naming system any way you'd like. For instance, you could put the word "slice" where the words "row/columns" currently are. The drop-down menus give you some options to choose from. When you are done, click the Set Defaults button to save.

You can also enter an alternate image description in this dialog box. Don't confuse this option with the Alt Tag description option found in the Object panel. The Alternate Image Description option in the Document Specific tab is used primarily for documents that don't use slices so the user can see a description in the browser as the image loads.

Export Options

Fireworks 4 makes many export options available to you. You can export whole pages, one image, multiple images, and images with the HTML code to put them all together again. You can export images for use in Flash, Dreamweaver, FreeHand, and many other applications. In this section, you will learn how to use each of the export options, and you will export the Atlantis document that you sliced in Chapter 11.

Alternate Tags

Alternate tags are displayed while an image is downloading or when a mouse cursor passes over the image. They are also helpful for people who browse with images turned off and for visually impaired users who use readers that read the descriptions to them. Your descriptions should be descriptive enough to communicate what the image represents. (If you've seen whole paragraphs used as Alt tags, you can assume the Web site is particularly concerned about making its services accessible to vision-impaired users.) I have also read that Alt tags can improve your search engine ratings with some of the search engines if you use good Alt tags.

Exporting Images Only

Many times, you will design images in Fireworks that you will place in an existing HTML page. Or, you may want to place the images into the HTML code
yourself. If you use Dreamweaver, it is very easy to place an image by simply
selecting Insert|Image and browsing to the image you want to place without
ever writing a bit of code. However, some of you wouldn't think of letting a
program handle your code; you want complete control over the way your image
is coded into the Web page. Whatever your reason to export only images, Fireworks makes it quite easy to export just one image or multiple images.

To export images only, follow these steps:

1. Select an image or Shift+select multiple images you want to export.

2. Choose File|Export and name your file.

3. Choose Images Only from the Save As Type drop-down menu, as shown
   in Figure 12.22.

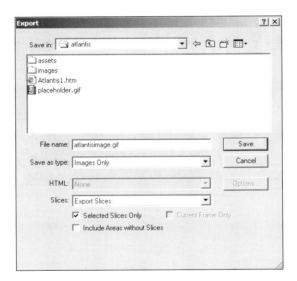

Figure 12.22
The Export dialog box with
Images Only selected.

4. Choose Export Slices from the Slices drop-down menu.

5. Select the Selected Slices Only option and deselect the Include Areas
   Without Slices option.

PROJECT Exporting Only the Images for the Horse Adventures Web Page

In this project, you will use the Horse Adventure Web site you've worked on in
Chapters 9 and 10. You will export just the images. By exporting just the images, you can manually place them into an HTML document or you can use
them for another purpose. This is a complex Web site as far as layout goes.
Many people prefer to place all the images in their own tables within

Dreamweaver or the HTML editor of their choice. This layout has a lot of images because of the many rollovers. To export the images only, follow these steps:

1. Open the HAimages.png file from the Chapter 12 resources folder.

2. You learned how to slice a document in Chapter 11. If you have images without slices, be sure to add them by right/Cmd-clicking the image and choosing Insert Slice or choose Modify|Insert Slice. Figure 12.23 shows the sliced images for this layout.

Note: The navigation symbols and the symbols below the line of icons all had slices added to them automatically when they were produced.

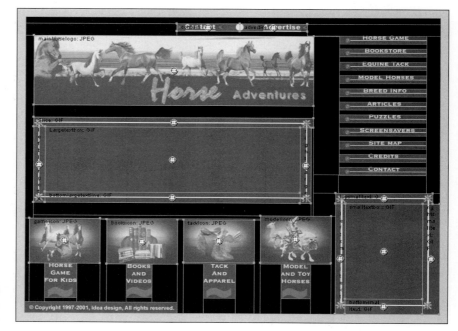

Figure 12.23
The sliced images for the Horse Adventures layout.

Note: If a designer were pressed for time on this project, the Export As HTML And Images would be a better option. It was tested and the page began loading within 5 seconds, which was acceptable for this Web page.

3. Choose File|Export. Choose Images Only from the Save As Type drop-down menu and Export Slices from the Slices drop-down menu, deselect Include Areas Without Slices, and select Selected Slices Only (see Figure 12.24).

4. Browse to the folder in which you want to save your images. Click Save. Figure 12.25 shows the contents of the ImagesOnly folder after the export. (I told you there would be a lot.)

Regardless of how you decide to export this site, it is now ready to have a Flash movie attached to it. A jigsaw puzzle is going to be added in the Flash section of this book (Chapter 17). You may recall in Chapter 1 that you made a puzzle shape in FreeHand that will be used in Flash.

Exporting HTML and Images

The Export HTML And Images option is a popular feature of Fireworks. It is a real timesaver for your workflow. You can lay out entire Web pages, and Fireworks will generate the HTML code and even the JavaScript for rollovers and

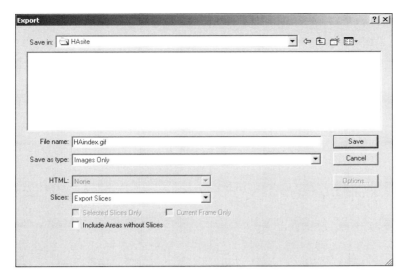

Figure 12.24
The export options for exporting images only.

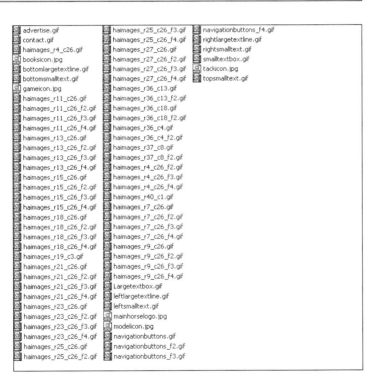

Figure 12.25
The contents of the ImagesOnly folder after exporting the selected images.

pop-up menus for you automatically. Even though the description says HTML, the JavaScript is exported as well, without any extra steps in the export process. To export an entire document, follow these steps:

1. Have a document that is sliced and ready to export. Choose File|Export.

2. Name your file and browse to the root folder of the site you are exporting into.

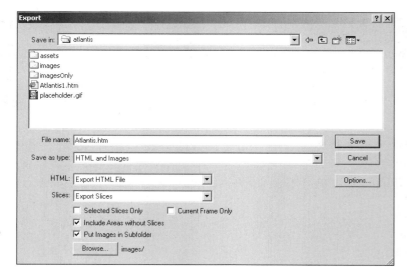

Figure 12.26

The Export dialog box with HTML And Images selected.

Areas Without Slices

If you select the Include Areas Without Slices option, the areas within the red lines automatically generated by Fireworks will be exported even if you haven't defined them as slices with the Slice tool. If you deselect the Include Areas Without Slices option, an area with an empty cell (or spacer depending on your HTML option setting) will be generated in the HTML code.

Pop-Up Menus

You can export pop-up menus using the HTML And Images option, but you can't export them as images only. Pop-up menus exist only as JavaScript that is exported from Fireworks; they are not actual graphics and can't be exported to Flash or Director. However, they can be used in Dreamweaver or other HTML editors when exported using HTML And Images.

3. Choose HTML And Images from the Save As Type drop-down menu; refer to Figure 12.26.

4. Choose Export HTML File from the HTML drop-down menu.

5. Choose Export Slices from the Slices drop-down menu.

6. Deselect the Selected Slices Only option, select the Include Areas Without Slices option, and select Put Images In Subfolder. Click Save.

PROJECT Exporting the Entire Atlantis Document

In this project, you will export the entire Atlantis document that you sliced in Chapter 11. Two disjoint rollovers have been added (Chapter 10) to demonstrate how the entire document (including the related JavaScript) is exported. You will preview the results at the end of the project. To export the Atlantis document, follow these steps:

1. Choose File|Open. Navigate to the Chapter 12 resources folder and select the AtlantisSliced.png file. Click Open.

2. Name your file Atlantis for this example. Browse to the root folder of the site you are exporting into.

3. Choose HTML And Images from the Save As Type drop-down menu.

4. Choose Export HTML File from the HTML Drop-down menu.

5. Choose Export Slices from the Slices drop-down menu.

6. Deselect the Selected Slices Only option, select the Include Areas Without Slices option, and select Put Images In Subfolder. Click Save.

Removing the Canvas Color

You can either export with the canvas color or choose Modify|Canvas Color and select Transparent. If you leave the canvas color, it will be exported with your image. To set the background color in an HTML editor or use a background image (which is available for this document), set the canvas color to Transparent before exporting. For your viewing pleasure, the canvas color was left for the screenshots so you don't have to view them with the checkerboard background.

To preview the file you just exported, open the Atlantis.htm file in Dreamweaver (or another editor) to see the table that has been generated. To view the working Web page, open it in a browser. Move your mouse over the first button in the second row of the button area to see the placeholder that says Image Goes Here. Move your cursor over the words "national museum", and the Image Goes Here placeholder becomes visible. Figure 12.27 shows the exported document open in a browser.

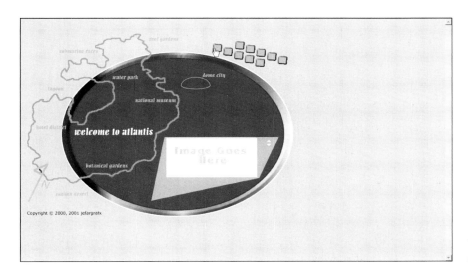

Figure 12.27
The Atlantis Web page exported and viewed in a browser.

Exporting to Macromedia Flash SWF

Exporting to SWF is becoming more popular with each passing day. It wasn't too long ago that GIF was still the animation option of choice, primarily because the user didn't need to download a separate plug-in to see a GIF as they had to do to view a SWF (Flash) file. Based on a recent survey that revealed 96.4 percent of all Web users have the Flash player, many more Web sites are featuring Flash animations instead of GIFs. SWF or Flash animations' greatest appeal is their tremendous flexibility in design capabilities, as well as their small file sizes.

You can export as a Flash SWF file or you can use a native Fireworks PNG file in Flash. To import into Flash, see the Flash section of this book. You can choose to import as a PNG file or as a SWF file, as well as edit bitmaps right from Flash. You will be amazed at the integration built in between Fireworks and

Flash—you can choose to import editable objects with options such as including text, guides, and images. Or, you can choose to flatten the image. A flattened image is brought into Flash automatically as a bitmap symbol and inserted into the Flash Library panel.

To export as Flash SWF, follow these steps:

1. Choose File|Export.

2. Select Macromedia Flash SWF from the Save As Type drop-down menu.

3. Click the Options button to set your export options. Figure 12.28 shows the Macromedia Flash SWF Export Options dialog box.

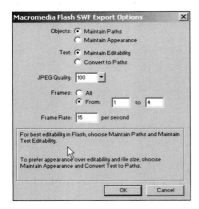

Figure 12.28

The Macromedia Flash SWF Export Options dialog box.

4. Choose the option you'd like in the Objects area. Maintain Paths converts paths into editable Flash paths, and Maintain Appearance converts paths into a bitmapped image.

5. Choose a Text option. Maintain Editability converts Fireworks text into text that is editable in Flash. Convert To Path converts the text into a bitmap.

6. If you are exporting a JPEG image, select the quality setting you'd like.

7. Select All Frames or just the frames you want to export.

8. Set the Frame Rate per second.

9. When you are done with your selections, click OK and then click Save in the Export dialog box.

You can use SWF exports from Fireworks as they are for Web viewing or insert them into Dreamweaver or another layout editor without even using Flash. But the real purpose of exporting as a Macromedia Flash SWF file is to reuse the artwork you made in Fireworks in Flash. Vector content remains vector in Flash, but effects you can choose in Fireworks will be lost when exported for use in Flash. Some of the things that are lost include Live Effects, opacity (objects with opacity become symbols with an alpha channel), blending modes, masks, slice objects, image maps, and behaviors such as rollovers. Also lost are features such as feathering, layers, and some text formatting. Anti-aliasing will not be maintained on export, because Flash automatically applies it to documents; so, that loss won't cause you any problems. If you keep in mind that the main reason to use a SWF export from Fireworks is to reuse the art, then you will experience few frustrations.

Exporting to PSD

If you want to open your Fireworks PNG files in Photoshop, or someone else needs to use Photoshop with your files, you can export the Fireworks files as PSD files. When you export as a PSD, you have the option of exporting with better editability over appearance or better appearance over editability. However, keep in mind that Fireworks paths will always be converted to a bitmap image. To export for Photoshop, follow these steps:

1. Choose File|Export.

2. Select Photoshop PSD from the Save As Type drop-down menu.

3. The Settings drop-down area gives you four options (see Figure 12.29):

   - *Maintain Editability Over Appearance*—Converts objects to layers and keeps effects editable and it converts text into editable text. Effects that don't have an equivalent in Photoshop are discarded.

   - *Maintain Fireworks Appearance*—Converts object into layers and renders the effects and text into an image.

   - *Smaller Photoshop File*—Flattens all the objects and layers into one layer, producing a smaller file size.

   - *Custom*—Allows you to select separate setting options for objects, effects, and text.

4. When you are done making your selections, click Save to export.

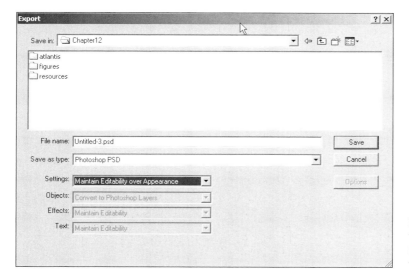

Figure 12.29

The Export dialog box when Photoshop PSD is selected as the export type.

Exporting or Copying as Vectors (Illustrator AI)

Using Fireworks vector objects in FreeHand, Illustrator, or Flash allows you to use the basic path, fill, and stroke information only. If you want to use the vector shape, this option is viable. To maintain the look of the object, it will be better to produce it in the program you want it for. Exporting as a vector object from Fireworks will cause the object to lose all effects, feathering, dither fills, slices guides, most text formatting, and blending modes. To export a vector shape for FreeHand, Illustrator, or Flash, follow these steps:

1. Choose File|Export.

2. Choose Illustrator 7 from the Save As Type drop-down menu. The options in the Export dialog box will change, as shown in Figure 12.30.

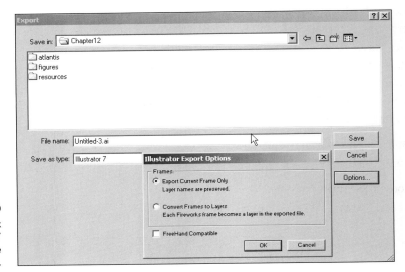

Figure 12.30
The Export dialog box after choosing the Illustrator 7 export option and clicking the Options button.

3. For more options, click the Options button (see Figure 12.30). To keep the elements on individual layers, select Export Current Frame Only. To keep each frame on a separate layer, select the Convert Frames To Layers option.

4. To make the export completely compatible for FreeHand, choose FreeHand Compatible. You will lose bitmap images. Gradients in FreeHand 10 are not lost.

5. You can also copy and paste a vector image into FreeHand, Flash, or Illustrator, but it will primarily maintain only the paths, strokes, and basic fill information.

Exporting to a Dreamweaver Library

You can export an HTML file with HTML code included as a Dreamweaver Library item (the new pop-up menus are an exception). Before you export as a Dreamweaver Library, you need to define a local site root folder in Dreamweaver and make a folder called Library (use a capital *L*). You export the Library item to this folder. You'll need to do this each time you are exporting a Dreamweaver Library into a new site. This step isn't necessary if you already have a Library folder in the root folder of the target site. To export as a Dreamweaver Library, follow these steps:

1. Choose File|Export.

2. Choose Dreamweaver Library from the Save As Type drop-down menu.

3. Locate the Library folder you want to export to.

4. To put the images into an image subfolder, select the Put Images In Subfolder option and click Save to export.

Exporting to CSS Layers

By exporting as CSS layers, you can produce style sheets that define how different elements appear on your Web page. CSS is usually used by more experienced users who want to have more control than simply using HTML code. By using CSS layers, you can overlap layers and stack them on top of one another, which you can't do with normal Fireworks HTML output. To export to CSS layers, follow these steps:

1. Prepare your document elements on layers, frames, and/or slices. Choose File|Export.

2. Choose CSS Layers from the Save As Type drop-down menu. Figure 12.31 shows the options that become available once you choose CSS Layers.

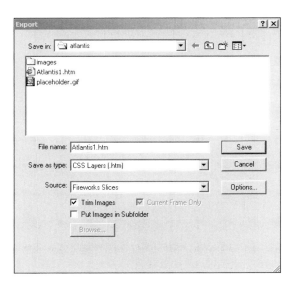

Figure 12.31
The CSS layers options.

3. From the Source drop-down menu, choose how you want to separate the elements. The choices are Fireworks Slices, Fireworks Layers, and Fireworks Frames.

4. Select the Trim Images option to discard excess canvas around the images.

5. To place the exported images in a subfolder, select the Put Images In Subfolder option.

Exporting Layers and Frames as Separate Images

You can export all the layers or all the frames of a Fireworks document. Each layer and each frame will export as a separate image. Figure 12.32 shows the Export dialog box when Layers To Files is selected.

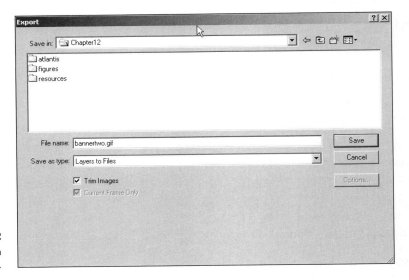

Figure 12.32
The Export dialog box with Layers To Files selected.

To export layers or frames as separate images, follow these steps:

1. Choose File|Export.

2. Select Layers To Files or Frames To Files from the Save As Type drop-down menu. You can use only one export option at a time; if you want layers and frames, you will have to do another export.

3. Select the Trim Images option to automatically trim the images to fit the objects on each layer (or frame). To keep the layer or frame the same size as the document, deselect the Trim Images option. When you are finished, navigate to the folder you want to export into and click Save.

Exporting an Area or Scaling an Image

In Fireworks, you don't have to export an entire slice or image. You have the option of exporting just a selected part of an image or document as well as cropping or scaling an image. When you use the Export Area tool or scale or crop an image, you don't alter the original image—just the exported one.

Export Area Tool

Sometimes you may want to export only portions of a document for use in a Web page. Or, you may want to export part of an image so you can assign specialized behaviors to it in an HTML editor. You use the Export Area tool to define the specific area of a document or image you want to export. The Export Area tool is in the fly-out attached to the Pointer tool. Click and hold the arrow in the corner of the Pointer tool icon and select the little camera icon to access the Export Area tool. To export just portions of a document or an image, follow these steps:

1. Select the Export Area tool.

2. Click and drag a marquee around the portion you want to export.

3. Click and drag the square handles to adjust the selection.

4. You can export in two different ways.

    • Choose File|Export, give the file a name, select Images Only from the Save As Type drop-down menu, and save your image.

    • You will have far greater control if you double-click inside the marquee surrounding the image you want to export. Doing so brings up the Export Preview dialog box, which gives you control over the size of the image area and the optimization settings. When you are finished, click the Export button. The same Save dialog box opens that you get by using the first option (File|Export); name the file and click Save.

Cropping and Scaling an Image

You can also crop or scale an image using the Export Preview dialog box. To scale or crop an image, follow these steps:

1. Choose File|Export Preview.

2. Click the File tab (see Figure 12.33).

> ### Using the Export Area Tool with Slices
>
> You can use the Export Area tool in a document that contains slices. When you select an area to export with the Export Area tool, either export option (double-clicking inside the image or exporting from the File menu) will give you a warning when you click the Export or Save button: "Slice objects will be ignored. To get sliced output and behaviors, choose Export Slices." To export the slices, use another export method. The Export Area tool will only export the selected area.

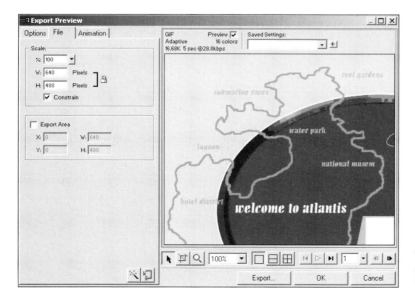

Figure 12.33

The options when the File tab of the Export Preview dialog box is selected.

3. To scale the image, you can use the percentage slider (%) or type in the desired width and height. If you select the Constrain option, your image will automatically maintain its proportions. With Constrain selected, you only have to change the height or the width—the other will be set for you. If you deselect the Constrain option, your image may be distorted.

4. To crop the image, look at the icons directly below the image preview. Next to the Pointer tool is an icon that looks like the Crop tool; it is called Export Area in the Export Preview window. Click the Export Area icon, and handles appear around the image area. Click and drag the handles to outline the area you want to export.

Moving On

In this chapter, you have discovered how to import a wide range of file formats from FreeHand and other applications, and what to expect with each format. You have also learned how to export your Fireworks documents for use in FreeHand, Flash, and Dreamweaver.

You will now move on to Section III, where Hillman Curtis will introduce you to the world of Flash. Then, you will begin in Chapter 14 with a few Flash basics.

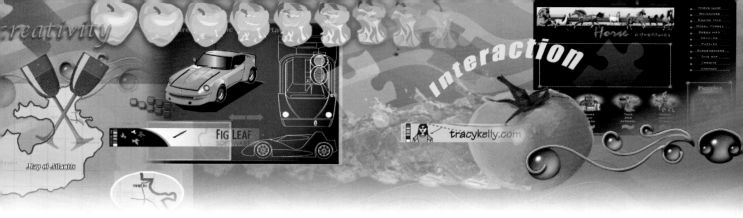

Integrating Flash,
Fireworks and
FreeHand Studio

*This Studio showcases many of this book's projects
made using the strongest features of Flash, Fireworks,
and FreeHand. Use this section for reference or inspiration.
When you see something you like, flip to that chapter and
start producing it. The source files for all these images
can be found on this book's CD-ROM, so you
can use them in the learning process.*

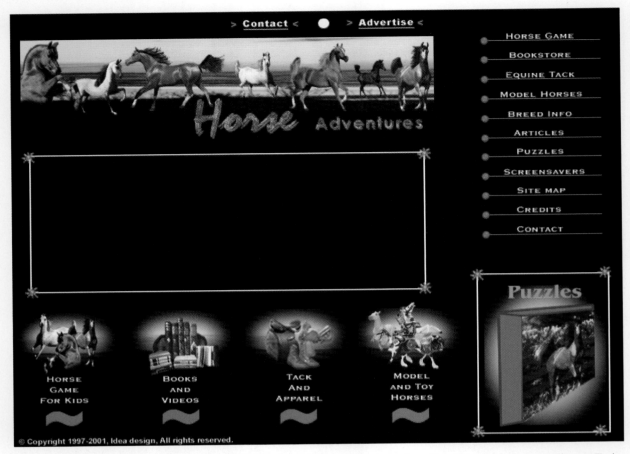

The images for the Horse Adventure Web page (**www.horseadventures.com**) are all made in Fireworks—the logo (Chapter 7), the collage and icon (Chapter 9), and the navigation (Chapter 10). You will slice, optimize, and export this page in Chapters 11 and 12. Placing this Web page into Dreamweaver is covered in Appendix A.

The Horse Adventures logo uses many different text effects, such as fills, textures, patterns, and drop shadows (see Chapter 7).

This image shows alternative navigation for the Horse Adventures Web page. The menu is made using the new Pop-Up Menu Wizard in Fireworks (see Chapter 10).

The collage for Horse Adventures uses masking techniques; the images are cut from their backgrounds with Fireworks selection tools (see Chapter 9).

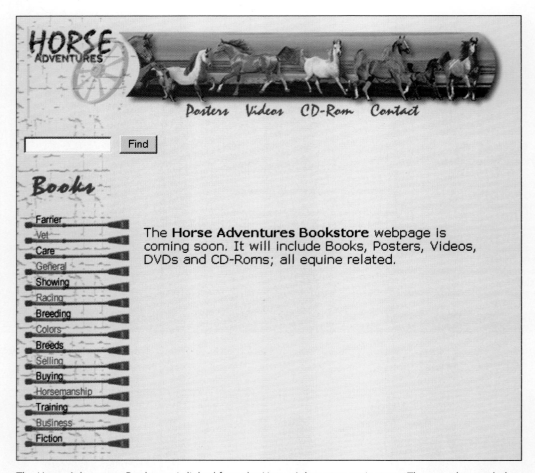

The Horse Adventures Bookstore is linked from the Horse Adventures main page. The same banner helps users identify that they are still in the same site. The design uses the same techniques from Chapter 9 as the original Horse Adventures Web page.

The header for the Horse Adventures Bookstore has its color changed using the Hue and Saturation effect in Fireworks (see Chapter 9). It is then taken to FreeHand, where the image is put inside the shape you see using the Paste Inside command (see Chapter 2). Once it is placed back into Fireworks, the Layer blend mode of Multiply is applied to help the colors blend better with the existing Web page background.

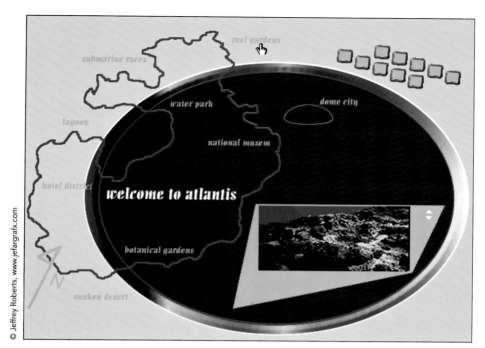

© Jeffrey Roberts, www.jefargrafx.com

The Atlantis Web page is done in Fireworks, except for the blue map, which is drawn in FreeHand (see Chapter 1). The disjointed rollover, where you see the photo, is done in Chapter 10. If you wanted to, you could just as easily place a Flash movie where the photo is.

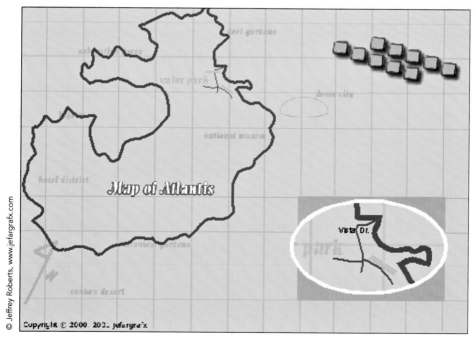

© Jeffrey Roberts, www.jefargrafx.com

This map page is accessed from one of the small buttons on the Atlantis home page. The detail area of the map is drawn in FreeHand. The magnified section and arrow are added in FreeHand as well (see Chapter 2). By deleting the center gradient and black circle, you change the look of the page but still keep the consistency of the site's look.

© Todd McPhetridge, www.cobaltgrahics.com

The background for this Flash movie is made in Fireworks. When the movie runs, the lure turns 360 degrees, which is performed in Flash (see Chapter 18).

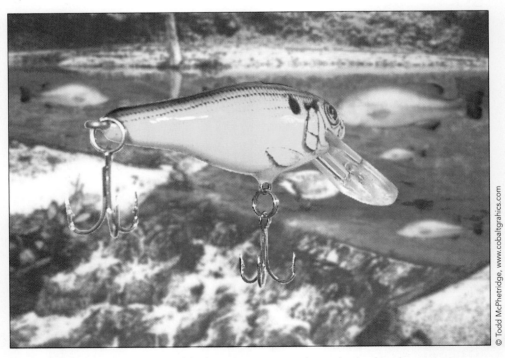

© Todd McPhetridge, www.cobaltgrahics.com

This figure shows one of the views of the lure as it turns around completely when the mouse is moved along the image. The effect is achieved in Flash by using invisible buttons and ActionScript (see Chapter 18).

The Horse Adventures Web page has a puzzle box in the right corner which links to this puzzle. The puzzle shapes are made in FreeHand (see Chapter 2), and the puzzle operation is done in Flash (see Chapter 18). The buttons on the bottom are used to load the puzzle Movie Clips into a different level than the main movie, keeping the buttons visible on each puzzle page.

This puzzle of a flower easily replaces the horse image without the need for additional ActionScript or image editing. The puzzle loads into the same level and uses a back button to return to the menu seen below.

A variation of the opening screen of the puzzles, this screen uses a Movie Clip on the same level as the main movie.

© Fig Leaf Software, www.figleaf.com

This is a banner for Fig Leaf Software. It features a color action that's new in Flash. This new action allows users to color the leaves different colors.

© Fig Leaf Software, www.figleaf.com

This banner features a print function. You will learn how to make printing available from your Flash movie in Chapter 19.

© Tracy Kelly, www.tracykelly.com

This variation of the new color function uses multiple objects to be colored instead of one duplicated object such as the leaves in the Fig Leaf banner.

This jukebox is traced in Flash (see Chapter 14). When a button is pressed, the artist's name, the song title, and the size of the file are all displayed (see Chapter 18).

© Darryl Larson Productions, www.darryllarson.com

The original photo

128 colors with a color tolerance of 156

256 colors with a color tolerance of 156

256 colors with a color tolerance of 255

The horse on the left is the original photo used in the Horse Adventures puzzle. Because this image is going to be placed on the perspective grid, it has to be a vector. The quickest way to convert this image into a vector is using the FreeHand tracing tool (see Chapter 2). The last three images show the results of the trace using different settings (see Chapter 2).

© Ian Kelleigh, www.freehandsource.com

Bar Wars is a Flash movie that has scrolling text similar to the opening scene of *Star Wars*. The background is designed in Fireworks, and the movie is then completed using FreeHand and Flash.

These wine glasses are made in FreeHand (Chapters 1 and 3), and then they are scaled and rotated and have a glow added all in Flash (see Chapter 14).

The wine in the image on the left is defying the law of physics, so the image is brought back into FreeHand where the wine is extracted and rotated in the glasses to look more realistic.

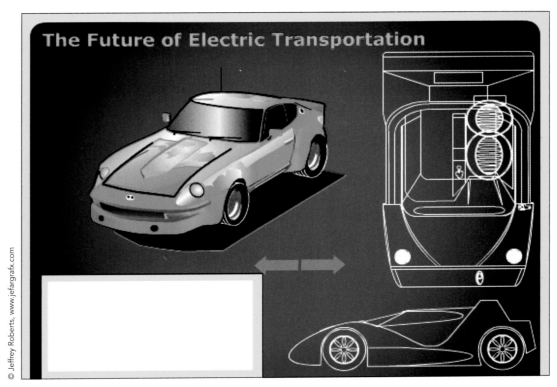

© Jeffrey Roberts, www.jefargrafx.com

The line drawings of the cars are done in FreeHand (see Chapter 1). The colored car is drawn in FreeHand and rendered in a 3D program. The car will be rotated in Flash (see Chapter 18).

Final image based on drawing © Jeffrey Roberts, www.jefargrafx.com

This car is drawn in Chapter 1 and is colored using the new contour gradient tool in FreeHand and other gradients as well.

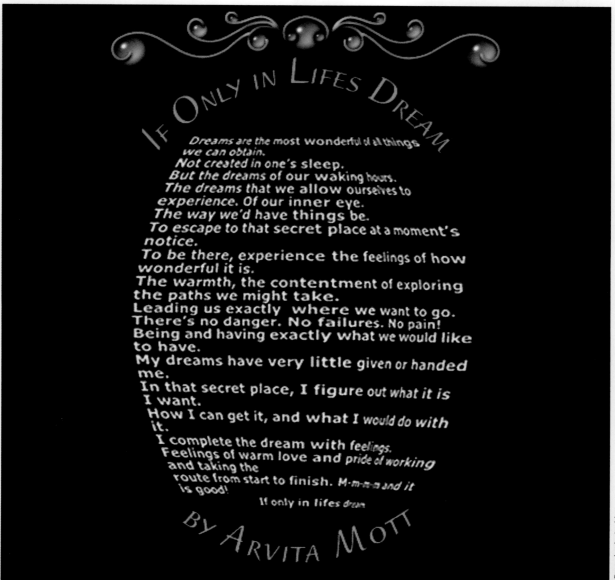

© Poem by Arvita Mott

This ornament and the text on this Web page are made in Fireworks (Chapters 7 and 9), and the poem is placed in an envelope to get the oval shape in FreeHand (see Chapter 2).

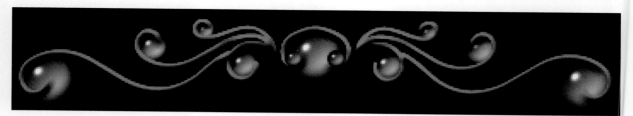

This ornament is made in Fireworks (see Chapter 9). The glassy spheres use three different gradients to achieve the shiny look.

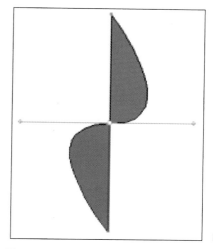 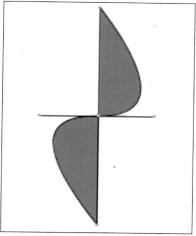 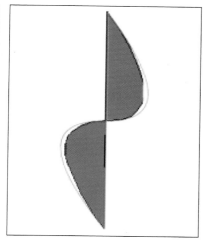

These curves were make by Ian Kelleigh in his "Exporting to Flash" project (see Chapter 6). The first curve on the left is an extreme curve drawn in FreeHand; the second is how curve looks when pasted into Flash. The third image is the FreeHand curve placed under the Flash curve; the red line indicates how the curve was altered. This phenomenon appears to happen in Flash only on extreme curves.

Both images © Ian Kelleigh, www.freehandsource.com

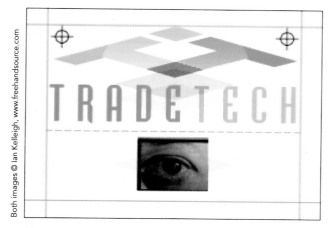 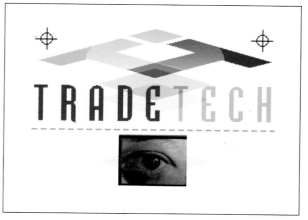

The logo on the left is made in FreeHand using CMYK colors and is opened in Flash. When compared to the logo on the right, there is a definite color shift because Flash converted the left image to RGB colors. The logo on the right is converted to RGB colors in FreeHand prior to opening in Flash (see Chapter 6).

This is a navigation bar in the Up state (left) and the Over state (right), which is made in Fireworks using a custom glass style (see Chapter 10).

The eaten apple is blended to the whole apple in FreeHand generating what looks like a shape tween (see Chapter 3). The blend is then taken into Fireworks where each apple is on a different frame and animated (see Chapter 12).

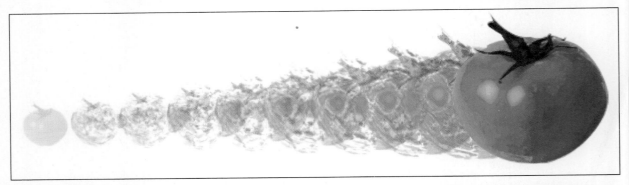

A shape tween is applied to the small green tomato in Flash, which then grows into a full-sized red tomato (see Chapters 14 and 15).

A Web page header for the *Fireworks 4 f/x & Design* Web site shown before you select the knock out feature of the Drop Shadow Effect (see Chapter 7).

The Web page header shown with the Drop Shadow options Knock Out selected.

The Eyeland Studio interface is provided for your use by Scott Hamlin of Eyeland Studio. All the objects are drawn in Fireworks (Chapter 8), and the interface and the sliding buttons are arranged and animated in Flash (see Chapters 14 and 15).

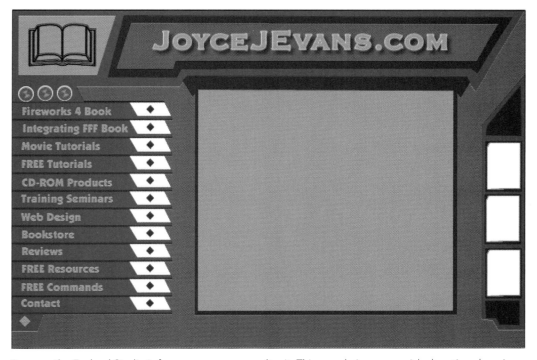

Because the Eyeland Studio is for your use, you can alter it. This sample is a very quick alteration changing color, name, links, and logo.

This horse is part of the Horse Adventure collage.

The rider is removed from this image using Firework's Rubber Stamp tool and other techniques taught in Chapter 9.

Part III

Flash

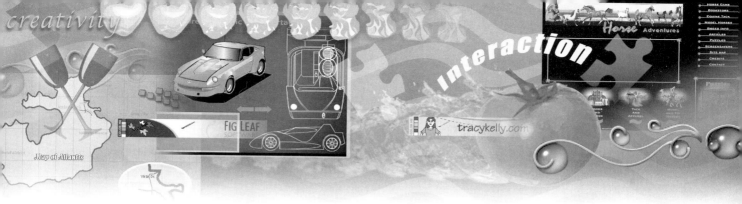

Chapter 13

Flash Introduction

This chapter provides a brief introduction to what you'll find in the Flash section of this book, as well as an introduction to using Flash by Hillman Curtis.

Flash

In this Flash section, it is assumed you know the basics of using Flash. We will not be discussing the interface or the toolbars at length unless they directly relate to a project for a particular topic. Because it's impossible to know what level of understanding each reader has when approaching Flash, some parts will be more basic than others.

Chapter 14 begins with some essential Flash concepts and shows you how Flash functions a bit differently in some areas than Fireworks and FreeHand. Chapter 15 will delve into symbols and a few animation concepts. Chapter 16 will discuss some ActionScript basics and essentials you will need to know to complete the projects presented in Chapter 17.

Once you get to the ActionScript chapter, you'll need to be quite comfortable working in the Flash environment. It would be preposterous to try to teach you all the ins and outs of ActionScripting in the limited space allowed, but you will learn the essentials to perform and, to some degree (depending on your knowledge of ActionScripting), understand what you are doing and why you are doing it. In any case, even if you don't understand all the whys, you'll be able to perform the exercises and projects and end up with working, usable Flash movies.

In Chapter 17, you will make the Flash movies for projects you began in Fireworks and FreeHand. You will also learn how to rotate a product display 360 degrees.

Chapter 18 contains two special bonus projects donated by Fig Leaf Software, a premier Web development and design company, and a leading Macromedia Authorized Training Partner. Chapter 19 wraps up the Flash section with the various methods of publishing your Flash movies.

Note: You can learn more about each contributor in the resource list in Appendix A.

You'll get the benefit of some real experts in the field of Flash in this section of the book. Scott Hamlin (author of *Flash 5 Magic*) provided an interface for your use and alteration, Fig Leaf Software supplied some super banners for you to make, and Tracy Kelly contributed the ActionScript for most of the projects.

I'm very happy to welcome Hillman Curtis (author of *Flash Web Design*), who has graciously agreed to write the opening pages for this section. Hillman is one of the most widely recognized new media designers in the world, with clients ranging from Adobe Systems Incorporated, to Intel, to **RollingStone.com**. His innovative work with Flash has garnered him and his company numerous awards and a growing reputation world wide.

An Open Letter to the Design Community from Hillman Curtis

When Joyce contacted me about writing this chapter, I initially thought I'd just run down the list of basic features that make Flash such a great tool. Then I thought, why do that? You can get that much off the back of this book or the Macromedia Web site. So I decided to focus on what makes Flash special to me as a designer, and why I think it's perhaps the most powerful application to come along since the Lumiere brothers invented motion pictures in 1895.

I started hillmancurtis, inc. as a Flash shop in 1998 after working as the art director at Macromedia for three and a half years. I'll never forget the first time I used the software. Macromedia had just gotten it in and I was asked to tool around with it, just to see what I could do. This was immediately after Flash hit the street, and most of us thought it was some kind of shareware. After a week of experimenting, I knew my life as a designer would never be the same again. I've loved graphic design since childhood, and in college I studied film theory; but it wasn't until Flash came along that I realized I could marry my two passions in my career. Flash re-introduced me to the power of motion and its uncanny ability to reinvent a static medium (in this case, the Web).

What the Lumiere brothers did for the photographic image, Flash did for graphic design. Design has always been the melding together of layout, typography, symbols, and color—and they're all important. But with Flash, you add motion; and with motion come rhythm, cadence, and repetition—the passage of time. In other words, by incorporating movement, the limitations of static imagery are shaken off. The design comes to life, giving it the power to transfix a viewer in the same way film can. The relationship between viewer and design is thus deepened through the nuances of gesture and action. Flash embodies the state of becoming, and that alone makes it a designer's dream.

But it's also an incredible scripting tool, making your work accessible on multiple platforms and browsers. Not only does Flash free you from the restrictions of HTML, allowing you to stretch the capabilities of a given browser, use all your fonts at once, and incorporate MP3s for voiceovers or music, it also increases your audience by spanning the Web with its universal appeal. And because you're working with the Web, you have an immediate means of posting your work. So you can experiment, put your designs online, have them shot down, rework them, and post them again. And if you're a fledgling designer, fear not. The Flash community, because of its youth and general lack of formal training, is incredibly supportive. We're all feeling our way and learning from each other as we go, making this a wonderful, educational time to be working in motion graphics. As for those who feel compelled to destructively criticize new work, they're few and relatively harmless, easily overshadowed by the warmth and encouragement you'll receive from most of your new media peers.

Less Is More

As with most powerful tools, discretion is just as important as know-how. The use of Flash must be moderate and deliberately careful. You have to justify its use because, despite what you read, plenty of people still don't have the necessary plug-ins, and making something unnecessarily complex is the exact opposite of your role as a designer. With Flash, it's really tempting to throw everything but the kitchen sink into your design, I know. But that's putting the messenger before the message to create nothing more than a pretty picture. And beyond breaking the first rule of graphic design—that it's not so much about your artistic talent, but what you're promoting—such overuse gives Flash a bad reputation for causing heavy and slow-to-load files, making sites crash, and wasting people's time. If used only for their own sake, interactivity and animation are just empty shells, cars without motors, tin-men without hearts.

I've judged a lot of design and Flash contests over the years, and one of my main rules regarding Flash spots is that they must load within 10 to 15 seconds. If one doesn't, I immediately give it a zero. Design has to respect its medium, environment, or function. Flash must stream well over the Web—and not just on DSL, cable, and T1 hook-ups, either. It must also be able to reach the millions of people with 56Kbps and slower connections.

But don't let this frustrate you. The Web's limitations are more liberating than restrictive, when you look at them the right way. In paring down a design, you make it simpler, more easily understood, and often more elegant. As I work, I question the inclusion of each and every element in what I'm doing. I ask myself if it will cause the spot to be too heavy, stutter, or stall the browser. I have an internal self-editor that's hyperaware of how bitmaps, audio, or intensely gradated vector images will affect the site's performance. I'm constantly looking for things to take out, asking myself how I can make the spot lighter by removing all the extraneous junk. My work has thus been described as "thoughtful" and "sublime." And although neither of those are particularly sexy descriptions, they mean a lot to me. They mean others realize that I put a lot of thought into my designs.

Self-editing, however, is one of the hardest skills to learn. Once you've created something, it's all too easy to become married to every part of it. Being able to see its unnecessary elements takes hard work and a humble spirit. Francis Ford Coppola used to write a script without stopping, just to see what he'd come up with. Then he'd go back through and eliminate everything that didn't support the story. As I began self-editing, just knowing he did that inspired me to do the same. Now it's practically second nature.

Use Your Wisdom

Flash is hip. It's still relatively new and exciting, and it's becoming ever more popular. More clients want it on their sites, more designers are learning to use it, and its capabilities are expanding. Although this means great things for the Flash designer, it also carries a potential handicap. For all the reasons I mentioned before, Flash isn't an inherently good thing. Sometimes, it quite simply isn't appropriate. As the designer, it's your responsibility to identify those instances, which may require your steering a client who's dead set on a Flash spot away from using it.

I typically start by asking them if "wowing" customers is really what the company is all about. Is it really in their best interest to make a dazzling, yet inaccessible Web site? I try to explain why I'd follow a different approach. If their company isn't about "wow," then why have a spot communicating just that? Once they see the contradiction, they almost always agree, and we can proceed in stride with one another.

Together, we then develop a rough to very-detailed storyboard, which gives us a kind of visual contract that keeps us on track. And because the client is involved in the design's development, both their satisfaction and my wish to communicate their message clearly are ensured.

Sometimes, of course, the client's desires and my comfort level are simply incompatible; at these times, I know that what they want won't work, but they want it anyway. If someone is set on having loud disco music, a bunch of balls bouncing around, and flamboyant pyrotechnics, I generally pass on the project. But this is a luxury many new designers can't afford, so my advice for those of you who are just starting is to use the tactics I mentioned earlier as much as possible. Ask if they really want their site to yell and scream. Try to reveal to them how certain effects might contradict their company's core values, and suggest ways of reflecting those values more truthfully. If they still don't get it, take the job anyway. God knows I have, many times. In the long run, every job is a good job. In other words, there's always something to learn.

That brings me to my final point. The beauty of graphic design is that it's a collaborative art. Working with other designers and clients alike, you have the opportunity to speak to thousands, sometimes millions through a visual language. And though collaborations can be a strain, causing you to wonder why you need to consult a non-designer on issues of design, it's the nature of commercial work. Like the Web, this too can be a liberating limitation. It gives you a framework, and through it, your designs will develop grace and consistency that are sure to garner the attention of both your fellow designers and future clients.

Moving On

Now that you know what to expect in the Flash section, you are probably ready to get at it, especially after reading Hillman's wonderful introduction to Flash. In Chapter 14, you will begin by looking at some essential terms and concepts of Flash, which will prepare you to begin writing ActionScript for this section's projects.

Chapter 14

Flash Essentials

This chapter is geared toward the user who may have intermediate-level skills in FreeHand and/or Fireworks but not Flash. You will learn some of the basics such as using layers, keyframes, and timelines. You will begin an animation and the Eyeland Studio interface.

Movie Properties

When you're making a movie in Flash, one of the first things you'll need to think through is the size you want your movie to be. For example, is it the whole Web site or part of a Web site? You should determine such things before you begin making your Flash movie. You'll also need to consider the color of the background. What is the color of the Web page you are embedding your movie into? Or, what color do you want the background of the Web page to be? The background color you choose is applied throughout the movie—you can't have different background colors for different scenes within the same movie in Flash.

You change the default size of your movie and choose a background color, dimensions, and ruler units in the Movie Properties dialog box. To access it, right-click/Ctrl+click the stage and select Movie Properties. You can also access it by choosing Modify|Movie (Ctrl+M/Cmd+M). Figure 14.1 shows the Movie Properties dialog box.

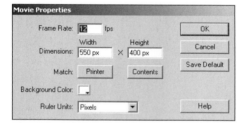

Figure 14.1
The Movie Properties dialog box.

The Frame Rate is 12 fps (frames per second) by default. As a result, it will take one second to play 12 frames of your movie. Change your movie dimensions by highlighting the default values and typing in the new dimensions. Match Printer sets the stage size to the default paper size of your default printer. Match Contents increases or decreases the stage size based on content, including anything that overlaps into the work area. Click the Background Color box to change the background color, and select the Ruler Units option you'd like to use.

Timeline

The timeline controls all aspects of timing, which determine how long your movie plays, when it plays, what plays, and basically everything involved in producing your Flash movie. What the viewer sees from the time the movie starts to when it stops is determined by where you place the content on the timeline.

The timeline sits on top of the stage area of your movie. Figure 14.2 shows the stage (the large white area) and the timeline on top. Figure 14.3 shows the timeline; I've undocked it and labeled some of the major areas for you. The left portion of the timeline is the layers section, which I'll label for you in the next section.

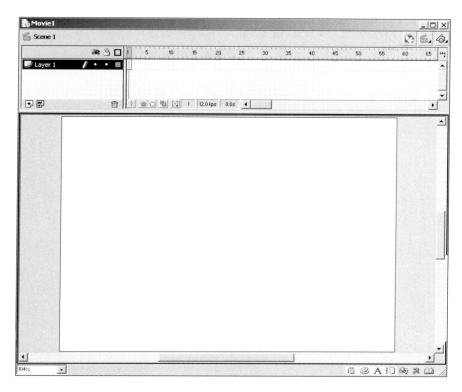

Figure 14.2
The timeline and the stage area.

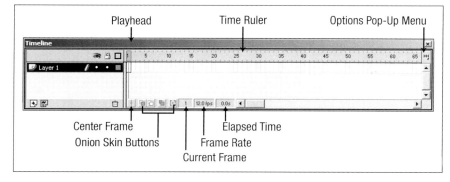

Figure 14.3
The timeline undocked
and labeled.

You can undock your timeline by clicking and dragging the icon to the left of
the Scene title. It's handy to be able to undock the timeline when you have two
monitors; you can move the timeline off the stage altogether onto a separate
monitor. This technique is a great way to view all the layers at the same time.

You'll see more of this portion of the timeline in the "Inserting and Deleting
Keyframes" section of this chapter.

Layer Basics

Layers help to separate and organize pieces of your content and actions. How
you use layers will depend on your workflow and work habits. It's a good idea
to separate different parts of your movies onto separate layers; otherwise, you'll
be amazed how quickly you can lose things. This section will show you how to

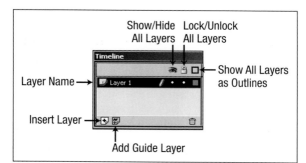

Figure 14.4
The layers portion of
the timeline.

name layers and will give you some organizational tips. Figure 14.4 shows the layers portion of the timeline.

Add

You can add a new layer in Flash several ways. You can choose Insert|New Layer or you can click the plus (+) icon (Insert Layer) on the bottom of the timeline, or right-click/Ctrl+click the layer name and choose Insert Layer from the context menu. All new layers are added to the top of the selected layer.

Delete

To delete layers, select the layer you want to delete and click the Delete Layer icon (the trashcan). Or, right-click/Ctrl+click and select Delete Layer from the context menu.

Move

To rearrange a layer, simply click and drag it to the location where you want it to be. Objects on the top layer will hide objects on the layer below them. Not all objects are obscured—just the object(s) directly below what's on the layer above. This fact in no way affects the way your movie plays. What appears in your movie and when it appears is controlled totally by the timeline and frames you use.

Visibility

You can turn off the visibility of each individual layer by clicking the dot in the column below the Eye icon. If you want to hide or show all the layers, then click the Eye icon. A red X in the layer indicates that the layer's visibility is turned off. The visibility of the layers does not affect the way the movie plays.

Lock

You can lock a layer/layers to prevent editing, if you'd like. Doing so is particularly handy when you are tracing items. You can lock the layer you want to trace so you don't accidentally alter it. To lock all layers, click the Lock icon. To lock individual layers, click the dot in the column below the Lock icon.

Name

It's a good idea to get in the habit of naming layers for easier editing and management of your movies. To name a layer, double-click the layer name and type the new name.

Select

A layer can be selected in several different ways. You can select a layer by clicking the layer name. If you select a frame, the layer it is on is automatically selected. If you select an action, the layer it is on is selected. Also, if you select an object on the stage, the layer it is on is automatically selected.

Organizing with Layers

If you are an experienced Flash user, I'm sure you already organize your layers. If you are new to Flash, it's a good idea to get in the habit of placing certain kinds of content and actions on separate layers. Following are some of the most commonly used layer names and functions that Flash developers use. You'll develop your own naming system that best suits the way you work:

- *Content Layers*—Content layers hold your art and things such as buttons, text, or sound. As you work through the Flash section of this book, you'll see how we put almost everything on its own separate layer.

- *Actions Layer*—If you keep all your frame actions on a layer named Actions, you'll be able to locate them easily.

- *Guide Layer*—If you right-click/Ctrl+click the layer name, you'll see a Guide option. On this layer, you can keep any guide you'd like to use. For example, you can set up guidelines for your movie and store them on this layer. You can also use shapes—perhaps a rectangle you'd like to arrange other objects around, or maybe a bitmap image of a mock-up to use as a guide. Whatever you put on the Guide layer does not export with the movie.

- *Motion Guide Layer*—In Chapter 15, you will see how to make motion tweens. When you make these tweens, you will use this layer. In short, when you select a tween object, right-click/Ctrl+click, and choose Motion Guide, the object is added above the layer the tween is on. When it's added, it is added as a Guide layer. The name is *Guide* plus the name of the layer it's a guide for. An Arch icon appears before the guide name, indicating it's a motion guide. You draw the path you want the motion to follow in the Guide layer. Remember, this layer doesn't export with your movie.

Keyframes and Frames

To make animations, you use the timeline. A frame-by-frame animation is similar to the flipbooks you may have played with as a child. (A series of images varies from page to page, and the images appear to move as you flip

Note: If you are not familiar with the concept of timelines and keyframes, you may want to start with a beginner's Flash book. Some suggestions are *Flash 5 Virtual Classroom*, *Flash 5 Visual Quickstart Guide*, and *Flash 5 Visual Insight*.

through the book.) Timelines work the same way; an image is placed in a keyframe each time a major change occurs in the animation.

A keyframe contains an object or objects. All the frames after the first keyframe up to and through the white rectangle contain the content of the first keyframe. Keyframes denote a change in the scene.

The best way to demonstrate how keyframes work within the timeline is to show you. We will walk through setting up a very simple animation of a green tomato maturing into a big, juicy, ripe tomato. You will need a starting point and an ending point, which will each be put in a keyframe. Each keyframe tells Flash that something important is in the frame.

To begin, you need to determine how long you want your tomato to take to grow. Twelve frames take one second, so let's set the tomato to grow over 20 frames. Follow these steps:

1. Flash opens with a new movie. If you don't have one open, choose File|New. Double-click Layer 1 and name it *tomatoes*.

2. Choose File|Import, navigate to the Chapter 14 resources folder, and select tomato.FH9. Click the stage. In the Info panel (Window|Info), change the Width to 60 and the Height to 62.

3. Choose Insert|Convert To Symbol (F8). In the Symbol Properties dialog box, name the symbol "tomato", choose Graphic, and click OK. Open the Effect panel (Window|Panels|Effect), choose Tint from the drop-down menu (or click on the Instance icon in the Launcher bar), and choose 40% and choose a green color.

4. Move the small tomato to the left corner. Figure 14.5 shows the position of the tomato. Also note the arrow; see the solid black dot that was added as soon as you added content? This is a keyframe. As soon as content is added to the first frame, a keyframe is automatically added.

5. You want the end of the movie to be the luscious, ripe tomato, and the animation will be 20 frames long. Right-click/Ctrl+click frame 20 in the tomatoes layer and choose Insert Keyframe. You need to add the content for this keyframe. Drag an instance of the tomato from the Library (Window|Library or Ctrl+L/Cmd+L). In the Info panel, change the Width to 140 and the Height to 142. Place the tomato on the right side of the stage. Figure 14.6 shows the red tomato in place; the arrow is pointing to the keyframe added to the timeline.

6. While you are still in frame 20, delete the small tomato—you don't want it to appear in frame 20. In Figure 14.6, notice the white rectangle in frame 19. It indicates that the next frame will be a keyframe. The red rectangle over the number 20 is the playhead; drag it to the first frame.

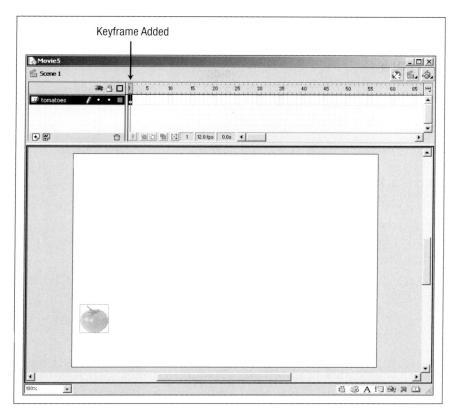

Figure 14.5
A keyframe added to
the timeline.

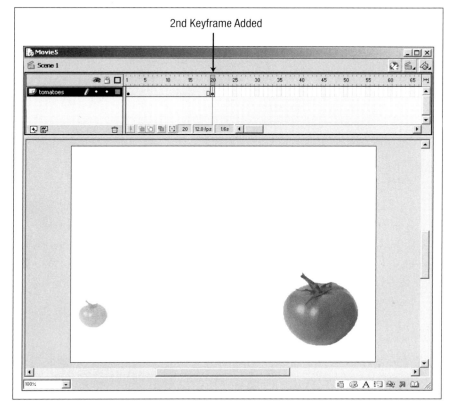

Figure 14.6
The large tomato in place
and a new keyframe added
to the timeline.

Note: You need to delete the small tomato because it was still on the stage when you added the keyframe to frame 20. You can avoid having to delete the small tomato if you insert a blank keyframe and then drag the instance onto the stage. If you want to see where the small tomato is in relation to where you want to place the large tomato, turn on the Onion Skinning option (the second icon to the right of the trashcan).

Note: The difference with a blank keyframe and adding a keyframe is that the blank keyframe will delete everything that was in the frame prior to inserting the blank. If you add a keyframe (F6), however, the content in the frame remains and you can alter it to suit the change you want to occur.

Note: To add multiple frames, select the frame you want to add, drag to increase the selection, and then choose Insert|Frame or press F5.

Notice that only the green tomato appears. Move the playhead over frame 2; still just the green tomato. If you move the playhead to frame 19, where the white rectangle is, every frame will contain the green tomato. Frame 20 contains the red tomato.

7. Test the movie so far by choosing Control|Test Movie (Ctrl+Enter/ Cmd+Return). You see the green tomato, and about one-and-a-half seconds later, you see the red tomato. You will finish growing this tomato in Chapter 15, in the section on tweening. To save your movie, choose File|Save As and save as mytomato.fla. A copy is saved for you in the Chapter 14 resources file as tomato.fla. Don't close the movie yet; the next section will discuss how to add and delete keyframes.

Inserting and Deleting Keyframes

If you need placeholder keyframes, or if you need to extend the length of time your movie plays, you may want to add frames. Of course, if you change your mind you can always delete them. Follow these steps:

1. While the movie is still open, let's look at a few more keyframe features. Right-click/Ctrl+click frame 25 and choose Insert Blank Keyframe from the context menu (or select frame 25 and press F7). A blank keyframe is basically a placeholder until you add content. If you have content on the page when you insert a blank keyframe, all the content is removed. Notice that a white rectangle appears in frame 24, indicating that frame 25 is a keyframe; but there is no solid black dot. Move the playhead to frame 20; you'll see the red tomato. Move the playhead to frames 21, 22, 23, and 24; the tomato is in all these frames, because the frames are filled with the content of the previous keyframe. Move the playhead to frame 25; it's blank, but independent of the previous keyframe.

2. Because you don't really need this keyframe, you can delete it. Right-click/Ctrl+click the frame you want to remove and choose Remove Frames. Delete frames 21 through 25.

3. Let's say you want to add two more frames after frame 5. To do so, select frame 5 and press F5 two times. Two new frames are inserted; they contain the same content as the previous frame. Notice that your keyframe in frame 20 has now moved to frame 22. You can delete any two frames or close the movie without saving—you'll need the unaltered version later.

Reversing Keyframes

Reversing keyframes comes in handy if you want to change the direction of an animation. For instance, the Eyeland interface has a button that slides open and then slides closed. This animation is accomplished by copying the keyframes (Shift+select) for the slide open, choosing Edit|Copy Frames, and then pasting in the next frame by choosing Edit|Paste Frames. To reverse the order, Shift+select the frames and choose Modify|Frames|Reverse.

PROJECT Assembling Eyeland Studio Static Elements

In Chapter 8, you drew the pieces for the Eyeland Studio Web page donated by Scott Hamlin of Eyeland Studio. You grouped the like colors together and saved them in individual files. In this project, you will put the pieces together. To assemble Eyeland Studio, follow these steps:

1. Choose File|New, choose File|Import, and navigate to the Chapter 14 Eyeland folder. Select base.png and click Open. A Fireworks PNG Import Settings dialog box will open (see Figure 14.7). Select Flatten Image and click OK.

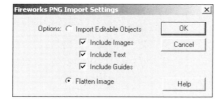

Figure 14.7
The Fireworks PNG Import Settings dialog box.

2. Double-click the layer name and name the layer "base".

3. Click the plus sign (+) to add a new layer. Choose File|Import and select light green.png from the same folder. Select Flatten Image from the Fireworks PNG Import Settings dialog box and click OK.

4. Double-click the layer name and change its name to "light green". If you click off the canvas, you will see a tad of black up by where the small circles go. This appears because the light greens are not in the correct position. Select the light green layer and press the left arrow key two times to nudge.

5. Click the plus sign to add another layer. Choose File|Import and select dark green.png from the same folder. Select Flatten Image and click OK.

6. Double-click the layer name and change it to "dark green".

7. Click the plus sign to add a layer. Choose File|Import and select white.png. Flatten Image should still be selected in the Fireworks PNG Import Settings dialog box; click OK.

8. The white layer's position is off quite a bit. With the white layer selected, press the right arrow key seven times and the up arrow key nine times, or until the small white boxes are lined up in the dark green boxes.

9. Double-click the layer and name the layer "white". Click the plus sign to add a new layer.

10. Choose File|Import and select pieces. Click Open, select Flatten Image, and click OK. Drag the logo to the top-left white square and position in the center. The three little circles will line up in the light green extension area.

11. Double-click the layer name and name the layer "pieces". Figure 14.8 shows the interface so far in Flash. Figure 14.9 shows the layers in the timeline. Notice the black dots in the first frame of every layer. A keyframe was automatically added to the first frame when content was added to each layer.

Figure 14.8
The Eyeland Studio interface imported into Flash.

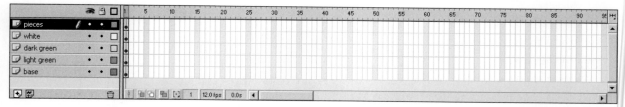

Figure 14.9
The layers in the timeline after Eyeland Studio was imported into Flash.

Drawing in Flash

Flash began as a vector-based program, but now you can use bitmaps as well. Bitmaps will add to the file size of the final movie, so use them judiciously. A vector image is generated by the computer using mathematical calculations. A bitmap or raster image contains pixels. When you enlarge a bitmap, new pixels have to be generated to fill in the expanded area, which usually results in a distorted image. Vector images generally have smaller file sizes.

Vector graphics are preferred because of their scalability and because you can use the same object numerous times while only waiting for it to load once. A vector object can be scaled to different sizes, opacity, and more, and it will still be the same object or symbol.

Drawing Tools Differ in Flash

We won't look at how to use the drawing tools in Flash, but rather at some of the differences from Fireworks or FreeHand. You can explore the basics of drawing in Chapter 1 (FreeHand) and Chapter 7 (Fireworks).

Stacking

In FreeHand and in Fireworks, when you place one object on top of another, each object remains separate. One covers or obscures the other, but both objects exist in their entirety. In Flash, if you place an object on top of another object of the same color on the same layer, the two objects become one object when you deselect. Figure 14.10 shows two circles with no strokes (or strokes that are the same color as the fill), each the same color; the bottom image is the resulting new shape.

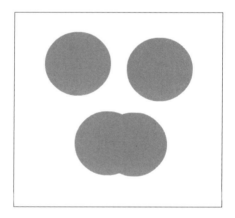

Figure 14.10
Two circles of the same color and the right circle placed halfway over the left circle.

If the objects are two different colors, the one you place on top will cut out the portion of the object below it, acting like a cookie cutter. Figure 14.11 shows two circles, each a different color. The circle on the right is placed over half of the left circle. The bottom image shows the result (after deselecting and then selecting and moving).

Tool Options

Another difference you will find in Flash are the tool options you can find in the Options portion of the Toolbox (Figure 14.12). The options you see with the Arrow tool selected are Snap To Objects, Smooth, Straighten, Rotate, and Scale.

More options are available in different panels (such as the Transform panel), but these frequently used options are easy to access from the Toolbox.

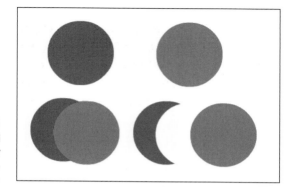

Figure 14.11

Two circles of different colors and the right circle placed halfway over the left circle, deselected, and then moved.

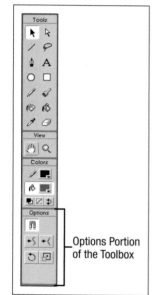

Options Portion of the Toolbox

Figure 14.12

The different options as seen in the Toolbox when the Arrow tool is selected.

Fills and Strokes

In Flash, a fill and a stroke are separate. This concept may take some getting used to. Draw a circle in Flash. With the Arrow tool, select in the center and move the circle. Do you see the stroke still in place, as in Figure 14.13? You can select the stroke by clicking the edge of the object. If the stroke or line around an object is a separate path, you can double-click the stroke to select all the lines. If you want to select both the object's fill and stroke, double-click to select.

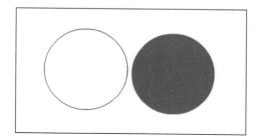

Figure 14.13

The fill selected and moved, with the stroke remaining behind.

No Fill, No Stroke

Setting no fill and no stroke in Flash is a bit tricky, but you'll like it once you see how it's done. You can't select None in the Fill panel, and there is no option for None in the Stroke panel. If you draw the shape first and select the color box next to the Stroke or Fill icons in the Toolbox, the red circle with the slash in it may or may not be available. The best way to get no fill and no stroke is to do the following:

1. Select the Drawing tool (don't draw yet).

2. Select the Stroke icon in the Toolbox and then click the No Color icon below the Fill icon (center one with a red slash).

3. Select the Fill icon in the Toolbox and then click the No Color icon.

4. Now you can draw your shape and the stroke and fill will be invisible.

If you want your fill or stroke to be transparent, you do this in the Mixer panel (Window|Panels|Mixer) and set the Alpha to the percentage you want. You can do this after the object is drawn. Don't use the Effect panel for fill transparency. The Effect panel will affect the entire Movie Clip if that's what you are working on.

Modify Shapes

You can do some interesting things by changing your strokes to fills. In this section, you will see a couple of different benefits of the Modify|Shape command.

Soften Fill Edges

The first shape command we will look at is Soften Fill Edges. You'll use it to add a glow to text. To add a glow to text, follow these steps:

1. With a new movie open in Flash, select the Type tool.

2. Click the stage and type the word "GLOW". On the bottom of the stage, in the lower-right corner, you will see an A. Click it to open the Character panel (or press Ctrl+T/Cmd+T). Use a large, thick font; I used 60-point, bold Verdana.

3. Choose Edit|Copy and then Edit|Paste In Place. Change the fill to a bright color; I chose a bright green.

4. Choose Modify|Break Apart, and then choose Modify|Shape|Soften Fill Edges. The Soften Edges dialog box opens. Choose a Distance value of 15 and a Steps value of 5 (see Figure 14.14). Because you want a glow on the outside of the text, choose the Direction value Expand. Click OK.

5. Choose Modify|Group and then choose Modify|Arrange|Send To Back.

6. To see how great this glow looks, choose Modify|Movie and change the Background color to black. Figure 14.15 shows the result, as well as a variation that uses a Distance value of 20 and 10 steps.

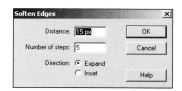

Figure 14.14
The Soften Edges dialog box and the settings used.

Figure 14.15

The results of expanding by 15 and by 20.

Convert Lines to Fills

You can convert your strokes or drawing lines into fills. You'll see a useful purpose for this command in this exercise as well as in the project following this
section. You will be using the car you traced in Chapter 1; a copy of the traced
car is in the Chapter 14 resources folder. You may wonder why you would want
to convert the lines to fills. You probably won't unless you want to scale down
the image. In Flash, when you scale down an image, the line width does not
scale down proportionately. Figure 14.16 shows the original drawing of the electric car; the scaled-down version is below it. Notice how thick the lines are.

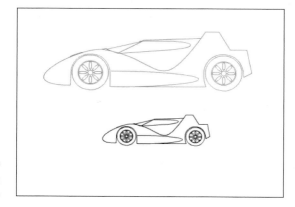

Figure 14.16

The electric car drawing and a scaled-down version.

To convert the lines to fills, follow these steps:

1. With a new movie open in Flash, choose Import. Navigate to the Chapter 14 resources folder, select the electriccar.FH9 file, and click Open.

2. Choose Modify|Break Apart. You'll have to do this numerous times on
   this particular drawing, because the different sections of the car are
   grouped together. Break apart the body three times, until you see the
   dotted black outline. Break apart the front tire twice, the back tire once,
   and the windshield twice. Select the line above and behind the windshield; break it apart twice. The left diagonal line of the windshield
   needs to be broken apart separately twice. Select the curved shape at
   the bottom of the car and break it apart twice.

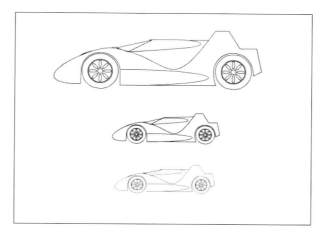

Figure 14.17
The original drawing, the original scaled down, and the original with the lines converted to fills and scaled down.

3. Marquee-select the car and choose Modify|Shape|Convert Lines To Fills. Choose Modify|Group. Select the Scale icon from the options in the Toolbox and scale down the car. Figure 14.17 shows the original car, the scaled-down version before converting the lines, and the scaled-down version after converting the lines to fills.

PROJECT Finishing the Wine Glasses

In this project, you will finish the wine glasses you began in Chapters 1 and 4. You will add the glow, and then rotate the glasses and scale them down. To finish the wine glasses, follow these steps:

1. Open a new movie in Flash, choose Modify|Movie, and choose a black background.

2. Choose File|Import and navigate to the Chapter 14 resources folder. Locate rotatedwine.FH9 and open it. Select Layers from the FreeHand Import dialog box. The image will open at the bottom of the stage. Marquee-select it, choose Modify|Group, and move it up to the center of the stage. Choose Modify|Ungroup.

3. Select the white part of the bottom of the glass. Choose Modify|Ungroup.

4. You should see little black dots all over the white edge. Choose Modify|Shape|Convert Lines To Fill, and then choose Modify|Shape|Soften Edges. In the Soften Edges dialog box, choose a Distance value of 8 and a Steps value of 20, select Inset, and click OK.

5. Choose Modify|Arrange|Send To Back. Select the dark blue area you see above the wine and choose Modify|Ungroup. Your wineglass should look like Figure 14.18.

6. Marquee-select the whole glass and choose Modify|Group. In the Info panel (Window|Info), change the Width to 35 and the Height to 100.

Note: It may take some practice with the settings to get the look you want. This stroke was so wide that I used Inset instead of Expand, because the glass will be made smaller and I didn't want such a large glow.

Figure 14.18
The glow added and the dark blue area fixed.

Note: You don't have to press the Enter/Return key in the Info panel to accept the changes like you do in Fireworks.

7. Select the Rotate icon from the Toolbox Options section and rotate to the left until the wine is horizontal. Choose Edit|Copy and Edit|Paste In Place. Choose Modify|Transform|Flip Horizontal. Use the keyboard right arrow to nudge the glass into place. Choose Modify|Group. Your finished glasses should look like Figure 14.19.

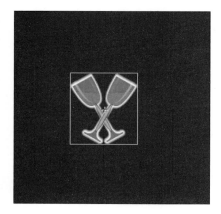

Figure 14.19
The completed wineglasses.

8. These glasses will be placed into the Bar Wars scene, so make this image into a symbol. Choose Insert|Convert To Symbol (F8). In the Convert To Symbol dialog box, name the symbol "wineglasses". Choose Graphic and click OK. (Chapter 15 provides more information on symbols.)

Panels

In this chapter, we will look at only a couple of the panels you will use in the Flash section of this book. You'll use the Info panel often, and the Align panel can be daunting if you haven't used it before.

Info Panel

You'll probably find yourself using the Info panel frequently. To access the Info panel, you can choose Window|Panels|Info; but the easiest way to open it is to select the first icon on the left in the Launcher bar (on the bottom of the stage area).

The Info panel in Flash is very similar to the Info panels in FreeHand and Fireworks. You can set the specific height and width of an object as well as determine its X, Y coordinates. This panel differs in the addition of the Alignment Grid option (see Figure 14.20). This grid has nine small squares representing a box around the selected item. Every object in Flash has this bounding box around it; the box encloses the entire object's shape. The grid allows you to position according to the upper-left corner or to the center of the bounding box. Click the position you desire.

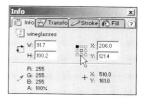

Figure 14.20
The Info panel with the arrow pointing to the Alignment Grid.

Align Panel

The Align panel is shown in Figure 14.21. From this panel, you align objects to each other and the stage. To access the Align panel, choose Window| Panels|Align (Ctrl+K/Cmd+K). Its different sections are as follows:

- *Align*—On the left are the horizontal alignment options: Align Left Edge, Align Horizontal Center, and Align Right Edge. On the right are the vertical options: Top Edge, Align Vertical Center, and Align Bottom Edge.

Figure 14.21
The Align panel.

- *Distribute*—The left set of options are Distribute Top Edge, Distribute Vertical Center, and Distribute Bottom Edge. The set on the right side are Distribute Left Edge, Distribute Horizontal Center, and Distribute Right Edge.

- *Match Size*—The options are Match Width, Match Height, and Match Width and Height.

- *Space*—The options are Space Evenly Vertically and Space Evenly Horizontally.

- *To Stage*—The option is Align/Distribute To Stage.

PROJECT Sliding Buttons for Eyeland Studio

The buttons for the Eyeland Studio interface will be made into a movie clip. Because they need to be added to the timeline and this process involves a lot of alignment, you'll set them up now and add the actions and make the movie clip in Chapter 15. To begin making the sliding buttons, follow these steps:

1. With a new movie open in Flash, choose Insert|New Symbol, choose Movie Clip for the Behavior, and name it "ButtonsMovie". Choose File|Import. Navigate to the Chapter 14 Eyeland folder and choose Buttonslide.png. In the Fireworks PNG Import dialog box, be sure Flatten Image is not selected and click OK. Make the window just large enough to view the button elements, and move it to the side.

2. Choose Modify|Movie and select a black background.

3. Drag the white button from the Buttonslide file onto the stage. Click your current movie title bar to make it active. The white button should still be selected; if it isn't, select it.

4. Open the Align panel. Select To Stage. In the Align area, select Align Horizontal Center and then the Align Vertical Center (the two center icons).

5. If you look in the timeline, you will see that a keyframe has been added to the first frame. Select frame 18 and choose Insert|Keyframe (F6). Double-click the layer name and name the layer "white bar". Figure 14.22 shows the timeline so far.

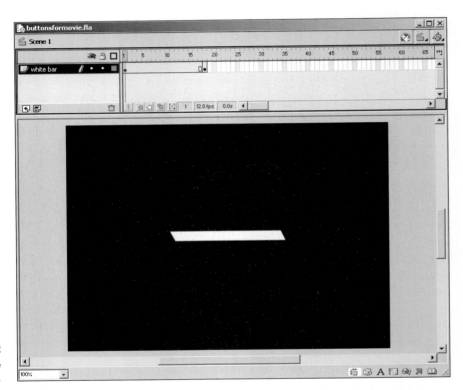

Figure 14.22
The timeline with the white bar added.

6. Add a new layer and name it "green bar". Drag the first green part of the button from the open Buttonslide.png file onto the stage. Select the current movie to make it active. In the Align panel, select To Stage. In the Align area, select Align Horizontal Center and then Align Vertical Center. Press the down arrow one time.

7. Select frame 2 in the green bar layer. Right-click/Ctrl+click to insert a blank keyframe. Drag the second green bar from the open Buttonslide

file. Select the current movie to make it active. In the Align panel, select To Stage. In the Align area, select Align Horizontal Center and then the Align Vertical Center. Press the down arrow one time.

8. Repeat Step 7 for all the remaining green bars. The only exception is that the last bar does not need to be nudged down. Figure 14.23 shows the timeline so far.

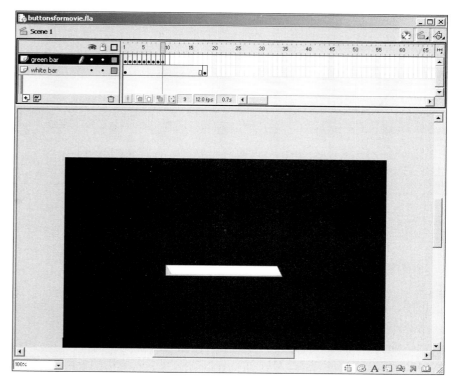

Figure 14.23

The timeline with the first nine keyframes added to the green bar layer.

9. Shift+select frames 1 through 9 and choose Edit|Copy Frames. Select frame 10 and choose Edit|Paste Frames.

10. Shift+select frames 10 through 18 and choose Modify|Frames|Reverse. Figure 14.24 shows the timeline with all the keyframes added to the green bar layer.

11. Select Scene 1 and you can now drag an instance of the ButtonsMovie Clip onto the stage if you want to, but it isn't necessary. Choose File|Save As and save the file as mybuttonsformovie. A file called buttonsformovie.fla is saved in the Chapter 14 Eyeland folder.

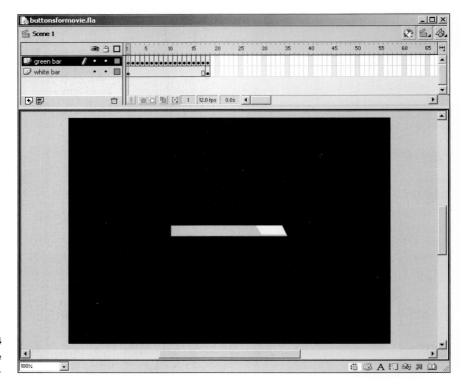

Figure 14.24
All the keyframes added to the green bar layer in the timeline.

Tracing Bitmap Images

If you want to convert a bitmap image in Flash to a vector, you can do so by tracing it with the Trace Bitmap command. This is a great way to produce a quick vector image from a bitmap, and you can get some pretty good traces. However, the better the trace, the larger the file.

To trace a bitmap, select it and choose Modify|Trace Bitmap. The Trace Bitmap dialog box opens, as shown in Figure 14.25. The options are:

- *Color Threshold*—The number of colors that will be used. Flash averages the colors to limit the number. The lower the number, the more colors used and the larger the file size.

- *Minimum Area*—The radius that Color Threshold uses to describe adjacent pixels. The smaller the number, the more detail.

- *Curve Fit*—Determines how smooth the curves are. If the bitmap has smooth curves, select Very Smooth; if it has a lot of angles, choose Very Tight.

- *Corner Threshold*—Similar to Curve Fit, except it refers only to corners.

Traces often have far more curves than you need for the image to be acceptable. To reduce the number of curves in the trace, choose Modify|Optimize. From the Optimize Curves dialog box, choose the amount of Smoothing you'd like and click OK. A window will open telling you how many curves you started with, how many you have now, and the percentage of reduction.

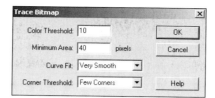

Figure 14.25
The Trace Bitmap dialog box.

Bitmap Trace Warning

When you import a JPEG file, it has already been compressed. When you export your Flash movie, Flash will compress this image again. Compressing JPEGs multiple times will frequently result in artifacts. To avoid this problem, select the image and open the Library (the last icon on the right in the Launcher). From the Options pop-up menu, choose Properties. The Bitmap Properties dialog box opens (see Figure 14.26); choose Lossless from the Compression drop-down menu and click OK.

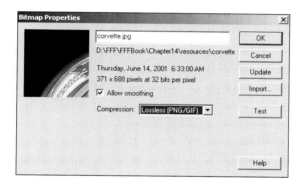

Figure 14.26
The Bitmap Properties dialog box.

PROJECT Tracing a Jukebox Image

The Game Gallery provided the image of the corvette jukebox for your use in this project. To trace the jukebox, follow these steps:

1. With a new movie open in Flash, choose File|Import. Navigate to the Chapter 14 resources folder and select corvette.jpg. Click the stage.

2. Choose Modify|Trace Bitmap.

3. In the Trace Bitmap dialog box, enter the following values:

   - *Color Threshold*—60

   - *Minimum Area*—40

   - *Curve Fit*—Very Smooth

   - *Corner Threshold*—Few Corners

   After you set your options, click OK.

4. The result is pretty good. I didn't want the whole jukebox for the movie that you will make in Chapter 17, so I copied the top part of the jukebox just below the pages and pasted it into a new movie. I then copy and pasted the bottom portion of the jukebox, pasted it in the new movie, and adjusted its position. The gradient was red next to the green, so I pasted from the original trace just below the green area of the first copy and pasted and positioned it on the new movie. Granted, you can get a lot more sophisticated in your repair, but for a quick trace this did the job.

5. Once the jukebox is the way you want it, marquee-select it all and choose Modify|Optimize. The Optimize Curves dialog box opens, and you can choose how much you want to optimize. The lower the setting, the larger the file size. As you can see in Figure 14.27, I chose Maximum because the number of curves in this image is huge. Figure 14.28 shows that there were originally 5,096 curves, and now there are 2,801 curves—a 45 percent reduction isn't bad, and the results are acceptable, as shown in Figure 14.29.

Figure 14.27
The Optimize Curves dialog box.

Figure 14.28
The message showing how many original curves, how many now, and the percentage reduction.

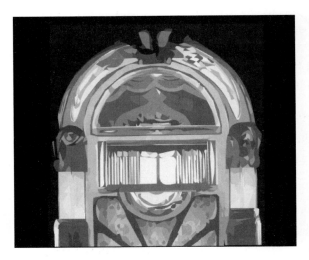

Figure 14.29
The result of the trace and the optimize.

Working with Text

You have all the normal text attributes available to you in Flash, such as font, alignment, color, kerning, size, and style. The text attributes are accessed in the Character panel. A quick way to open the Character panel is to click the A in the Launcher bar. Or, you can choose Window|Panels|Character or press Ctrl+T/Cmd+T. Flash includes several kinds of text.

Device Fonts

Fonts are embedded, and the outlines are exported with your Flash movie. But Flash does not necessarily support all fonts. It's easy to do a quick test to see if the fonts you want to use are acceptable. Choose View|Antialias Text: If the text appears jaggy, it isn't compatible. If the text you need isn't design critical, you can use a device font: The _sans font is similar to Arial and Helvetica, the _serif font is similar to Times Roman, and _typewriter is similar to Courier. These fonts are the top three in the font drop-down menu of the Character panel. You reduce the file size by using device fonts; they will use the closest font match from the user's system, so no fonts are embedded in the movie.

Text Line

When you select the Type tool and begin to type, the text box expands as you type. If you don't press the Enter/Return key, it keeps expanding horizontally. As you press Enter/Return, the text box expands to accommodate.

Text Block

You can also define the size of a text block by dragging it out with the Text tool. The block has a set width that is determined by how far you drag. The text in a text block automatically wraps. You can also set the size for the text block by using the Info panel.

Input Text Box

Input text boxes enable users to input text in forms or surveys. To make an input text box, drag the size you'd like or select a current text box and open the Text Options panel (Window|Text Options). This panel contains the Static Text, Dynamic Text, and Input Text options. Choose Input Text. You will be presented with many options, which are beyond the scope of this book.

Dynamic Text Boxes

Dynamic text boxes access a database to display dynamically changing text, such as sport scores and weather reports. Dynamic text can also be provided from another part of your Flash movie by using variables and assigning actions. You make a dynamic text box the same way you do an input text box, but you choose Dynamic Text in the Text Options panel. In Chapter 17, you will finish adding the music to the jukebox. The song title, the artist's name, and the file size will be displayed dynamically when the appropriate button is clicked.

Moving On

In this chapter, you have reviewed some of the basic functions of Flash. You have begun to make your first movies by getting a tomato ready to grow and putting the Eyeland Studio interface's static pieces in place. You've also learned how to trace bitmaps and reviewed the different types of text boxes in Flash.

In Chapter 15, you will learn about invisible buttons, how to make movie clips, and how to assign instance names.

Chapter 15

Symbols and Animations

In this chapter, you will learn how to produce all three kinds of symbols in Flash. You'll see how to use the Movie Clip symbol; Button symbols, including an invisible button; and Graphic symbols.

Libraries and Symbols

Symbols are the main reason that file sizes in Flash can be kept to a minimum. Symbols are usable elements that are stored in the Library with other assets, such as sound and video. When a symbol is produced, it is automatically added to the movies Library. You can drag an instance (a copy) of the symbol into your movie as many times as you'd like. Because Flash uses multiple instances of the same symbol, the file size is much smaller. The symbol only needs to be loaded in a browser once for all copies. Libraries can be shared between movies and even be made available to all movies.

Libraries

The Library contains all the symbols for your movie. When you make a Movie Clip symbol, Button symbol, or Graphic symbol, it is automatically added to the Library, along with bitmaps, sound, and video files. Every Flash movie has its own Library, but you can drag a symbol or other asset from one open Flash movie into another. Figure 15.1 shows the Library for the jukebox you'll finish in Chapter 17.

Figure 15.1
The Library specific to the jukebox project.

Common Libraries

Flash uses another type of Library, which may confuse you. If you choose Window|Common Libraries, you will see the six options shown in Figure 15.2. These Libraries are common and available to all movies. If you have a Library in a movie and you'd like to make it into a common Library, then simply save your Flash file with a descriptive name and place it in the Libraries folder of the Flash program on your hard drive. You can delete such Libraries anytime you decide you don't want them any longer. As soon as you drop the file into the Libraries folder, it is available in Flash; you don't have to close and reopen the program.

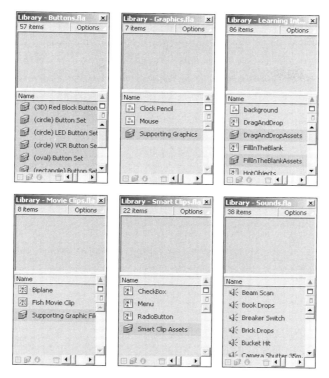

Figure 15.2
The six default common Libraries
that ship with Flash.

Sharing Libraries between Movies

As I mentioned before, if you have more than one movie open, you can drag assets from one to another. But if you don't have other files open and you don't need them open, you can still borrow the assets of another movie. Choose File|Open As Library, navigate to the file that contains the Library you want, select the file, and click Open. Only the Library will open—not the whole file. Common Libraries work in a similar way, but this method lets you "use as you need" instead of making Libraries permanently available.

Using Libraries

Your symbols are automatically added to the movies Library when you produce them or when you drag one from another Library. To add sound, bitmaps, vectors, or QuickTime movies, you import them into your movie; Flash adds them to the Library.

To use a symbol or other asset from the Library, you simply drag an instance (a copy) of the symbol or asset to the stage.

Symbols

Flash uses three types of symbols: Movie Clip, Button, and Graphic. When you make a symbol, it is automatically stored in the movie's Library. To insert the object into the movie, you drag instances of it onto the stage from the Library. Placing an instance of a symbol on the stage causes little to no addition to the file size.

You can alter these instances so that they appear different, when in fact they are still instances of the original symbol. The movie has to call the symbol only once, and then Flash stores information about any size, color, or transparency changes you make.

Symbols also save you a great deal of editing time. When you edit the original symbol, all instances are changed automatically. You'll love this feature if you've ever had to change an element in a large Web site that didn't use symbols.

Once you start making symbols, you should develop your own (or a company) naming convention. In Chapter 14, we named every layer to make editing easier and more logical. With symbols, it's even more important—in fact, it's vital—that you name them carefully. The symbols must be named so you can reference them when you add ActionScript. Because symbols are stored in the Library, it's vital that you understand how to use the Library; refer to the section on "Libraries" earlier in this chapter.

Movie Clip Symbols

Each Movie Clip symbol has its own timeline and layers. Movie Clips can be used in a single frame on the main timeline. One of the best advantages of Movie Clips is that they play independently of the main timeline. Because you can add actions to Movie Clips, they offer infinite possibilities. You can include dynamic animation generated during playback, such as an object that moves when the user presses keys on the keyboard.

You can make a Movie Clip symbol by following these steps:

1. Open a new Flash movie.

2. Choose Insert|New Symbol (Ctrl+F8/Cmd+F8). The Symbol Properties dialog box will open (see Figure 15.3).

Figure 15.3
The Symbol Properties dialog box.

3. In the Symbol Properties dialog box, select Movie Clip, which is the default. Click OK.

4. The stage is empty, because you are now in Symbol Editing mode. In the upper-left corner in Figure 15.4 you can see the name "Scene 1", but the word "Symbol 1" (or whatever you named your symbol—in Figure 15.4, it's "Tomato") appears in a white box to indicate that you are in the Symbol Editing mode. The stage and the timeline you see are both for the

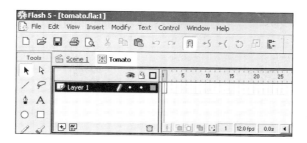

Figure 15.4
The stage in Symbol Editing mode.

Movie Clip you are about to make. All you need to do now is add the graphics you want to make into a symbol by choosing File|Import and selecting tomato.jpg from the Chapter 15 resources folder.

5. Return to the main timeline by selecting Scene 1. You'll be making Movie Clips and other symbols in the following chapters.

6. The Movie Clip symbol is now in the Library, ready to be inserted into the main timeline of a movie. Select the Movie Clip, open the Instance panel (Window|Panels|Instance), and give it an instance name.

If you have made a small movie and you want to make it a Movie Clip, follow these steps:

1. Open the movie you'd like to convert into a Movie Clip.

2. Check to be sure no layers are locked or invisible.

3. Choose Edit|Select All.

4. Choose Insert|Convert to Symbol (F8).

5. In the Symbol Properties dialog box, choose Movie Clip.

6. The movie is now a Movie Clip in the Library. It contains all the layers, timelines, and actions of the original movie.

7. You can now drag this Movie Clip into a new Flash movie.

Button Symbols

Button symbols are extremely popular and are useful for navigation buttons. You can add sound, animation, and actions with event handlers to Button symbols (as discussed in Chapter 16). To make a Button symbol, follow these steps:

1. With a new Flash movie open, choose Insert|New Symbol. In the Symbol Properties dialog box, select Button and click OK.

2. You are now in Symbol Editing mode. Take a moment to look at the timeline (see Figure 15.5). Notice the Up, Over, Down, and Hit tabs. Up is the default. Draw a button or drag on or import a button graphic.

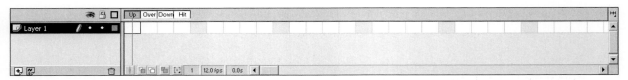

Figure 15.5

The timeline as seen in the
Button Symbol Editor.

3. Select the frame under the Over tab and choose Insert|Keyframe.
    Change the button's appearance for the Over state.

4. Repeat Step 3 for the Down state.

5. Select the frame under the Hit tab and choose Insert|Keyframe. The user
    can't see what you draw here. Draw a rectangle large enough to cover
    the button; otherwise, only the text will be the *hit area*. If the mouse
    passes over this area, the assigned action—in this case, a rollover—will
    be triggered.

6. Notice that your button is a symbol in the Library. If you didn't name
    your button in the Symbol Properties dialog box, you can do so now by
    double-clicking the symbol name and giving the button a suitable
    name. Click Scene 1 to return to the main movie. To use your button,
    drag an instance from the Library to the stage.

Invisible Button Symbols

Invisible buttons are not a separate or different kind of symbol. Because they
are used so frequently as hit areas, I need to mention them. An invisible button is a hotspot that you can assign actions to. You put invisible buttons over
other objects. Because of their transparent blue color, you can position them
easily. You will also use this type of button in the Eyeland Studio interface in
Chapter 16. To make an invisible button, follow these steps:

1. With a new movie (or your current movie) open, choose Insert|New Sym-
    bol. In the Symbol Properties dialog box, select Button and click OK.

2. Select the frame below the Hit tab and choose View|Insert Keyframe (F6).

3. Draw the shape of your invisible button. It is added to the Library.

4. Click Scene 1 to return to your main movie. You can drag the invisible
    button from the Library onto the stage. It isn't invisible to you, so you
    can easily position it.

Graphic Symbols

Graphic symbols have the fewest capabilities in Flash. They are great for repeating static elements or for simple animations, but you cannot add actions or attach
sound to a Graphic symbol. To make a Graphic symbol, follow these steps:

1. With a movie open, choose Insert|New Symbol. In the Symbol Properties
    dialog box, select Graphic and click OK.

2. You are now in Symbol Editing mode. You can draw, drag, or import the content for the symbol. It will be added to the Library.

3. To return to the main timeline, click Scene 1. Drag an instance of the Graphic symbol onto the stage wherever you want it, as many times as you want to.

Graphic symbols and Movie Clips differ in several important ways. Graphic symbols are static images, which you can also place in separated frames on the timeline of the main movie, for things such as an animation. The animation will play in the main movie only and not independently of the main movie like a Movie Clip will. When you set the instance properties such as height, color, rotation, and so on in a Graphic symbol, you can do it in the Effect and Instance panels, where you can preview in realtime. You can't do this with Movie Clips. But you can't change the properties on the fly after design time as you can with a Movie Clip.

In addition, if you have a static image and it will receive ActionScript, then it needs to be a Movie Clip or a Button. In the banner ad project in Chapter 18, you will add ActionScript to a Movie Clip.

If you have a Graphic symbol and decide to add some ActionScript to it, such as a mouseover, you can always convert it. To convert any of the symbols, select the symbol, open the Instance panel, and change the Behavior.

Animation Basics

The focus of the Flash section of the book is primarily on using ActionScript for the projects, so we won't be spending a lot of time on animation. However, I want to at least mention a few basics, such as how to make a motion tween, and look at frame-by-frame animations. I'll also recommend some great Flash books I have personally reviewed and used in this section; a complete list appears in Appendix B.

Motion Tweening

A motion tween has a beginning and an ending symbol; Flash completes the in-between steps for you. The shapes between the two symbols are based on changes you make to the symbols, such as location, size, rotation, color, and transparency. The two symbols have to be the same, but you can change their characteristics.

Adding motion to the tomatoes you began working on in Chapter 14 is very simple. To finish that animation, follow these steps:

1. Open the tomato.fla file in your Chapter 15 resources folder on the companion CD-ROM.

Note: I've seen other good names for this technique. Instead of *motion tweening*, Russell Chun calls it *instance tweening* in his book *Macromedia Flash Advanced*. In *Flash 5 f/x & Design*, Bill Sanders calls it *symbol tweening*. (You are really tweening instances of symbols.)

Figure 15.6
The Frame panel.

Note: Other options appear in the Frame panel when you choose Motion, but for the most part, they are self-explanatory. Easing is explained in the "Shape Tweening" section.

2. If you recall from Chapter 14, you made both tomatoes into symbols. You don't have to use symbols for a motion tween—you can use a grouped object or a text block, as well. The difference is that a grouped object or text can't tween colors or alpha (transparency). Select a tomato and open the Frame panel if it isn't open already (Window|Panels|Frame or Ctrl+F/Cmd+F). The Frame panel can be seen in Figure 15.6.

3. In the Tweening drop-down menu, choose Motion. The Shape option won't work on the tomato file right now, because you are using symbols—shape tweens only work on drawings. You'll see a solid line with an arrow, and the frames are now purple, indicating a successful motion tween.

4. If you'd like to see the in-between steps of the motion, click the Onion Skin icon on the bottom of the timeline. Over the playhead, you'll see a crescent shape with a little ball. Drag the right side to the end of your animation (frame 20 in this example), and you can see all the transitions. Figure 15.7 shows the motion tween. Of course, in black and white it will be difficult to see the color change; but if you try the technique yourself, you can.

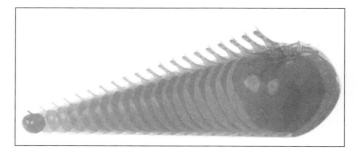

Figure 15.7
The onion skin view of the motion tween.

This is just a basic motion tween. You can tween along a path, use multiple guided layers, and perform a motion tween around a closed path. For more in-depth discussions of Flash features, I recommend consulting the books mentioned earlier or the ones listed in Appendix B.

Shape Tweening

Shape tweening follows the same steps as motion tweening, with a few exceptions. You can't shape-tween a bitmap, a grouped object, or text blocks unless you break them apart first. If you are going to tween more than two objects, they must all be on the same layer. If the shapes are complex, you can control the resulting tween by using shape hints (which we won't discuss here). Figure 15.8 shows the Frame panel and the options available when you select Shape.

Figure 15.8
The options available in the Frame panel when Shape is selected.

The options are:

- *Easing*—Positive values of 1 to 100 will ease out the tween: Changes occur quickly at the beginning and ease out toward the end. To ease in, choose a negative value.

- *Distributive*—Use this option in the Blend drop-down menu when you don't want to preserve any of the straight lines or curves.

- *Angular*—Use this option in the Blend drop-down menu to preserve the corners and straight lines in the in-between shapes.

If you'd like to try a shape tween, follow these steps:

1. Open a new movie. Choose File|Import and select the greentomato.FH9 file from the Chatper 15 resources folder; select Flatten in the FreeHand Import dialog box and click OK. Marquee-select the tomato and choose Modify|Group (Ctrl+G/Cmd+G).

2. In the Info panel, change the size to 35 by 37 pixels. Move the green tomato to the lower-left corner of the stage.

3. Choose Modify|Ungroup and then choose Modify|Break Apart.

4. For this tween, you will place the large tomato over the small one. Choose View and select Rulers. Pull a horizontal guide and a vertical guide to the center of the green tomato. These guides will help you place the large red tomato.

5. Select frame 20 and choose Insert|Keyframe.

6. Choose File|Import and select tomato.FH9 from the Chapter 15 resources folder. Select Flatten and click OK. Marquee-select the red tomato and choose Modify|Group.

7. In the Info panel, change the size to 150 by 152. Center the tomato on the cross of the guides.

8. Choose Modify|Ungroup and Modify|Break Apart.

9. Select any frame between the two keyframes. In the Frame panel, select Shape and accept the defaults. Press F12 to preview the animation in the browser. This file is saved for you in the Chapter 15 resources folder as tomatoshape.fla.

It isn't an attractive shape tween. Shape tweens can be tricky, and they frequently need finessing. I did a shape tween with the tomato to the side (shapetween.fla in the Chapter 15 resources folder) so you could see the steps more easily with onion skinning turned on. The results are shown in Figure 15.9.

Preparing the Tomatoes

The green tomato's hue and saturation were changed in Fireworks. Both tomatoes you will use in this exercise were traced in FreeHand, and their backgrounds were removed. For instance, the red tomato was a JPEG file, so it had a white background. The image would shape-tween, but as a rectangle. In FreeHand after the trace, the white background was deleted.

Figure 15.9
The shape tween of the tomato with onion skinning turned on.

Frame-by-Frame Animation

Frame-by-frame animation is the traditional way of making animations such as cartoons. Every frame has a slightly different image on it to produce the appearance of movement. This is a long and tedious process, but at times it is the only way to achieve the desired results. We won't practice this technique; frankly, I'm not an artist and wouldn't even want to attempt it. If you are artistically inclined, Flash is capable of producing top-notch, fast-loading animations—that is, unless you add an extreme number of frames.

Note: The text on the perspective and the Flash movie was supplied by Ian Kelleigh of The FreeHand Source (**www.freehandsource.com**). I added the wine glasses and text and used Ian's directions to complete this project.

 ## Completing the Bar Wars Scene

You began the Bar Wars scene in Chapter 5, where you prepared the text on the perspective grid. The wineglasses, which are simply decorative, were made in Chapters 2 and 4 and finished in Chapter 14.

To complete this movie, follow these steps:

1. Open a new Flash movie. Choose File|Import and select sky.gif from the Chapter 15 resources folder.

2. Choose File|Open As Library and select the finishedwineglasses.fla file. Only the Library will open. Click the plus (+) sign to add a new layer and name it "glasses". Drag an instance of the glasses onto the stage and place in the upper-left corner. Choose View and select Rulers if they are not visible. Drag a horizontal guide to where you want the glasses to sit. Drag another instance of the glasses for the opposite side of the stage. Figure 15.10 shows the results so far.

Figure 15.10
The wineglasses added to the stage.

3. For the next part, choose View|Work Area and be sure the work area is selected. You'll be working in the area off the stage. Add a new layer and name it Text. Choose File|Import and select the barwarstext.FH9 file from the Chapter 15 resources folder.

4. Select the text and Shift+select each line. Choose Modify|Group. Select the Scale tool from the Toolbox and press the Shift key to constrain the scale. Pull out on a corner square until the text is just under where the movie stage is visible, as shown in Figure 15.11. Choose Modify|Ungroup.

Figure 15.11
The text scaled and placed below the stage.

5. Add a new layer and name it Guide. Right-click/Ctrl+click on the layer name and choose Guide from the menu. Select both lines, choose Edit|Cut (Ctrl+X/Cmd+X), and paste (Ctrl+V/Cmd+V) into frame 1 of the Guide layer. Double-click one of the lines; you'll be editing a group. Double-click again until you see dots all over the line; change the Stroke color to white. Repeat for the other line, so you can see what you are doing. You may need to position the lines as shown in Figure 15.12.

6. To make the text into a Graphic symbol, select the text and press F8. In the Symbol Properties dialog box, name the symbol "text" and select Graphic. Click OK. The text will now appear as a symbol in the Library.

7. With the text still selected, open the Effect panel if it isn't already open (Window|Panels|Effect). From the drop-down menu, choose Tint. You can choose any color you'd like; to use the colors Ian used, enter the RGB values shown in Figure 15.13 (R 253, G 204, B 10). You are ready to animate this movie.

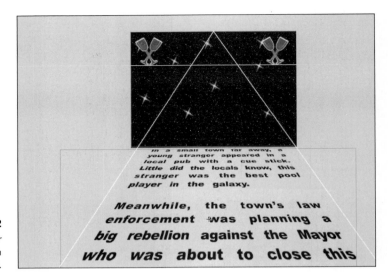

Figure 15.12
The lines with the color changed and in position on the Guide layer.

Figure 15.13
The effects used in the Effect panel.

8. While the text is still selected, choose Modify|Transform|Edit Center to make the center point of the symbol editable (the place in Figure 15.14 where the white arrow is pointing). Drag it up to where the two guide lines intersect (the place in Figure 15.15 where the white arrow is pointing). If Snap To Objects (View|Snap To Objects) is turned on, this step is quite easy.

Figure 15.14
The white arrow is pointing to the center.

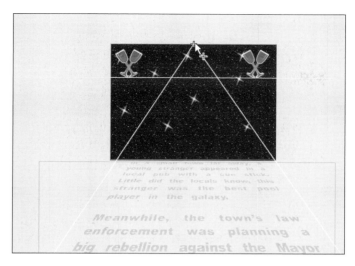

Figure 15.15
The center moved to the top of the guide lines.

9. In the timeline's Background layer, add 405 layers to make a smooth and slow scroll toward the top. Select frame 405 and press F5.

10. On the Text layer, select frame 385 and insert a keyframe (F6). This keyframe now contains the same text symbol. With the symbol still selected, activate the scale handles (click the Scale icon in the Toolbox) and click-drag one of the corner handles until the symbol is at the top of the movie stage and shrinks enough for your needs. Did you notice how the object scales after you change its center point (Step 8)? Figure 15.16 shows where I placed the text, because I'll be adding a title at the top of the stage.

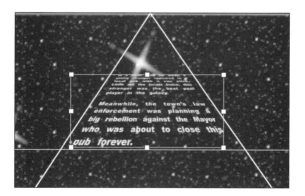

Figure 15.16
The text in place near the top of the stage.

11. You will now add the motion tween to make the symbol in the first keyframe of the Text layer scroll up to the symbol in frame 385 (the smaller text). Click any frame without a keyframe in the Text layer and open the Frame panel if it isn't already open (Window|Panels|Frame). Choose Motion and use the settings in Figure 15.17.

Figure 15.17

The settings of the motion tween in the Frame panel.

Note: The Swish Movie Clip will begin to play at whatever frame you place it in. There is also a demo for SWFX, which has a lot more preset text effects. You have to use the LoadMovie action, however, and positioning is trickier with the SWFX program.

12. To finish the text effect, fade the smaller text to invisibility. Select the keyframe in frame 385 just to select the text. Select frame 405 and insert a keyframe (F6). Double-click the text to enter symbol editing mode. In the Effect panel, choose Alpha at 100%.

13. Select any frame between the last two keyframes. In the Frame panel, select Motion. That's it. You can test your movie by pressing F12. A copy named barwars.fla is saved for you in the Chapter 15 resources folder. You'll add the title in the next section.

Add a Title

I added a quick title using a program called Swish (**www.swishzone.com**); a free demo is included on the CD-ROM. I won't go through how the title was made; it's quite simple and the instructions at the Swish Web site are easy enough to follow. I made a quick title using one of the preset effects and exported it as a SWF movie (in the Export tab, check the Offset Movie option). To insert the SWF movie, follow these steps:

1. There are several ways to insert the SWF file made in Swish into the Bar Wars movie. We will use the Movie Clip method, because it makes positioning easier. We import the movie into a Movie Clip and then place an instance on the stage. Choose Insert|New Symbol, choose Movie Clip, and name it "Title".

2. Choose File|Import, navigate to the Chapter 15 resources folder, and select title.swf.

3. Return to Scene 1 and add a new layer.

4. Select the first frame and drag an instance of title from the Library onto the stage.

5. Position the text where you'd like it and test the movie.

Moving On

In this chapter, you have learned how to make all three of the Flash symbol types: Graphic, Button, and Movie Clip. You have also reviewed some of the basic types of animation in Flash that do not require ActionScript.

In Chapter 16, you will begin to learn some of the essential actions and terminology of using ActionScript.

Chapter 16

ActionScripting Essentials

In this chapter, you will learn how to add ActionScript to your frames, buttons, and Movie Clips. You will see how to change properties and learn some of the basic terms used in ActionScript. You'll also learn about the new dot syntax.

Opening the Actions Panel

Like most things in Flash, there are numerous ways to access panels. You should access the Actions panel using the technique that works best for you. You can open the Actions panel by double-clicking the frame, choosing Window|Actions, or pressing the keyboard shortcut Ctrl+Alt+A/Cmd+Option+A. I prefer to double-click the frame or frames. This method doesn't work for an object, though; in that case, I like to use the arrow icon in the Launcher Bar to quickly access the Actions panel.

Overview of Adding ActionScript

This section of the chapter will cover some of the main aspects of using ActionScript. The following sections will deal with the specifics of different parts of ActionScript; they act as a reference for the techniques used in the project chapters (Chapters 17 and 18). You may want to refer back to this chapter if you don't understand what you are doing or why you are doing it.

This section's overview will cover more information than you'll need for the techniques you will use in the following chapters; but if you happen to be new to ActionScript, it will help you grasp some of the concepts and terms.

Adding Actions to Buttons and Frames

ActionScript is written into the Flash Action window in the Actions panel. The name of the Actions panel varies, depending on which event handles are selected. For instance, if you select a frame, the panel is called Frame Actions (see Figure 16.1). You add ActionScript either by using menus (on the left) or by choosing Expert mode (Options pop-up menu, which is the menu accessed from the right-pointing arrow) and typing your own syntax. ActionScript can be added to frames, buttons, or objects.

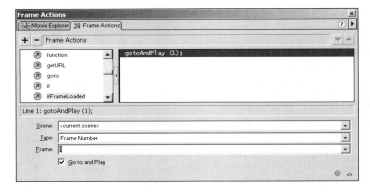

Figure 16.1
A frame is selected in the Actions panel, so the panel's name becomes Frame Actions.

To add ActionScript to a frame or a Button symbol, follow these steps:

1. With a new movie open, draw a simple rectangle on the stage and select the frame that will receive the ActionScript.

2. Open the Actions panel (see tip, "Opening the Actions Panel").

3. Click on the Basic Actions book to open it. Double-click Go To; doing so adds the syntax to the right pane. You can also drag the action into the right pane. An alternative way of selecting the action is to click the plus sign (+) and choose from the resulting menu to add the syntax automatically to the right pane. Figure 16.2 shows the Go To action added to the right pane. The parameters available with the action are covered in the "Go To" section of this chapter.

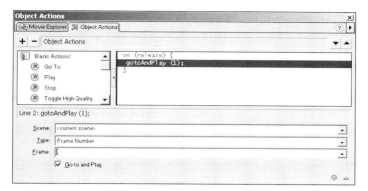

Figure 16.2
The Go To action added to a Button symbol.

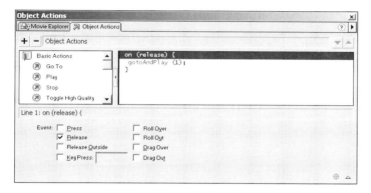

Figure 16.3
The **on (release)** line of code selected and the parameters area open showing the list of events to choose from.

If you attach the same Go To action to a Button symbol, the code will vary slightly. Figure 16.3 shows the additional code added to a Button symbol. The event (**release**, in this example) specifies which type of user interaction will make the action occur. You can change the event by selecting the **on (release)** line of code (which is clicking the mouse button) and choosing a different event from the Event list, as shown in Figure 16.3. To access the parameters area, click the little white triangle in the lower-right corner of the Actions panel.

Usually, a button click should take the user somewhere, such as to another page. You have two options: You can go to another frame within the same movie or to a different HTML page outside the Flash movie. You can access another frame of the movie by using the Go To action we just looked at. To use a hyperlink instead, you would use the getURL action, by following these steps:

1. Select a Button symbol.

2. Open the Actions panel, open the Basic Actions book, and choose Get URL.

3. The code you see is:

```
on (release) {
    getURL ("http://www.JoyceJEvans.com");
}
```

Type the URL address in the URL box in the parameters area. You will see the address added to the syntax between the quote marks as you type.

4. In the Window box of the parameters area, select the target for the URL to open into.

Movies and Movie Clips

In this section, we will look at using Movie Clips, embedding Movie Clips inside other Movie Clips, and accessing or giving instructions to these various Movie Clips.

Before we begin looking at the awesome power of using Movie Clips, let's discuss loading movies (not Movie Clips) into your Flash movie. Multiple Flash movies can play at the same time in your main movie. You accomplish this result by using different levels for each movie. For instance, the main movie is level0 (zero), the bottom level. You then use the LoadMovie action from the Basic Actions book to open another movie. The movie you want to open must be on another level, such as level1, so it will play on top. If you tried to open this movie and it was on level0, it would replace the original movie. You can have only one movie per level, but you can have as many Movie Clips as you'd like on the same level.

The big advantage of using Movie Clips over just loading movies is that a Movie Clip runs independently of the main movie. It has its own timelines and actions and is in effect a "mini movie." You have a lot of control over a Movie Clip—you can change its color and position, and even make it disappear (using transparency).

Movie Clips are controlled by the instance name (in the Instance panel). You add ActionScript to a Movie Clip by referencing its instance name. You can also place a Movie Clip inside another Movie Clip. You name the path to the second Movie Clip the same way you'd add hyperlinks. See the "Paths" tip.

To target a Movie Clip named title2 inside a Movie Clip named title, the path would be:

```
title/title2
```

Sending instructions from a Movie Clip to another Movie Clip is quite similar to linking to a Movie Clip inside a Movie Clip. For instance, let's say you are in a Movie Clip called text on the main timeline, and you want to send instructions to title2, which is inside title. The path would be a relative path and would look like this:

```
../title/title2
```

Paths

The following examples use *slash syntax*. This syntax was used prior to Flash 5 and is still used sometimes. Flash 5 has added a new syntax called *dot syntax* (more on this later in the chapter). The following examples use the older slash syntax only to demonstrate how the paths to your Movie Clips closely resemble a path in an HTML document. You will also see the dot syntax version in the "Dot Syntax" tip later on in this section.

Dot Syntax

More information about dot syntax appears at the end of this chapter, but demonstrating the difference between the slash syntax and the dot syntax in context here may help you see the differences. Basically, the slashes are replaced with dots. However, there are also a few differences in the way the paths are accessed. The dot syntax for the title movie clip would be **title.title2**.

The relative path would replace the **../** with **_parent** and look like this:

```
_parent.title.title2
```

The absolute path replaces the forward slash with **_root** and looks like this:

```
_root.title.title2
```

To access level2, the dot syntax would look like this:

```
_level2.title.title2
```

You could type the dot syntax for the paths into the TellTarget Action parameters area, but it's much easier to simply type the path into the Actions syntax window in Expert mode. Here's an example that accesses title, which is on level2, and then plays title2, which is a Movie Clip inside title:

```
on (release) {
_level2.title.title2.play();
}
```

As you can see, the syntax closely resembles the way paths are written in Dreamweaver. Another variation is an absolute path. Absolute targets follow the path from the root, which is the main timeline. For absolute paths, add a forward slash (/) before the path, like this:

```
/title/title2
```

You can also target Movie Clips on different levels. To do so, simply add the level number you want to target before the path, like this:

```
_level2/title/title2
```

ActionScript

Flash 5 uses ActionScript (a scripting language) to add interactivity to your movies. ActionScript is used for things such as navigation, arcade-style games, puzzles, sound, banners, communication with a server for things like chat, or e-commerce activities like login and registration. ActionScript is a powerful scripting language, yet it's relatively easy to learn.

ActionScript is based on JavaScript, which is an object-oriented language; so, if you know JavaScript, you will learn ActionScript very quickly. JavaScript controls the browser; ActionScript controls the objects in a Flash movie. Version 5 of Flash also uses a syntax called *dot syntax*, which is similar to the format most programmers are familiar with. Not only will a programmer be more comfortable using dot syntax, but it also adds much more power and flexibility to Flash 5. You'll see more about the dot syntax later in this chapter.

As with any new language, you'll experience a learning curve as you learn the rules of ActionScript. If you tell Flash, "move the ball", it can't comply—it doesn't understand. You'll have to tell Flash how big the ball is, how far to move it, which direction to move it, and how long it should keep moving. Are you beginning to see how much you need to think about before you write your first piece of ActionScript? Thinking through all the specifics of what you want to happen is the first step to making your Flash movie—before you write any code.

You will learn some of the essential terms and aspects of ActionScript in this chapter. We will focus primarily on the concepts and actions you'll need to understand to complete the projects in Chapters 17 and 18. The most difficult part of writing one chapter about ActionScript is deciding what to include and what not to include; after all, whole books are written on the subject. Be sure to check Appendix B for a list of the books I use and recommend for further study. It is also impossible for me to know what knowledge level you have as you use this book. You may be an intermediate Flash user but new to ActionScript, and so we will begin with some general terms. You may find that some of these instructions and descriptions make more sense after you begin using the actions in real projects.

Properties

Movie Clips, frames, and symbols have properties that you can control using ActionScript. You can control changes such as position, color, transparency, and so on. To set a property, follow these steps:

1. Select a Movie Clip.

2. Open the Actions panel (use the arrow icon from the Launcher Bar).

3. Select the Properties book and choose the property you want to control. Add it to the right pane by double-clicking your choice.

4. Open the parameters area and type in an expression.

You'll use the following properties in the projects in Chapters 17 and 18:

- **_visible**—Visibility is either true or false.

- **_x** or **_y**—The X, Y coordinates of the object.

- **_droptarget**—The target path of a draggable Movie Clip that must be dropped on a specific target.

An example of changing properties of a Movie Clip could be to move a clip by so many pixels. Let's say you wanted to move the title2 Movie Clip by 20 pixels. First, you'd locate the clip, and then you'd set the new value (more on setting values in the "Variables" section). The getProperty action (Actions|SetProperty) finds the property's current value from the Property drop-down menu; choose _X (X position). In the Target field, type in the target path (or use the Insert Path icon in the bottom-right corner of the Paramenters pane) and the property name in quotes, followed by your new value. To move title2 Movie Clip 20 pixels, the code would be:

```
_root.title.title2._x=20
```

If you try to enter this code directly into the setProperty value box, it wouldn't work. If it's entered in the value box, Flash thinks it's a value—but it isn't. Flash needs to do a calculation to determine the value (expression); so, check the Expression box by the value of the setProperty action.

You can save even more time if you type your code into the right pane using Expert mode. If you wrote your own syntax, it would look like this:

```
title.title2._x=title.title2._x+20
```

This bit of code yields the same result—moving title2 by 20 pixels.

Variables

Variables are the information containers of ActionScript. The container is the variable's name, which remains constant; however, the content can change. Variables can record user input and evaluate if a condition is true or false.

Flash remembers data and the label that identifies the data. The data and its label form the variable. Every variable has a name, also called a label, which is used to access the data it contains. To put information into the container (variable), the syntax is:

```
variable Name = Value;
```

variable Name is the name of the variable, and **Value** is the data. For example:

```
message="Hi";
```

Here, **message** is the variable name, the text (**Hi**) is the value, and the equal sign (=) is the assignment operator that assigns the value on the right side to the variable name on the left side. In this example, the value type is text. The value type can also be mathematical. Your code can be attached to a frame, keyframe, button, or Movie Clip.

Using Expert Mode

When you're first learning how to write your own syntax, you can tell Flash to check the syntax for you by choosing Check Syntax from the Actions panel Options pop-up menu. If an error is found, an Output dialog box opens and any errors are described. When you are beginning to write code, you should check it often by pressing Ctrl+Enter/Cmd+Return; the Output dialog box will then show any errors. If you are still having problems with your code, you can use the Debug option by choosing Control|Debug Movie.

Note: Declaring or setting the variable is a good habit to get into, but if you don't, then Flash will do it automatically. If you come from a programming background, you can name your variables with a **var** prefix if you'd like. Setting the variable yourself lets you specify your own naming conventions.

To set or declare a value, you can type in the variable's name or use an action (see note). The Set Variable action is in the Actions book; double-click Set Variable, and you'll see a message telling you that the variable must be named—for instance, **MyName**. If you type "Joyce" in the value box, the syntax reads:

```
MyName = "Joyce";
```

Variables are stored in the target where they are declared. So if you have

```
TitleName="Integrating Flash, Fireworks and FreeHand f/x & Design"
```

in both a Movie Clip named title and a Movie Clip named title2, there won't be a problem.

Movie Clips can share variables by using target paths to say where they are. Recall that in the ActionScript overview we used title and title2 Movie Clips, and title2 was inside title. If you want to change the value of TitleName in the Movie Clip title2 from the main timeline (level0), the code would look like this:

```
_level0.title.title2.TitleName="New Value"
```

Data Types

The data types are as follows:

- *Strings*—A string consists of text or numbers or both enclosed in quotes (""). When you're using numerical calculations, the quotes are not present in the code—the quote marks indicate a string. For example, *"6" + "2"* would be interpreted as 62.

- *Expressions*—Expressions contain more than one element; the elements can be numbers or calculations. For instance, **Total=6+2** would be interpreted as 8. An expression is a formula that combines variables.

- *Boolean*—Boolean variable values are either true or false, yes or no, or 1 or 0. Boolean values are used in either/or situations, such as toggle switches.

- *Number*—The number data type includes any value (or expression value) that refers to a numeric value in Flash. Number data does not have quotes around it in the syntax.

Actions and Event Handlers

Interactivity begins with an event such as a mouse click being performed, resulting in a behavior or action happening. You can apply many actions in Flash, but for them to execute, you must "tell" them to act. You do so using an *event handler*, such as:

```
on (rollover) or on (release)
```

The Actions panel makes adding commands easy. You select the action you want or type your own code (in Expert mode). If you select a frame, the panel is called Frame Actions (see Figure 16.4). If you select an object, the panel is called Object Actions (see Figure 16.5). In this book, it is referred to simply as the Actions panel.

Note: Every time you access the Actions panel, it will default back to the Normal mode. Most of the examples in this book will be using the Expert mode. If you'd like to remain in Expert mode and not have to keep selecting it manually, you can change a Preference. Choose Edit|Preferences, the General tab. At the bottom in the Actions Panel Mode drop-down, choose Expert Mode.

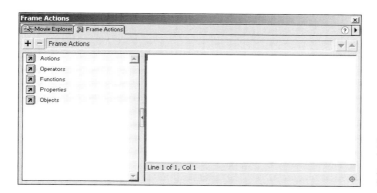

Figure 16.4
The Actions panel is called Frame Actions when an event handler frame is selected.

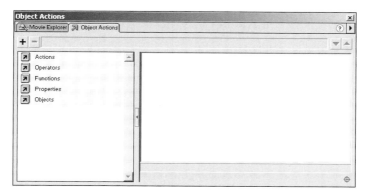

Figure 16.5
The Actions panel is called Object Actions when an event handler object is selected.

Normal mode is the default. You'll see a list of actions grouped in categories or *books* in the left pane of the Actions panel. To switch to Expert mode, click the right-pointing arrow and choose Expert Mode from the Options pop-up menu (a check mark appears next to it when it's selected). Or, use the keyboard short-cut: Ctrl+E/Cmd+E. In Expert mode, you can type or copy and paste custom code into the right pane of the Actions panel. You also can combine your custom code with the pre-built actions by double-clicking the action from the left pane or dragging the action into the right pane.

Deprecated Actions

You will notice some of the actions in the Actions panel are highlighted in green. This highlight means the actions are deprecated. If you don't see highlighted items such as TellTarget, then check your Publish settings (File|Publish Settings; see Chapter 19); if the Publish settings are set for Flash 5, you will see the deprecated items highlighted in green. The Flash 5 player will support these actions, but better options are now available, such as using dot syntax instead of TellTarget. You'll see yellow highlights in the Actions panel if the action isn't supported at all with the Flash Player (the version number) you have set up in the Publish settings.

Flash Pre-built Actions

You can access actions in several different ways. Open the Actions panel by choosing Window|Actions (Ctrl+Alt+A/Cmd+Option+A). You also can click the arrow icon in the Launcher Bar. To add an action to a frame, you can double-click the frame to open the Actions panel.

Once the Actions panel is open, you can add actions several ways. You can open the appropriate book and double-click an action to add it to the right pane, or you can click-and-drag the action to the right pane. You can click the plus sign (+) and choose from that list. Once you make a selection, the code is automatically added to the right pane. You also can choose Expert Mode from the Options pop-up menu and type in your own code.

Basic Actions

Basic actions include simple actions used with navigations such as play and stop. Such actions assign mouse responses, play different frames, or load a movie.

The basic actions are listed in groups in the Actions panel according to function. The first group controls the playback of movies, the second handles sounds and visual quality, the third loads external files, and the fourth communicates with Movie Clips and controls the display of movies while downloading.

Go To

When added to the right pane, the Go To action looks like this:

```
gotoAndPlay (1);
```

This statement says to go to a specified frame, indicated by the number in parentheses, and play. The other variation of the Go To action is gotoAndStop, which goes to a specified frame and stops. These actions are frequently used with buttons.

Actions that contain parameters you need to specify will have the parameter choices in the parameters area. For instance, the Go To action has parameters, but the Play action doesn't. To access the parameters of an action, click the little white triangle at lower right in the Actions panel (see Figure 16.6). Figure 16.7 shows the Go To action selected and the parameters area open.

The parameters for Go To are:

- *Scene*—You can choose various scenes.

- *Type*—You choose the Frame Number, Frame Label, Expression, Next Frame, or Previous Frame to be the target of the action. The choices are self-explanatory, except for Expression. Expressions are used to dynamically assign targets of Go To actions.

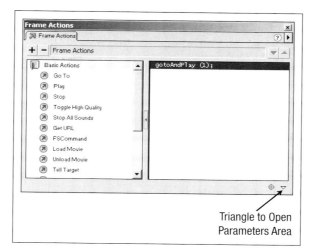

Triangle to Open
Parameters Area

Figure 16.6
The triangle to click to open the
parameters area.

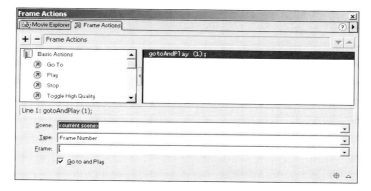

Figure 16.7
The parameters area open for
the Go To action.

- *Frame*—This area varies depending on the Type you select. If you choose Frame, enter the frame number here. If you choose Frame Label, enter the label name.

- *Go To And Play*—If you deselect this option, the action changes to gotoAndStop.

A practical use of the Go To action is a simple preloader. If your movie takes more than a few seconds to open, a preloader will be needed; a preloader indicates that the movie is loading and perhaps how much time is still left. Often a preloader contains a little bit of entertainment while the user waits for the loading of the movie.

Actions

The Actions book includes the basic actions plus more. In Expert mode, you don't see the Basic Action book; these actions are combined in the Actions book. These actions manipulate variables, expressions, and conditional statements.

Evaluate

The action we'll be using in the puzzle project in Chapter 17 is Evaluate. We will use Expert mode to type in the code. The Evaluate action will check to determine if the puzzle piece is dragged to its proper position. The Evaluate code looks like this:

```
if (eval(this._droptarget)==_root.base1)
        this._x=_root.base1._x;
        this._y=_root.base1.y;
```

This code asks that a check be made to see if the values are equivalent. The two equal signs (==) check the operands on the right and the left to see if they are the same. The **root.base** value accesses the main timeline, which is called **root**. The number following is the number of the **root.base** item. In this case, it will be the puzzle piece number. The **x** and **y** code elements check the X, Y coordinates of the drop target to verify the puzzle piece is in the correct position.

<aside>
Note: If your code doesn't work, check to be sure there are two equal operators; this is the first place to look; programmers often put in only one equal (assignment) operator by mistake.
</aside>

if Statement

The **if** statements are conditional. The **if** statement contains one or more substatements that execute only when specified conditions are met. For example, if the condition is true, the action is executed. If it's false, the action isn't executed. A good use for such statements would be password-protected sites.

else Statement

An **else** statement is an extension of an **if** statement. Using the **if** statement in conjunction with the **else** statement is a better way to protect a passworded site. The **else** statement says that if a condition is met, do this; otherwise, do this. An example would be opening the site URL if the password matches, or else returning an error page.

Print

The Print action allows you to print the content on the main timeline or from the timeline of a Movie Clip. It's a good idea to use Movie Clips to contain the content you'd like to print. Assuming you are using a Movie Clip, you'll need to specify which frame or frames you want to print. Enter Symbol editing mode by double-clicking the Movie Clip, choose the keyframe you'd like to print, and label it #P. To label the keyframe or keyframes you'd like to print, open the Frame panel and enter a label name of #P. The #P designates which keyframe to print. If you want to print the entire timeline, don't add any labels.

We'll look at some of the parameters that need to be set for the Print action. After you add the print action to a print button or text in the main movie (Scene 1), you'll need to set the parameters. From the Print drop-down menu, choose As Vector or As Bitmap; in the Location filed, enter or locate the Target (Path). The Bounding Box field determines what prints; you can define its values three ways:

- *bframe*—The bounding box of each frame to be printed is set individually to match the contents. Every frame's content scales to fill the printed page.

- *bmax*—The area that the content occupies forms the general bounding box. The content of each frame is scaled on the printed page relative to the bounding box.

- *bmovie*—This option specifies a cropping area. All printed frames will be the size of a designated frame in the target clip. The frame that is designated as the bounding box is labeled with #b. The printable area is controlled by using Flash's Movie Bounding Box option and the frame labels #b and #P. The #P designates which frames to print instead of the default of all frames.

Objects

Objects are a collection of properties; all *properties* have a name and a *value*. You can change and access object characteristics using ActionScript. There are user-defined objects as well as pre-defined objects. An instance of a symbol must be placed on the stage to have an object action applied to it; actions are not applied in Symbol Editing mode. A few of the pre-defined objects follow.

Array

Arrays are a special type of variable new to Flash 5. They consist of numbered images and forms, which are used frequently in JavaScript. These variables have one or more dimensions and are considered objects. The array method is **New Array**, with an optional argument for array length. For example, if you have a customer list with a list of names, such as

```
Name ="Sally";
Name2="Gerald";
Name3="Sue";
Name4="Hank";
```

a new array would appear as

```
customers=New Array(Sally, Gerald, Sue, Hank);
message="Thank you for your order" + customers[3];
```

The result of this small piece of code is *Thank you for your order Hank*.

Color

The method of the color object is **SetRGB**, which sets the color of the color object. The argument is **0X*RRGGBB***. The zero x (**0x**) is an escape code for hexadecimal values and is always used prior to the hexadecimal values. You replace ***RRGGBB*** with the hexadecimal values of the color you want to use. You can find the hexadecimal values in the Mixer panel.

You can manipulate the color attributes of a Movie Clip instance two ways: the hexadecimal value and the RGB code. We will look at the hexadecimal value; the RGB values are in decimals from 0 to 255 and translate to 0 to FF in hexadecimal.

To define a color for a Movie Clip, you'll need to set your variable using the **New Color** statement. (You will use this statement in Chapter 18, when we make a banner using the color functions.)

Math

The math actions access trigonometry functions. All the math objects prepare read-only values and are written in all-capital letters. The trigonometry functions for sine, cosine, tangent, logarithmic, mathematical, and constant are beyond the scope of this book. However, you will use the **math.round** statement in the jukebox project. **math.round** is just what it sounds like—it rounds to the nearest integer.

The code you will use is as follows:

```
math.round(this.getBytesTotal()/1000)
```

This code rounds off the byte size of object you are editing to the nearest byte. In this case, it is the size of a song, which will be a Flash movie. At the end of the code line, **/1000** tells Flash to divide by 1000 so we get the number of kilobytes instead of bytes.

Movie Clip

Movie Clip is one of the pre-defined objects in Flash. Movie Clips are objects with characteristics you can access and control. Some of the properties you have control over specify appearance, such as transparency, visible, color, size, and position. Movie Clips are added to your movies by dragging an instance onto the stage from the Library.

getBytesTotal

You saw briefly in the "Math" section how getBytesTotal works. This action does exactly what it sounds like: It gets the total bytes of the object it is assigned to. Another popular use of getBytesTotal is in conjunction with getBytesLoaded. Together, these actions determine the progress of a file's loading, such as in a Flash movie preloader.

startDrag and stopDrag

startDrag and stopDrag do just what they sounds like: They let you drag a Movie Clip and stop dragging the Movie Clip, respectively.

Dot Syntax

Dot syntax is one of the most exciting new additions to Flash 5. The short version is that dot syntax replaces slashes (/) with dots. You saw a few of the other variations is the "Dot Syntax" sidebar in the section "Overview of

Adding ActionScript," such as ../ being replaced with **_parent** and **_root** instead of just a forward slash.

The dot syntax has expanded the possibilities of Flash far beyond previous versions. The dot syntax is the method of writing ActionScript. It allows much more flexibility and power for programmers, but it isn't too difficult for non-programmers to grasp, either. Although Flash 5 maintains menu-driven actions, which are extremely easy to use, the addition of dot syntax appeals to pro-grammers who want more control over their objects.

Dot syntax is a scripting language that adheres closely to the specifications based on JavaScript. It's an object-oriented programming language with code that looks like this:

```
object.property=value;
```

or

```
object.methods();
```

In this statement, four things need defining: the object, properties, values, and methods. For example, a Movie Clip object has properties (characteristics) that can be changed. The data, which goes with the properties, is the value.

PROJECT Finishing the Eyeland Studio Interface

In Chapter 14, you put the button graphics on the timeline for the slide animation. The Button symbol itself is about done. The original file (emerald.fla) supplied by Scott Hamlin of Eyeland studio is included in the Chapter 16 Eyeland folder. This file uses some deprecated code (because it was originally designed in Flash 4), which is replaced in this project with the dot syntax. The original file also has diamonds on the button Movie Clip. You won't add them, because they follow the same techniques you used to add the button graphics to the timeline. The diamond graphics are supplied in the Eyeland folder if you'd like to add them. All the files you're making are saved separately (in the Eyeland folder in the Chapter 16 folder) from the original, which you can use as a guideline. To finish the button Movie Clip and add it to the Eyeland interface, follow these steps:

1. From the Eyeland folder in the Chapter 16 folder, open buttonsformovie.fla. This is the Button symbol you started in Chapter 14. Click the plus sign (+) to add a new layer. Double-click the layer name and name the layer "Controls".

2. Select frame 1 of the Controls layer, open the Actions panel, choose Basic Actions, and double-click Stop. Figure 16.8 shows the code added in the right pane.

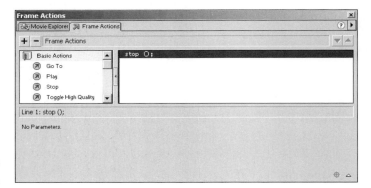

Figure 16.8
The Stop action added to frame 1.

3. Select frame 9 and Choose Insert|Blank Keyframe. In the Actions panel, choose Stop from the Basic Actions book and double-click to add it to the right pane.

4. Select frame 18 and choose Insert|Blank Keyframe. In the Actions panel, select Go To from the Basic Actions book and double-click to add it to the right pane. Figure 16.9 shows the timeline for the button.

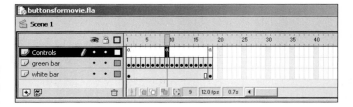

Figure 16.9
The timeline with the controls added to the button Movie Clip.

Note: Normally, you would make this button Movie Clip right in the main movie; we did it in a separate file to demonstrate using the Open As Library option.

5. Select the Control layer and Shift+select all layers. Choose Insert|Convert To Symbol. In the Symbols property box, select the Movie Clip Behavior and name it "ButtonMovie". A copy called buttonmovieclip.fla is saved in the Chapter 16 Eyeland folder.

6. Open the eyeland.fla file from the Eyeland folder in Chapter 16 on the CD-ROM. Click the plus sign to add a new layer. Double-click the layer name and name the layer "Anim buttons".

7. Choose File|Open As Library, navigate to the Eyeland folder, and choose buttonmovieclip.fla. Click OK.

8. Drag 12 instances of the buttonmovieclip onto the Eyeland layout. A button goes between each of the green lines on the left side. Place the top button just below the top dark green line and the last button just above the bottom dark green line. Use the Align panel (Window|Panels|Align) to space the buttons evenly. Shift+select each button, select Align (Align Left Edge), select Distribute (Distribute Bottom Edge), and nudge the button into position. Figure 16.10 shows the button instances in place.

Figure 16.10
The button instances added to the Eyeland layout.

Name each button. Select the top button, open the Instance panel (the icon to the right of the A in the Launcher Bar), and name the button "button1". Repeat for all 12 buttons, ending with button12. Figure 16.11 shows the Instance panel with button6 being named.

Figure 16.11
The Instance panel with button6 being named.

9. To add the invisible buttons for the hit area of your button Movie Clips, click the plus sign to add a new layer and name it "invisi buttons".

10. Choose Insert|New Symbol. In the Symbols dialog box, choose Button Behavior and name the button "Invisible". Select the Hit state frame and insert a keyframe (F6). Use the Rectangle tool and draw a rectangle. Select the rectangle and set its size to 200×20 in the Info panel. The invisible button is added to the Library. Click Scene 1 to return to the main movie.

11. Drag an instance of Invisible on top of every button and align as you did in Step 8. Figure 16.12 shows the invisible buttons added. They are represented by a transparent blue rectangle that isn't visible when viewed in the movie.

12. Click the plus sign to add a new layer. Double-click the layer name and name the layer "Text". Open the Character panel (Window|Panels| Character). Select the Text tool and type the link names. The font used in this example is 12-point Times in all Caps with a color of black. The link names used are:

  - WEB SITE DESIGN

  - ANIMATION DESIGN

  - INTERFACE DESIGN

Figure 16.12

The invisible button symbols in place.

- GAME DESIGN
- GAME LICENSING
- GAME SAMPLES
- ONLINE PRODUCTS
- CD-ROM PRODUCTS
- SAMPLE & DEMOS
- FREE TUTORIALS
- FREE RESOURCES
- CONTACT

Center all the text over their respective buttons. Now it's time to add the ActionScript to each button.

13. Select the first invisible button. In the Actions panel, choose Expert Mode and type in this syntax:

```
on (rollOver) {
button1.gotoAndPlay(2);
}
on (rollOut) {
button1.gotoAndPlay(10);
}
on (rollOver) {
screentext.gotoAndStop(10);
}
on (rollOut) {
screentext.gotoAndStop(1);
}
```

To demonstrate that you can actually write the ActionScript in different ways and get the same results, look at the following code; it is a bit more compact but performs the same function.

```
on (rollOver, dragOver) {

_root.button1.gotoAndPlay(2);
_root.screentext.gotoAndStop("Websitedesign");
}

on (rollOut, dragOut) {
_root.screentext.gotoAndStop("Default");
_root.button1.gotoAndPlay(10);
}
```

Remaining in Expert Mode

If you use Expert Mode often, which you will do in Chapter 17, you can change your Preferences so you don't have to manually select Expert Mode (although, the instructions I give don't assume you've changed your Preferences). Choose Edit|Preferences|General. At the bottom, in the Actions panel area, choose Expert Mode from the drop-down menu.

On rollover, this code tells button1 to play frame 2; on rollout, it plays frame 10, ending with a sliding button. This is the dot syntax versus the **tellTarget** used in the original emerald.fla file. The next rollover deals with the text in the middle of the interface. On rollover, the text changes with frame 10 of the screentext Movie Clip.

14. Copy and paste this code into every invisible button. Change the button number for each one, as well. You also need to change the rollover value of screentext on each button and increase the frame number by 10 for every button, ending with (120). You will need to select Expert Mode every time; it's a hassle, but it switches back to Normal mode as soon as you change buttons (see "Remaining in Expert Mode" tip). This file was saved in the Eyeland folder as eyeland2.fla.

Moving On

In this chapter, you have learned some of the key principles and vernacular of speaking the language of Flash—ActionScript.

In Chapter 17, you will use the actions in projects that you began to build in either FreeHand or Fireworks.

Chapter 17

Projects Using ActionScript

In this chapter, you will learn how to add ActionScript to projects you began designing in Fireworks and FreeHand, such as a jigsaw puzzle. You'll rotate a product demo 360 degrees and add music to a jukebox.

Adding ActionScript

You began adding a bit of ActionScript to the Eyeland Studio interface in Chapter 16. In this chapter, you will be completing projects you began in both Fireworks and FreeHand. All the steps needed are included, although for multiple Movie Clips that follow the same instructions, you will make one sample with the book and the rest on your own. We will deconstruct the title Movie Clip in the jukebox project so you can see how it's done, and you'll make the song sound files into a Flash movie. Most of these instructions were supplied by Tracy Kelly (**www.tracykelly.com**; see her bio in Appendix B). I rewrote them and added formatting. I also added details such as how some of the Movie Clips were made, along with notes, tips, sidebars, and variations when appropriate. I encountered a few problems along the way, and I share why and how to correct them.

PROJECT Finishing the Jukebox

You will use the jukebox image you traced in Flash in Chapter 14. When you click one of the numbered buttons, a song will play; when you click the Stop button, the song will stop. The title, artist name, and file size will all display dynamically (using dynamic text boxes) as each song is selected. To complete this project, follow these steps:

1. Open jukeboxstart.fla from the Chapter 17 jukebox folder.

2. Double-click the layer name and name the layer "jukebox".

3. You are done with this layer and don't want to make modifications to it; lock it by clicking the red dot under the Lock icon (the center dot). The red X over the Pencil icon indicates that this layer is not editable.

4. Click the plus sign (+) to add a new layer. Double-click the layer and name it "data".

The Movie Clip named "title" is already in the Library, but you will take a little sidetrack to make the Movie Clip "title" yourself.

Title Movie Clip

There is a movie named Jukebox1.mov in the Movie Tutorial folder on this book's CD-ROM that covers this next section. Open the Library (click the Book icon in the Launcher Bar) and double-click the title symbol to enter Symbol Editing mode so you can see what is involved in this Movie Clip. To return to the main stage and begin making the Movie Clip, follow these steps:

1. Click Scene 1. You could delete the title Movie Clip from the library and make your own; but just in case, let's leave it there and make a new Movie Clip. Select the data layer.

2. Choose Insert|New Symbol, choose Movie Clip for the Behavior, and name it "title2".

Warning

If you are used to working on symbols in Fireworks, be sure to save your files often. In Fireworks, when you are done editing a symbol, you close the editor by clicking the X in the upper-right corner. If you do this in Flash, you close your movie. In Flash, click Scene 1 to return to the movie.

Note: In Fireworks, every time you enter values into a panel, you must press Enter/Return to set the value. In Flash, you don't need to do this in the Info panel and many other panels. However, I did run into problems with the Instance panel and the Frame panel in Flash if I didn't press the Enter/Return key. It's not a bad habit to get into; it's quite frustrating to troubleshoot when an instance name you "know" you typed isn't there.

Note: When you add new layers, be sure the top layer is selected if you want to add a new one on top of it. A new layer is placed above the currently selected layer. You can move layers by clicking and dragging them to any position you'd like.

3. Select the Oval drawing tool (don't draw yet).

4. Select the Stroke icon in the Toolbox. Click the No Color icon at the bottom of the Color section on the Toolbox (center icon with a red slash). Figure 17.1 has an arrow pointing to the correct icon.

5. Draw your shape without a stroke anywhere on the stage. Press the Shift key as you draw the oval to constrain to a perfect circle. Open the Info panel and set the size to 193×193.

6. To set the fill to a 50% transparency, open the Mixer panel (Window| Panels|Mixer). With the circle selected, click the fill color box and choose a light gray; then change the Alpha value to 50%, as shown in Figure 17.2.

7. Select the Rectangle tool and draw a rectangle over the bottom portion of the circle. Because of the stroke (make sure your stroke color is different than the fill color), the rectangle will slice off the part of the circle you are covering (see Figure 17.3). Select the fill of the rectangle and delete it. Double-click the stroke and delete it. In the Info panel, adjust the height of your half circle to 84 pixels.

Figure 17.1
The No Color icon.

Figure 17.2
The Mixer panel with the Alpha set to 50%.

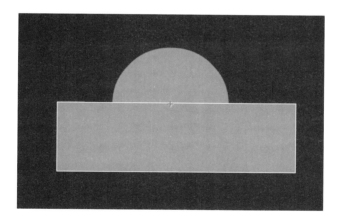

Figure 17.3
The rectangle cuts the circle in half.

8. In the Movie Tutorial folder is a movie called Jukebox2.mov, which covers this next portion. Select the oval, and in the Info panel, set the X coordinate to 0.0 and the Y coordinate to 2.

9. You will now add the text that is needed for this Movie Clip. Open the Character panel (Window|Panels|Character or Ctrl+T/Cmd+T). Choose 14-point, bold, black Times New Roman for the font and deselect Kern. Select the Text tool and type "Length:"; deselect and then type "K".

10. To position the text, select Length:. In the Info panel, set X to -24.8 and Y to 27.9. Select K and change X to 29.4 and Y to 27.9. Your sym-

> **Note:** You could also cut the circle in half using a line, as long as the stroke is a different color. I find it easier to use a rectangle.

bol is now the same as the one called title in the Library. You can delete your symbol if you want to use the one supplied. The finished Movie Clip can be seen in Figure 17.4. Return to the main movie by selecting Scene 1.

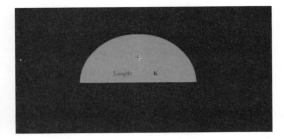

Figure 17.4

The title Movie Clip with the text added and in position.

PROJECT Jukebox Steps, Continued

Before we took the side trip to make the Movie Clip, you were ready to drag the Movie Clip called "title" onto the stage. You can do that now (be sure the data layer is selected). Then, follow these steps:

1. You can watch the Jukebox3.mov file for this portion of the project. It's in the Movie Tutorial folder on the CD-ROM. With the title instance still selected, change its location using the Info panel. Enter "249.6" for the X value and "313" for Y. You are done with this layer for now, so lock it (click the red circle below the lock).

2. Click the plus sign to add a new layer, and name the layer "buttons".

3. The buttons in the Library were originally made in FreeHand and imported into the Symbol Editor, but you can make them just as easily here in Flash. Choose Insert New Symbol, select Button for the Behavior, and name it "1a". (The Library already contains a 1, and you won't need to use this sample Button symbol.)

> **Note:** You can look at the completed button by double-clicking the number 1 in the Library.

4. Your button will only have an Up state, which is selected by default (see Figure 17.5).

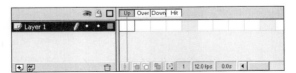

Figure 17.5

The Up state is active when the button's Symbol Editor opens.

5. Open the Stroke panel; choose a Solid stroke with a size of 3.5 and a color of #660000. In the Fill panel, change the fill color to #6B8B8C. Select the Rectangle tool and draw a little rectangle. Set the size in the Info panel to 18.5×18.5. Figure 17.6 shows your button so far.

6. Select the Text tool. In the Character panel, select a 12-point, bold Arial font with a color of #660000 and type the number "1". Center the text in the button, as shown in Figure 17.7. If you were making your own buttons, you'd repeat Steps 3–5 for buttons 2 through 4. The Stop button is the same, but it has a red rectangle in the center instead of a number. Click Scene1. You can delete this button now.

Figure 17.6
The button with a fill and a large stroke.

7. From the Library, drag all four Button symbols onto the stage. Drag the stop Button symbol onto the stage, as well. Select each button and enter these coordinates in the Info panel:

- *Button 1*—X: 185, Y: 368

- *Button 2*—X: 215, Y: 368

- *Button 3*—X: 245, Y: 368

- *Button 4*—X: 275, Y: 368

- *Stop*—X: 330, Y: 368

The jukebox so far can be seen in Figure 17.8.

Figure 17.7
The finished number 1 button.

Figure 17.8
The jukebox with the buttons added.

Adding the Dynamic Text Boxes

You will now begin to add the interactivity for the jukebox (Jukebox4.mov) by following these steps:

1. Click the plus sign to add another layer, and name the layer "actions". You will now add the text boxes to display the artist name, the song, and the song's file size.

2. Unlock the data layer and double-click the title symbol. You are now in Symbol Editing mode for this Movie Clip. The title Movie Clip has one layer called "background". Select background and click the plus sign to add a new layer; name it "dynamic text boxes".

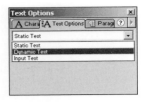

Figure 17.9
The Character, Paragraph, and Text Options panels are in the same group in your work area.

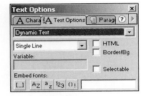

Figure 17.10
The Text Options panel after Dynamic Text is selected.

3. Select the Text tool from the Toolbox and open the Character panel (it should already be open). Choose a 14-point, bold, black _serif font. Click the Paragraph tab and select the Center Justify Align button (second from the left).

4. Select the Text Options tab (Figure 17.9) and choose Dynamic Text from the drop-down menu. Figure 17.10 shows the Text Options panel after you select Dynamic Text.

5. With the Text tool selected, draw a rectangle above the text (length) in the title Movie Clip. In the Info panel, change its Width value to 110, Height to 17, X to 8, and Y to 10.

6. In the Text Options panel, be sure the default of Single Line is selected and the other boxes are left deselected. Change the Variable name to "title_artist".

7. Select the text box you just added and choose Edit|Duplicate. In the Text Options panel, use the same settings as in Steps 5 and 6, but change the variable name to "title_name". In the Info panel, change X to 8 and Y to -10.

8. Choose Edit|Duplicate again. In the Info panel, use these settings: Width 20, Height 17, X 8, and Y 30. In the Text Options panel, name the variable "title_size". In the Paragraph panel, choose the Right Justify button. Figure 17.11 shows the text boxes added.

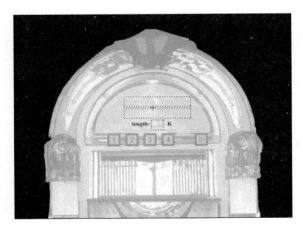

Figure 17.11
The dynamic text boxes added.

9. Lock the dynamictextboxes layer. Return to the main movie by clicking Scene 1. Now would be a good time to save your movie.

Setting the Variables for the Dynamic Text Boxes

The file is now set up to receive data from the dynamic text boxes. The next step is to declare some default values in those boxes that will appear before a user picks a song to play. To do this, you need to set variables, which are the storage containers to hold these default values. These values will then pass into the dynamic text boxes on the stage.

The default values will be listed in the dynamic text boxes until a song is selected from the jukebox. When the song is selected, the variables will update to contain the information about that song. (We will worry about that part a little later.) Your first goal is to send information from the variables you set in this Flash movie into the dynamic text boxes. See the Jukebox5.mov movie for this portion of the project. Follow these steps:

1. You should now be in the main movie. You need to give the title Movie Clip a distinctive instance name so you can talk to it programmatically. Select the title Movie Clip. In the Instance panel (Window|Panels|Instance or icon in the Launcher Bar), name it "title". Press Enter/Return.

2. Double-click frame 1 of the actions layer to open the Actions panel. From the Options pop-up menu, choose Expert Mode.

3. Click inside the right pane so you can type in some ActionScript. You need to set a variable that can be accessed by the title Movie Clip. To do this, you must ask yourself two questions: "What do I need to do?" and "Where do I need to do it?"

4. What you need to do is set a variable. In the right pane of the Actions panel, type:

```
_root.title.title_name="Song Title Here";
_root.title.title_artist = "Artist";
```

5. Save your file. A copy of the finished file is in the Chapter 17 jukebox file jukebox.fla.

Preparing the Music

You will load songs as needed instead of including them in the movie. To do this, each song will be an individual Flash movie. If you placed the sound files in the jukebox movie, all the songs would have to load before the jukebox displayed. The way we are using the sound files is only one way to do it; I chose this technique because of the file-size savings, which should always be a major consideration.

The group called PPK (**www.English.ppk.ru**) donated the song "I Need Rhythm 2001" that will be used in this example. (It reached number 2 on the MP3 chart. See Appendix B for more information about this group.) Sound clips 2 through 4 were donated by Gazelleboy from Austin, Texas (see Appendix B for more about him).

All the sound files are for your practice and enjoyment: They are not to be distributed. With this in mind, I did not edit the MP3s. They are far too large for the Internet, but are files for you to use on your system. To make the sound movies, follow these steps:

1. Open a new movie. Double-click Layer 1 and name the layer "sound". Click the plus sign to add a new layer; name this one "actions".

2. Choose File|Import. From the Chapter 17 jukebox folder, choose ineedrhythm2001ppk.mp3 file. The sound will be imported and placed in the Library.

3. If the Library isn't open, click the Book icon in the Launcher Bar. Select the ineedrhythm2001ppk.mp3 sound file. Click the Play button in the viewer part of the Library (see Figure 17.12), and you should hear the sound playing. Click the Stop button after you test the sound file.

4. Select frame 1 of the sound layer and drag an instance of the sound file onto the stage. A straight black line appears in frame 1 of the sound layer. This line is a visual reminder that a sound is in this layer (see Figure 17.13).

Figure 17.12

The Library with the sound file selected and the Play button visible.

Figure 17.13

An instance of the sound file added to frame 1 of the sound layer, indicated by a little horizontal line.

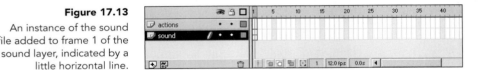

5. The sound is now added to the timeline. You need to set values so that the title, artist, and file size appear in your dynamic text boxes when the song is selected. Double-click frame 1 of the actions layer to open the Actions panel. From the Options pop-up menu, choose Expert Mode.

6. You need to ask yourself the same questions as before: "What do I need to do?" and "Where do I need to do it?" You need to send data that can be accessed by the Movie Clip named "title". To answer the "What do I need to do?" question, you must set the dynamic text boxes with the correct data about this particular sound. When you play a sound, the text box should display the correct song name and artist. You need to change the text in the dynamic text boxes to reflect the correct file and artist name changes.

Answering the second question, "Where do I need to do it?" will take a bit of explanation. The dynamic text boxes are in the jukebox in a Movie Clip called "title". In Chapter 16, you may recall that the code **_root** speaks with the main timeline. That won't work in this case, because **_root** talks to the main timeline of the movie you are in—and you are currently in a totally different movie (song movie) than the jukebox.

To explain what code you need, I need to outline the process of loading the movie that contains the sound into the jukebox. Flash has a feature called *levels*. Levels allow you to place one SWF file into another. You can load the SWF file on top of the current movie at a higher level, or you can replace the movie that is currently there by using the same level number. It just depends on which level you load the movie. Remember, only one movie can be on each level.

The timeline of the main movie (jukebox) is level0 (zero). When you click a button on the jukebox, the song SWF file will be loaded into the jukebox movie. Because you don't want the current movie (the jukebox) to be replaced, you must load the song movie to a level higher than level0. Any number higher then zero will do just fine (we will use level1).

You need to communicate with the jukebox. Remember, you must send the artist name, song title, and file size to those dynamic text boxes located in the title Movie Clip. The jukebox is on the first level (**_level0**); the name of the Movie Clip that contains the dynamic text box is "title". To summarize where you need to do it, the dynamic text boxes are located at **_level0.title**.

7. **title_name** and **title_artist** are the names of the variables in the juke-box that need to change when the user clicks a song. In the right pane of the Actions pane, type the following code; it sets the dynamic text boxes to the correct name and title.

```
_level0.title.title_name = "I Need Rhythm 2001";
_level0.title.title_artist = "PPK Vera Feat";
```

To recap, you just told Flash that when this file loads, it should place the data listed here into the title_name and title_artist dynamic text boxes inside the title Movie Clip in the jukebox. But you aren't done yet! You need to send the jukebox the size of the song movie.

8. The dynamic text box that will contain the file size is called "title_size". It is in the title Movie Clip in the jukebox. Under the code you already have in the Actions panel, type this:

```
_level0.title.title_size = ;
```

9. Now that you are targeting the correct dynamic text box, you need to figure out how to get the size of the song movie. Between the equal sign and the semicolon, type:

```
Math.round(this.getBytesTotal () /1000)
```

The finished line of code will look like this:

```
__level0.title.title_size = Math.round(this.getBytesTotal()/
1000) ;
```

That's a bit of scary ActionScript code, so let's take a closer look at it. **this.getBytesTotal()** contains **this**, which is a special keyword in ActionScript that tells Flash you are referring to the object you are in. Because you are in the main timeline of the song movie, **this** refers to the entire movie. **getBytesTotal()** is a bit of ActionScript that allows you to display the total bytes in your movie.

But this ActionScript returns the total bytes, not the total kilobytes that people are much more used to. That is why you divide the number returned by 1,000. By doing so, you get the total number of kilobytes in the movie.

Finally, you place that whole bit of code in the **Math.round** brackets. **Math.round** does exactly what you think it does: It rounds to the nearest integer. This way, you don't have any ugly decimals in the dynamic text box. See? The code wasn't so scary after all. The final code looks like Figure 17.14. Figure 17.15 shows the timeline when you finished.

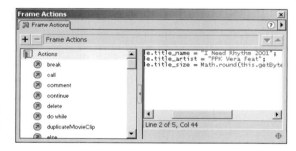

Figure 17.14
All the ActionScript for the song movie.

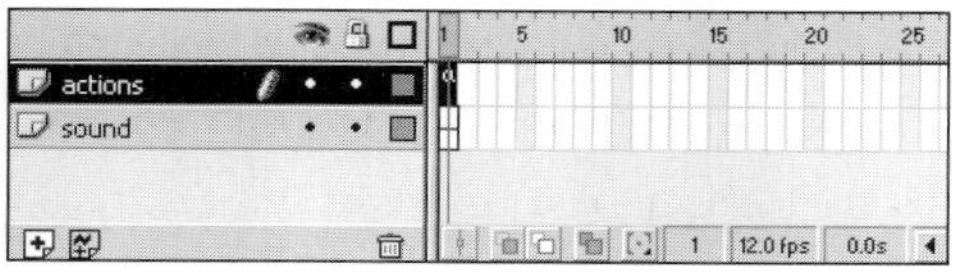

Figure 17.15
The final timeline when the ActionScript is added to the song movie.

Note: The song file needs to be saved in the same directory as the jukebox file.

Finish with these steps:

10. Save the movie as song1.fla (a copy is already in the Chapter 17 juke-box folder).

11. You need an SWF of the song1.fla file. The quickest way to make it is to test the movie and choose Control|Test Movie; an SWF file is automatically generated in the same folder as the song1.fla file.

12. Repeat these steps for song2, song3, and song4. Or, use the song files in the Chapter 17 jukebox folder. Just copy them to the same directory you are saving your files in.

Making Music

The last thing you need to do before you have music available in the jukebox is to add the actions to make the buttons work and get the songs to load. To finish with the music, follow these steps:

1. In the main timeline (Scene 1), unlock the button layer and select button1. Open the Actions panel (the Arrow icon in the Launcher Bar) and select Expert Mode from the Options pop-up menu. Enter this code:

```
on (press) {
loadMovie ("song1.swf", 1);
}
```

   The **loadMovie** line of code loads the song1.swf file in the jukebox to level1.

2. Repeat Step 2 for the other numbered buttons. You can copy the same code from song1 and paste it into the Actions panel (in Expert mode). The only thing you'll have to change is the song number. You may wonder why you are loading all the songs into the same level. If you recall, only one movie can be played per level. By loading all the movies into the same level, you ensure that only one movie can be played at a time.

3. Select the Stop button. In Expert mode, type the following code:

```
on (press) {
unloadMovie (1);
}
```

4. Stopping the song is as easy as unloading the movie from the main movie. Save and test your movie. When you click the numbered buttons, the songs should play, and the song title, artist, and total size should fill in the dynamic text boxes. When you click the Stop button, the song will stop playing.

PROJECT Making a Jigsaw Puzzle

This puzzle is linked from a puzzle box in the Horse Adventures children's Web site. The puzzle pieces were made in Chapter 1, and a copy of the file is in the Chapter 17 puzzle folder. The finished project can be seen in Figure 17.16. In addition, four movie tutorials are available on the CD-ROM (Puzzle1.mov–Puzzle4.mov) to help you with this project.

Most of the instructions for the basic puzzle were supplied by Tracy Kelly (**www.tracykelly.com**; see her bio in Appendix B). I added the variations. To make a puzzle out of the horse image, follow these steps:

1. Open a new Flash movie. Double-click Layer 1 and name the layer "puzzle base".

2. Choose Modify|Movie. Change the dimensions to 650×600 and leave the background white.

Figure 17.16
The finished puzzle project.

3. Choose File|Import and navigate to the Chapter 17 puzzle folder. Select horseimage.jpg. Move the image off the stage for now.

4. Choose File|Import and navigate to the Chapter 17 puzzle folder. Select puzzle.FH9. In the FreeHand Import dialog box (Figure 17.17), select Flatten and accept the defaults.

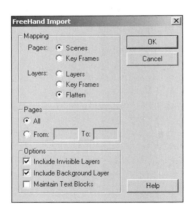

Figure 17.17
The FreeHand Import dialog box.

5. Marquee-select the puzzle shapes and group (Ctrl+G/Cmd+G). Select the horse image and open the Align panel. Click the To Stage button, followed by the Center Horizontal and the Center Vertical buttons. Repeat for the puzzle pieces.

6. The two images are aligned. Choose Edit|Select All. In the Align panel, deselect To Stage (very important). Click the Match Width And Height button, and then click the Center Horizontal and Center Vertical buttons. The horse image and the puzzle shapes should be in the same X, Y position, and they should be the exact same size—but they aren't.

What would happen if you continued this project at this point and followed the steps to cut out the pieces separately? Some of the pieces would still be connected. Check the sidebar "Troubleshooting the Puzzle" to see another reason why the pieces might be connected. With the puzzle shape taken care of in FreeHand, you would still run into a problem at this point. Some pieces are connected because of the size issue. The image and the shapes *must* be the exact same size and position. Why the Align panel is off a tad, I couldn't tell you. But the next step resolves the problem.

7. Select just the puzzle shapes (which are still grouped) and open the Info panel. Notice the Width value is 386.6 (the horse image's is 386.5) and the X coordinate is 321.1 (the horse image's is 321.0). To check the horse image yourself, select the image: You'll see the Width is 386.5, which is OK; leave it. The X coordinate is 321.1; change it to 321.0. Select the puzzle again and change its size to 386.5. They are now both the same size and aligned.

8. Select the puzzle pieces and ungroup them (Ctrl+Shift+G/Cmd+Shift+G).

9. These puzzle shapes, which were made in FreeHand, are horizontal and vertical lines that are grouped. You can select each line of shapes individually and ungroup, but it's much faster to Shift+select all the lines and then ungroup. Be sure you select only the grouped lines, indicated by a light blue rectangle shown when you select. If you accidentally select the image instead of the puzzle line, you will see a thin dotted line. Figure 17.18 shows how the selection will look when you are done. The result after ungrouping will look like Figure 17.19. Notice the little dots in the lines; this shows they are now ungrouped. Once they are ungrouped and you deselect (don't deselect yet!), the puzzle will be behind the horse image—why, I don't know, but it doesn't matter.

> **Note:** If the X and Y coordinates are different for you, that's fine, just be sure that they are the same for the puzzle shapes and the horse image.

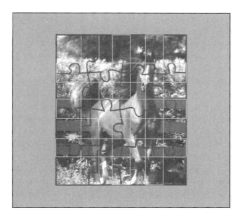

Figure 17.18
The puzzle's horizontal and vertical lines selected.

Figure 17.19
The puzzle pieces aligned
and ungrouped.

10. Choose Edit|Select All.

11. With everything still selected, choose Modify|Break Apart. You will see a shadowed dotted overlay on the puzzle. When you deselect and select each puzzle piece, they should be individual pieces. I say "should be" because it's possible you will have pieces connected; this can be quite trying. See the sidebar "Troubleshooting the Puzzle" to see what causes pieces to be connected and how to fix the problem.

12. You have 16 individual puzzle pieces. Select the upper-left piece and choose Insert|Convert To Symbol (using the keyboard shortcut F8 will be much faster for this many pieces). Select Movie Clip as its Behavior and name it MC1. Repeat for each piece, ending with MC16.

Figure 17.20
The Movie Explorer with the
Show Graphics, Buttons And
Movie Clips button selected.

13. You need to remove the jigsaw overlay. Open the Movie Explorer (the icon with a magnifying glass in the Launcher Bar). Be sure the Show Graphics, Buttons And Movie Clips button is selected (second from the left). The Movie Explorer can be seen in Figure 17.20.

14. In the Movie Explorer, select MC1 from the puzzle base layer and Shift+select all the Movie Clips through MC16. Choose Edit|Cut (Ctrl+X/ Cmd+X). From the stage, double-click the puzzle shapes and press the Delete key. Choose Edit|Paste In Place to return your puzzles pieces. Lock the puzzle base layer.

Troubleshooting the Puzzle

When you design the puzzle shapes, you have to be very careful that there are no openings. Each of the horizontal and vertical lines must touch the edges. Even if they touch, you may have to adjust them a bit. Don't let any lines overlap the bounding shape. I had to fix the puzzle shape (the one supplied doesn't need adjusting) and then test it in Flash, then alter again where the shapes were connected, then edit, and so on. Of course, some of the testing problems could have been the alignment discrepancies discussed in Steps 6 and 7, which weren't discovered until after the puzzle shapes were altered.

15. Select the puzzle base layer and click the plus sign to add a new layer on top. Name this layer "puzzle pieces".

16. Select frame 1 of the puzzle pieces layer and choose Edit|Paste (Ctrl+V/Cmd+V). The pieces are now on the new layer. Move the pieces off the image in the puzzle base; in other words, to the white area. Your canvas will be too small, but that's real life. You'll take care of it in a bit. Be sure none of the puzzle pieces touch the puzzle base image.

17. You need to set instance names for the puzzle targets so you can use those names when you add the ActionScript. The puzzle targets are the location of each piece in the puzzle base. Lock the puzzle pieces layer.

18. Unlock the puzzle base layer. In the Movie Explorer, select MC1 in the puzzle base layer (see Figure 17.21).

19. Open the Instance panel using the Launcher Bar icon. Give the puzzle piece an instance name of "base1" and press Enter/Return. Repeat for the rest of the pieces, ending with "base16". Figure 17.22 shows the instance names added in the Movie Explorer. The name is added automatically after you type it in the Instance panel.

20. Check to be sure the puzzle pieces layer is locked. Choose Edit|Select All. Open the Effects panel (Window|Panels|Effects) and choose Alpha, with a setting of 40%.

Making the Pieces Draggable

You will make the puzzle pieces in the puzzle pieces layer draggable by using the **press** and **release** mouse events of buttons. To set up the puzzle pieces, follow these steps:

1. Unlock the puzzle pieces layer and lock the puzzle base layer. In the Movie Explorer, double-click MC1 from the puzzle pieces layer. You will now be in Symbol Editing mode. You can see MC1 on the stage, and it isn't muted like the rest; select it and choose Insert|Convert To Symbol with the Behavior value of Button.

2. With the new Button symbol still selected, open the Actions panel (arrow on Launcher Bar). Select Expert Mode from the Options pop-up menu and enter this code:

```
on (press) {
this.startDrag();
}
on (release,releaseOutside) {
this.stopDrag();
}
```

This code makes the puzzle piece draggable.

Figure 17.21
The MC1 puzzle piece selected in the Movie Explorer.

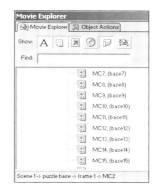

Figure 17.22
The instance names of the Movie Clips added to the Movie Explorer.

Note: If you did the Select All and chose an Alpha of 40% and you see puzzle pieces that are not transparent, then you missed them when you moved the pieces to the side. If this happens, unlock the puzzle pieces layer and move them.

Variations

You might want to skip ahead a bit and look at Variation 3. If you like this feature, which snaps the piece back to its original position if it's in the wrong place, then use the finished code from that variation. Also, if you want to use the snap-back feature and you plan to resize this image, then skip to the "Resizing" section before you add the code to each button. Otherwise, you will have to do every button over again with new X, Y coordinates. To add the ActionScript after resizing, just double-click the puzzle piece and select it to enter Symbol Editing mode. Open the Actions panel and enter the final code in Expert Mode.

Note: Don't forget to convert the Movie Clips to Button symbols—the mouse events you are adding won't work on the Movie Clip. After you add the ActionScript to each button, click Scene 1 and then double-click the next Movie Clip to convert. For the names of the buttons and the base targets, just look in the title bar to see the number of the puzzle piece you are working on.

3. Next, you must determine if the puzzle piece is in its proper place over the puzzle target. To do so, you will utilize the **_droptarget** Movie Clip property. The **_droptarget** command returns the name of the object on the stage that the selected puzzle piece is over. After **this.stopDrag();**, press Enter/Return and add this code:

```
if(eval(this._droptarget)==_root.base1){
this._x=_root.base1._x;
this._y=_root.base1._y;
}
}
```

This piece of code checks to see if the item you are dragging is on top of the base1 instance on the stage. If the piece is in the right place, the code sets the X and Y positions of the piece to the base instance on the stage. The finished code looks like this:

```
on (press) {
this.startDrag();
}
on (release,releaseOutside) {
this.stopDrag();
if(eval(this._droptarget)==_root.base1){
this._x=_root.base1._x;
this._y=_root.base1._y;
}
}
```

4. Save your file (a copy called horse.fla is saved for you in the Chapter 17 puzzle folder). Test the movie (Control|Test Movie). You should be able to select the puzzle piece you just placed ActionScript on and place it over the correct target in the puzzle base. The puzzle piece should snap into place. If errors occur, you will be notified in a dialog box. The most likely errors are typos—check your code carefully. Before you perform Step 5, check the tip "Variations."

5. Repeat these steps for the rest of the puzzle pieces. It's easiest if you copy the ActionScript from the piece you just finished, edit the base name in the ActionScript, and change the button names when you make each symbol.

6. Save and test your movie. You can change the base layer to an Alpha of 0 if you don't want it to be visible.

Resizing

Of course, you could have resized the horse before you started, which would have been ideal; but in real life, sometimes you'll run into problems such as this. So, I made the file larger to demonstrate a point. Make the following changes to the horse.fla files.

1. Open the horse.fla file and then the puzzle.fla file, and unlock both layers.

2. Choose Modify|Movie and change the stage size to 550×400.

3. Choose Edit|Select All; select the Pointer tool and then the Scale tool. Press the Shift key to constrain the scale and drag in one of the corners until the puzzle is the size you want.

4. Deselect and rearrange the pieces. I saved this new version as horseresize.fla. Test the movie to generate the SWF file. The resized horse puzzle can be seen in Figure 17.23.

Figure 17.23
The horse puzzle resized, with a Back button added.

Variation 1

You will make a Flash movie with two buttons, so you can have multiple puzzles. The first thing you will do is change the puzzle picture: Doing so is simple! Then, you'll load the puzzle of choice from the main movie.

To swap any image with this puzzle (that's right, swap—no additional coding required), the other image must be the exact same size as the horse image. The flower.jpg file is in the same puzzle folder with the horse puzzle; you'll use that one. Do as many images as you'd like. To swap the image, follow these steps:

1. Open horseresize.fla from the Chapter 17 puzzle folder. Open the Library panel, right/Ctrl+click horseimage.jpg, and choose Properties. In the Properties dialog box, choose Import and select flower.jpg; click OK. That's all there is to it—you now have a new puzzle (see Figure 17.24). Notice that it even worked on this scaled version of the image.

Figure 17.24
The horse puzzle changed into a flower puzzle.

2. Save the puzzle as flower.fla and test the movie to automatically make an SWF file. Close the file.

3. Open a new Flash movie and choose Insert|New Symbol. Choose a Button Behavior and name the symbol "horsebutton". You will now import buttons made in Fireworks and exported as JPEGs.

4. Choose File|Import and select button1.jpg from the Chapter 17 puzzle folder.

5. Return to Scene 1 and choose Insert|New Symbol. Choose a Button Behavior and name the symbol "flowerbutton". Return to Scene 1, choose File|Import, and select the smflower.jpg from the Chapter 17 puzzle folder. Repeat for the smhorseimage.jpg image. These pictures were shrunk and shadows were added in Fireworks, as well. Drag the symbols for the buttons and pictures from the Library panel onto the stage. Use Figure 17.25 as a placement guide.

Figure 17.25
The main movie for the puzzles.

6. Select the Text tool and add any text you'd like. To load the movies, select the Horse button, open the Actions panel, and choose Expert Mode. Add this code to the Horse button and the Flower button (change the file name on each):

```
on (press) {
loadMovie ("horseresize.swf", 0);
}
```

Note: If you are using any other file name, such as horse3.swf, that you make in a later variation, be sure you change the name here.

This code should look familiar by now: It is identical to the code you used to load the sound files in the jukebox (with the file name changed, of course). The puzzle loads into level0 and will overwrite the file.

It would be ideal if you could put a Back button on each of the puzzle pages. A smart clip to do this is in development, but it isn't working at this time—check the Flash exchange when you get this book and see if it's available. Meanwhile, you'll add some code that will do the trick; you'll also see another variation in which you wouldn't need a Back button.

Continue with these steps:

7. Save your file as puzzle.fla. Open horseresize.fla. Choose Insert|New Symbol and then File|Import, and select backbutton.jpg from the Chapter 17 puzzle folder. Name it "backbutton" and give it the Behavior value of Button.

8. Click Scene 1 to return to the main movie. Drag an instance of the button from the Library and position it either at the top of the page or at the bottom, or anywhere you'd like. With the button selected, open the Actions panel and insert this code into Expert Mode:

```
on (press) {
loadMovie ("puzzle.swf", 0);
}
```

Look familiar? It's the same code with the file name changed. Test the horse and the flower movies to generate new SWF files (the Back buttons won't work yet). Then, test puzzle.fla and click the buttons; all will work.

Variation 2

This variation is similar, except it doesn't need Back buttons. The buttons will be visible on the same page with the puzzles open. In this example, you will load the movie to level1. Follow these steps:

1. Open a new file and choose Insert|New Symbol. Name the symbol "button1" and give it a Behavior value of Button. Choose File|Import and

select button1.jpg from the Chapter 17 puzzle folder. Click Scene 1 to return to the main movie. Drag an instance from the Library to the lower-left area of the movie. Repeat for button 2; place it at the lower-right side. Position the buttons so they look good to you; the puzzle will load in the top portion. Save this file as puzzle2.fla.

2. Open horsefinal.fla. With both layers unlocked, choose Edit|Select All and click the Scale icon. Using the Shift key to constrain, drag in one of the corners. Make the puzzle small enough to leave room at the bottom for the buttons you just added in the main movie and save as horse2.fla. Repeat for flowerfinal.fla and save as flower2.fla. Move any pieces around, if you want to.

> **Note:** Change the file name according to the version number or your own file name.

3. In the main movie (puzzle2.fla), select the Horse button (button1) and open the Actions panel in Expert Mode. Type in this code:

```
on (press) {
loadMovie ("horse2.swf", 1);
}
```

You'll have this code memorized pretty soon. It tells Flash to open the horse puzzle file in level1. If you recall from Chapter 16, when a movie loads into the same level, it replaces the current movie; but when it loads into a different level, the main movie is still present. By putting the buttons on the bottom of the stage, you can still see them when the smaller puzzle loads. Select the Flower Puzzle button (button2) and add this code to the Actions panel in Expert Mode:

```
on (press) {
loadMovie ("flower2.swf", 1);
}
```

Figure 17.26 shows the buttons at the bottom of the stage in level0, and the horse puzzle loaded in level1.

Variation 3

This is one of my favorite functions of the puzzle. You will add a bit of code to the draggable symbols, which will check the location of the puzzle piece. If it is dragged to the wrong spot, it will snap back to its original position. Because it is a tedious job to paste the ActionScript into each button, you may want to make this decision at the time you are adding the **onpress** and **eval** actions in Step 3 of "Making the Pieces Draggable."

Figure 17.26
The buttons visible while
a movie is loaded.

In Step 3 of "Making the Pieces Draggable," the final code looked like this:

```
on (press) {
this.startDrag();
}
on (release,releaseOutside) {
this.stopDrag();
if(eval(this._droptarget)==_root.base1){
this._x=_root.base1._x;
this._y=_root.base1._y;
}
}
```

To make the pieces snap back to the original location, the final code is as
follows:

```
on (press) {
this.startDrag();
}
on (release,releaseOutside) {
this.stopDrag();
if(eval(this._droptarget)==_root.base1){
this._x=_root.base1._x;
this._y=_root.base1._y;
} else {
setProperty (this, _x, 66.9);
setProperty (this, _y, 191.3);
}
}
```

I highlighted the last two } symbols and replaced them with

```
} else {
setProperty (this, _x, 66.9);
setProperty (this, _y, 191.3);
}
}
```

This bit of code says that if the puzzle piece isn't dropped in this location, return it to its previous location. The **else** statement checks to see whether the drop target is correct; if it isn't, the code returns the piece to its original location. To determine the X and Y positions for each button, first select the puzzle piece and open the Info panel. You will see the puzzle piece number; write it down, along with its X and Y values.

When you are done preparing your code for the draggable puzzle pieces, just add the finished code shown earlier and change the X, Y values for each button.

This file is saved as horse3.fla. It is the size of puzzle that goes with puzzle2.fla; its buttons are on the bottom, and the puzzle loads at the top. The files supplied in the puzzle folder include the horse3.fla with the snap-to code added. The snap-to code has not been added to the puzzle2.fla file yet, so you get to practice some more by adding it to the puzzle2.fla file yourself.

PROJECT Three-Dimensional Product Display

This is a great technique to display merchandise from different viewpoints. In this project, you will view a fishing lure. The photos of the lure and the background were provided by Todd McPhetridge of MfgQuote, Inc. (**www.mfgquote.com**). The ActionScript instructions were provided by Tracy Kelly. As usual, I provided the formatting, tips, and so on.

The finished demo can be seen in Figure 17.27. To do this project, follow these steps:

1. Open a new movie. Double-click Layer 1 and name the layer "background". Choose File|Open As Library and choose luredone.fla. You will now have a Library open with the assets needed for this project.

2. Drag a copy of the background symbol from the Library. In the Info panel, change the size to 550×400. You will use a lot of symbols, so I'll review briefly how they are made. Open a copy of the original GIF file on the stage, make any changes (I changed sizes), and then choose Insert|Convert To Symbol (F8). The background and lure images all use the Graphic Behavior.

3. Lock the background layer and click the plus sign to add a new layer. Name this layer "fishing lure". You will now make a Movie Clip for the lure.

Note: You can use any background you want; this one was prepared and sized in Fireworks. The photos of the lure were cropped and sized in Fireworks, as well. If you are using this technique for a project display, you may want to use a plain-colored background and possibly a small movie to display in a pop-up window.

Figure 17.27
The finished lure project.

4. Choose Insert|New Symbol to enter Symbol Editing mode. Double-click Layer 1 and name the layer "pictures". From the Library, drag in lure1.

5. Open the Align panel (Window|Panels|Align). Select To Stage and click Align Horizontal Center and Align Vertical Center.

6. Select frame 2 and choose Insert|Blank Keyframe (F7). Drag a copy of lure2 from the Library and align it as in Step 5.

7. Repeat Step 6 for all eight lure symbols, placing each one on a new frame. (Lure3 goes on frame 3, and so on.) When you are done, move the playhead to see the movement of the lure.

8. You need to add some simple actions. You are still working on the lure Movie Clip. Add a new layer and name it "actions". Select frame 1 and open the Actions panel (arrow on the Launcher Bar). In the Basic Actions book, double-click Stop.

9. Select frame 2, insert a new keyframe (F6), and double-click Stop. Repeat this step for frames 3 through 8. (You may wonder why you add all these Stop actions. A Movie Clip plays independently of the timeline. By placing a Stop action into each frame that also contains a graphic, you can control exactly when each of the graphics in the Movie Clip appears.) Figure 17.28 shows the Movie Clip's timeline.

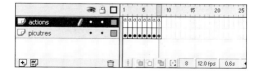

Figure 17.28
The timeline of the lure Movie Clip.

10. Save your file and click Scene 1 to return to the stage.

11. Drag a copy of lure movie from the Library onto the stage and set the position in the Info panel to X 330 and Y 200.

12. You need to give the Movie Clip an instance name so you can talk to it later with ActionScript. With the Movie Clip still selected, open the Instance panel (from the Launcher Bar) and name it "lure"; press Enter/Return.

Invisible Buttons to Make the Lure Turn

You will make buttons on the main timeline, which will contain the actions to trigger the movement of the fishing lure on the stage. Because you do not want any visual representation of these buttons in the main movie, you will make them invisible. Invisible buttons are simply buttons that contain a Hit state, or a clickable area. The Up, Over, and Down states of the buttons don't exist. To finish this project, follow these steps:

1. In the main movie, click the top layer. Click the plus sign to add a new layer and name it "buttons". To make invisible buttons to move the lure, select the Rectangle tool. Click the Stroke icon and then click the No Color icon below the Fill icon.

2. Drag a rectangle on the stage. In the Info panel, give it a Width of 30 and a Height of 280. Set X to 165 and Y to 206.

3. With the rectangle still selected, choose Insert|Convert To Symbol. Choose a Behavior of Button and name it "invisible". Double-click the button to enter Symbol Editing mode.

4. Right now, the rectangle you drew is in the Up state of the button. For the button to be invisible, it must be in the Hit state only. Place your mouse over the Up state in the timeline and wait for the Hand icon to appear. Click and drag to the Hit state. If you prefer, you can cut and paste from the Up state to the Hit state.

5. Select Scene 1 to return to the main movie. Notice that your rectangle has turned light blue. This is the same way a hotspot looks in Fireworks and Dreamweaver. It's just a visual representation and won't appear this way in your movie.

6. To add the actions to this invisible button, open the Actions panel and open the Object book. Click the Movie Clip category and double-click **gotoAndStop** to add it to the right pane. Figure 17.29 shows the code in the right pane. The red line indicates that you must enter some data.

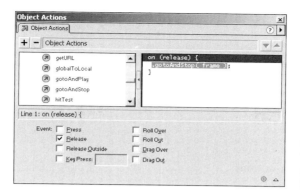

Figure 17.29
The Actions panel with **gotoAndStop** added to the invisible button.

7. Select the **on (release)** line of code, as shown in Figure 17.29. In the Parameters panel, deselect Release and select Roll Over and Drag Over. These options will allow the actions between the curly brackets to occur when the mouse rolls over this invisible button on the stage.

8. Select the **gotoAndStop(frame)** line. In the Parameters area in the Expression box, replace the word *frame* with the number 1. Still in the Expression box, place your mouse before the dot (.) in **gotoAndStop(1)** and click the Insert A Target Path icon (the one in the lower-right corner that looks like a crosshair).

9. The Insert Target Path dialog box will open. Set Notation to Dots and Mode to Absolute. Locate the lure Movie Clip in the top area of the dialog box, select it, and click OK. Figure 17.30 shows the Insert Target dialog box with the settings selected.

> **Note:** The target button helps you set the ActionScript needed to talk to a particular item on the stage. You need the target to tell Flash that when your mouse moves over this invisible button, a particular frame in the fishing lure Movie Clip should display.

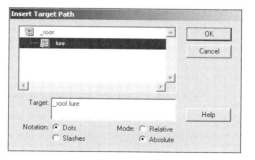

Figure 17.30
The Insert Target Path dialog box with the correct settings selected.

This is the code that is generated:

```
    _root.lure.gotoAndStop( 1 );
}
```

Root is the name of the main timeline. To talk to the lure Movie Clip that exists on the main timeline, you say **_root.lure**.

Note: Lure is the instance name of the fishing lure Movie Clip that is on the stage. Instance names help Flash understand the exact Movie Clip you want to perform actions on.

10. You may need to move the Actions panel out of the way for now. Duplicate the invisible button by pressing the Alt/Option key, and drag a new copy. In the Info panel, set X to 195 and Y to 206. You need a total of nine invisible buttons. The X and Y values for buttons 3 through 9 are:

    - *Button 3—X: 225, Y: 206*
    - *Button 4—X: 255, Y: 206*
    - *Button 5—X: 285, Y: 206*
    - *Button 6—X: 315, Y: 206*
    - *Button 7—X: 345, Y: 206*
    - *Button 8—X: 375, Y: 206*
    - *Button 9—X: 405, Y: 206*

11. Select invisible button 2; the same ActionScript is already added to the copy because you duplicated button 1. All you need to do is change the frame number from 1 to 2 (in Expert Mode). Repeat this process for buttons 3 through 8. In invisible button 9, leave the frame number set to 1—you want the first and last buttons to target the first frame for a smoother motion.

12. Test the movie to generate a SWF file. To make the lure turn, run your mouse back and forth horizontally and it will turn.

PROJECT Point of Purchase Interface

This is more of a mini project. I promised in the FreeHand section of the book that we'd rotate the red car in Flash. Doing so is very simple—you will use the same techniques you did in the fishing lure project. Jeffrey Roberts (**www.jefargrafx.com**) supplied this design. To rotate the car, follow these steps:

1. Open the pop_start.fla file from the Chapter 17 Pop folder.

2. A Movie Clip named "cars" is in the Library. To make this Movie Clip, choose Insert|New Symbol with a Behavior of Movie Clip and the name "cars2" (it needs to have a different name so you can practice on it—all the code is for cars, which is supplied). Select frame 1, choose File|Import, and select carleft.gif from the Chapter 17 Pop folder.

3. Select frame 2 and insert a keyframe (F6). Choose File|Import and choose carright.gif from the Chapter 17 Pop folder. Name this layer "cars".

4. Add a new layer and select frame 1. Open the Actions panel, click the Basic Action book, and double-click Stop. Select frame 2, add a keyframe (F6), add the Stop again, and return to the main movie.

5. Drag a copy of the cars Movie Clip (it's identical to the one you made for practice) onto the stage and place it in the center. While it is still selected, open the Instance panel and give your Movie Clip the instance name "cars". Press Enter/Return.

6. On the arrows layer, select the left arrow and open the Actions panel. Add this code in Expert Mode:

```
on (press) {
_root.cars.gotoAndStop(1);
}
```

7. Repeat Step 6 for the right arrow, but change the frame number to 2. Save and test your movie. Figure 17.31 shows the final design.

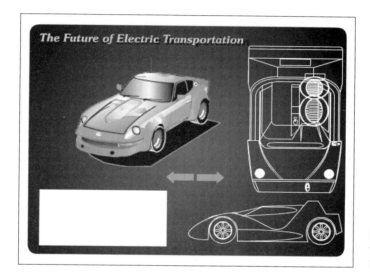

Figure 17.31
The finished Point of Purchase interface.

Moving On

In this chapter, you have learned a lot of reusable pieces of ActionScript. You can now load separate SWF files, drag pieces, and rotate an object 360 degrees.

In Chapter 18, you will learn about two great new features of Flash 5: the print-from-Flash function and the Color object.

Chapter 18

Special Projects

The projects in this chapter are donated by Fig Leaf Software. In one project, you will use the new Flash 5 feature that lets you print a brochure from a Flash movie. Another project uses the new Color object, which allows you to color an image in a movie.

Rich Media

This chapter is devoted to two projects that are a bonus donated for your learning by Fig Leaf Software (**www.figleaf.com**; you'll find more information about this company in Appendix B, "Resources.") The chapter also presents one variation of the color banner ad by Tracy Kelly.

Macromedia's Web site includes a section that offers information on what it calls *rich media* (**www.macromedia.com/solutions/richmedia**); at this link, you'll find a ton of information and inspiration. It speaks about the emerging technologies for banner ads, which let you integrate animation, sound, interactivity, and even e-commerce. Jupiter Media Metrix predicts that by the year 2005 almost 30 percent of online media spending will be dedicated to rich media or streaming advertising. That's quite a prediction, and it's worth checking into. The projects in this chapter will get you started in adding interactivity to your banners using the newest features in Flash 5.

Color Objects

The Color object is a new feature of Flash 5. In a banner ad, a Color object can encourage user involvement by drawing a user to your banner and encouraging them to enter your site. It's also great for kids' sites, cartoons, and just plain fun. Another useful technique involves changing the color of products, such as shirts, hats, pants, and so on. If you combine the changing color of an item with the ability to drag and drop, as you did with the puzzle in Chapter 17, you can try clothes on a model and change the color.

These two projects reference techniques you have already used in Chapter 17; I won't teach them again step by step. The main purpose in these projects is to introduce and show you how to use the new print and color functions of Flash 5.

PROJECT A Banner Ad

In this banner ad, you will be able to change the color of a Movie Clip. You will set the colors in the color palette dynamically, capture a color when you click your mouse on it, and then set the color of a leaf in the banner ad. To begin, follow these steps:

1. Open the banner_start.fla file from the Chapter 18 color folder. The banner layout is already done for you (see Figure 18.1). You can change the graphics, if you wish, to customize the banner. You will add the ActionScript that will make the banner functional.

> **Note:** Most of the layers in the main timeline are for the graphics, and you will not deal with the graphics in this project. These graphics are useful only to the company the ad is intended for.

Figure 18.1
The banner ad as seen in Flash.

2. Double-click the color palette on the stage (the little square boxes) to open Symbol Editing mode. The outlines and invis button layers are already made invisible (see Figure 18.2). Only the color layer is visible. Select near the top of the white bar, and the first little rectangle will be selected (there are six little rectangles; each one is a Movie Clip named palletecolor with a rectangle in it).

Selecting the Small Rectangles

If you find selecting the little rectangles difficult, you may want to increase your magnification for easier selection by choosing View|Zoom In. You can also make the outlines layer visible (click on the red X) and then lock it (click the dot below the Lock icon).

Note: If you'd like to know what is on a layer, click below the Eye icon to make the other layers invisible (red X). If you make all the other layers invisible, you will see exactly what is on that layer. To return the visibility, just click the red X again; the black dot will return and the contents will be visible once again.

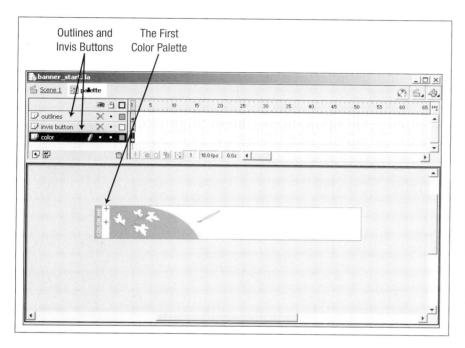

Figure 18.2
The outlines and invis button layers are invisible, and the first color palette is selected.

3. Open the Actions panel in Expert mode and type this ActionScript (see Figure 18.3):

```
onClipEvent(load) {
palleteColor=new Color(this);
palleteColor.setRGB(0x003399);
}
```

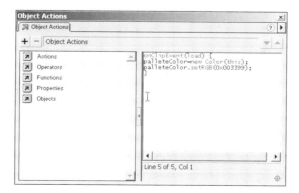

Figure 18.3
The Actions panel with the code added to the right pane for the first color palette.

The new color generates a new instance of the Color class on the stage and sets the Movie Clip to a blue color. If you recall from Chapter 17, the numbers or letters or both after the **0x** are Hexadecimal numbers.

4. Select each of the other five color palettes and add the same code, but with different color numbers:

   - *2*—0xFFCC33

   - *3*—0x91CE44

   - *4*—0xFF6600

   - *5*—0x9900CC

   - *6*—0xFFFFFF

5. Save and test the file. All the colors in the palette should be changed.

6. You must now capture the value of the colors in the palette when you click them. You have to set a variable that will store the color. Make sure you are on the main timeline (click Scene 1). Add a new layer to the top of the stack and name it "actions".

7. Select frame 1 (you will initialize the variable that sets the color to white) of the actions layer and open the Actions panel. In Expert mode, type the following ActionScript (see Figure 18.4):

```
mycolor=0xFFFFFF;
```

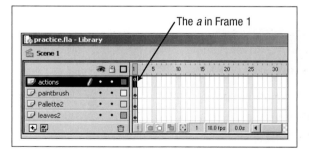

Figure 18.4

The *a* in frame 1 of the actions layer indicates that ActionScript is attached to that frame.

8. Double-click the palette graphic to return to Symbol Editing mode. Lock the color layer and unhide the invis button layer. Select the first button on the palette and in Expert mode, type in the Actions panel:

```
on(press){
_root.mycolor=0x003399;
}
```

9. Place the same code into the other five color palettes, using these colors:

   - *2*—0xFFCC33
   - *3*—0x91CE44
   - *4*—0xFF6600
   - *5*—0x9900CC
   - *6*—0xFFFFFF

10. Select Scene 1 to return to the main timeline. Double-click any one of the leaves; you are now in Symbol Editing mode.

11. The outlines and invis button layer are already hidden. Unlock the fill layer and select the white leaf.

12. Open the Instance panel and give the leaf an instance name of "leafy" (see Figure 18.5). Press Enter/Return. Lock the fill layer.

13. Unhide the invis button layer and select the invisible button on the stage. (It will be a bit darker than the other leaves. It is actually a light blue that you can see through.) With the button selected, type this code into the Actions panel in Expert mode:

```
on(press){
leafColor=new Color(this.leafy);
leafColor.setRGB(_root.mycolor);
}
```

Note: The leaf is simply a leaf graphic that was converted into a Movie Clip symbol.

Figure 18.5
The Instance panel with the instance name added for leafy.

14. Return to the main movie (Scene 1). Save and test your file. To test, click with your cursor on any color and then click on any leaf. You can color any leaf with any of the colors.

15. Now you will make it possible to dip the paintbrush into the paint and color the leaves with the brush. You will actually hide the cursor so the paintbrush will move with it. Select (don't double-click) the paintbrush on the stage.

16. Open the Actions panel and type this ActionScript in Expert mode:

```
onClipEvent(load){
Mouse.hide();
this.startDrag(true);
}
```

Figure 18.6
The finished banner as seen in the Flash movie test.

17. Save and test the file. It should work the same as color.fla supplied in the Chapter 18 color folder. Figure 18.6 shows the banner after it is loaded in the test movie.

Variation

You will most likely want more than one Movie Clip to color in your project. The previous example uses the leaves, which of course are instances of the same symbol. This next ad is a quick example that Tracy Kelly made for you to demonstrate coloring a girl's hair and shirt. Figure 18.7 shows how the banner ad looks in the start file.

Figure 18.7
The banner ad as it looks in the start file.

You need to make the following adjustments to the previous instructions to add an additional area to color:

1. Open the tkstart.fla file from the color folder and perform Steps 2 through 9 from the previous Fig Leaf banner project.

2. Select Scene 1 to return to the main timeline. Double-click the girl's shirt; you are now in Symbol Editing mode. The shirt is a Movie Clip named girlmovieclip.

3. The outlines and invis button layer are already hidden. Unlock shirtMC and select the white shirt. Figure 18.8 shows the layers of girlmovieclip in Editing mode.

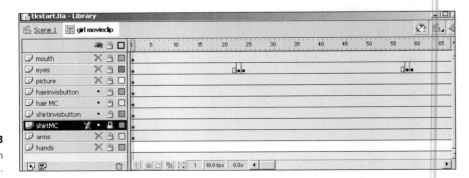

Figure 18.8
The layers of the girlmovieclip in Editing mode.

4. Open the Instance panel and give the shirt an instance name of "myshirt". Press Enter/Return. Lock the shirtMC layer.

5. Unhide the shirtinvisbutton layer and select the invisible shirt button on the stage. With the button selected, type this code into the Actions panel:

```
on(press){
  shirtColor = new Color(myshirt);
  shirtColor.setRGB(_root.mycolor);
}
```

6. Lock the shirtinvisbutton layer, unlock the hairMC layer, and select the hair in the banner.

7. Open the Instance panel and give the hair an instance name of "myhair". Press Enter/Return. Lock the hairMC layer.

8. Unlock the hairinvisbutton layer and select the invisible hair button on the stage. With the button selected, type this code into the Actions panel:

```
on(press){
  hairColor = new Color(myhair);
  hairColor.setRGB(_root.mycolor);
}
```

9. Return to the main movie (Scene 1). Save and test your file. To test, click any color with your cursor and then click the shirt.

10. There is no paintbrush in this file, but it is in the Library. Open the Library and drag an instance of the paintbrush Movie Clip onto the stage near the girl's left shoulder (see Figure 18.9).

> **Note:** As you can see from the instructions, you simply make a Movie Clip of each object you want to be able to color and put it in its own layer; then, you make an invisible hit state button of each item in its own layer. If you don't recall how to make invisible buttons, see the project "Three-Dimensional Product Display" in Chapter 17, in which you made invisible buttons to turn the fishing lure. Then you simply repeat Steps 2 through 8 of this variation project for each additional Movie Clip you want to be able to color.

Figure 18.9
The paintbrush moved onto the banner.

11. To make it possible to dip the paintbrush into the paint and color the shirt and hair with the brush, select (don't double-click) the paintbrush on the stage.

12. Open the Actions panel and type this ActionScript in Expert mode:

```
onClipEvent(load){
Mouse.hide();
this.startDrag(true);
}
```

That's all there is to adding more Movie Clips to be colored.

Figure 18.10

The appearance of the print start file before you begin.

PROJECT A Print Banner Ad

This little ad can be put on almost any Web site that has a brochure to print. Of course, the techniques are the same for an article or anything you'd like to make available for printing from within the Flash movie. Follow these steps:

1. Open the print_start.fla file (see Figure 18.10) from the Chapter 18 print folder on the CD-ROM.

2. Select the movie layer and click the plus (+) icon to add a new layer. Name the layer "brochure" and press Enter/Return. Move this layer below the movie layer (at the very bottom) as shown in Figure 18.11.

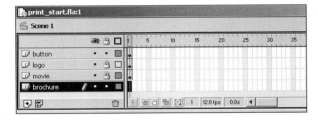

Figure 18.11

The new layer named "brochure" moved to the bottom of the stack.

Note: This is a spot that caused me problems. If you test the movie after you complete this lesson and the brochure isn't visible, come back to this step to verify that the instance name brochure is there. If you forget to press Enter/Return, Flash will not set the instance name. It's all too easy in Flash to forget when you have to press Enter/Return, because most of the time you don't have to.

3. The Library contains a Movie Clip named "print". It consists of a 576-by-756 pixel rectangle with a light fill and some text added. (Do your users a favor and don't use a background color; I printed this brochure and kept working, not realizing I had just printed a full page of solid color. Believe me, your users won't appreciate it.) The image was then converted into a Movie symbol and named "print". Select the print Movie Clip from the Library and drag it onto the stage.

4. In the Info panel, set the X and Y values to -70 (see Figure 18.12).

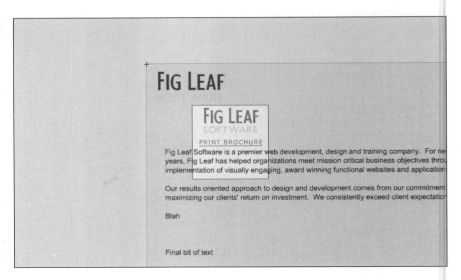

Figure 18.12

The brochure with the X and Y values changed.

5. Open the Instance panel and give the print Movie Clip the instance name "brochure". Press Enter/Return. Lock and hide the brochure layer.

6. To make the Print Brochure button on the stage print the brochure Movie Clip that you just placed on the stage, select the button and open the Actions panel. Type this code (see Figure 18.13):

```
on(press){
print("brochure", "bmovie");
}
```

This code prints the Movie Clip brochure. **bmovie** makes the printable size of the Movie Clip the size of the frame indicated by a frame labeled #b. You will do this shortly.

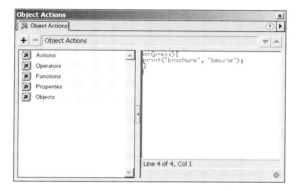

Figure 18.13

The Actions panel with the ActionScript for the Print Brochure button.

7. Select the brochure layer and add a new layer; name it "actions".

8. You need to set the visibility of the print Movie Clip to false, making it invisible. This Movie Clip is used to determine the size of the page that will be printed. Select frame 1 of the actions layer and in the Actions panel type (see Figure 18.14) the following:

```
_root.brochure._visible=false;
```

Figure 18.14

The ActionScript added to the Actions panel in frame 1 of the actions layer.

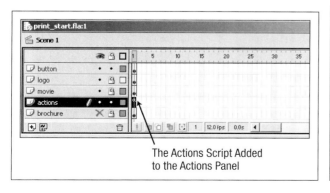

The Actions Script Added to the Actions Panel

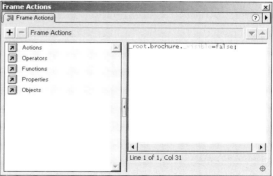

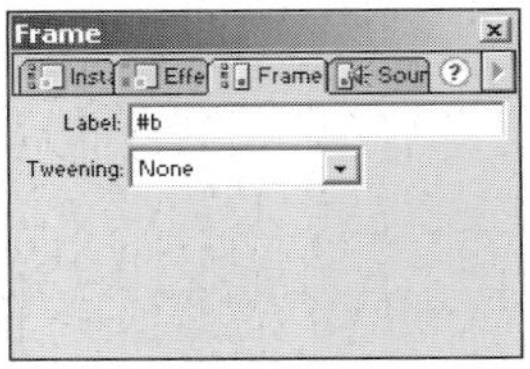

Figure 18.15

The Frames panel with
the name #b added.

9. Open the Frames panel (Window|Panels|Frame) and give frame 1 of the actions layer the name "#b" (see Figure 18.15). Press Enter/Return.

10. Unlock and unhide the brochure layer. Double-click the brochure to Center Symbol Editing mode. Select the light green Movie Clip and open the Instance panel. Give the print Movie Clip the instance name of "size" and press Enter/Return.

11. Save and test the file. When you click the Print Brochure button, the brochure should print. Figure 18.16 is how the ad looks in Flash when the movie is tested. A copy of the finished ad is saved in the Chapter 18 print folder and is called print.fla.

Figure 18.16

The finished print brochure ad
as seen in the movie test.

Moving On

In this chapter, you got to try two of the newest features of Flash 5. You used the Color object to make a color palette, and you colored objects on the stage. You also learned how to make a brochure available from Flash for print.

In Chapter 19, you will learn what you need to know to publish your SWF movies.

Chapter 19

Publishing Your
Flash Movies

*In this chapter, you will learn optimizing tips for getting
your movies ready for the Internet and then how to publish
them. You will explore many of the Publish options as well
as the Debugger and the Bandwidth Profiler.*

Publishing

At this point, you are probably ready to put some of your newly generated movies onto your Web server. The first thing you'll need to do is consider the size of your SWF movie file and its performance.

Optimization

We'll be looking at a series of tips and tricks to optimize your images. It is beyond the scope of this book to teach you all the finer points of optimization, but the tips should point you in the right direction so that you know what areas to check. This way, you'll know the areas you need to brush up on, and you'll be able to find more specific information. Remember, you'll find a whole resource list in Appendix B.

Carefully optimizing the individual elements in your movie and following some of the tips listed here will go a long way toward reducing the size of your SWF movie.

Bitmaps

If you absolutely have to use large bitmaps, which is discouraged, only use them as static background images. You shouldn't use large bitmaps in an animation because of the large size of the files. However, you can use small bitmaps sparingly and animate them with a motion tween.

You'll get better results if you edit your bitmaps in Fireworks before you place them into Flash. For instance, the horse puzzle you made in Chapter 17 really should have been made smaller in Fireworks before being imported into Flash, instead of being scaled in Flash. I checked the file size of a movie I made of the horse using a bitmap that was resized prior to using it in Flash versus the size of the scaled version done in Flash—the version done in Flash was almost 2KB larger. Not much, I agree, but every little bit adds up.

I prefer to optimize bitmaps in Fireworks prior to using them in Flash, because more control is available. For instance, I love the new Selective JPEG Compression feature: I can optimize portions of an image at a higher setting and optimize less important areas at a lower setting.

Keep in mind, though, that when you export your Flash movie, Flash will compress the image again. JPEGs that are compressed multiple times will frequently result in artifacts. To avoid this problem, right-click the image name in the Library list (the last icon on the right in the Launcher Bar will open the Library). From the Options pop-up menu, choose Properties. When the Bitmap Properties dialog box opens, choose Lossless from the Compression drop-down menu and click OK (see Figure 19.1).

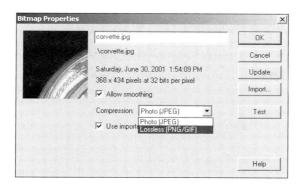

Figure 19.1
The Bitmap Properties
dialog box.

Tracing Bitmaps

If you trace complex images, the file size of the traced image may be considerably larger than the original version because of the complex curves. You traced a bitmap image of a jukebox for use in the Jukebox project in Chapter 17. The trace was used only to demonstrate how to use the tool. To test the comment about how bitmaps could be the better choice, I swapped out the traced image in the jukebox.fla file (Chapter 17, jukebox folder) with a bitmap I optimized in Fireworks. I then published the movie—and it was almost half the size of the file using the traced image. The file size with the trace is acceptable for some of us non-artist types, but it could really be decreased by using a line drawing done in FreeHand.

Animations

In animations, it's best to use symbols as much as possible and then use tweens on the symbols. If you animate frame by frame, each keyframe has to load; but if you animate using a motion tween or a guided motion tween, only the symbols have to load.

Symbols

You should tween symbols instead of groups. If you ungroup your elements, fewer paths are involved for Flash to handle. Plus, if a symbol doesn't contain any groups, then any effects you apply will be applied to the symbol as a whole rather than to groups within the symbol.

Paths

When you make vector images in FreeHand or other vector programs, simplify the paths as much as possible while still maintaining the paths' integrity. You should optimize the paths of vectors you make in Flash, as well (Modify|Optimize).

Fonts

Fonts are embedded, and the outlines are exported with your Flash movie. But Flash does not necessarily support all fonts. It's easy to do a quick test to see if the fonts you want to use are acceptable: Choose View|Antialias Text. If the text appears jaggy, it isn't compatible. If the text you need isn't design-critical, you can use device fonts: _sans (similar to Arial and Helvetica), _serif (similar to Times Roman), and _typewriter (similar to Courier). These fonts are the top three in the font drop-down list in the Character panel. You reduce the file size by using device fonts because they will use the closest font match from the user's system—no fonts are embedded in the movie.

Gradients

Solid fills add the smallest amount to your file size. Gradients should be used sparingly. Flash can make gradients consisting of up to eight colors; after that, the additional colors will be broken into separate shapes, which will add to your file size.

Alpha vs. Tint

Adding an Alpha effect to a symbol increases the file size. Tint adds less to the size, if it will do the trick for you. This isn't the better option if you need any transparency, though; tints are opaque. Try to limit the number of Alpha effects you include in the same symbol.

Layers

Layers are a great way to keep your movies organized. You can place images on a layer, buttons on another layer, actions on another, and so on. Use all the layers you want or need; they do not add to the finished SWF movie file size.

Sound

Covering all the aspects of sound could take a very large chapter. If you want to use sound often, it would behoove you to get one of the excellent reference books listed in Appendix B.

If you want streaming sound, place it in the main movie timeline and not in a Movie Clip. In the main timeline, the sound will begin at the appropriate frame and play immediately. If it's in a Movie Clip, the entire file has to load before play begins. This is why you loaded a separate SWF song file for use in the Jukebox project from Chapter 17. If you placed it in a Movie Clip within the main timeline, the user would have to wait for all the songs to load before using the interface. When you have your sound file in the Library, right-click and choose Properties. Be sure under the Export Settings area that the Use Document Default is unchecked. If you use the Default, the file will be much larger than needed. You'll get better results if you edit your sound files prior to importing them into Flash. MP3 is the smallest and best format to use for sound.

In the Publish Settings dialog box's Flash tab, you can compress for Audio Stream and Audio Event separately. Doing so lets you have higher quality for music and lesser quality for sounds that go with buttons.

Debugging

The most frustrating part of making a Flash movie happens when you choose Control|Test Movie and the movie doesn't work. The most common error I find is incorrect spelling. When writing your own ActionScript, you need to take extra care to spell things correctly each time you use it to reference instances of Movie Clips, and so on. Fortunately, Flash provides some tools you can use to track down additional problems. For example, it's easy to forget to select a frame in an actions layer, or attach a button action to a frame that doesn't contain a button—this, of course, will return an error when you test your movie. Let's look at some of the debugging tools available to you.

Debugger Panel

You can activate the Debugger panel by choosing Control|Debug Movie (see Figure 19.2). The top portion of the Debugger panel is the Display List with the absolute paths and nesting of all the current timelines, including all Movie Clips. You can also access properties and variables from their respective tabs. The Watch tab lets you monitor specific variables on any timeline.

Figure 19.2
The Debugger panel.

You can now access the Debugger panel to debug your movie from a Web browser. In the Publish Settings dialog box's Flash tab options, if you choose Debugging Permitted, you can access the Debugger panel from the Debug Movie environment or from a browser that has the Flash plug-in. (You'll need to install the Flash Debug Player plug-in or ActiveX control. You can find it in the Players folder of your Flash 5 application folder.)

Output Window

When you test your movie, the Output window will automatically open and list any errors. Figure 19.3 shows the Output window when I didn't select the correct frame to attach a button behavior to.

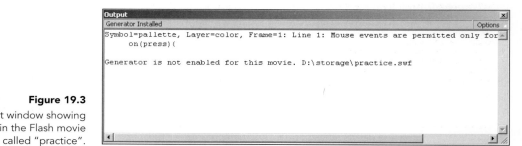

Figure 19.3
The Output window showing an error in the Flash movie called "practice".

Whenever you test your movie, even if there are no errors, a Debug menu item is added to the menu bar. This menu offers three choices:

- *List Objects*—You can use List Objects in Test Movie or Debug Movie mode to obtain a list of every element present on the stage. This list can be extremely helpful when you're checking target names. Figure 19.4 shows an Output list.

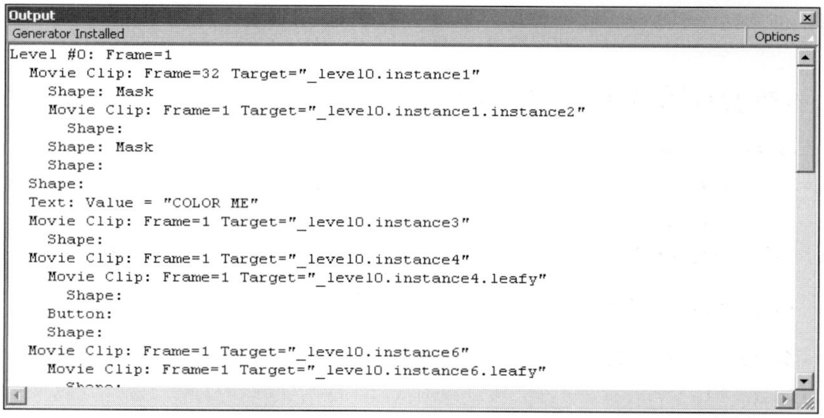

Figure 19.4
The Output window with a list of elements in your movie.

- *List Variables*—Again, if you are in Test Movie or Debug Movie mode, you can access a list of all variables in your movie and see their locations and values, as shown in Figure 19.5. You can use this list to check the location of a variable on the timeline.

- *Trace*—You can add a trace action to send the value of an expression to the Output window during Test Movie or Debug Movie mode. You enter the trace action into the Actions panel like any other action. For instance,

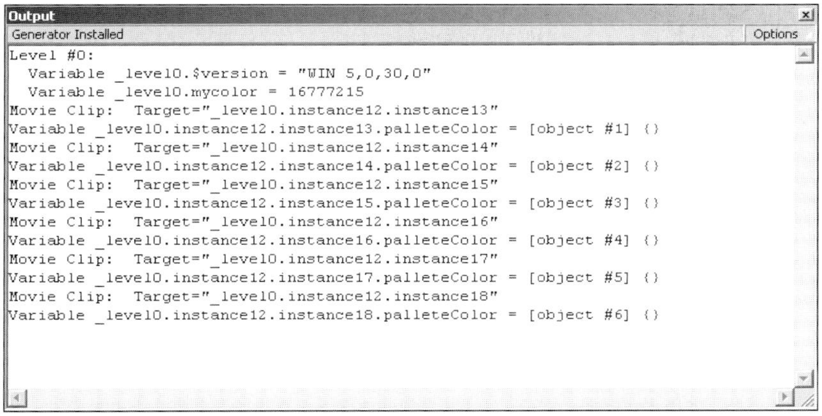

Figure 19.5
The Output window with a list
of variables and their locations
and names.

let's say you have an instance of a circle on the stage that has **color** and
xPosition properties, and you want to check the properties. You type the
following into the Actions panel in Expert mode:

```
mycircle = new circle (0x660000, 40);
trace (mycircle.color); //the trace return in the Output window
would be 660000
trace (mycircle.xPosition);  //the trace return would be 40
```

If you don't get a return, you know to check for errors.

Bandwidth Profiler

You can use the Bandwidth Profiler to determine how long users with modems
will take to load your movie. In the Profiler, you can simulate how long it will
take a user to see your movie using different modem or cable speeds. To use the
Bandwidth Profiler, follow these steps:

1. Open the horse2.fla file from the Chapter 17 puzzle folder.

2. Choose Control|Test Movie and choose View|Bandwidth Profiler (see
   Figure 19.6).

3. Choose Debug and select the modem speed or custom speed you've
   defined that you'd like to simulate.

4. Choose View|Show Streaming. You will see a simulation of the time it
   will take for your movie to load. With the horse2.fla file and a 28.8Kbps
   modem, you will see that it takes a while to load. This is a file that
   would benefit from a preloader so users will see something while they
   wait for the puzzle to load.

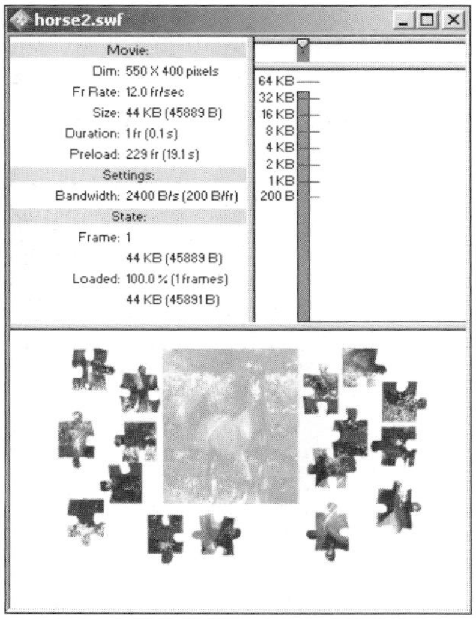

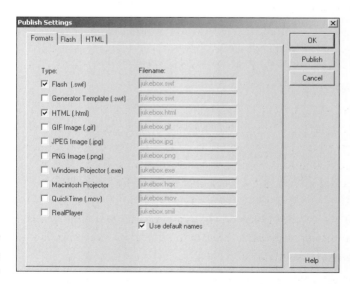

Figure 19.6
The Bandwidth Profiler.

Publish Settings

You can access the Publish Settings dialog box by choosing File|Publish Settings. Once your settings are done, simply click the Publish button in the HTML tab to put your movie in an HTML page or choose File|Export for a SWF movie.

Formats Tab

The default tab that opens in the Publish Settings dialog box is Formats (see Figure 19.7). The Flash (.swf) and HTML (.html) options are selected by default. SWF is the only format that will maintain full functionality of your movie and ActionScript.

Figure 19.7
The Formats tab in the Publish Settings dialog box.

Flash Tab

The Flash tab offers a lot of control over your movie settings. This tab and its options can be seen in Figure 19.8. We will look at each option separately:

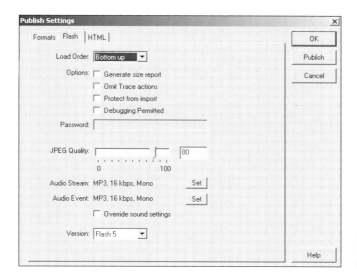

Figure 19.8
The Flash tab in the Publish Settings dialog box.

- *Load Order*—If you select this option, you can determine how your frames load. Bottom Up, which is the default, loads in ascending order: The lowest layer displays first, then the second lowest, and so on. If you select Top, the frames load in descending order.

- *Generate Size Report*—The size report can be quite useful in determining problem areas involving bandwidth concerns. If you select this option, the Publish command exports a simple text (Mac) or TXT (PC) file.

- *Omit Trace Actions*—If you used trace actions while you were developing your movie, you should select this option. The Flash player ignores any trace actions used in ActionScripting. The trace actions will open the Flash Output window for debugging purposes.

- *Protect From Import*—Selecting this option will protect your Flash SWF file from being downloaded and imported into Flash. However, Macromedia Director can import and use even protected SWF files. Hacker utilities can get at a protected file, as well. SWF files can be read in Notepad to see variables names and values. Because of this vulnerability, you should never include sensitive information such as passwords in your source file. The bottom line is that protecting your movies only helps discourage the general audience from using them; those who know how and are determined to steal your work can do so.

- *Debugging Permitted*—With this option selected, you can access the Debugger panel from the Debug Movie environment or from a browser that has the Flash plug-in. (You'll need to install the Flash Debug Player plug-in or ActiveX control. You can find it in the Players folder of your Flash 5 application folder.)

- *Password*—If you select Debugging Permitted, then the Debugger panel can be accessed from an Internet browser. You also should select the Password option if you want the Debugger panel to be accessed only with a password.

- *JPEG Quality*—The slider from 0 to 100 determines the JPEG compression applied to bitmap images. The higher the value you choose, the less compression is applied. But if you choose the Lossless compression option (no loss of data, your JPEG won't be compressed again) in the Library properties, this setting will not override the choices made in the Library.

- *Audio Stream*—The values you see listed are the current audio compression scheme for Audio Steam. If you click the Set button, you can alter the compression scheme in the resulting dialog box (see Figure 19.9). Like bitmap properties, the Audio Stream settings do not override the compression value if any other compression than the default is applied in the Sound Properties dialog box in the Flash Library.

Figure 19.9
The Set button options for Audio Stream.

- *Audio Event*—The values listed are the current scheme for Audio Event. The Set button allows you to alter the settings. Audio Event works very much like Audio Stream. As you can see in Figure 19.10, the options are the same.

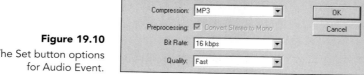

Figure 19.10
The Set button options for Audio Event.

- *Override Sound Settings*—This option allows you to override any settings you made to the sound properties in the Flash Library.

- *Version*—This option allows you to specify which version you want to be compatible with. If you choose version 4, then any of the new Flash 5 features will be ignored, such as the dot syntax. Which means, if you designed in Flash 5, most of your ActionScript may not work and you won't be able to use the Debugger because it won't be able to understand Flash 5 ActionScript either.

HTML Tab

The settings in this tab control the way Flash publishes its movie into an HTML page. A lot of the options shown in Figure 19.11 are self-explanatory if you understand how HTML works. We will discuss a few of them, however.

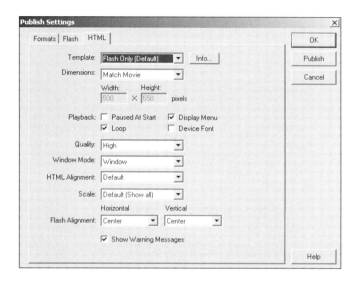

Figure 19.11
The options in the HTML tab.

- *Template*—These options give you choices such as Image Map. You can then click the Info button, which gives a description of the option and a bit of instruction, as shown in Figure 19.12. If you haven't done so yet, it's a good idea to check out the Info buttons for each option to familiarize yourself with everything you can do. The Default template uses the <OBJECT> and <EMBED> tags to insert your Flash movie into the HTML document, but there are no browser detections. You can, however, make your own custom templates using customized tags that will search for Flash version installed, browser, and so on.

Figure 19.12
The result of clicking the Template option's Info button with Image Map selected.

Note: The Dimension choices are closely tied into the choices you make in the Scale options category.

- *Dimensions*—The choices you make in this section control how your Flash movie is viewed. It does not change the physical size of the original SWF movie. The Width and Height of the <OBJECT> and <EMBED> tags are affected by the dimension settings. The settings you choose will alter the viewing area of the movie.

  - *Match Movie*—This is the option to choose if you want the viewer to see your movie in the exact proportions you designed it in Flash.

  - *Pixels*—You determine a specific Height and Width in pixels for the movie to display.

  - *Percent*—The movie scales to the percentage of the browser you choose. Scaling to 100% is probably the most used option of all the dimension choices. You can however use a percentage of the browser window.

- *Scale*—Scale works together with the Dimension choices you have made.

Note: If you do not alter the default choices of Flash and HTML in the Formats tab, then the Flash and HTML tabs are the only ones available. The rest will be grayed out in the File|Publish Preview list. The tabs discussed in the next few sections are visible if you first select their corresponding option in the Formats tab.

  - *Default*—The entire Flash movie will fit into the dimensions you have chosen. If there is space in the dimensions you chose that are empty, you will get a border added around the movie, but there is no distortion of the movie.

  - *No Border*—The area you defined in Dimensions will be filled with no borders. You may, however, get some cropping of the movie.

  - *Exact Fit*—Your movie will fill the area you defined in Dimensions exactly, even if it means distorting your movie.

  - *Window Mode*—Applies only to ActiveX controls and only to 32-bit Windows versions of Internet Explorer.

GIF Tab

Graphics Interchange File (GIF) format was developed by CompuServe. GIF is used primarily for images with a lot of flat color and when you want a transparent background. Its main limitation is the fact that it supports only 256 colors.

The options in the GIF tab (Figure 19.13) will format your Flash movie into a GIF animation, which can be used if a user doesn't have a Flash player installed.

The options in the GIF tab are pretty standard. If you need more information about the settings, refer to Chapter 11, which discusses the GIF options in more detail.

JPEG Tab

Joint Photographic Experts Group (JPEG) format is best used on images with more than 256 colors, such as photographs. Although gradients don't have that many colors, they also look better as JPEGs. A gradient in a GIF will usually have banding, but as a JPEG, it will look great.

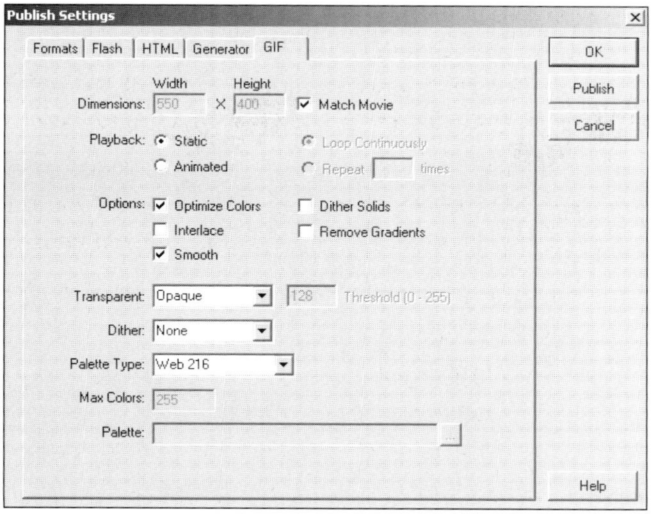

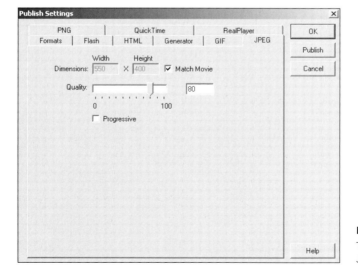

Figure 19.13
The GIF tab options.

JPEG images are compressed and then decompressed when they are opened. As a result, although the file size is small, more memory is needed to decompress the image in the browser than is required for a GIF image.

Figure 19.14 shows the JPEG options available. If you need more information about the settings, refer to Chapter 11, which discusses JPEG options in more detail.

Note: Remember that the JPEG options in the Publish Settings area do not override the settings you choose for an individual image in the Library under Properties. These settings are for static JPEG images you may want to export for the Flash movie.

Figure 19.14
The JPEG options available with JPEG selected in the Formats tab.

PNG Tab

Portable Network Graphics (PNG) format was developed as an improvement over GIF and JPEG, which it would be *if* all browsers supported its wonderful features. Its biggest advantage is that you can have transparency and lossless

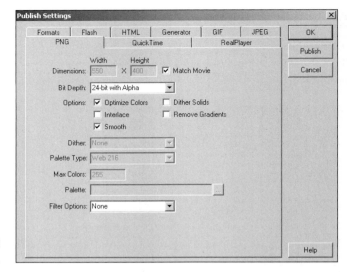

Figure 19.15
The PNG options.

compression. Unfortunately, these features are not yet fully supported in the major browsers. Until they are, the PNG format will not be used widely on the Internet. Figure 19.15 shows the options available on the PNG tab. These settings also apply to exporting a static image of your Flash movie.

QuickTime Tab

QuickTime 4 includes built-in support for Flash SWF files as well as something called a *Flash track*. Flash can import QuickTime movies, add Flash content, and then export the whole movie as a QuickTime movie. If you want to publish your Flash movie as a QuickTime movie, then select the QuickTime option in the Formats tab. Figure 19.16 shows the QuickTime options. Although you can export as a QuickTime movie, a QuickTime movie cannot play within a Flash movie (the same for RealPlayer).

Note: QuickTime 4 can play Flash 3 content; QuickTime 4 does not support Flash versions 4 and 5. You can only edit QuickTime movies with the Pro version of QuickTime, but it's fairly straightforward to use. You can still open QuickTime movies in Flash 4 and 5, but you can't use any actions or ActionScript, because they did not exist in Flash 3. QuickTime 5 supports Flash 4.

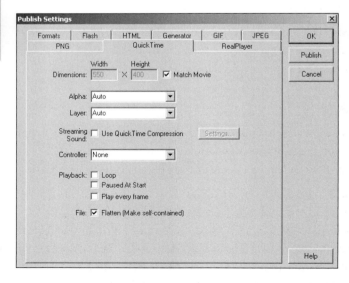

Figure 19.16
The QuickTime options.

RealPlayer Tab

To turn tuned SWF files into RealAudio files from the Stream Sync audio used in your Flash movie, select the RealPlayer option in the Formats tab. Figure 19.17 shows the RealPlayer options.

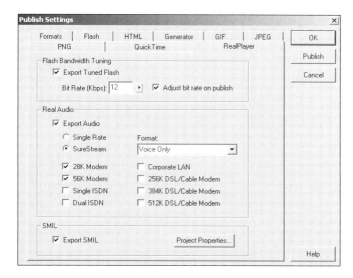

Figure 19.17
The RealPlayer options.

Export

Once you have optimized your movie the best you can, debugged it, checked the download speeds in the Bandwidth Profiler, and set your options in the Publish Settings dialog box, you are ready to export.

After you've set your Publish Settings options, the export is one step: File|Export. This command exports your movie as a SWF file. If you want Flash to make your movie an HTML page, choose File|Publish. An HTML file with your Flash movie embedded will be generated automatically.

If you have selected other options in the Formats tab of the Publish Settings dialog box, such as QuickTime, and so on, those formats will be generated as well when you choose File|Export Movie or File|Export Image.

Moving On

In this chapter, you learned how to optimize your Flash movies to reduce their file sizes as much as possible, so they load more quickly in the user's browser. You have explored many of the settings available and the Export options you can use.

This concludes the main portion of the book. Be sure to check Appendix B for plenty of recommended resources and tools that I use in the design process. Appendix A discusses using Dreamweaver with Fireworks. The Horse Adventures Web site has many images, which were placed into Dreamweaver. You will also see how to edit Fireworks images from within Dreamweaver, how to insert Fireworks code into Dreamweaver, and how to use Fireworks pop-up menus in Dreamweaver.

Appendix A

Incorporating Fireworks 4 HTML Code and Images into Dreamweaver

This appendix shows you how to get your Fireworks 4 HTML code into a Web layout program in Dreamweaver. Fireworks 4 pop-up menu placements are dealt with in detail, helping you to position these menus so that they appear where you want them.

Fireworks Integration

Fireworks is great for generating Web-ready images. These images and their code then need to be moved to a Web layout program or HTML editor, to prepare them for Web presentation.

Dreamweaver is the preferred choice of many developers because of its tight integration with Fireworks. You will discover in this appendix the many ways Dreamweaver makes getting your Fireworks designs onto the Web easy.

Placing Exported HTML and Images from Fireworks into Dreamweaver

You can find a demo of Dreamweaver 4 at **www.macromedia.com/downloads**; this demo is fully functional for 30 days. Even if you don't use or don't want to use Dreamweaver, it may benefit you to evaluate the code and placement techniques for use in other editors. When the term *Dreamweaver* is used, it refers to any application of Dreamweaver 4.

Preparing a Dreamweaver Web Page

You can place your Fireworks code into any existing Web page or use the Fireworks-generated HTML file as your template. To make all the exercises in this appendix easier to follow, you will be told when to add a new folder and what to name it. If you want to skip that step, you can use everything in the Appendix A exportingsamples folder. A practice file called DWsample.htm is included.

> **Note:** You will need the folders and files included on this book's CD-ROM to complete all the exercises in this appendix. Copy the entire exportingsamples folder in the Appendix A folder to your hard drive.

In order for some of the inserted code to be recognized, the site's root directory must be defined. Also, for correct placement of inserted images, you will set your margins to zero so that no margin exists in the browser. To define the site and set the margins, follow these steps:

1. Open Dreamweaver 4. Choose Modify|Page Properties. The only things to be concerned about for this exercise are the margins; type "0" for all four. These settings will ensure that no browser border appears around your placed images. Even though all the margins are blank before you specify zero, a 2-pixel default border exists when you view in a browser.

2. You need to define this site so that some of the examples in the rest of this appendix will work, such as using the Library item that I exported for you to practice with (exporting Dreamweaver Library items from Fireworks is discussed in Chapter 12). Choose Sites|Define Site or Site|New Site and click the New button. In the window that opens, click the yellow folder icon to locate the exportingsamples folder, and then click Select.

   Click OK. A window will open saying that the cache will be created; click OK and then click Done.

3. Choose Insert|Table or use the Object Inspector's Common category (see Figure A.1). In the window that opens, specify one row, two columns, 100%, CellSpacing and CellPadding both to 0, and a Border value of 0. Click the OK button.

4. Place your cursor over the dotted vertical lines in the center of the table, and click and drag to the left. Figure A.2 has an arrow pointing to the lines to move. To view the code and see the design area at the same time, click the Show Code And Design Views icon; the cursor is pointing to the icon in Figure A.2.

5. Place your cursor in the first column and click. Figure A.2 shows the portion of the code visible when you click in the first cell. Notice the code that looks like this:

```
<td width="22%"> </td>
<td width="78%"> </td>
```

Figure A.1
The Object Inspector's Common category in Dreamweaver.

Your numbers will vary, but this is the code to look for. Highlight **22%** (or whatever percentage you have in the first **<td>** tag) and change it to **200**. The code will now look like this:

```
<td width="200"> </td>
<td width="78%"> </td>
```

You have made the first column a fixed width, and the second column is a percentage table. By making the second column a percentage, it will stretch to fit a browser's size. By having the first column fixed, whatever is placed in it will always remain in the same position no matter the browser size. This step is particularly important for placing Fireworks 4 pop-up menus later in this appendix.

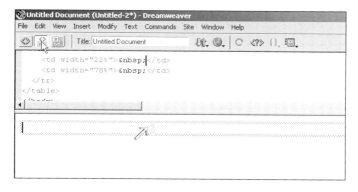

Figure A.2
The Design view, the line being moved, and the Show Code And Design Views icon.

That is the important part of this Web page. You can save it or you can use the one completed for you in the exportingsamples folder, named DWsamplefile.htm. It includes a simple text layout so that you can see how the second column stretches in some of the exercises in which you will use this file.

Placing Fireworks 4 HTML Code into a Dreamweaver 4 Web Page

A few different ways exist to get your Fireworks code into a Dreamweaver Web page. You can simply use an insert command, or you can copy and paste the code into the correct areas.

Inserting the Fireworks 4 HTML Code into Dreamweaver

In the Fireworks section, Chapter 12, you learned how to export your Fireworks projects as HTML and images and how to export with images only. In this section, you will see how to insert a navigation bar with its code intact from a Fireworks-generated HTML file into Dreamweaver. To insert the Fireworks code of a pop-up menu I have supplied (files are in the popup folder in the exportingsamples folder), follow these steps:

1. Open Dreamweaver 4, choose File|Open, and navigate to the exportingsamples folder on this book's CD-ROM. Choose DWsamplefile.htm and click Open. Figure A.3 shows the file the way it looks so far.

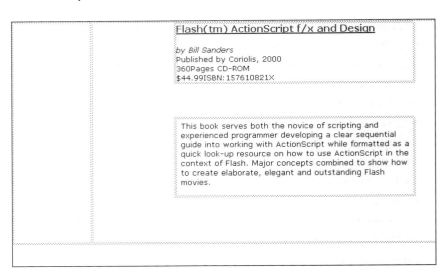

Figure A.3
The appearance of the sample Web page before Fireworks code is inserted.

2. Place your cursor in the first column and click. Choose Insert|Interactive Images|Fireworks HTML. Or, use the Insert Fireworks HTML icon in the Common section of the Object Inspector, as shown in Figure A.4.

3. In the window that opens, click the Browse button. Navigate to the exportingsamples folder and open the popup folder. Click the popupsample.htm file. Don't select the Delete File After Insertion option, because you will be using the file again. (When you are doing this on a real Web page, you will usually delete the file after it is placed— there is no need for an additional HTML file, because the code is integrated into the file where you placed the Fireworks HTML.) When you are finished, click OK. The completed file is shown in Figure A.5.

Figure A.4
The Insert Fireworks HTML icon.

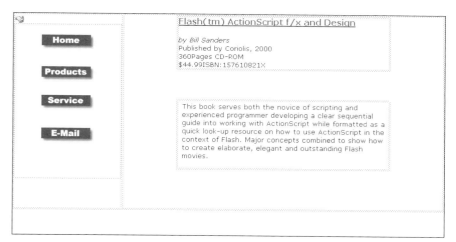

Figure A.5
The sample Web page with the Fireworks 4 HTML code added.

4. Choose File|Preview In Browser or the Globe icon on the same row as the HTML code icons below the menu bar, and select the browser you want to view in. Pass your cursor over the Products button. The menu will pop out, but notice the red X in Internet Explorer or a blank square in Netscape Navigator next to the first menu's items. The instructions had you use DWsamplefile.htm in the exportsamples folder to demonstrate this point: You see the X or blank area because the arrow image that goes in the menu is missing. It's in the image folder of the popup folder. The files that access the pop-up menus need to be in the same folder as the fw_menus.js file and the image folder. Choose File|Save As and save this file in the popup folder. Now, if you preview, the arrows will be there. A copy of the file has been saved for you in the popup folder and is called popupinserted.htm.

Using the Fireworks 4 HTML File

If you think inserting the Fireworks 4 HTML code into an existing Dreamweaver layout was easy, you'll find using the native Fireworks 4 HTML file (after you exported it from Fireworks) even easier. If you don't yet have a current Web page into which you want to insert your Fireworks code, then you can simply open the HTML file that Fireworks generated when you exported. You can use the Fireworks 4 HTML file as a Dreamweaver template.

Copying and Pasting Fireworks 4 HTML Code into Dreamweaver
When you are going to use Fireworks 4 HTML, you need to choose the generic Export As HTML And Images option. To copy and paste the pop-up menu sample provided, follow these steps:

1. In Dreamweaver, choose File|Open, navigate to the exportingsamples folder, select DWsamplefile.htm (the copy without any menus inserted), and click Open.

2. Click the second icon below the menu bar, Show Code And Design Views, to view the code and the Web page. Choose File|Open, navigate to the popup folder inside the exportingsamples folder, select the popupsample.htm file, and click Open. To see just the HTML code in this file, click the first icon below the menu bar, called Show Code View. Listing A.1 shows the top portion of the HTML code.

Listing A.1 The **\<head\>** portion of the HTML code of the pop-up menu.

```
<html>
<head>
<title>popupsample.gif</title>
<meta http-equiv="Content-Type" content="text/html;">
<!- Fireworks 4.0  Dreamweaver 4.0 target.  Created Mon Jan 22
   12:45:36 GMT-0600 (Central Standard Time) 2001->
<script language="JavaScript">
<!-
function MM_findObj(n, d) { //v3.0
  var p,i,x; if(!d) d=document; if((p=n.indexOf("?"))
  >0&&parent.frames.length) {
    d=parent.frames[n.substring(p+1)].document;
   n=n.substring(0,p);}
  if(!(x=d[n])&&d.all) x=d.all[n]; for
 (i=0;!x&&i<d.forms.length;i++) x=d.forms[i][n];
  for(i=0;!x&&d.layers&&i<d.layers.length;i++)
x=MM_findObj(n,d.layers[i].document); return x;
}
function MM_nbGroup(event, grpName) { //v3.0
  var i,img,nbArr,args=MM_nbGroup.arguments;
  if (event == "init" && args.length > 2) {
    if ((img = MM_findObj(args[2])) != null &&
!img.MM_init) { img.MM_init = true; img.MM_up =
args[3]; img.MM_dn = img.src;
      if ((nbArr = document[grpName]) == null) nbArr =
document[grpName] = new Array();
      nbArr[nbArr.length] = img;
      for (i=4; i < args.length-1; i+=2) if
 ((img = MM_findObj(args[i])) != null) {
        if (!img.MM_up) img.MM_up = img.src;
        img.src = img.MM_dn = args[i+1];
        nbArr[nbArr.length] = img;
    } }
```

```
  } else if (event == "over") {
    document.MM_nbOver = nbArr = new Array();
    for (i=1; i < args.length-1; i+=3) if
  ((img = MM_findObj(args[i])) != null) {
      if (!img.MM_up) img.MM_up = img.src;
      img.src = (img.MM_dn && args[i+2]) ? args[i+2]
  : args[i+1];
      nbArr[nbArr.length] = img;
    }
  } else if (event == "out" ) {
    for (i=0; i < document.MM_nbOver.length; i++) {
      img = document.MM_nbOver[i]; img.src = (img.MM_dn)
   ? img.MM_dn : img.MM_up; }
  } else if (event == "down") {
    if ((nbArr = document[grpName]) != null)
      for (i=0; i < nbArr.length; i++) { img=nbArr[i];
  img.src = img.MM_up; img.MM_dn = 0; }
    document[grpName] = nbArr = new Array();
    for (i=2; i < args.length-1; i+=2) if
  ((img = MM_findObj(args[i])) != null) {
      if (!img.MM_up) img.MM_up = img.src;
      img.src = img.MM_dn = args[i+1];
      nbArr[nbArr.length] = img;
  } }
}


function MM_preloadImages() { //v3.0
 var d=document; if(d.images){ if(!d.MM_p)
  d.MM_p=new Array();
   var i,j=d.MM_p.length,a=MM_preloadImages.arguments;
   for(i=0; i<a.length; i++)
   if (a[i].indexOf("#")!=0){ d.MM_p[j]=new Image;
  d.MM_p[j++].src=a[i];}}
}


function fwLoadMenus() {
 if (window.fw_menu_0) return;
   window.fw_menu_0_1 = new Menu("Product 1",77,17,
  "Verdana, Arial, Helvetica, sans-
serif",10,"#0000cc","#009900","#009900","#0000cc");
   fw_menu_0_1.addMenuItem("Sample 1");
   fw_menu_0_1.addMenuItem("Sample 2");
    fw_menu_0_1.hideOnMouseOut=true;
   window.fw_menu_0_2 = new Menu("Product 2",81,17,
  "Verdana, Arial, Helvetica, sans-
serif",10,"#0000cc","#009900","#009900","#0000cc");
   fw_menu_0_2.addMenuItem("Sample 1");
   fw_menu_0_2.addMenuItem("Sample  2");
    fw_menu_0_2.hideOnMouseOut=true;
 window.fw_menu_0 = new Menu("root",76,17,"Verdana,
  Arial, Helvetica, sans-serif",10,"#0000cc",
  "#009900","#009900","#0000cc");
 fw_menu_0.addMenuItem(fw_menu_0_1);
```

```
    fw_menu_0.addMenuItem(fw_menu_0_2);
    fw_menu_0.hideOnMouseOut=true;
    fw_menu_0.childMenuIcon="images/arrows.gif";

    fw_menu_0.writeMenus();
} // fwLoadMenus()

//->
</script>
<script language="JavaScript1.2" src="fw_menu.js"></script>
</head>
```

The area that is grayed out is the code that you copy from the Fireworks 4 HTML–generated code and paste into the **<head>** section of the Web page you want to use it in. Paste this code below the **<title>** and **<meta>** tags but before the **</head>** (end head) tag. The code you are copying and pasting is the JavaScript for the rollovers.

3. The next section to copy and paste is needed only when images are coded to preload. Listing A.2 shows the code from the pop-up menu sample you are using. If this code is not present in a document you are copying, skip this step. The top gray area shown in Listing A.2 is the only part you need to copy right now.

Listing A.2 The code in the body background section and the table code.
```
</head>
<body topmargin="0" leftmargin="0" marginheight="0"
  marginwidth="0" bgcolor="#ffffff"
onLoad="MM_preloadImages('images/popupsample_r2_c2_f2.gif',
'images/popupsample_r2_c2_f3.gif',
  'images/popupsample_r6_c2_f2.gif',
  'images/popupsample_r6_c2_f3.gif',
  'images/popupsample_r8_c2_f2.gif',
  'images/popupsample_r8_c2_f3.gif');"> <script
language="JavaScript1.2">fwLoadMenus();
</script>
<table border="0" cellpadding="0" cellspacing="0" width="200">
<!- fwtable fwsrc="popupsample.png" fwbase="popupsample.gif"
fwstyle="Dreamweaver" fwdocid = "742308039" fwnested="0" ->
  <tr>
    <td><img src="images/spacer.gif" width="43" height="1"
    border="0"></td>
    <td><img src="images/spacer.gif" width="116" height="1"
    border="0"></td>
    <td><img src="images/spacer.gif" width="41" height="1"
    border="0"></td>
    <td><img src="images/spacer.gif" width="1" height="1"
    border="0"></td>
  </tr>
```

```
 <tr>
  <td colspan="3"><img name="popupsample_r1_c1" src="images/
popupsample_r1_c1.gif" width="200" height="12"
 border="0"></td>
  <td><img src="images/spacer.gif" width="1" height="12"
 border="0"></td>
 </tr>
 <tr>
  <td rowspan="8"><img name="popupsample_r2_c1" src="images/
popupsample_r2_c1.gif" width="43" height="288"
 border="0"></td>
  <td><a href="#" onMouseOut="MM_nbGroup('out');"
onMouseOver="MM_nbGroup('over','popupsample_r2_c2',
 'images/popupsample_r2_c2_f2.gif',
 'images/popupsample_r2_c2_f3.gif',1);" onClick="MM_nbGroup
 ('down','navbar1',
 'popupsample_r2_c2','images/popupsample_r2_c2_f3.gif',1);
 " ><img name="popupsample_r2_c2"
 src="images/popupsample_r2_c2.gif" width="116" height="45"
border="0"></a></td>
  <td rowspan="8"><img name="popupsample_r2_c3" src="images/
popupsample_r2_c3.gif" width="41" height="288"
 border="0"></td>
  <td><img src="images/spacer.gif" width="1" height="45"
 border="0"></td>
 </tr>
 <tr>
  <td><img name="popupsample_r3_c2"
 src="images/popupsample_r3_c2.gif" width="116"
 height="15" border="0"></td>
  <td><img src="images/spacer.gif" width="1"
 height="15" border="0"></td>
 </tr>
 <tr>
  <td><a href="#" onMouseOut="FW_startTimeout();"
onMouseOver="window.FW_showMenu(window.fw_menu_0,149,83);
 " ><img name="popupsample_r4_c2"
 src="images/popupsample_r4_c2.gif" width="116"
 height="44" border="0"></a></td>
  <td><img src="images/spacer.gif" width="1"
 height="44" border="0"></td>
 </tr>
 <tr>
  <td><img name="popupsample_r5_c2"
 src="images/popupsample_r5_c2.gif" width="116"
 height="14" border="0"></td>
  <td><img src="images/spacer.gif" width="1"
 height="14" border="0"></td>
 </tr>
 <tr>
  <td><a href="#" onMouseOut="MM_nbGroup('out');"
onMouseOver="MM_nbGroup('over','popupsample_r6_c2',
 'images/popupsample_r6_c2_f2.gif',
```

```
          'images/popupsample_r6_c2_f3.gif',1);"
onClick="MM_nbGroup('down','navbar1','popupsample_r6_c2',
     'images/popupsample_r6_c2_f3.gif',1);" >
     <img name="popupsample_r6_c2"
     src="images/popupsample_r6_c2.gif" width="116" height="45"
border="0"></a></td>
       <td><img src="images/spacer.gif" width="1"
     height="45" border="0"></td>
     </tr>
     <tr>
       <td><img name="popupsample_r7_c2"
     src="images/popupsample_r7_c2.gif" width="116"
     height="19" border="0"></td>
       <td><img src="images/spacer.gif" width="1"
     height="19" border="0"></td>
     </tr>
     <tr>
       <td><a href="#" onMouseOut="MM_nbGroup('out');"
onMouseOver="MM_nbGroup('over','popupsample_r8_c2',
     'images/popupsample_r8_c2_f2.gif',
     'images/popupsample_r8_c2_f3.gif',1);"
       onClick="MM_nbGroup('down','navbar1',
     'popupsample_r8_c2','images/popupsample_r8_c2_f3.gif',1);
     " ><img name="popupsample_r8_c2"
     src="images/popupsample_r8_c2.gif" width="116" height="45"
border="0"></a></td>
       <td><img src="images/spacer.gif" width="1" height="45"
     border="0"></td>
     </tr>
     <tr>
       <td><img name="popupsample_r9_c2"
     src="images/popupsample_r9_c2.gif" width="116"
     height="61" border="0"></td>
       <td><img src="images/spacer.gif" width="1"
     height="61" border="0"></td>
     </tr>
</table>
</body>
</html>
```

The code to copy is located in the body background area. The code to locate in the target Web page is similar to this:

```
<body bgcolor="#FFFFFF" text="#000000" leftmargin="0"
  topmargin="0">
```

Delete the last closing symbol (>) and paste the two grayed lines of code, as shown in Listing A.2, starting with **onLoad** and ending with **</script>**.

4. The last chunk of code to copy and paste contains the buttons and their table. Refer to the second gray area in Listing A.2 and copy all the way through the </**table**> tag. Locate the code (it's close to the <**body**> tag) and then paste what you just copied, just before the </**td**> that you see in this portion of code:

```
<table width="100%" border="0">
<tr>
<td width="200
" valign="top">  </td>
```

You have just pasted the table containing the buttons and surrounding image slices into the first column.

Using Exported Dreamweaver Library Objects

Dreamweaver Library items simplify the process of editing and updating a frequently used Web site component, such as a navigation bar. A Library item is a portion of an HTML file located in a folder named library at your root site. Library items appear in the Dreamweaver Library palette. You can then drag a copy to any page in your Web site. To place a Library item in a Web page, follow these steps:

1. In Dreamweaver, open the Web page in which you want to place a Library item. For this exercise, open the DWsample.htm file in the exportsamples folder. I exported a sample Library item into the library folder of exportsamples (see Chapter 12, which explains how to export a Library item).

2. If the Library category isn't open, choose Window|Library or Window|Assets; in previous versions of Dreamweaver, the Library was in its own panel, but now it is a category in the Assets panel. You will see the Navbarsample in the Library. Drag either the image or the text (which one doesn't matter) into the first column. That's all there is to it. Using Dreamweaver really is the simplest way to integrate your Fireworks 4 HTML code.

You cannot edit a Library item directly in the Dreamweaver document; you can edit only the master Library item. Then, you can have Dreamweaver update every copy of that item as it is placed throughout your Web site using the Update option found by clicking the right-pointing arrow in the Library panel.

Using Exported Images Only

In the Fireworks section, Chapter 12, you learned how to export images only. A sample file of images only is in the imagesonly folder in the exportsamples folder for you to practice on. To add images only to a Dreamweaver page, follow these steps:

1. Open the DWsamplefile.htm file located in the exportsamples folder.

2. Place your cursor in the first column (left side) and click. From the Object Inspector, click the Insert Image icon (a little tree) or choose Insert|Image. Navigate to the imagesonly folder in the exportsamples folder, select the first image (navbarsample_rw2_c2.gif), and click Select.

3. Press the Enter/Return key, click the Insert Image icon again, choose the second image, and click Select. Repeat for the next two buttons.

4. Select the first button and, if the Property inspector isn't open, choose Window|Properties. Figure A.6 shows the Property inspector with the Home button selected. Add your link and alternative text here.

5. Repeat Step 4 for each button.

Figure A.6
The Property inspector.

 Horse Adventures Layout in Dreamweaver

In this project, you will place all the Horse Adventures images, including the navigation, into Dreamweaver. This project was written by Brad Halstead, a frequent contributor and a great help to many people in the Project Seven forum. You can learn more about Brad in Appendix B.

Horse Adventures Comparison

The objective of this project is to compare the generated outputs of Dreamweaver and Fireworks in relation to complexity of code, ability to be modified, and file size, all based on Dreamweaver's built-in behaviors, commands, and objects.

You already have learned how to make all the graphics and navigation for the Horse Adventures Web site in the Fireworks section, so you are familiar with the various exported images.

I assume you have a working knowledge of Dreamweaver 4 and know your way around the different panels, commands, objects, and behaviors. It is beyond the scope of this appendix to teach Dreamweaver 4.

Before you begin, copy the HA-Dreamweaver folder from the Appendix A folder to your hard drive.

Setting Up the Site

The first thing you should do when working on a new site is to define it.

1. Open Dreamweaver. If a Site Definition dialog box doesn't automatically open, choose Site|Define Site. Click New.

2. Figure A.7 shows a Site Name of HA-Dreamweaver. Click the yellow folder to the right of Local Root Folder to select the HA-Dreamweaver folder you copied to your hard drive. Leave all other Site Definition items at their default for this exercise. Click OK and then click Done.

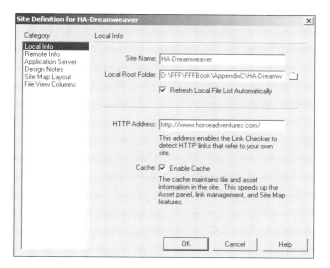

Figure A.7
The Site Definition dialog box.

3. The Site Manager opens, as shown in Figure A.8. Using it, add the following folders (File|New Folder) in your site, adjusting the path name according to where you copied the sample folders to your hard drive. See the tip "Filling the Folders" after you add these folders:

   - *source*—c:\HA-Dreamweaver\source. This folder holds all the source files for the site, the Fireworks PNG file (if you have one), and any other related materials used to build the site. The tracing image is also stored here (layout.jpg).

   - *images*—c:\HA-Dreamweaver\images. This folder houses all of the exported images from the Fireworks PNG files.

4. Add a new file (File|New) and name it "index.html". Double-click the index.html file to open it for editing.

Note: This file automatically becomes the site map layout homepage in the site definition.

Filling the Folders

After you add the new folders, you can drag the images from the starter folder (in the HA-Dreamweaver folder) into the image and source folders you just added to the HA-Dreamweaver folder. You won't need the starter folder any longer, so you can delete if you'd like.

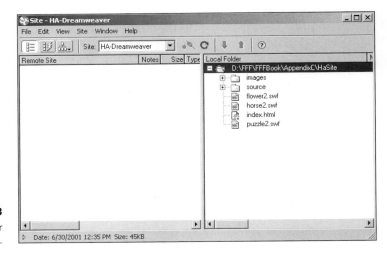

Setting the Page Properties

Next, you will define the page properties. With index.html open for editing, choose Modify|Page Properties (Ctrl+J/Cmd+J) and use these specifications:

- *Title*—HA–Dreamweaver

- *Background*—#000000

- *Text*—#FFFFFF

- *Left Margin*—0

- *Top Margin*—0

- *Margin Width*—0

- *Margin Height*—0

- *Tracing Image*—source/layout.jpg (This file will be removed once the page is completed and is used strictly to see how your content lines up with the Fireworks-created image.)

- *Image Transparency*—50%

Click the Apply button, and then click OK. Figure A.9 shows the Page Properties dialog box for the HA-Dreamweaver site. Figure A.10 shows the tracing image at 50 percent transparency.

Note: The tracing image has *no* display properties on the Web; it is strictly a background image on which to base your alignment and positioning within Dreamweaver.

Laying Out the Page

To set up the layout of the page, follow these steps:

1. Insert a table with the following specs:

   - *Rows*—2

   - *Columns*—2

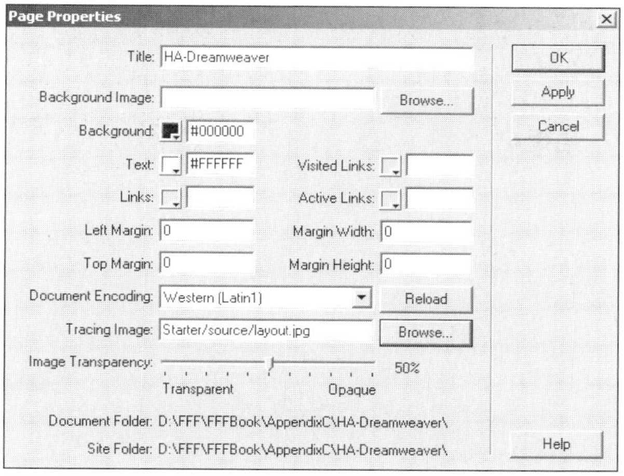

Figure A.9

The Page Properties dialog box for the HA-Dreamweaver site.

Figure A.10

The layout.jpg file being used for a tracing image at 50 percent transparency.

- *Width*—750 pixels

- *Cell Padding*—5

- *Cell Spacing*—0

- *Border*—1

In the Property inspector, make the border white for visibility. You'll change it later.

Figure A.11 shows the Insert Table dialog box with the settings added. You've just added the table with a maximum and minimum display size of 750 pixels.

Note: The Border is set to 1 and Cell Padding to 5 for visual purposes only in the development and layout of this page. If you didn't use these settings, it would be very difficult to add the nested table to the second column because you wouldn't be able to see it. The Border and Cell Padding will be set to 0 when the layout is complete.

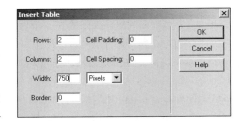

Figure A.11

The Insert Table dialog box.

2. You will use the **<td>** tag for image positioning. Place your cursor in row 1, column 1, and select the **<td>** tag in the Tag Selector (bottom-left corner **<td>**) to set the following properties (Figure A.12 shows the Property inspector where you enter the values):

   - Horizontal Alignment—Center

   - Vertical Alignment—Top

   - Width—750

Figure A.12

The Property inspector with the <td> values entered.

3. You will use the **<td>** tag for table positioning. Place your cursor in row 1, column 2, and select the **<td>** tag in the Tag Selector to set the Vertical Alignment to Top.

4. To insert a nested table into row 1 of column 1, place your cursor, click, and insert a table with the following properties:

   - *Rows*—3

   - *Columns*—1

   - *Width*—100%

   - *Cell Padding*—0

   - *Cell Spacing*—0

   - *Border*—0

   When you click OK, the Property inspector will change and you can name the table. Name it "contenttable".

5. To place the top image, position your cursor in the content table, row 1, column 1; choose the Insert icon in the Object inspector (the little tree); and navigate to the images folder and select banner.gif. In the Property inspector, name the image "banner" and give it a Border of 0, as shown in Figure A.13.

Figure A.13
The Property inspector with the image named and a Border of 0.

6. To make the Contact area of the banner into a hotspot to receive a link, select the rectangular hotspot tool from the Property inspector and draw a rectangle over the word "Contact". You will see a transparent blue rectangle. This is only a visual representation of the area. In the Property inspector, add these properties:

- *Link*—mailto:contact@somewhere.com
- *Alt*—Contact us for more information

7. Repeat Step 6 for the word "Advertise" and give it the following properties:

- *Link*—mailto:advertise@somewhere.com
- *Alt*—Advertise your horse with us!

8. To insert the header, position your cursor in the content table, row 2, column 1, and insert header.jpg from the image folder with these properties:

- *Alt*—Horse Adventures
- *Border*—0

9. To insert the Textbox image, position your cursor in the content table, row 3, column 1, and insert box1.gif from the images folder. In the Property inspector, add these properties:

- *Name*—textbox
- *Border*—0

10. Add a line break for spacing purposes. Select the content table; if you are not sure how or where to locate the nested table, look at the Tag Selector area at the bottom-left corner of the document window. Figure A.14 shows the second **<table>** tag selected; by selecting this **<table>** tag, your table will be selected. Press the right arrow key one time to place your cursor after the content table. Press and hold the Shift key, and then press Enter/Return. Doing so positions a line break (**
**) after the table so that you can insert the next table and have the little bit of space you need to position the content. 

`<body> <table> <tr> <td> <table> <tr> <td>`

Figure A.14
The second **<table>** tag selected.

Warning

The Macromedia built-in behavior called Swap Image has
the capability of assigning
more than one image swap on
the same event. If you decide
to use this functionality, it is
best to disable the Swap
Image Restore, because
Netscape Navigator won't
perform multiple Swap Image
Restores on the same event.
To overcome this limitation,
simply use a second swap
image to restore the two or
more images to their original
state. Ensure that the Behavior
panel is using onMouseOver
for the swap image behavior
and using onMouseOut for the
restore image behavior; otherwise, the image swap will work
only in Internet Explorer!

Inserting the Bottom Navigation System

Insert a table with the following properties (enter the last item in the Property inspector):

- *Rows*—2
- *Columns*—4
- *Width*—100%
- *Cell Padding*—0
- *Cell Spacing*—0
- *Border*—0
- *Name*—bottomnav

Inserting the bottomnav Images

In the bottomnav table, insert the information as detailed in Table A.1.

Adding the bottomnav Rollovers

Select the image in row 2, column 1. To add the Swap Image behavior, open the Behaviors panel (Window|Behaviors or Shift+F3), click the plus (+) sign, and choose Swap Image. Figure A.15 shows the Swap Image dialog box with the following properties selected and filled in:

- *Swap Image*—images/gameover.gif
- *Preload Images*—Selected
- *Restore Images onMouseOut*—Selected

Repeat this procedure for the remaining three images on the bottom row, as indicated in Table A.2.

Table A.1   Data for the bottomnav table.

Row	Column	Image	Name	Border
1	1	images/kids_bh.jpg		0
1	2	images/video_bh.jpg		0
1	3	images/tack_bh.jpg		0
1	4	images/model_bh.jpg		0
2	1	images/gameup.gif	kidsgame	0
2	2	images/videoup.gif	bookvideo	0
2	3	images/apparellup.gif	tack	0
2	4	images/modelup.gif	toyhorse	0

Table A.2   Bottom row images.

Row	Column	Swap Image
2	2	images/videoover.gif
2	3	images/apparellover.gif
2	4	images/modelover.gif

Figure A.15

The Swap Image dialog box filled with the first swap image.

Inserting the Right Navigation System

Remember how you added a border, border color of white, and cell padding to the base table? Now is the time you'll be glad you did. You should be able to see the right column with a white border around it. If only the cell padding is visible, manually move the column to the left. Place your cursor inside and click, and insert a table with the following properties:

- *Rows*—14
- *Columns*—1
- *Width*—183 pixels
- *Cell Padding*—0
- *Cell Spacing*—0
- *Border*—0
- *Name*—rightnav

Setting Up the rightnav Table

Select the spacer in row 1 of the table. In the Property inspector, set the height to 24 and the width to 159. Select the spacer in row 13; in the Property inspector, set the height to 30 and the width to 159. You are setting the dimensions for the first and last row so the table won't collapse; the spacer is used for positioning. In the rightnav table, insert the information as detailed in Table A.3.

Adding the rightnav Rollovers

Select the first navigation element called horsegame-up.gif in row 2 and add the Swap Image behavior with the following properties:

- *Swap Image*—images/horsegame-over.gif
- *Preload Images*—Selected
- *Restore Images onMouseOut*—Selected

Repeat this procedure for the remaining 10 images on the bottom row, as indicated in Table A.4.

> **Note:** To get this table to align to the top, you will need to do a bit of hand coding. Look in code view, select the rightnav 14-row table, and select the **<td>** just prior to the table. Change the **<td>** to this:
>
> ```
> <td valign=top width=183>
> ```
>
> It has nothing to do with the table per se, but with the cell holding the table, which is controlled by the **<td>** tag. Alternatively, you also can change the code by selecting the<td> prior to the table in the Tag Selector area and entering 183 in the width box, and the valign=top code.

Table A.3 Right navigation.

Row	Image	Name	Alt	Border
1	images/spacer.gif			0
2	images/horsegame-up.gif	horsegame	Horse Game	0
3	images/bookstore-up.gif	bookstore	Bookstore	0
4	images/equinetack-up.gif	equinetack	Equine Tack	0
5	images/modelhorses-up.gif	modelhorses	Model Horses	0
6	images/breedinfo-up.gif	breedinfo	Breed Info	0
7	images/articles-up.gif	articles	Articles	0
8	images/puzzles-up.gif	puzzles	Puzzles	0
9	images/screensavers-up.gif	screensavers	Screen Savers	0
10	images/sitemap-up.gif	sitemap	Site Map	0
11	images/credits-up.gif	credits	Credits	0
12	images/contact-up.gif	contact	Contact Us	0
13	images/spacer.gif			0
14	images/box2.gif	puzzlebox	Puzzle	0

Table A.4 Right navigation rollovers.

Row	Image
3	images/bookstore-over.gif
4	images/equinetack-over.gif
5	images/modelhorses-over.gif
6	images/breedinfo-over.gif
7	images/articles-over.gif
8	images/puzzles-over.gif
9	images/screensavers-over.gif
10	images/sitemap-over.gif
11	images/credits-over.gif
12	images/contact-over.gif

Inserting the Copyright Information

Let's go back to the content table. Position your cursor at row 2, press Shift+Enter/ Return to add one space, column 1. Using the Object panel, select the Character category and insert a copyright symbol. Press the right arrow once (doing so takes focus off the copyright symbol; this is a "feature" when inserting objects from the Object panel that leaves them selected after adding). Type the following (without quotation marks): "Copyright 1997-2001, Idea design, All rights reserved." The text formatting will be addressed later in this project.

Inserting the Flash File Links

Select the puzzles-up.gif image in the rightnav table. In the Property inspector, click the yellow folder near the Link box, browse for the puzzle2.html file, and select it. In the Select Target area, choose _blank. Repeat for the box2.gif image. You have now set both images to open the Flash puzzles, which have been exported from Flash as HTML files.

Note: If the viewer's browser does not have the Flash plug-in, then the user will be prompted to download and install it. However, recent statistics show that over 96 percent of users have the Flash plug-in.

Adding the Content Text Layer

Select the <**body**> tag in the Tag Selector (lower left) and choose Insert|Layer. In the Property Inspector, change the properties to:

- *Layer ID*—box1content
- *L*—34px
- *T*—196px
- *W*—471px
- *H*—155px
- *Z-Index*—1
- *Overflow*—Hidden

Position your cursor inside the layer and type the following, without the quotes, "This is where your content would go for this nice little text box that is housed in a layer on top of the box image." You could make a table for the box and make this text part of the table, but doing so adds a lot of code to the page and therefore a lot of overhead to the download time. As it is, some of the images, although compressed, will cause you to go over the target page weight of 40 to 50KB. Due to the nature of the site, the users (mostly children) will not mind the wait (probably)! Kids using the Sim horse games want photos and lots of them!

Notice how the content will overflow the specified area, because you haven't applied any style to the text. This step will be covered in the next section, "Cascading Style Sheet." Do not adjust the layer or reposition it, because it will fit when you are done. So you can see what's happening, press F12 now: The content is hidden if it is outside your defined size. To fit it all, you will apply a custom style to that block of text. You could also make this area of text scroll, but you won't do that here.

Cascading Style Sheet

Open the CSS panel (Window|CSS Styles or Shift+F11) and click the Edit Style Sheet icon at lower right. Select New, and populate the defined fields with the following properties (see Figure A.16):

- *Name*—.copyr (That's period[.]copyr)
- *Type*—Make Custom Style (Class)
- *Define In*—This Document Only

> **Note:** We originally tried to link to the puzzle.swf file directly; it worked in all browsers except for Netscape 6. You can't directly link to the SWF file because the Flash file is not properly embedded in the link. To overcome this problem, you make the puzzle2.html file, which is generated by Flash 5 on export, and you simply link to this file. All PC-based browsers that were tested were happy with this file. Browsers tested were IE 5.5, Netscape 4.77, Netscape 6.01, and Opera 5.11.

> **Note:** You will not be able to select any properties for the layer until it is inserted on the page. To select any layer, use the Layer panel and click once on the layer.

Layer Positioning

After you have completed the instructions for "Adding the Content Text Layer," your layer should be positioned above the box1.gif image, equally spaced on all sides of the box image. If it is close, make adjustments using the four arrow keys until you are satisfied with its position.

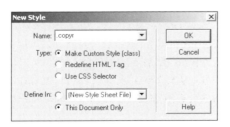

Figure A.16
The New Style dialog box with the properties filled in.

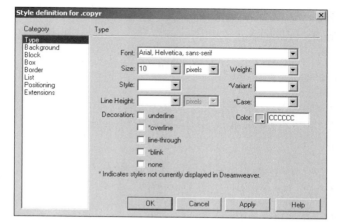

Figure A.17
The Style Definition For
dialog box.

Click the OK button to bring up the Dreamweaver style editor (Figure A.17) where you can define the properties for the custom class .copyr. Following the definitions, populate the CSS fields as follows:

- *Font*—Arial, Helvetica, sans-serif

- *Size*—10

- *Unit of Measure*—Pixels

- *Color*—CCCCCC

Click the Apply button, and then click the OK button.

Repeat the previous steps, using the following values:

- *Name*—.tbox1

- *Font*—Verdana, Arial, Helvetica, sans-serif

- *Size*—12

- *Unit of Measure*—Pixels

- *Color*—CCCCCC

Click Apply, click OK, and click Done. Your completed style sheet block should look like this in code view:

```
<style type="text/CSS">
<!-
.copyr {  font-family: Arial, Helvetica, sans-serif; font-size:
  10px; color: #CCCCCC}
.tbox1 {  font-family: Verdana, Arial, Helvetica, sans-serif;
  font-size: 12px; color: #CCCCCC}
->
</style>
```

Note: You use pixels as the unit of measure because it gives you the most control over the font size when the remote viewer views the page. This is a rule of thumb; if the user has a custom style sheet defined in their browser, it may override your definitions and cause some discrepancy during remote viewing. We used a light gray color because stark white on a black background is difficult to read.

Applying the Styles

To apply the styles, follow these steps:

1. Position your cursor in the layer. Using the Tag Selector, select the **\<div>** tag. Click .tbox1 in the CSS panel.

2. Position your cursor in the copyright notice area in the content table, row 2, column 1, and select the **\<td>** tag from the Tag Selector. Click .copyr in the CSS panel.

3. Select the base table, the first \<table> tag in the Tag Selector. In the Property inspector, change the Border to 0 and the Cell Padding to 0.

4. Press Ctrl+S/Cmd+S to save the page—you are done. Preview the page in your browser using F12 to see that everything is working just fine. Notice that the rollovers are all functional in both navigation systems and that the layer content now is completely displayed in the layer.

This comparison shown in Table A.5 is based on the Fireworks source file provided to me by Joyce Evans. This source file is subject to change and modification to be more optimized, but as of this writing these numbers are accurate and complete.

Conclusion

Fireworks provides you with the ability to generate really nice graphically oriented pages with rollovers fairly effortlessly and gives you the option of exporting as images with the HTML file—all with a couple of clicks. The code may be slightly bloated, due to the Fireworks JavaScript contained within the pages and because of additional slices if you choose the Include Areas Without Slices option. This option will add images even if they are blank background areas. The file size will be improved by altering the HTML settings to use a spacer.gif or non-breaking space.

Macromedia, being a forward-thinking company, has given us the ability to produce in one product and edit in another. The company calls this *round trip HTML*. You'll notice that when you select an image in Dreamweaver, the Fireworks symbol is shown in the Property inspector. This means that

Table A.5   The comparison.

Comparison Criteria	Fireworks	Dreamweaver
Size of HTML file	17KB	10KB
Number of images	85	39
Total size of images	110.0KB	81.3KB

Note: Do not manually manipulate Fireworks navigation systems unless you are absolutely comfortable with layers, or your menus will cease to function accurately.

Note: Kids don't mind the additional download time. This site gets more than 200 e-mails per day, and no complaints have been received to date about it taking too long to load. In fact, young visitors have stolen the site in its entirety four times that we are aware of.

Browser Compatibility

At the time I performed the browser compatibility tests in this appendix, they worked in IE5, and some worked in Netscape 6. I hope that by the time you try this technique, Netscape 6 (maybe 7) will be more compatible. Always be sure to test your menus in the major browsers. The pop-up menus will not work in the Opera browser. The positioning may be a bit different in Internet Explorer and Netscape browsers. Making these pop-up menus compatible with both platforms is the most challenging part of using them. As a designer, you need to evaluate the pros and cons of one browser versus another and whether the new Fireworks pop-up menus will be suitable to your audience.

double-clicking the image will open Fireworks with that image and allow you to edit it and update the PNG file at the same time. So, you can produce in Fireworks, export as HTML and images, and then update, manipulate, and clean up the page in Dreamweaver—and the Fireworks source is updated to reflect the changes.

No matter which option you choose, please note that this project exceeds the target page weight of 45 to 50KB for acceptable rendering time on a 56Kbps modem. In this particular instance, this sort of site may be acceptable because it is a target site (meaning the audience will always be people, usually children, who are interested in horses and are probably used to high-quality images taking a little time to display).

Compatibility

This page has been tested and is compatible with:

- Internet Explorer 5.5 Service Pack 1—PC
- Opera 5.11—PC
- Netscape Communicator 4.77—PC
- Netscape Communicator 6—PC

I was not able to test the output on a Mac.

I'd like to thank **Brad** for his wonderful insight and for the time and effort he obviously put into this project.

Positioning Fireworks 4 Pop-Up Menus

To place the pop-up menus generated by Fireworks 4, you use the same methods that you use to insert regular Fireworks HTML code. A special section is devoted to placing the pop-up menus not because the placement is any different, but because we need to address some of the problems you may encounter. Centering the pop-up menus on the page is a common problem. Some of the options involved in centering pop-up menus will be discussed in this section. But, just in case you decide to skip portions of the introductory explanations, you should know before you start experimenting that you cannot center the image containing pop-up menus or the table you place them into.

Absolute Positioning

The first thing to understand about the Fireworks 4 pop-up menus is that they use *absolute positioning*. Fireworks 4 generates a JavaScript file, which generates CSS layers. The JavaScript code assigns absolute positioning of each pop-up menu CSS layer. It does so to keep the menus and the submenus in the same location in relation to the buttons they are linked to. When the button is moved to another location, the menus stay where they were designed to be. The coordinates that are written into the HTML code of the pop-up menus are relative to the position zero pixels from the top-left corner of the browser. If the pop-up menu is not the same position in the Web page, then the menus will not be positioned correctly. Several options are available to solve some of these problems, and you can choose which works best for your situation.

Changing the Coordinates

You change the coordinates of the menu's positioning via the HTML inspector in Dreamweaver. To change the coordinates, follow these steps:

1. Open insertedpopup.htm from the popup folder in the exportingsamples folder. To change the coordinates in Dreamweaver, open the HTML inspector. If you are using version 4 or the demo, then click the Show Code And Design Views icon. Locate the line of code that is highlighted in Figure A.18. You can find it in the **<body>** part of the code, not in the **<head>** part. The following is the code you are looking for:

```
onMouseOver="window.FW_showMenu(window.fw_menu_0,145,82);"
```

Note: This is the code from the exercise where you inserted the pop-up menu code into the sample HTML page. The saved file is in the Appendix A exportedsamples popup folder and is named insertedpopup.htm.

Figure A.18

The code from the body section.

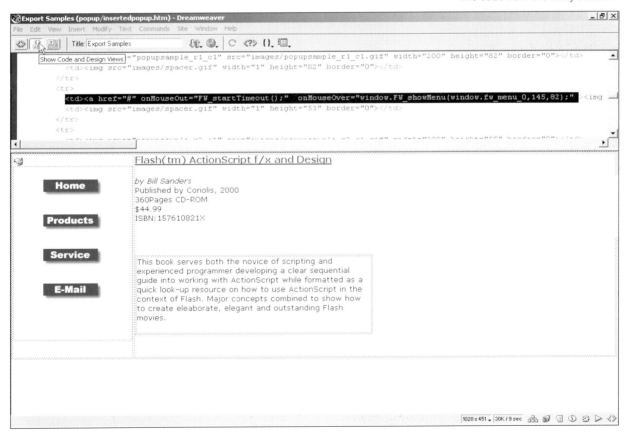

2. The second two sets of numbers in the preceding code represent the X, Y coordinates of the menu. You can change them according to where you would like the menus positioned. Along these lines, you can open the file in Fireworks and use the Info panel (Window|Info) to determine the exact location of the menu.

   You may ask, "How do I know what to change the coordinates to?" Good question. Open the file you designed in Fireworks, open the Info panel (Window|Info), and place your cursor in the top-left corner of a menu. Look in the Info panel, and you will see the X, Y coordinates.

Designing in Fireworks

Another option is to place the menus in Fireworks in the location you want them to appear in the Web page. In other words, if your menu will start at 200 pixels down the Web page, then start your design in Fireworks at that point. When the page is exported and placed in an editor, the menus will be positioned properly. This technique works great for centering a top navigation bar.

Trial and Error

You can also reopen the menu in Fireworks, move the position of the menu, export it again, insert it into the Web page again, and then preview. Repeat this process until the menu is where you want it.

Using Layers and Coordinates

This procedure worked every time it was tested in IE5 and Netscape 4.5, 4.7x, and 6. Follow these steps to use a layer:

1. Open the DWsamplefile.htm file located in the exportingsamples folder. Place your cursor in the first column on the left and click.

2. Choose Insert|Layer. When the layer is placed, click and drag it over the first column. In the Code inspector, locate this code:

   ```
   <div id="Layer1" style="position:absolute; width:209px;
      height:108px; z-index:1; left: 11px; top: 10px"></div>
   ```

3. The only reason you dragged the layer a bit was to add the **left:** and **top:** code. If you didn't drag the layer, these coordinates won't be in your code and you'll have to add them by hand coding. The numbers will vary, of course. In this example, change **left: 11px** to **0 px**, and change **top: 10px** to **0px**.

4. Place your cursor in the layer, click to place your cursor in the correct position, and choose Insert|Interactive Images. Locate the file you want to insert and click OK.

Note: You can also place a top navigation bar in a layer in a fixed center cell (not a centered table) to center a header. This technique also should work in Netscape browsers, but always check. A lot depends on how you designed the top navigation bar in Fireworks and your coordinates.

Positioning Facts

The pop-up menus will not display properly if you center the main table or a nested table that you insert the menu into. If you use a percentage table and don't set a fixed-width cell or column, then the pop-up menu will reposition as a browser resizes, causing the menus to be incorrectly positioned. Be sure that the cell or table into which you place the Fireworks 4 pop-up menu code has an absolute pixel size and is not centered.

Working with Images in Dreamweaver

The integration between Fireworks 4 and Dreamweaver 4 offers you a lot of time-saving editing features that let you edit Fireworks source files without leaving Dreamweaver. If you are using Fireworks 4 and Dreamweaver 4 Studio, the integration files are added to Dreamweaver.

Optimizing Images from within Dreamweaver

You can optimize an image without leaving Dreamweaver. If you decide you'd like to change the optimization settings, you can access a version of the Fireworks optimization settings by following these steps:

1. Open a Web page in Dreamweaver that has images you made in Fireworks. Or, make a new page. If you make a new page, save it at least once before trying to edit images.

2. Choose Commands|Optimize Image In Fireworks. If a window opens telling you that you need to save, then you didn't save in Step 1.

3. The first time you use this command, you may be asked to enter the Fireworks serial number again. If you can't get your hands on it quickly, open Fireworks and choose Help|About Fireworks. Click in the area that scrolls, and your serial number will be displayed.

4. A Find Source dialog box opens (see Figure A.19) asking if you want to use the source image; you also have the option of selecting Always Use Source PNG, Never Use Source PNG, or Ask When Launching. Dreamweaver will try to find the source file; if it can't, you can browse to locate the PNG file or any other format yourself.

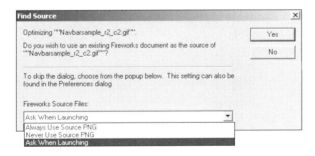

Figure A.19
The Find Source dialog box.

5. A version of the Optimize panel opens. Figure A.20 shows how many options are available without leaving Dreamweaver. When you are done making changes, click the Update button. The changes you made are now updated in Dreamweaver.

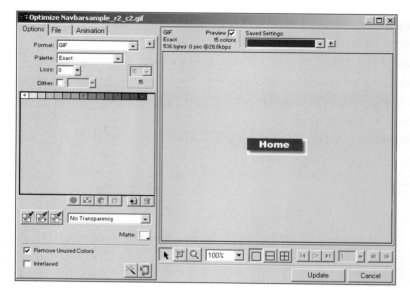

Figure A.20
The Optimize window in Dreamweaver.

Editing Images in Dreamweaver

You can change anything in your image. You can change the fill, effect, style, or whatever else suits your needs. To edit an image while in Dreamweaver, follow these steps:

1. Open a page in Dreamweaver and click an image to edit.

2. In the Property inspector (Window|Properties), click the Edit button. Fireworks opens and you are given the opportunity to locate the image file.

3. Make any changes as you normally would in Fireworks. Notice that the top bar of the document in which you are editing your image says Editing From Dreamweaver (see Figure A.21). When you are done making changes, click the Done button.

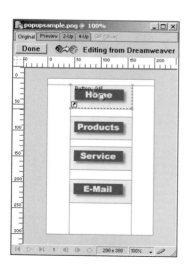

Figure A.21
The Editing From Dreamweaver label displayed in Fireworks.

4. Changes you've made in Fireworks will be updated in Dreamweaver, except for one: If you changed the physical size of the image, it isn't automatically updated in the Dreamweaver code. The image may appear distorted or blurry. In the past, you had to right-click the image to access this availability, but a great new feature has been added in Dreamweaver 4. Figure A.22 shows the Property inspector, which now has a Reset Size button. Click it, and the size is changed for you.

Be sure to check out Appendix B for more references and resources for Dreamweaver.

Figure A.22
The Property inspector's Reset Size button.

Appendix B

Resources

This appendix provides links to Flash, Fireworks, and FreeHand resources, such as tutorials, commands, and plug-ins. A list of resources and product descriptions of software/hardware may aid you in the design process. Short "reviews" describe items such as digital cameras, easy 3D text applications, and third-party plug-ins.

Contributors

I am listing the contributors to this book and their contact information first because their contributions added tremendously to the value of this book. Instead of trying to do it all myself, I requested input from others and used their expertise in particular areas. Musicians have donated music for your use, and horse farms and a photographer have donated photos. The software contributors for the CD are mentioned in the "Software" section. I am listing the other contributors alphabetically here so as not to slight anyone. The descriptions provided, for the most part, have been provided by the contributors:

- *Shafgat Ali*—**www.designwithphotoshop.com**. Because Ali didn't send me any material about himself, I'll tell you what I know. His site is one of my favorite Photoshop and all around inspirational sites. The site loads very slowly, but the wait is worth it. The ornament that you made in Fireworks was originally done in Photoshop, and Ali allowed me to remake it in Fireworks.

- *Hillman Curtis*—**www.hillmancurtis.com**. See Chapter 13 for more information about Hillman Curtis and read his wonderful introduction to Flash. hillmancurtis, inc., a New York City-based firm, specializes in design across a wide range of mediums for a broad client base. The firm's body of work includes broadcast spots, Web design, corporate identity work, motion design, and has garnered such acclaim as the One Show Gold Award, Communication Art's Award of Excellence, and the Clio Awards Short List. For additional information on hillmancurtis, inc., visit the Web site at **www.hillmancurtis.com** or call (212) 226-6082.

- *Fig Leaf Software*—**www.figleaf.com**. Fig Leaf Software is a premier Web development and design company. It specializes in dynamic, transactional, and data-driven Web and e-business applications. Fig Leaf's unique approach to Web-site development, leveraging database technology with client-side scripting, sets it apart from the competition. The applications Fig Leaf designs combine the latest in graphics and multimedia technology with dynamic programming. The focus on a rich graphical user interface makes Fig Leaf applications look great while at the same time obtaining the level of functionality that clients need. The company has crafted Web-based solutions for corporations including AOL, Estee Lauder, FannieMae, T. Rowe Price, and Verizon. Government clients include the FAA, the Federal Reserve Bank of Atlanta, and the United States Mint. Fig Leaf also serves numerous trade and non-profit organizations including the American Petroleum Institute, the American Chemical Society, the National Association of Counties, and the World Resources Institute.

  Fig Leaf is also the leading Macromedia Authorized Training Partner. It has written six of the certified curriculum for Macromedia, including the Fast Track to JavaScript, Fast Track to SQL, Intro to Flash 5, and Generator 2.

The company's staff have contributed to best-selling books on Flash 4, Flash 5, ColdFusion, and Macromedia Spectra. Examples of their work can be viewed at **www.figleaf.com** or **demo.figleaf.com**.

- *Game Gallery*—**www.rockolabubbler.com**. The Game Gallery graciously allowed us to use the picture of the jukebox for tracing and distribution on the CD so you could practice with it as well.

- *Gazelleboy*—Gazelleboy is William T Bozarth from Austin, Texas. Part Zen gardener, part mad scientist, he makes his songs from bits and pieces found in reality and reassembled with electronic glue. You can find him at bozarthwilliamT@hotmail.com and mp3.com under gazelleboy.

- *Brad Halstead*—**www.prettylady2.net**. Brad is a jack of all trades, master of none in the computer industry. He has been interested in and has been dabbling in Web design for several years and has recently become engrossed in it. Brad enjoys the challenges and the rewards that Web development brings him.

- *Scott Hamlin*—**www.eyeland.com.** Scott Hamlin is the author of *Flash 5 Magic* book (New Riders) and contributed the Eyeland Studio interface for your use in this book. Eyeland Studio has a lot of Flash goodies, interfaces, buttons, and more. Be sure to check it out.

- *Ian Kelleigh*—**www.freehandsource.com**. Ian Kelleigh is a designer and Web-site developer who loves to work on cool stuff like this book. He's experienced with print, Web, and multimedia design and production. He loves to try new and exciting things and tends to learn them on his own during his free time. You can find out more about Ian at his personal site linked from his FreeHand Source Web site.

- *Tracy Kelly*—**www.tracykelly.com**. Tracy Kelly has been a full-time Macromedia trainer at Fig Leaf Software primarily teaching Macromedia Flash and Dreamweaver. She graduated from Seton Hall University with a BA in Liberal Studies in 2000. Before working at Fig Leaf, Tracy spent several years working on political campaigns at the national level. She is a co-author of the Macromedia Authorized Training materials for Flash and the book *Inside Flash 5* (New Riders Press). She resides in Washington, Delaware.

- *Darryl Larson Photography*—**www.darryllarson.com**. Darryl Larson is a photographer and produces videos. She does equine photography and donated some of the horse photos we used in the Horse Adventures Web site.

- *Todd McPhetridge*—**www.cobaltgraphics.com**. Todd has been a photographer for more than 10 years and has more than 4 years' experience in Web design and the graphic arts. His services include (but are not limited to) Web design, photo manipulation, and graphic design, with a special focus on nature and projects related to the outdoors. Todd is a consultant for major corporations as well as small, family-owned businesses. You can reach him by phone at (770) 684-2688 or send email to **todd@colbaltgraphics.com**.

- *Arvita Mott*—**www.dted-online.com**. Arvita runs a small graphic-design studio in Spokane, Washington.

- *Paragon Arabians*—**www.paragonarabians.com**. Paragon Arabians is home to the world-renowned stallion Shah Azim, featured on the cover of *Arabian Horseworld Magazine*, as well as U.S. National Top Ten Stallion, Showkayce, both sires of halter and performance champions.

- *Platinum Arabians*—**www.platinumplusarabians.com/**. Platinum Plus Arabians is a small Bask line breeder with the integrity of this awesome sire always in mind. Platinum Arabians honors the Bask Legacy, and strives to continue his destiny through his get.

- *PPK vera feat*—**www.english.ppk.ru**. PPK, a duo from Moscow, Russia, has so far attracted more than 2 million fans from around the world. They are among the most-downloaded artists on the Web and are the first Russian band to climb to number one on the biggest Internet music chart, **MP3.com**'s Music Top 40.

- *Jeffrey Roberts*—**www.jefargrafx.com**. Jeff is a conventional artist with an expertise in illustration for technical manuals and book design. Computer vector illustration seemed the natural progression for his work. His years of experience in pen and paper drawing fully prepared him for new media. Web design grew from his experience with multimedia interface and software information architecture.

- *Ron Rockwell*—**www.nidus-corp.com**. Ron is a technical illustrator and the author of *FreeHand 10 f/x & Design*. He offered advice about FreeHand.

Flash Resources

At the top of any resource list for any of the Macromedia products are Macromedia's own support pages. Also check out the exchange, where you can find fantastic extensions and commands. These and a few other resources are listed here, but a huge list is available at the Macromedia Support site:

- www.macromedia.com/support/flash

- www.macromedia.com/exchange/flash

- www.flashkit.com/

- www.virtual-fx.net/

- www.flashlite.net

- www.flashcentral.com

- www.ultrashock.com

- www.mock.org/asdg

Fireworks Resources

The community of Fireworks users is growing each day. As the program develops and becomes more powerful, more and more designers are discovering they can't work without it. With the release of Fireworks 4 and increasing numbers of new Fireworks users came a growing number of people seeking answers and help with the program. Currently, the number of sites devoted solely or primarily to Fireworks is limited.

Macromedia Fireworks Forum

The Macromedia Fireworks Forum (**www.macromedia.com/support/fireworks**) should be at the top of your list when you run into a snag and need help. The forum has helpful, courteous people available to assist you. You can frequently find Macromedia technical support hanging out, as well.

Commands/Tutorials

The supply of Fireworks tutorials is scarce. The following list includes commands and tutorials I found for Fireworks 4, including the Web site I set up for this book:

- Fireworks 4 f/x & Design *companion Web site*—**www.JoyceJEvans.com.** *Fireworks 4 f/x & Design* updates, tutorials, and product reviews are provided on this site.

- Integrating Flash, Fireworks, and FreeHand f/x & Design *companion Web site*—**www.JoyceJEvans.com.** This book's companion Web site.

- *Pretty Lady*—**www.prettylady2.net**. This site offers Dreamweaver and Fireworks commands, behaviors, objects, tutorials, and interfaces, based on the original work of Eddie Traversa.

- *Playing with Fire*—**www.playingwithfire.com**. The Playing with Fire site has a nice assortment of beginner's tutorials, along with a Fireworks bulletin board.

- *Project Fireworks*—**www.projectfireworks.com**. Project Fireworks has an archive of downloadable commands, patterns, textures, and symbols.

- *Escogitando*—**www.escogitando.it**. Japi Honoo owns this site. It is available in Italian, Spanish, and English.

- *About.com*—**www.graphicssoft.about.com/compute/graphicssoft/cs/ fireworks/. About.com** provides a list of Fireworks tutorials and resources at this site. Not much is available for Fireworks 4 yet, but check now and then to see what is available. Tutorials for Fireworks 3 will often work if you are familiar enough with the Fireworks work environment to know what has changed and where to find each tool.

FreeHand

Visit Macromedia's support site at **www.macromedia.com/support/freehand**.

The finest FreeHand tutorial site is The FreeHand Source, at **www.freehandsource.com**.

Dreamweaver

Here are several outstanding Dreamweaver resources you may want to check out:

- *Macromedia's support site*—**www.macromedia.com/support/ Dreamweaver**.

- *DreamweaverFAQ.com*—**www.dreamweaverFAQ.com**. All you ever wanted to know about Dreamweaver!

- *Project Seven Development* —**www.projectseven.com**. A Dreamweaver resource site that contains tutorials, extensions, and templates for Dreamweaver. The site includes a very active forum, as well.

- *Massimo Foti*—**www.massimocorner.com**. You can download objects, behaviors, and other files related to Dreamweaver, Dreamweaver UltraDev, and Fireworks from this site. Massimo won the Macromedia award for the Best Extension Developer.

Books

This section lists the books I recommend that are currently available. I own almost all of the recommended books. I've put an asterisk by the ones that I don't own but that I am confident will be good when they are published, based on my experience with the series or the author. I've posted reviews for many of these books at **books.je-ideadesign.com**.

Flash

Check out these Flash titles:

- *Flash Web Design: The v5 Remix*. Hillman Curtis. New Riders. ISBN 0735710988.

- *Flash 5 Magic: With ActionScript*. J. Scott Hamlin and David J. Emberton. New Riders. ISBN 0735710236.

- *ActionScript: The Definitive Guide*. Colin Moock. O'Reilly & Associates. ISBN 1565928520.

- *Flash 5 Advanced for Windows and Macintosh Visual QuickPro Guide*. Russell Chun. Peachpit Press. ISBN 0201726246.

- *Flash 5 Bible*. Robert Reinhardt and Jon Warren Lentz. Hungry Minds. ISBN 0764535153.

- *Flash 5 f/x & Design*. Bill Sanders. The Coriolis Group. ISBN 1576108163.

- *Flash ActionScript f/x & Design.* Bill Sanders. The Coriolis Group. ISBN 157610821X.

- *Flash 5 Virtual Classroom.* Doug Sahlin. Osborne. ISBN 0072131152.

- *Flash 5 Cartoons and Games f/x & Design.* Bill Turner, James Robertson, and Richard Bazley. The Coriolis Group. ISBN 1576109585.

- *Flash 5 Cartooning.* Mark Clarkson. Hungry Minds. ISBN 0764535471.

Fireworks

Check out these Fireworks titles:

- *Fireworks 4 f/x & Design.* Joyce J. Evans. The Coriolis Group. ISBN 1576109968.

- *Fireworks 4 for Windows and Macintosh: Visual QuickStart Guide.* Sandee Cohen. Peachpit Press. ISBN 0201731339.

- *Fireworks 4 Bible.* Joseph Lowery. Hungry Minds. ISBN 0764535706.

- *Playing with Fire.* Linda Rathgeber. Hungry Minds. ISBN 0764535498.

FreeHand

Check out these FreeHand titles:

- *Macromedia FreeHand 9 Digital Illustration.* "Against the Clock" series. Prentice Hall. ISBN 0130325244.

- *FreeHand 9 Authorized.* Tony Roame. Peachpit Press. ISBN 0201700344.

- *Macromedia FreeHand 9 for Windows and Macintosh: Visual QuickStart Guide*.* Sandee Cohen. Peachpit Press. ISBN 0201354896.

- *FreeHand 10 f/x & Design*.* Ron Rockwell. The Coriolis Group. ISBN 1588801640.

Dreamweaver

Check out these Dreamweaver titles:

- *Dreamweaver 4 Magic.* Al Sparber. New Riders. ISBN 0735710465.

- *Dreamweaver UltraDev: The Complete Reference.* Ray West, Tom Muck, and Tom. AllenMcGraw-Hill. ISBN 0072130172.

- *Dreamweaver 4 Bible.* Joseph Lowery. Hungry Minds. ISBN 0764535692.

- *Dreamweaver 4: The Complete Reference.* Jennifer Ackerman Kettell. Osborne/McGraw Hill. ISBN 0072131713.

- *Dreamweaver 4 f/x and Design.* Laurie Ann Ulrich. The Coriolis Group. ISBN 1576107892.

- *Dreamweaver 4 Virtual Classroom.* Robert Fuller and Laurie Ann Ulrich. McGraw-Hill. ISBN 007213108X.

- *Dreamweaver 4 Hands On Training.* Lynda Weinman and Garo Green. Peachpit Press. ISBN 0201741334.

Third-Party Plug-ins

Plug-ins that I have tested personally are noted in this section. In addition, links are listed for you to explore on your own. Some of the plug-ins are free, some are demos, and some are for sale only.

Puzzle Pro 1.2

Puzzle Pro is a very cool plug-in from AV Bros. (**www.avbros.com**) that makes producing puzzles quick and easy. It offers a wide range of flexibility, with all kinds of options for puzzle shapes, bevels, and more. Figure B.1 shows the interface. Figure B.2 shows the second interface screen, which allows you to edit even further. The price is $39.95.

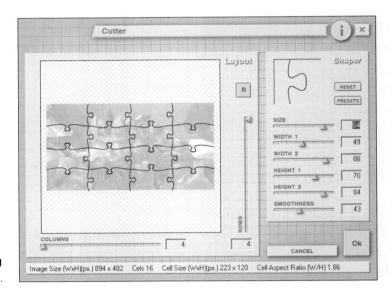

Figure B.1
The Puzzle Pro interface.

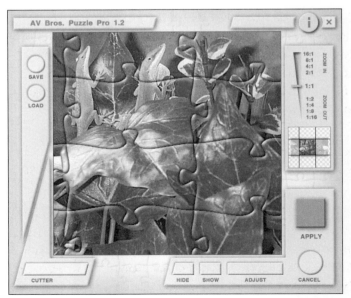

Figure B.2
The Puzzle Pro Edit interface.

Auto FX Software Plug-ins

Auto FX Software (**www.autofx.com**) offers a variety of special-purpose plug-ins, some of which are listed here:

- *AutoEye*—A demo of AutoEye (Figure B.3) is included on this book's CD-ROM. AutoEye is similar to Auto Levels in Fireworks, but it uses a different algorithm and brings out detail a bit differently. I found that in some cases it has a tendency to over-sharpen, but it brings out a tremendous amount of detail in very dark pictures.

- *Photo/Graphic Edges 10,000+*—A demo of Photo/Graphic Edges 10,000+ (Figure B.4) is on this book's CD-ROM. You can find more edges in this product than you could possibly ever use, but it certainly is great to be able to pick from so many. The manual helps you locate the type of edge you'd like, and once you find it on the CD-ROM, you can alter it before it's applied to your image.

- *Studio Bundle Pro 2.0*—Studio Bundle Pro 2.0 (Figure B.5) contains 11 of Auto FX Software's most popular products in one integrated package for $199.95. This package is worth more than $1,250 if the products are sold separately. The effects in this package include Typo/Graphic Edges; Ultimate Texture Collection Volumes 1, 2, and 3; Photo/Graphic Patterns; Universal Animator; Universal Rasterizer; Photo/Graphic Frames Volumes 1 and 2; Page/Edges; and WebVise Totality.

Alien Skin Software Plug-ins

Alien Skin Software (**www.alienskin.com**) is very well known for two of its spectacular products: Xenofex and Eye Candy 4000. These two plug-ins offer some really great effects that are fully customizable before you apply them to an image:

- *Eye Candy 3SE*—This special edition of Eye Candy 3 contains 21 fully-functional filters that will help you produce stunning effects in seconds. View your work in an advanced preview that zooms, resizes, and gives you instant access to any part of the original image. Save and restore your settings for each filter or use one of over 200 presets for quality effects with minimal clicks. In addition, Eye Candy's filters take full advantage of Photoshop's Actions feature.

  This special edition of Eye Candy 3 does not time out. It will, however, entitle you to a special discount on the award-winning Eye Candy 4000.

- *Eye Candy 4000*—A demo version of Eye Candy 4000 by Alien Skin Software (Figure B.6) is on this book's CD-ROM. Samples are given in Chapter 10 using only the filters that ship with Fireworks 4. Eye Candy has many other great filters, so be sure to check out Alien Skin's Web site, which has a great interface enabling you to see each of the included 23 filters in use. The price of Eye Candy 4000 is $169, or an upgrade price of $69 is offered for registered users of Eye Candy 3.

Figure B.3
AutoEye, from Auto FX Software.

Figure B.4
Photo/Graphic Edges 10,000+, from Auto FX Software.

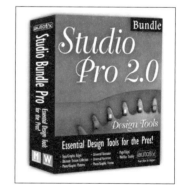

Figure B.5
Studio Bundle Pro 2.0, from Auto FX Software.

Figure B.6
Eye Candy 4000, from
Alien Skin Software.

Figure B.7
Xenofex, from
Alien Skin Software.

- *Xenofex*—A demo of the Xenofex plug-ins (Figure B.7) is included on this book's CD-ROM, and a sample is provided in Chapter 10. The Xenofex filters from Alien Skin have a collection of 16 filters and 160 presets. Be sure to check out the filters at the company's Web site. The price is $129.

Flaming Pear Software Plug-ins

Flaming Pear Software (**www.flamingpear.com**) offers the free Primus plug-in you may have tried in Chapter 10. The company has a very nice, innovative collection of plug-ins:

- *Tachyon*—This filter reverses the brightness and keeps the colors.   You can find Tachyon on Flaming Pear's site by clicking the Download link on its home page and going to the Free Plugins category.

- *SuperBladePro*—In September 2000, Flaming Pear released SuperBladePro, adding new effects such as dust, moss, waterstains, and abrasion, as well as features such as an undo tool and a graphical preset browser. Flaming Pear plans to offer more texture packs, presets, and tutorials for SuperBladePro, and to continue developing intriguing and useful plug-ins. SuperBladePro is available via download and online purchase for $30. Registered users of the original BladePro can purchase an upgrade for $15.

Helpful Accessories

When you work with graphics, a few items may make your job easier. I have tested some hardware and accessories, and only those worthy of mention (and worth the money) are listed here.

Matrox Millennium G450 32MB DualHead Graphics Card

If you are tired of moving panels and palettes around your screen all the time, you have to try dual monitors—it's great. I have Fireworks, or one of the other programs, running on one monitor and the panels on another. Sometimes I keep Fireworks on one monitor and open Word on the other. Doing so made writing this book much easier, because I could perform the tutorials on one monitor and write on the other.

Some of the highlights of the Matrox G450 (Figure B.8) are that you can use monitors with separate resolutions, or a monitor and a TV. The Matrox G450 is also compatible with LCD flat screens.

To read more about the benefits of this new chip, go to **www.matrox.com/mga**.

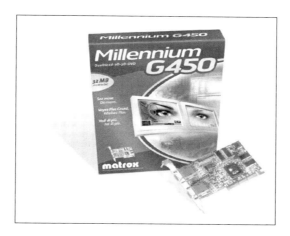

Figure B.8
Matrox Millennium G450.

Wacom Graphire Tablet

A pressure-sensitive tablet comes in handy with a program like Fireworks or FreeHand (see Figure B.9). Many of the strokes and the Brush tool take advantage of pressure sensitivity, speed, and the direction you draw with. What's nice about the Graphire tablet (**www.wacom.com/graphire/index.html**) is that it takes up the same amount of desk real estate as a mouse pad. The price of $99.95, which includes the pen tool and cordless mouse, makes it a great deal for novice users. You can trace images on the tablet, design your own innovations, or sign your name. If you make the occasional map, a tablet makes the job much easier.

Figure B.9
Wacom Graphire tablet.

The Graphire tablet's key features are as follows:

- The tablet is connected to the computer via a cable to either the USB or a serial port.
- It includes a patented cordless and batteryless pen and mouse.
- The pen features a pressure-sensitive tip, two side switches, and a pressure-sensitive eraser.
- The mouse features three buttons and a rubberized scrolling wheel.
- It features an ambidextrous mouse design.
- The no-ball mouse design always tracks smoothly and never clogs up.
- All buttons and switches can be set to user's preference.
- The mouse scrolling wheel's speed is customizable.
- The tablet features a clear-plastic overlay for tracing.
- The tablet pen stand is detachable.
- It comes with a great software bundle including Photoshop LE, Corel Painter, and more.

Software

I have found a few programs that are reasonably priced and are beneficial for making Web sites. You may enjoy checking out some of these products.

SWFX 1.03

A demo of SWFX (Figure B.10; **www.wildform.com/swfx/**) is included on this book's CD-ROM. This is a very easy to use and versatile tool to make quick text animations for use in Flash. It is a standalone application that comes with 100 different preset text animations to use and customize. Another 100 presets are available from Wildform's Web site. All this costs only $19.99.

Figure B.10
SWFX from Wildform.

Flix 1.52

A demo of Flix (**www.wildform.com/flix/**) is in the Wildform folder on the CD-ROM. You can also see a demo of a Flix banner in action in the Appendix B wildform folder.

Flix lets you do the following:

- Stream video to over 96 percent of Web browsers without a download—even through firewalls

- Embed links in video files

- Produce hassle-free video banner ads and video e-mails

- Integrate video into customized media players and UIs

- Embed video into HTML web pages, or larger Flash movies

SnagIt

I began using SnagIt by TechSmith (**www.snagit.com**) when I received it for writing a review for *Web Review*. I have used it ever since. It was used for all the screen shots taken for this book. You can also capture video and text, and add sound, annotations, and watermarks. I like the AutoScroll feature, which captures a whole Web page—even the part you can't see. You get all these features and more for only $39.95. You can find a shareware version, which is fully operational, at the SnagIt Web site. If you'd like to see the full review I wrote about the product, go to **www.webreview.com/2000/12_22/designers/index03.shtml** (if you don't want to type in that long address, just go to **www.webreview.com** and type "Joyce Evans" into the search box).

Note: In order to make the movies compatible with both Windows and Macintosh, the AVI movies from Camtasia were opened in QuickTime 5 and converted into MOV files.

Camtasia

Camtasia, another product of TechSmith (**www.camtasia.com**), was used to produce the movie tutorials for *Fireworks 4 f/x & Design* as well as *Integrating Flash, Fireworks, and FreeHand f/x & Design*. Some of the movies are included on this book's CD-ROM.

EZ Motion

EZ Motion is made by Beatware; you can download a demo at **www.beatware.com**. It includes dozens of templates such as animated banners, buttons, and other graphics. You can use them as is or customize them. A library of graphic objects is also available, including 3D and 2D objects, animated objects, designs, gradients, and images. You can do more than just simple animations like movement and fades; you can animate text on a curve and change font size, outlines, fills, shearing, and spacing. You can change the size, shape, and opacity, and the elements remain editable. EZ Motion sells for $99.99.

Hemera Technologies

A demo including 500 free Hemera Photo-Objects (**www.hemera.com**) is included on this book's CD-ROM. These images are on transparent backgrounds and are ready to be added to any document you are working on.

The interface that you use to access the objects is very easy to use and is quite impressive. After you install the application, you open the program, and an image browser opens. You can scroll to find images, but with 50,000 of them (if you purchase the package), scrolling could take forever. Instead, you can search for the items you want. When you locate something of interest and click it, you will be told which CD-ROM to insert. With the Hemera Photo-Objects 50,000 Premium Image Collection, you get eight CD-ROMs and a manual; the package has 80 categories. The 50,000 Premium Image Collection is available for both Windows and the Mac, for $84.99.

Photoshere

PhotoSphere (**www.photosphere.com**) offers you thousands of professional, royalty-free stock images to use in your print and online design projects. All photos are model and property released, and can be used in a variety of projects. EyewireEyeWire (**www.eyewire.com**) has a lot of resources, if you have time to search for them. You can access photos, illustrations, audio, type, and more. Photo-Disc CDs are available, along with art from Art Parts and Artville, and tutorials and tips. You can purchase individual images or, in some cases, buy images on a CD.

IrfanView

IrfanView (**www.irfanview.com**) is a thumbnail image browser for PCs that allows you to view hundreds of images in a folder without logging out. The best part is, it's freeware. Give it a try to easily and quickly locate your image files.

Digital Cameras

A digital camera is a great way to obtain the images you need for Web pages. The cameras available today are even suitable for print work, but are more than suitable for Web design. The cameras listed here are those that I have personally used and tested. They are not the highest-priced versions because, frankly, you don't need the top of the line for Web work. Of course, if you're going to use the camera for high-end print work or very large printed pieces, you need a camera with higher resolution.

Kodak

Besides taking great pictures, the Kodak DC3400 is extremely easy to use (Figure B.11; **www.kodak.com**). This 2.3 megapixel camera has resolutions of 1,760×1,168 (High) and 896×592 (Standard) and image quality settings of Best, Better, and Good. You can print up to 8×10-inch prints with the High resolution.

Figure B.11
The Kodak DC3400.

The learning curve is less than half an hour (based on my family). This is the camera my husband and kids grab when they want to take photos.

Don't let the ease of use fool you, though, because this camera is also powerful. It has an LCD screen to view pictures taken, an autofocus lens, different lighting settings, different flash settings, and even a 3x digital zoom. The pictures taken don't require a lot of time to set up. If you want to, you can make a few adjustments for the lighting and distance, and you are ready to shoot. I like the fact that it's easy to use, but I also like having control over the lighting, flash, and zoom.

Note: If you want to save on batteries and don't want to buy an adapter, I highly recommend getting a card reader. They are wonderful. I found one for only $25 (prices vary). You simply put the CompactFlash Card in the reader. The images are almost instantly available on your hard drive. Delete them from the card, and you are ready to shoot again.

Nikon CoolPix 800

The Nikon CoolPix 800 camera I have is a 2.11 megapixel with a resolution up to 1200×1600 (Figure B.12; **www.nikonusa.com**). The first impression I had right out of the box was that this camera felt and looked like a "real" camera. What I particularly like about Nikon cameras is the control I have over the white balance. I also have noticed that the background detail is better than with some of the cameras I've used. This is probably because of the Nikkor lens, which has a reputation for being top-notch. You can add wide-angle, fisheye, and telle converter lenses to the camera, which add to its value.

Figure B.12

The Nikon CoolPix 800.

The learning curve for CoolPix is a bit steeper than for some other cameras because of all its options. The LCD is easy to see, and I like the Autofocus feature as well.

This camera has a lot of bang for the buck. I found it on Pricewatch (**www.pricewatch.com**) for as low as $345 in June 2001. The price may be lower when you read this. Nikon has released new versions that have brought the price down for the 800. But if you are primarily doing Web work, you won't need more than the CoolPix 800 camera provides. Of course, only you can determine your needs versus your budget.

Moving On

Be sure to check the companion Web site for *Integrating Flash, Fireworks, and FreeHand f/x & Design*, **www.je-ideadesign.com/fireworksbook.htm**, for updates, new tutorials, and news.

Index

C

Canvas Color, 257

Cascading Style Sheets

 Dreamworks, 405–407

 exporting Fireworks files to CSS layer, 261–262

Centerpoint option, 27

Check Syntax action, 318

Chun, Russell, 303

Circle Hotspot tool, 222

Clipping path, 97–98, 104

Clone, 21, 67

Closed paths, 4, 9

CMYK color mode, 62

 converting to RGB, 103

Collage techniques, 185–187

Color

 applying in FreeHand, 65–66

 changing, 158, 362

 CMYK, 62

 dithering, 225

 gradients, 125–127

 hex numbers, 124, 324, 362

 hue adjustments, 131, 179

 Indexed Palette options, 225

 modes available in FreeHand, 62

 objects, 323–324, 360

 reducing, 225

 RGB, 62

 saturation adjustments, 131

 tables import and export, 64

Color Mixer

 selecting color, 12

 opening, 62

 Swatches panel, 62, 63–64

Color mode option, 37

Common libraries, 298

Composite images, 185

Connector points, 4

 control handle movement, 6

Control handles, 5

 Bezier curve, 147

 dragging, 6

editing, 14

 gradients, 126

Contour gradient, 66, 74–75

Converet Lines to Fills command, 287

CorelDRAW files, 248

Corner points, 4,

 moving handles independently, 5

CSS layers, 261–261

Cursors

 changing, 148

 smart, 5

Curtis, Hillman, 267, 269–271

Curve points, 4

 selecting, 5

Curves

 changing a straight line to, 11

 changing to a straight line, 11

 drawing with Bezigon tool, 7–9

 drawing with Pen tool, 6–7

 editing, 10–16

Cut paths, 119

D

Darryll Larson Productions, 185

Debugger panel, 373

Debugging Permitted option, 377

Deprecated actions, 320, 325

Designing for Flash, 269–271

Detach from Path option, 117

Dialog box entries, 158

Dimensions options, 380

Disjointed rollovers, 202–203, 220

Distorting text, 122

Distributive blend option, 305

Dithering, 225

Dot syntax

 compared to slash syntax, 314

 description of, 315, 325

Drawing. *See also* Shapes.

 curves, 6–16

 ellipse, 71, 118

 tools in Flash, 283–287

HILLMAN CURTIS

MTIV:

PROCESS, INSPIRATION & PRACTICE

IN BOOKSTORES EVERYWHERE FEBRUARY 2002.

WWW.HILLMANCURTIS.COM

Expand your creative skills with these Creative Professionals Press titles

Fireworks® 4 f/x & Design

by Joyce J. Evans
Media: 2 CD-ROMs

ISBN #: 1-57610-996-8
$49.99 U.S., $74.99 CAN.

Fireworks® 4 f/x & Design teaches how to use some of the more advanced aspects of an image editor. Readers will obtain knowledge needed to produce professional level images, buttons, animations, and graphical interfaces for the Web. This guide goes beyond explaining the functions of Fireworks by showing how to produce usable elements that can be effectively incorporated into a professional Web site. This book includes two CD-ROMs containing trial versions of Dreamweaver®, Flash®, and FreeHand®; over 12,000 comping images; plus many other extras.

FreeHand® 10 f/x & Design

by Ron Rockwell
Media: CD-ROM

ISBN #: 1-58880-164-0
$49.99 U.S., $77.99 CAN.

FreeHand® 10 f/x & Design teaches how to trace scanned images for use in printable or Web-ready illustrations. Learn how to construct an object from drawings, sketches, or actual objects into three-dimensional renderings, plus much more. The CD-ROM includes demo versions of FreeHand 10 and Flash 5, a library of electronic symbols used in electronic schematic drawings, plus a gallery of other photos for use when trying out these techniques.

Photoshop® 6 In Depth

by David Xenakis and Benjamin Levisay
Media: 2 CD-ROMs

ISBN #: 1-57610-788-4
$59.99 U.S., $89.99 CAN.

Takes the mystery out of the new Photoshop® functions! Readers will learn layering, channel selection, color corrections, prepress integration with other applications, and how to prepare images for the Web. The linear format in each chapter addresses individual topics, allowing readers to select according to their needs and skill levels. This book includes two CD-ROMs containing a collection of third-party software such as filters, plug-ins, stock photos, and fonts, as well as three additional chapters covering third-party filters, ImageReady, and how to prepare graphics for the Web.

Deciphering Web Design

by David Robison
Media: CD-ROM

ISBN #: 1-58880-146-2
$49.99 U.S., $77.99 CAN.

Deciphering Web Design addresses specific solutions and strategies of Web design through more than 24 projects based on real Web sites employing HTML, JavaScript, and Cascading Style Sheets. The author focuses on issues of text formatting and typography, image generation and optimization for Web delivery, layout strategies, navigation design, browser considerations and compatibility, and guidelines for efficient strategies in Web development. This book will empower the newly arrived Web designer, as well as provide valuable insight and affirmation to the established professional. Demo versions of Dreamweaver, Photoshop, and Fireworks; up-to-date versions of Internet browsers—Internet Explorer, Netscape Navigator, Opera, and Lynx (browser for the visually-impaired); clipart; and Web page templates designed for use with Dreamweaver fill the accompanying CD-ROM.

Flash Forward with Coriolis Books

Flash™ 5 Visual Insight

Authors: Sherry London and Dan London

Audience: Novice to Intermediate Flash™ users

- Fundamentals of Flash™ 5 through a graphically oriented format.
- Projects showing the full range of the product's capabilities.
- Color section illustrating features of Flash™.
- Teaches Flash™ tools and their options, then guides readers to create their own movies.

Flash™ ActionScript f/x and Design

Author: Bill Sanders

Audience: Intermediate to Advanced Flash™ users

- Combines major concepts to show how to create more elaborate, elegant, and outstanding Flash™ 5 movies
- Teaches strategies to integrate ActionScript into Flash™ movies producing desired effects.
- Shows basic algorithms for creating movies not possible without ActionScript.

Flash™ 5 f/x and Design

Author: Bill Sanders

Audience: Intermediate to Advanced Flash™ users

- Newest features of Flash™, with case studies and tutorials.
- Contains advanced topics, including how to use data from external sources, text files, HTML pages, or servers.
- CD-ROM with 50 Flash™ 5 movies in FLA and SWF formats, and trial versions of Flash™, Dreamweaver®, Fireworks®, and FreeHand®.

Flash™ 5 Cartoons and Games f/x and Design

Authors: Bill Turner, James Robertson, and Richard Bazley

Audience: Intermediate to Advanced Flash™ users

- Reveals very beneficial Flash code and authoring source files.
- Learn cartooning with the use of lip-synching with Magpie Pro® and storyboarding in Flash™.
- CD-ROM includes demo versions of Flash™, SmartSound®, Magpie Pro®, and complete authoring files for animation and games, plus numerous games.

Flash™ is the leading vector technology for designing high-impact, low-bandwidth Web sites that deliver motion, sound, interactivity, and graphics. Vector-based Flash™ content downloads faster, is scalable, and boasts higher quality than other graphic formats. The Web experience becomes more attractive and compelling than ever before through the use of Flash™.

©2001 The Coriolis Group, LLC All Rights Reserved. SS

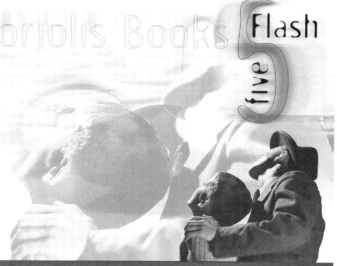

Visit us at creative.coriolis.com
Available at book and computer stores worldwide.

What's on the CD-ROM

The Integrating Flash, Fireworks and FreeHand f/x & Design's companion CD-ROM contains elements specifically selected to enhance the usefulness of this book, including:

- *The tutorial images in the book, arranged by chapter*—The images needed to complete the projects.
- *Tutorial movies*—Demonstrating some of the project techniques from the book.
- *AutoEye by Auto FX demo for Mac and PC*
- *Photo/Graphic Edges by Auto FX demo for Mac and PC*
- *Alien Skin's Eye Candy 3, Special Edition for Mac and PC*
- *Alien Skin's Xenofex demo for Mac and PC*
- *Hemera Photo-Objects 50,000 Premium Image Collection Trial Version 1.5 for Mac and PC*—500 images are included for your use.
- *Wildform SWFX 1.03 demo for PC*
- *Wildform Flix 1.52 demo for PC*
- *Swish demo for PC*

Note: The following software (not included on this CD) is required to complete the exercises and tutorials (downloads available at **www.macromedia.com/downloads/**):

- Macromedia Dreamweaver 4 demo for Mac and PC.
- Macromedia Fireworks 4 demo for Mac and PC.
- Macromedia FreeHand 10 demo for Mac and PC.
- Macromedia Flash 5 demo for Mac and PC.

System Requirements

Windows

- Intel Pentium grade processor running Windows 98, ME, 2000 or NT 4 (with Service Pack 5) or later
- 64 MB of RAM plus 100 MB of available disk space
- 800×600 pixel resolution, 256-color display (1024×768 resolution, millions of colors recommended)
- a mouse or digitizing tablet
- a CD-ROM drive.

Macintosh

- Power Macintosh (G3 or higher recommended), running System 8.6, 9.x, or later
- 64 MB of RAM plus 100 MB of available disk space
- Adobe Type Manager 4 or later for using Type 1 fonts
- a color monitor (1024×768 resolution, millions of colors recommended)
- a mouse or digitizing tablet
- a CD-ROM drive.